6/12

Aftermath

Aftermath

Deportation Law and the
New American Diaspora

DANIEL KANSTROOM

OXFORD
UNIVERSITY PRESS

OXFORD
UNIVERSITY PRESS

Oxford University Press, Inc., publishes works that further
Oxford University's objective of excellence
in research, scholarship, and education.

Oxford   New York

Auckland   Cape Town   Dar es Salaam   Hong Kong   Karachi
Kuala Lumpur   Madrid   Melbourne   Mexico City   Nairobi
New Delhi   Shanghai   Taipei   Toronto

With offices in

Argentina   Austria   Brazil   Chile   Czech Republic   France   Greece
Guatemala   Hungary   Italy   Japan   Poland   Portugal   Singapore
South Korea   Switzerland   Thailand   Turkey   Ukraine   Vietnam

Published by Oxford University Press, Inc.
198 Madison Avenue, New York, New York 10016

www.oup.com

Oxford is a registered trademark of Oxford University Press

Library of Congress Cataloging-in-Publication Data
Kanstroom, Dan.
Aftermath : deportation law and the new American diaspora / Daniel Kanstroom.
p.   cm.
Includes bibliographical references and index.
ISBN 978-0-19-974272-1
1. Deportation—United States. 2. Emigration and immigration law—United States.
3. Rule of law—United States. 4. Deportees—United States. I. Title.
KF4842.K38   2012
342.7308′2—dc23   2011045708

1 3 5 7 9 8 6 4 2

Printed in the United States of America
on acid-free paper

For Julie, Emily, and Hannah

CONTENTS

Preface   ix

1. Introduction: "What Part of 'Illegal' Do You Not Understand?"   3

2. The Goals of Deportation: Border Control, Social Control, or "Out of Sight Out of Mind"?   28

3. The Major Methods of Deportation   50

4. Accomplishments and Problems: Does Deportation Work Within the Rule of Law?   81

5. The Effects of Deportation in the United States and in the New Diaspora: The Challenge to "All That Makes Life Worthwhile"   135

6. Law in the New Diaspora: Deportees and the Space/Time Continuum   164

7. Reconceptualizing the Law for Deportees: Discretion, Human Rights, and the "Spirit of Fair Play"   210

Index   239

PREFACE

Prisoner, hear the sentence of the Court. The Court decides, subject to the approval of the President, that you never hear the name of the United States again.

—Edward Everett Hale (1863)[1]

This book is about how deportation has worked in the United States, a "nation of immigrants."[2] In one sense, it is a book of stories—many sad, some frustrating or infuriating, but some inspiring—about people who have had to leave one home only to be forcibly removed, often years later, from another. The stories are also about the United States itself, which has undertaken a radical social experiment with massive deportation enforcement. I call this a radical experiment because, although deportation is at least as old as the modern nation-state, we have never before seen an immigration enforcement system of the size, ferocity, and scope that has been built, ironically, in one of history's most open and immigrant-friendly societies. The experiment has now continued for more than a decade. It is time to consider what it has accomplished and what it has wrought.

Deportation, at first glance, would seem to be mostly about border enforcement. To citizens of affluent nation-states, this generally seems an important and protective function. Borders aim to safeguard culture, identity, social peace, security, and relative wealth. They serve as semi-permeable membranes, enabling governments to control the movements of people, especially workers.[3] Most basically, though, border enforcement seeks to keep various forms of foreign turmoil at bay, as it separates "us"—the citizens—from "them"—the foreigners, the outsiders, the aliens, and from various Hobbesian international realities.[4] Neither globalization, international legal tribunals, supra-national entities like the European Union, the Internet, social networking, nor the "flatness" of the world have fundamentally changed this reality.[5] Reports of the death of the nation-state, in short, have been exaggerated, as have reports of the irrelevance of national borders.[6] The importance of geographic space may have diminished somewhat with the advance of transportation and new communication technologies.[7] But the poor and the oppressed of the world encounter a tighter regime of state regulation—with fewer migration possibilities—than many would have found in the past.[8]

And yet all boundaries—especially physical borders—are inevitably imperfect and porous.[9] This fact creates not only a certain anxiety, but also enforcement dilemmas. Control of the physical border is equated with such elastic but viscerally powerful goals as "national security" and compliance with the "rule of law." But there are always, inevitably, many of "them" among "us." In the United States, this has led to a particularly harsh situation: the lives of many millions of noncitizens without legal status—and of many others with legal status but who may have violated certain legal rules—are starkly different from those of all but the most marginalized citizens.[10] A knock on the door in the early morning, a uniformed government agent at the workplace, the flashing light of a police car due to a minor traffic violation, or a simple dispute with a landlord or an employer can mean the end of all life plans, arrest, detention, separation from loved ones, poverty, physical danger, and permanent banishment.

The most common justification for imposing such a precarious existence on noncitizens is rhetorically resonant but complex: these people, it is said, have violated the "rule of law."[11] No nation-state in history has more strongly associated itself with law than the United States. As Tocqueville asserted long ago, America could be well-described as "a Nation of people who aspire to live according to the rule of law."[12] Today, "rule of law" discourse, though often crudely deployed, marks virtually all debates about border enforcement and deportation. As one well-known proponent of strict enforcement responded to those who supported mercy and compassion for undocumented noncitizens: "They broke the law. Period."[13] But the law is not so simple; and its complexity suggests that a question mark rather than a period should follow the assertion that "they broke the law." Laws have certainly been broken. But what should we do about it?

The answer requires fundamental rethinking of both ends and means. As Seyla Benhabib has noted, we are like "travelers navigating an unknown terrain with the help of old maps, drawn at a different time and in response to different needs."[14] We must rethink the norms and goals of deportation as we also examine enforcement mechanisms in light of current realities. The agency that now controls most U.S. deportation is the Department of Homeland Security (DHS), its very name a fitting blend of aspiration and atavism. DHS asserts that we need a "smarter, more holistic approach that embeds security and resilience directly into global movement systems." The agency itself recognizes, however, that these goals of security and resilience must include protection of "civil liberties and the rule of law."[15] The hard task is to sort out what this really means in practice, both within and outside U.S. territorial borders.[16]

The outside, extraterritorial space has become especially important because of a phenomenon that I term, somewhat provocatively, the *new American diaspora*.[17] The United States deportation system has created a forcibly uprooted population of people with deep and cohesive connections to each other and to the nation-state from which they were removed. Around the world, from Haiti and the Dominican Republic to Brazil, from Mexico and Guatemala to the Azores, from Cape Verde to Cambodia, there are now hundreds of thousands of former long-term legal resident deportees who were raised and fully accultur-ated in the United States. In addition to their moral claims and the complex policy implications of their very existence, their legal rights are a problem that demands serious attention.

Let me make something clear at the outset: this book does not argue for com-pletely open borders, for the abolition of the nation-state, or against all immigration enforcement. Its call is for critical, thorough, humane analysis and reconceptuali-zation of a deportation system that has become shockingly large, unnecessarily harsh and, in many ways, dysfunctional. Once a relatively seldom-used and legally nuanced, flexible process, deportation in the United States has developed into a huge, expensive, and rigid enterprise. Its goals are elusive to define, and its positive effects are difficult to measure, especially when compared to its substantial negative collateral consequences. It has thrived in its current form for nearly two decades, having developed an impressive politico-legal momentum despite opposition from critics on the left and the right. It was, after all, not an immigrant rights organi-zation, but the editorial board of the Wall Street Journal who argued presciently—a decade ago—that deportation "would break up families [and] would disrupt busi-nesses that depend on foreign labor for jobs that Americans don't want. . . . "[18] Still, the system endures.

Deportation law is part of the U.S. constitutional legal system, though the fit is complicated and imperfect. It offers a salient example of the deep tension between the best ideals of liberal universalism and human rights and the realities of restricted membership in this nation-state.[19] Simply put, it mediates the line between our highest aspirations and our most basic fears. And yet it has largely done so without drawing the critical attention it deserves. Indeed, compared to the famous late eighteenth-century debates over the Alien and Sedition Acts, the biting controversies over Chinese exclusion and deportation laws in the late nineteenth century, ideological deportation episodes after World War I, and mas-sive repatriations of Mexicans in the mid-twentieth century, there has been insuf-ficient sustained recent consideration of deportation as a matter of fundamental principle. After many years of laboring in this system, teaching law students about it, and studying its history and nature, I realized that it evoked for me Marshall McLuhan's old adage, "I don't know who discovered water but it wasn't a fish."[20] To the extent that we think about it at all, many of us have now simply come to accept deportation as a background fact of normal modern life. But the nature of the current system demands that this be challenged.

Nearly a century ago, Raphael Lemkin, a Jewish lawyer from Poland, began developing a powerful new idea.[21] As he later put it: "New conceptions require new terms." His proposed term, "genocide," defined a new international crime, "the destruction of a nation or of an ethnic group."[22] The idea was so powerful that it is now considered one of the pillars of the modern human rights law regime.[23] In short, Lemkin changed the way we think about law and about basic human rights. The aims of this book—while much more modest—are inspired by this sort of history. Deportation does not require us to conceptualize a new term, but to *fundamentally rethink new forms of an old phenomenon*—to see how the system has developed, incrementally, into something in urgent need of major reform. My hope is that this work—at the very least—will inspire serious thought about the basic rights of deportees and their families, broadly defined. Of course, their rights claims are not simple. Most deportees are, by definition, not completely innocent victims, and many (though not all) have violated the law. Still, they have powerful moral and legal claims. Their life stories transcend the boundaries of the nation-state, and their voices should be heard. The size and consequences of the current deportation system have rendered the traditional "out of sight, out of mind" approach unjustifiable.

One of the redeeming joys of working in the often depressing realm of deportation law is a moving tradition of camaraderie and solidarity and an inclusive vision of human rights. In my last book, *Deportation Nation*, I sought to highlight a history of noncitizens' rights discourse that ranged from Jefferson and Madison to Charles Sumner; from Louis Post and Frances Perkins to immigration lawyers Jack Wasserman, Louis Boudin, and Carol King. It has included such poets as Henry Wadsworth Longfellow and Emma Lazarus; such singers as Woody Guthrie, Paul Robeson, Harry Belafonte, and Pete Seeger; and such activists as Harry Bridges, Carey McWilliams, Gordon Hirabayashi, Fred Korematsu, Minoru Yasui, César Chávez and Dolores Huerta, along with many, many others. I have been deeply inspired by their work and, my modest hope is to be able to continue its best traditions.

I owe debts of gratitude to more people than I can name who have helped with my research, writing and understanding of this project over many years. I am particularly grateful to Deans John Garvey and Vincent Rougeau, Interim Dean George Brown, and to my colleagues at Boston College Law School for their ideas and support. Special thanks are also due to Jacqueline Bhabha, Susan

Bibler-Coutin, Jessica Chicco, Jennifer Chacon, Julie Dahlstrom, Matt Gibney, Elspeth Guild, Kent Greenfield, Susan Gzesh, Don Hafner, David Hollenbach, Don Kerwin, Steve Legomsky, M. Brinton Lykes, David Martin, Nancy Morawetz, Hiroshi Motomura, Gerald Neuman, Michael Olivas, Vlad Perju, Julia Preston, Rachel Rosenbloom, Telma Silva, Nina Siulc, Debra Steinberg, Jacqueline Stevens, Maunica Sthanki, David Thronson, and Mike Wishnie, as well as to many government officials and employees of nongovernmental organizations from the Azores, Cambodia, Cape Verde, Ecuador, El Salvador, Guatemala, and Mexico who were generous with their time and provided helpful background materials. Emily Dix, Dhriti Pandhi, and Mariah Rutherford-Olds provided excellent research assistance and Dan Maltzman and Judy Yi helped mightily with various logistics. The project was much improved by feedback I received during presentations at American University, Washington College of Law, the Council on Foreign Relations, the biannual Immigration Law Teachers' Conference, at DePaul University, Harvard University, Stanford Law School, Temple University, Beasley School of Law, the University of Buenos Aires, UCLA, the University of Massachusetts, Boston, and the University of Oxford. I am very grateful to my editor, David McBride, who slogged through my early ramblings, and to various anonymous reviewers at Oxford University Press who offered sharp questions and invariably useful suggestions. Finally, I thank my students for helping me to clarify my thinking, and my clients and those deportees I have interviewed for sharing their lives and their truths with me.

Notes

1. Edward Everett Hale, *The Man Without A Country*, ATLANTIC MONTHLY, vol. 12, issue 73 (published anonymously December 1863), at 667.
2. For recent examples of the genre, see DANIEL KANSTROOM, DEPORTATION NATION (Harvard University Press 2007); BILL ONG HING, DEPORTING OUR SOULS: VALUES, MORALITY, AND IMMIGRATION POLICY (Cambridge University Press 2006); THE DEPORTATION REGIME: SOVEREIGNTY, SPACE, AND THE FREEDOM OF MOVEMENT (Nicholas De Genova & Nathalie Peutz eds., Duke University Press 2010).
3. As Zygmunt Bauman has put it, "Traveling for profit is encouraged; traveling for survival is condemned." ZYGMUNT BAUMAN, SOCIETY UNDER SIEGE 84 (Cambridge: Polity Press 2002).
4. *See* ROBERT GILPIN, WAR AND CHANGE IN WORLD POLITICS 7 (Cambridge University Press 1981) (cited in JOHN RAWLS, THE LAW OF PEOPLES 28 (Harvard University Press 1999)).
5. The European Union, often cited as a counterexample vis-à-vis its member states, confirms the basic point clearly against, for example, migrants and refugees from Africa. See Jacqueline Bhabha, *"Get Back to Where You Once Belonged": Identity, Citizenship, and Exclusion in Europe*, 20 HUMAN RIGHTS Q. 592–627 (August 1998). *See also* THOMAS L. FRIEDMAN, THE WORLD IS FLAT: A BRIEF HISTORY OF THE TWENTY-FIRST CENTURY (2005). As Giorgio Agamben once piquantly put it: humanity itself has, for border control purposes, become a dangerous class. *No to Bio-Political Tattooing*, LE MONDE, Jan. 10, 2004, at 3. (quoted in

Ronen Shamir, *Without Borders? Notes on Globalization as a Mobility Regime*, 23(2) Sociological Theory 197–217 (2005).

6. *See, e.g.,* Bryan S. Turner, *Enclosures, Enclaves, and Entrapment*, 80(2) Sociological Inquiry 241–60 (May 2010) (noting important trends toward increased immobility of people
across borders due to enhanced methods of tracking and containing people and a greater
emphasis on securitization by the state); *see also* Bryan S. Turner, *The Enclave Society: Towards
a Sociology of Immobility.* 10(2) Eur. J. of Soc. Theory 287–303 (2007); Ronen Shamir,
Without Borders? Notes on Globalization as a Mobility Regime, 23(2) Sociological Theory
197–217 (2005) (suggesting that the emergence of a global mobility regime, oriented to clo-
sure and to the blocking of access, is premised not only on national or local grounds but also
on a principle of perceived universal dangerous personhoods, "a paradigm of suspicion." The
aim of this mobility regime is "to maintain high levels of inequality in a relatively normatively
homogenized world."); Rogers Brubaker, *The 'Diaspora' Diaspora*, 28(1) Ethnic & Racial
Stud. 9 (January 2005) ("states have gained rather than lost the capacity to monitor and
control he movement of people by deploying increasingly sophisticated technologies of identification and control including citizenship, passports, visas, surveillance, integrated databases and biometric devices"); John Torpey, The Invention of the Passport:
Surveillance, Citizenship and the State (Cambridge University Press 2000).

7. As Paul Virilio noted, "speed-space" has replaced "time-space" as the most relevant operative
concept. Virilio Live: Selected Interviews 71 (John Armitage ed., 2001).

8. Brubaker, *The 'Diaspora' Diaspora*, *supra* note 6, at 9 (citing Paul Hirst and Grahame
Thompson Globalization in Question 30–31, 267 (Cambridge: Polity Press1999).

9. Nevertheless, a main purpose of the nation-state is still "to guard the selectivity of osmosis."
Bauman, *supra* note 3, at 82. *See* Gabriel Sheffer, Diaspora Politics: At Home
Abroad 22 (Cambridge University Press 2003) (noting the "unprecedented porosity" of
borders).

10. *See, e.g.,* Yasemin Soysal, Limits of Citizenship: Migrants and Postnational Membership in Europe 3 (University of Chicago Press 1994) (describing the rights of noncitizens); *see also* Devon W. Carbado, "Racial Naturalization," in Legal Borderlands: Law
and the Construction of American Borders 41 (Mary L. Dudziak and Leti Volpp
eds., Johns Hopkins Press 2006).

11. *See* Matthew Gibney, *Precarious Residents: Migration Control, Membership and the Rights of
Non-Citizens*, UNDP. Human Development Research Paper, 2009/10 ("Precarious residents
can be defined as non-citizens living in the state that possess few social, political or economic
rights, are highly vulnerable to deportation, and have little or no option for making secure
their immigration status.")

12. Alexis de Tocqueville, 1 Democracy in America 278 (Knopf 1945); *see* Austin Sarat,
"At the Boundaries of Law: Executive Clemency, Sovereign Prerogative, and the Dilemma of
American Legality," in Legal Borderlands: Law and the Construction of Ameri-
can Borders 21 (Mary L. Dudziak & Leti Volpp eds., Johns Hopkins Press 2006).

13. U.S. Representative Steve King, R-Iowa, quoted in Elizabeth Llorente, "Steve King Asks What
Part of the 'Rule of Law' Don't We Understand?" *Fox News Latino*, January 7, 2011, *available at*
http://latino.foxnews.com/latino/politics/2010/12/14/key-force-immigration-congress-
vows-focus-enforcement/.

14. *See* Seyla Benhabib, The Rights of Others 6 (2004).

15. U.S. Department of Homeland Security, Quadrennial Homeland Security Review Report: A
Strategic Framework for a Secure Homeland, Washington, DC, February 2010, at 16.

16. For insightful consideration of how this actually works in the United States, see Ayelet
Shachar, *The Shifting Border of Immigration Regulation*, 3 Stan. J. C. R. & C. L. 165 (2007); *see
also* Huyen Pham, *When Immigration Borders Move*, 61 Fla. L. Rev. 1115 (2009).

17. I fully realize that this is a complex and, for some, problematic word choice. As Rogers Brubaker has noted, the "latitudinarian 'let-a-thousand-diasporas-bloom' approach may have
rendered the category stretched to the point of uselessness." *See* Brubaker, *The 'Diaspora' Diaspora, supra note 6. See also* the Introduction in this volume for my justifications; Diaspora
and Transnationalism: Concepts, Theories and Methods (Rainer Bauböck &
Thomas Faist eds., 2010).

18. As the editorial continued: "The U.S. needs policies in place that recognize the economic realities that come with a long, porous border between an immensely rich country and a poor one. We need programs that will legalize the status of foreigners who are here already and contributing to our economy. We need more legal channels, such as temporary work programs, to handle future arrivals. And we need to speed up family reunifications." *The GOP's Immigration Fumble*, WALL ST. J., August 4, 2002.

19. *See, e.g.,* Mark Tushnet, *Essay-Review: United States Citizenship Policy and Liberal Universalism*, 12 GEO. IMMIGR L. J. 311 (1998).

20. McCluhan repeated many versions of this maxim in public talks as well as in print. *See, e.g.,* MARSHALL MCLUHAN AND QUENTIN FIORE, WAR AND PEACE IN THE GLOBAL VILLAGE 175 (1968) ("they have no anti-environment which would enable them to perceive the element they live in"); MARSHALL MCLUHAN, CULTURE IS OUR BUSINESS 191 (1970) ("Fish don't know water exists till beached.").

21. The concept, which Lemkin had earlier referred to as "the crime of barbarity," was crafted from the root words *genos* (Greek for family, tribe, or race) and *cide* (Latin for killing).

22. RAPHAEL LEMKIN, AXIS RULE IN OCCUPIED EUROPE: LAWS OF OCCUPATION—ANALYSIS OF GOVERNMENT—PROPOSALS FOR REDRESS 79–95, ch. IX: "Genocide a New Term and New Conception for Destruction of Nations" (Washington, DC: Carnegie Endowment for International Peace, 1944).

23. *See* the Convention on the Prevention and Punishment of the Crime of Genocide. 78 UNTS 277 (1951).

Aftermath

Introduction

"What Part of 'Illegal' Do You Not Understand?"

As to its cruelty, nothing can exceed a forcible deportation from a country of one's residence, and the breaking up of all the relations of friendship, family, and business there contracted.
—Supreme Court Justice Stephen J. Field (1893)[1]

Fear is the parent of cruelty.
—James Anthony Froude (1876)[2]

Picture a woman—let's call her Marie—who came to the United States twenty years ago as a refugee with her 1-year-old son, Marc. Marie is poor and speaks very little English. She has struggled to make a good life, but she never became a citizen, nor did Marc. They were both legal permanent residents of the United States, with "green cards."[3]

Marie always saw Marc as a good boy; he was polite and a decent student. But they lived in a tough neighborhood, and in high school, Marc fell in with a bad crowd. Arrested by state police with some of the drug called ecstasy in his pocket, he pled guilty to "aiding and abetting the possession of a controlled substance."[4] According to his criminal lawyer, this was a very good deal—he was sentenced to one year of probation. He had no other criminal record. Marie was frustrated and angry with him, but she figured he would learn his lesson.

However, when he went to meet his probation officer one day in 2005, Marc was arrested by federal Immigration and Customs Enforcement (ICE)[5] agents, placed in mandatory detention with no right to even ask for bail, and told he faced inevitable deportation as an "aggravated felon" (a technical term under U.S. immigration law that can include many types of crimes, including some drug offenses). He was to be sent to the country from which he and his mother had fled, but where they have no contacts and no more family.[6] When Marie went to visit him in ICE detention, Marc told her that he had thought they were the same as U.S. citizens, if he had ever thought about it all.[7] His appointed criminal lawyer said she could not help him with his deportation case as it was not part of her job. Marie had no money for an immigration lawyer, and the lawyers with whom she talked said it seemed there was probably nothing they could do for him anyway. One day, Marc was transferred to another facility two thousand miles away from her. Then, a few months later, he was deported and banned from the United States for life.

Marie, now almost 60 years old, was devastated. She was especially upset to learn that after Marc's removal, the U.S. Supreme Court had ruled that his offense never should have been classified as an aggravated felony and that he should have been able to ask an immigration judge for a discretionary waiver of the deportation order. But Marc's situation was even worse than Marie had imagined. Soon after Marc was deported, Marie learned that he was HIV-positive and that, after deportation, he would be held in his home country for at least two weeks in a filthy, overcrowded, and corrupt prison with no access to medication.[8] Now completely alone and fearing that her son had, in effect, been sentenced to death, she asks a legal expert if there is anything that can possibly be done to bring him back to the United States. The answer, essentially, is "no."

This story must surely be troubling even to those who favor strict immigration enforcement. Reflecting more than the personal tragedies of a mother left alone and a son condemned perhaps to die in what, for him, is a foreign, unknown place, it raises deep questions of law and justice. Should people who immigrate as young children—legally or not—be forever subject to deportation if they do not become citizens? Should there be a statute of limitations for deportation? Should immigration authorities and courts balance the gravity of the offense against other factors such as legal status or foreseeable hardship to the deportee or his/her family? How should legal mistakes or changes in law be addressed? These questions, and many more like them, are the subjects of this book. Though they have complicated and technical aspects, they also present some of the most compelling politico-legal and ethical dilemmas of our time.

This book advocates a dramatic change of focus in our thinking about immigration admissions and enforcement. Historically, much of the U.S. system was a comparatively optimistic enterprise. Entry and admission were the key concepts, and the widespread assumption was that those who came here would succeed, stay, and become citizens. Of course, as I have previously shown, exclusion and deportation were always critical parts of this enterprise.[9] Indeed, the systematic control of foreign laborers, particularly those from Asia and Latin America who entered in irregular ways or who lack legal status, has long been oppressive. In recent decades, however, removal has become such an overwhelming and integral component of the U.S. immigration system that it now vies with admission and naturalization as a central operating principle. For many millions of noncitizens, the threat of deportation now looms at least as large as the promise of permanent residence and citizenship. For millions of others, the reality of deportation has already destroyed such opportunities, and it has done so in ways that are unprecedented in their harshness. This is not to say that deportation can never be warranted. If one accepts the basic legitimacy of the nation-state, then deportation as a tool of *extended border control* is logical and at least potentially justifiable.[10] Also, for severe human rights abusers, violent terrorists, and serious criminals (all terms in need of very careful definition), deportation may be a necessary enforcement tool. But acceptance of some forms of deportation in principle surely does not require acceptance of the current system, which has vastly exceeded any historical precedent in terms of its size, its ferocity, its disproportionality, its disregard for basic rights, and its substantial negative effects.

How might we best understand and reform the system? Anecdotes alone, no matter how compelling they may be, are insufficient. For every story like that of Marc and Marie (and there are many), others offer chilling counter-narratives. Reports of foreign terrorist plots and crimes by "illegal aliens" inspire strong public reactions. One website even features "America's Most Forgotten," dedicated "to all of the innocent people and their families who have been victimized by illegal aliens as a result of the refusal of our elected officials to enforce United States immigration law and to secure our borders." A particularly tragic story describes a 21-year-old Marine corporal home on leave for Thanksgiving from Iraq who was killed by "an illegal alien with a blood alcohol level four times the legal limit."[11] The site also includes a list of "must reads" such as "School Bus Tragedy Ends in Death At the Hands of Illegal Alien Driver," "Drunk Illegal Alien Causes Christmas Eve Crash: Three Family Members Die" and "13-Year-Old Strangled by Illegal Alien."[12] As we shall see, the data about immigrants and crimes indicate no need for substantial concern about noncitizen criminality.[13] Still, such stories have a certain logic and an obvious emotional appeal: "if these people, who have no right to be here, had been deported, then this never would have happened."[14]

So how can we better understand deportation? Theories about the border and the nation-state are important starting points, but too abstract to yield specific policy solutions. Statistics are essential, but perhaps not so different from anecdotes in their malleability. Cost-benefit analyses may be useful but—like such research in the criminal justice system—famously complex. As two researchers once put it: "Estimating the social costs and benefits of competing transportation or environmental policies is no analytical picnic. But estimating them for imprisonment and other sentencing options is a certain analytical migraine."[15] This is at least equally true of deportation research. Ultimately, we must consider such strong normative claims as those of basic rights to dignity, family, proportionality, and equality. This approach, too, may cut in different directions, however. Marc and Marie undoubtedly have powerful rights claims.

But so do others in the society in which they live, including perhaps rights to self-determination,[16] to define the nature of membership,[17] to associate with each other as citizens in a nation-state[18] and against drug-dealing in their community. These claims, however, are subject both to internal limits (set by the "members" themselves) and to fundamental principles.[19] To ignore such principles is to risk a profound, well-recognized historical danger: "the rule of citizens over non-citizens, of members over strangers is probably the most common form of tyranny in human history."[20]

Clearly, deportation is a complex subject with many facets, complicated roots, and many possible permutations. Even a quick look in a thesaurus for synonyms for the word, "deportation," yields a moving litany: banishment, displacement, expatriation, expulsion, relegation. A list of "related words" is similarly evocative, including: ostracism, diaspora, dispersion, scattering, emigration, ethnic cleansing, transportation, dispossession, ejection, and ouster.[21] To understand deportation, then, we must carefully blend many analytical methods.

A central focus of our inquiry must be on the idea of the "rule of law." As we shall see, rule of law discourse—both domestic and international—is far more than a rhetorical trope deployed by those who support greater border control or strict internal enforcement. It crystallizes and renders specific critical aspects of the deep debate over the nature and effects of deportation. It incorporates the data and bridges the gaps between anecdotes and statistics, between normative values and cost-benefit calculations, between raw majoritarian power and legitimacy.[22]

Human rights are no less a part of the coercive power of the rule of law than government enforcement power.[23] For deportees, however, rights are very much works-in-progress that require textured and nuanced thought, not only about the rights they may have due to their humanity, but also by virtue of their residence in the United States.[24]

The U.S. Department of Homeland Security (DHS) states that it is imperative to its mission to know who lives and works within U.S. national borders.[25] This might, of course, include constant oversight of everyone, but DHS focuses mostly on noncitizens. Its major aims include deterrence of immigration violations.[26] A large part of this task involves "removing those who violate our laws." DHS accepts that this must be done not only with "efficiency," but also with "fairness, and integrity."[27] The hard question, simply put, is how to define and balance these three criteria. This, as we shall see, involves both legal rules and the related concept of discretion. The Obama administration has, for example, interpreted "family" to include gay and lesbian couples and has developed important new guidelines for prosecutorial discretion. Indeed, in August 2011, the Administration announced a bold new initiative to stop focusing on people who are "low priorities for deportation." This includes young people who were brought to this country as small children as well as military veterans and the spouses of active-duty military personnel.[28] If this program works as described (its exact procedures and parameters are unclear as of this writing), it will be a major step forward—albeit a belated and perhaps temporary one—toward a smarter and more humane enforcement regime.[29]

Still, the hard basic facts of deportation must be confronted. Since its reinvigoration in the late 1990s, deportation has torn through many communities like a capricious tornado: touching down suddenly from dark clouds and leaving a trail of devastation in its wake, while sweeping away tens of millions of people from our midst. It has had profound and still-understudied effects on individuals, families, and communities, both in the United States and in the countries to which deportees are sent. This book therefore considers the nature of deportation, its justifications, its accomplishments, and its failures. It then considers its consequences, its *aftermath*. We must engage in as thorough, objective, and careful an empirical study as the data permit.

But let us also listen to the voices of deportees and try to see the system as they do. Here is how one deportee, Jose Angel Carachuri, whose legal case is discussed in Chapter 4, was described in the government's legal brief before the U.S. Supreme Court:

> Petitioner is a citizen of Mexico. After obtaining lawful permanent residency in the United States, he committed a variety of crimes. He was convicted . . . of two state drug possession offenses. The Department of Homeland Security charged petitioner with being removable. . . .[30]

Compare that laconic description with one written by Mr. Carachuri's lawyers:

> Petitioner was born in Mexico and immigrated to the United States with his parents. He later became a lawful permanent resident, and has worked as a carpet installer from the time he was seventeen years old. Petitioner is engaged to a U.S. citizen, with whom he has four children, each also a U.S. citizen. In addition, petitioner's mother and two sisters live in the United States. Petitioner has no family in Mexico, and before the government removed him from the country, petitioner had made no visits to Mexico since childhood.[31]

This narrative dissonance reflects more than the skills of legal advocates. Our perceptions of deportation vary depending on how we view the deportees themselves. Are they objectified "illegal aliens"—who bear their illegality existentially and permanently—or do they have life stories to which attention must be paid? For those unaccustomed to hearing the voices of undocumented migrants, their eloquence can be both surprising and moving. As one Salvadoran mother put it, "[The] laws say that a person who crosses [the border] is a criminal. It's more criminal to let your children starve to death. If I have to lose my life, at least I wanted to try rather than let my children die of hunger."[32] Deportees, when their voices are heard, often describe their plight with poignant simplicity. A 26-year-old man, raised in the United States, was deported to Haiti in 2011 because of a conviction for possession of cocaine. Suddenly he found himself living in a tent along with thousands of Haitians, amid the horrors of an earthquake that had ravaged the country, facing cholera, chaos, abject poverty, and permanent banishment. He observed, "I wouldn't wish Haiti on my worst enemy. . . . I'm used to being treated like a human being, but a human life has absolutely zero value in Haiti."[33]

Of course, every large government system has its horror stories. Those of deportation, however, have been distressingly common, both predictable and predicted. Thirty-four-year-old deportee Wildrick Guerrier had been nicknamed "Black Jesus" because of his attempts to assist other struggling inmates. While detained in a Port-au-Prince police station after his deportation, Guerrier displayed cholera-like symptoms of diarrhea, weakness, and vomiting after tending to other sick and wounded detainees. Other detainees reportedly begged the police for medical care for Guerrier. But there was to be no help. Several deportees interviewed by the Associated Press said the police told them: "This is what you came here for: to suffer."[34] As one attorney noted, during his pre-deportation detention in Louisiana, Guerrier had expressed grave concerns that he had no family in Haiti, that he had not been to Haiti for a very long time, and that he was afraid of what would happen to him amid a cholera outbreak. In retrospect, she sadly intoned, "he was right to be terrified."[35]

This book thus revisits fundamental legal questions about deportation: Does it demand proportionality?[36] How powerful a legal value is "finality"? How does deportation fit within our constitutional legal system? What are its limits in time and in territorial space? How should we understand the increasingly pervasive idea of "discretion"?[37] But deportation also raises questions that transcend the nation-state, evoking considerations of "globalization," "post-nationalism," and "transnational families."[38] Most important, deportation has created a large foreign population of people who were raised in the United States, who speak English as their primary language, who often have deep family ties in the United States, and who are culturally and socially American. In effect, this is a new, unplanned *diaspora*. The use of this term in this uncommon, somewhat polemical way requires explanation. Though an ancient and useful idea, the term diaspora has, in recent years, become popular to the point where no single, exact definition is possible.[39] As Rogers Brubaker has suggested, we face a "'diaspora' diaspora," in which there are such a wide variety of meanings in "semantic, conceptual and disciplinary space" that the term itself may be lost.[40] The original, core meaning of diaspora related to Jewish dispersion, and was then applied to such "classical" examples as the Armenian and Greek diasporas.[41] Most basically, the term has signified displaced populations that have maintained strong racial, religious, or ethnic ties to what they recognize as their original homeland. But recent usages have ranged more widely to include political communities, labor migrants, and many others. Thus, some write of "Dixie," white, liberal, gay, queer, and even digital diasporas.[42] The attempt in this work is to relate the contemporary situation of U.S. deportees to the traditional meaning, but with a unique twist: the deportees' identity is based on their upbringing, socialization, culture, and family connections to the United States, *despite* their lack of formal citizenship status. The U.S. deportation *diaspora* consists of a forcibly uprooted population of people with deep, cohesive social and cultural connections to each other and to the nation-state from which they have been involuntarily removed.[43] The term, I suggest, may appropriately apply to the hundreds of thousands of (former) long-term legal resident deportees who were raised and acculturated in the United States.[44] These people, now widely scattered, share features that constitute the core of the generally accepted use of the term: First, they have faced a "traumatic dispersion."[45] Second, as we shall see, many of them maintain deep connection to their former homeland (the United States) as an "authoritative source of value, identity and loyalty."[46] (This distinguishes them from those around the world who may voluntarily undertake "second-generation" return.)[47] But what about "boundary-maintenance?"[48] Historically, scholars have viewed the preservation of a distinctive identity in host societies as the *sine qua non* of a diaspora.[49] The basic idea is that of a "separate society or quasi-society in a larger polity."[50] Describing U.S. deportees as a diaspora community may thus depend upon the extent to which they eventually reintegrate into the countries to which they are deported. Various governments now have programs to facilitate such reintegration, as do some international nongovernmental organizations.[51] However, the success of such efforts has been sporadic and, on the whole, minimal. Given the fact that the current U.S. deportation experiment, though massive and radical, is less than two decades old, we shall have to wait and see what the future research holds. In the meantime, one could view the term *diaspora* in this context as an idiom, a stance, or a tentative claim as much as an objectively settled description of deportation phenomena.[52] It is worth noting, however, that some deportees themselves use the terminology of diaspora—indeed, a group of young people in Massachusetts have created an organization called *Deportation Diaspora* with which I have worked. Of course, what is especially tricky here is that deportees, by definition, have not been U.S. citizens or had full membership rights in U.S. society. Can people be "diaspora-ed" from a homeland that never granted them full membership? The question seems the converse of Groucho Marx's pledge never to join a club that would have him as a member. Can deportees legitimately identify with the club that has, in effect, declined their application for membership? Perhaps. But the problem runs deeper than terminology.

This brings us back to the rule of law. Proponents of strict deportation laws argue that noncitizens have lesser rights in general than citizens and especially tenuous claims to stay in a country if they have violated the law.[53] As to the undocumented who face deportation, the argument may be simpler still: *"what part of illegal do you not understand?"*[54] Some use a trespassing metaphor to describe those who have arrived on U.S. territory without permission.[55] Others, expressing frustration with "porous borders" and ineffective immigration control, offer a more general utilitarian goal of respect for law.[56] To be sure, many in the United States seem to be more upset by the *failure* of immigration enforcement than by its excesses. Thus, it is unsurprising that the Clinton, Bush, and the Obama administrations have all strongly supported deportation, albeit focusing in different arenas and using rather different methods.[57]

One might accept the potential validity of some such arguments without adopting the simplistic solution of deportation for all undocumented noncitizens and other deportees. There is, in fact, much about the strange concept of human illegality that many supporters of strong deportation laws do not seem to understand. The basic legitimacy of the nation-state and its borders does not demand absolute, disproportionate or arbitrary power.[58] The assertion that someone has broken a law is the *beginning* of a conversation, not the end of one.[59] The passage of time, for example, may surely erode "the moral right of states to deport irregular migrants."[60] Colonial history, past aggressions, and massive wealth disparities may likewise render certain deportations highly questionable.[61] And if the regime of international human rights means anything, it surely means that there are limits on what a government may do even to noncitizens within its borders.

From this perspective, we might accept that *some* types of exclusion and deportation laws are theoretically justifiable.[62] Border control, security, respect for immigration laws, and certain aspects of public safety are legitimate democratic goals.[63] Admission and exclusion laws are foundational systems that relate to "the deepest meaning of self-determination." And large numbers of irregular migrants may damage the state's efforts to maintain minimum labor standards and other aspects of social justice.[64] But again, these are starting points—not the end of discussion.

This book thus considers the U.S. deportation system *as it works and as it might work more justly and fairly.* We shall examine its costs, its systemic impacts, and its harms to individuals, families,[65] U.S. communities, and the countries of the deportees.[66] Costs can, of course, be measured in a variety of ways: some rather general (such as the cost of racial profiling); some indirect (such as effects on children whose parents are deported); and some quite specific (such as the costs of the immigration detention system). The task is undoubtedly multilayered and complex. But the failure even to attempt it would be unjustifiable.

And what of the rule of law? The system in action forces us to think about the breadth and depth of law in practice. Much of U.S. deportation law has long been formalistic and rigidly categorical, a vestige of nineteenth-century doctrinal roots.[67] The system, for example, is said to be civil, not criminal, and its sanctions are often defined as nonpunitive. As a result, many constitutional rights, such as a right to appointed counsel or a clear right against retroactive legislation, do not apply.[68] Law and discretion are separated and proportionality is largely ignored. This book suggests that deportation law should be more grounded in well-developed principles of constitutional and international human rights law, including ameliorative discretion and strong safeguards against disproportionate harshness, unforeseen consequences, and mistakes.

Although, as Kal Raustiala has noted, "[t]erritoriality is so intuitive that we rarely question it,"[69] it remains a central feature of U.S. deportation law. The border, in short, often marks the line where the rule of law ends for deportees.[70] But this line is not consistently or carefully drawn. Indeed, as we shall see, territoriality has been a fluid and contingent legal idea, deployed in various ways to achieve often completely contradictory results.[71] Post-deportation law (the rule of law for those who have actually been deported) is thus a tortuous, complicated enterprise in which government lawyers have long sought to restrict the reach of legal norms.[72] Many deportation cases, including those with major mistakes, are largely insulated from review, leaving the affected individuals and their families with no effective remedies.[73] Such situations challenge the ideal of the rule of law as much as unauthorized entry by individuals.[74] The Board of Immigration Appeals, denying jurisdiction over the legal claims of deportees who have been physically removed from U.S. soil, has intoned: "Removed aliens have, by virtue of their departure, literally *passed beyond our aid*."[75] Surely we can do better than this. The basic task is to strike a balance between the "needs of organized society" and justice.[76] This cannot be done with territorial formalism or mechanical, unvarying rules.[77]

So, let us now begin to examine this strange system in greater detail. Modern deportation law has evolved from diverse antecedents, including colonial restrictions on the movement of poor people, transportation and banishment of criminals, fugitive slave laws, race-based laws, and ideological social controls.[78] It has thus long implicated powerful normative concerns, racial categories, complex legal interpretation problems, and inherent tensions in the self-definition of the United States as a "nation of immigrants." However, in recent years, the system has changed dramatically. The most important changes took place in 1996, when two laws known by their acronyms, AEDPA (Antiterrorism and Effective Death Penalty Act) and IIRIRA (Illegal Immigration Reform and Immigrant Responsibility Act), reconfigured the U.S. deportation system. Among other features, the 1996 laws (retroactively) expanded many grounds for exclusion and deportation, created mandatory detention for many noncitizens, invented new "fast-track" deportation systems; eliminated judicial review of certain types of deportation (removal) orders; discarded some and limited other discretionary "waivers" of deportability; and vastly increased possible state and local law collaboration. As a direct result of these laws, hundreds of thousands of people have been excluded and deported from the United States who would have been allowed to become legal permanent residents and (probably) naturalized citizens under prior laws.[79] Budgets for the enforcement agenda have increased steadily as the dominant political reality remains the failure of "Comprehensive Immigration Reform" during the George W. Bush administration to become law.[80] Despite the statements of candidate Barack Obama (who once said "we cannot—and should not—deport 12 million people"),[81] the number of annual deportations (technically called removals) increased significantly in the first years of the Obama administration. The most recent statistics from ICE show more than 392,000 total "removals" in FY 2010, a term which, as we shall see, includes a variety of mechanisms.[82] Indeed, as the following (Chart 1.1) shows, the last few decades have witnessed a stunning increase in deportations of all types. Though the best available statistics are far from perfect, involving some double-counting and some recidivist border crossers, the numbers are still quite impressive. If we include "returns"—some of which are technically called "voluntary" and many of which occur at or near the border—we see a ten-fold increase in total deportation events from the period 1961 to 1970 (when the totals were 101,205 forced removals and 1,334,528 returns) to 1971 to 1980 (240,235 forced removals and 7,246,812 returns) to 1991 to 2000 (946,506 forced removals and 13,588,193 returns) to 2001 to 2010, when the force removal totals rose sharply to 2,794,946 along with 9,378,880 returns.

Simply out, the system, as a whole, is huge and has grown dramatically. As I write this book, U.S. federal deportation authorities will incarcerate more than twenty-nine thousand noncitizens on any given day, (with more than one thousand added each day) and oversee more than 1.6 million people in various stages of immigration removal proceedings.[83]

The size of the deportation system may also be understood by considering the population it governs. The number of foreign-born people residing in the United States now approximates the highest levels in history (see chart 1.2). As a percentage of the U.S. population, the current number—some 12 percent—had not been reached since the turn of the twentieth century. Of the roughly 38 to 40 million foreign-born residents in the United States, about 17 million are naturalized U.S. citizens, essentially immune from deportation.[84] The rest, about 22 million

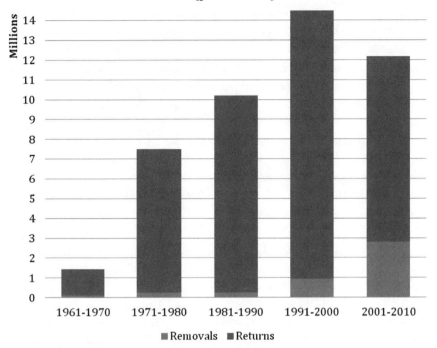

Total Removals and Returns Since 1961 (per decade)

■ Removals ■ Returns

Chart 1.1 Total Removals and Returns Since 1961 (per decade). Source: United States Department of Homeland Security, Yearbook of Immigration Statistics: 2010. Washington, DC. Table 36 available at: http://www.dhs.gov/files/statistics/publications/YrBk10En.shtm

people, are not citizens.[85] There are some 170 million legal "nonimmigrant" entries into the United States each year. Though this number counts many who enter and leave repeatedly, the number of tourists, students, workers, and so forth is still impressive.[86] Moreover, about a million new legal immigrants arrive each year as legal permanent residents.[87] Millions more live in a variety of complex tenuous, quasi-legal statuses.[88] Whatever else it may be, deportation was not designed to be—nor does it work as—an anti-immigration system as such.[89] This is part of its complexity. Still, for many millions of people in the United States, Cicero's famous observation about Damocles may remain apt: "[T]here can be nothing happy for the person over whom some fear always looms[.]"[90]

Among the many aspects of deportation that one might reasonably fear, the problem of mistakes looms large. Accuracy, while not the only criterion by which one measures the quality of a legal system, is surely critical. The well-known and highly influential Innocence Project, which focuses on the wrongly convicted, was not called the "Disproportionality Project" for good reasons. Data about wrongful deportations indicate substantial systemic problems.[91]

Foreign Born Population and Foreign Born as Percentage of the Total US Population, 1850 - 2009

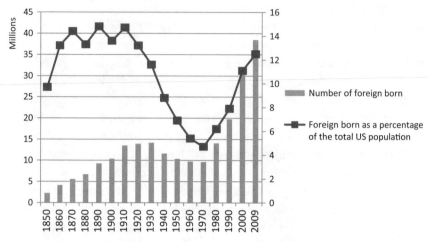

Chart 1.2 Foreign Born Population and Foreign Born as Percentage of the Total US Population, 1850–2009. Source: Migration Policy Institute, MPI Data Hub, available at http://www.migrationinformation.org/datahub/charts/final.fb.shtml.

Indeed, even U.S. citizens have found themselves deported—a situation that violates more laws and more legal principles than one can count.[92] As Jacqueline Stevens has poignantly reported, "U.S. citizens who previously had been housed and self-sufficient or cared for by their families have been found bathing in the Tijuana River and eating garbage; drifting among Latin American shelters and obtaining nourishment and liquid from roadside soda cans in El Salvador; and, in a somewhat surreal reversal, eking out livings as day laborers in Mexico or telemarketing in the Dominican Republic."[93]

How can such strange things happen? Consider Pedro (also known as Peter) Guzman, a United States citizen, born and raised in California, who was arrested one day for the misdemeanor of trespassing. Mr. Guzman, then 29 years old, has a cognitive disability. He attended special education classes as a child, cannot read or write, and has serious difficulty processing information. While in the custody of the Los Angeles County Sheriff's Department, he apparently signed a document stating that he was a citizen of Mexico and had no legal status in the United States. The Sheriff's Department administrator who obtained Mr. Guzman's signature on the document checked a box indicating that Mr. Guzman had read the statement himself, in Spanish. On the basis of this signature alone, Mr. Guzman was transferred to ICE custody and was transported to the streets of Tijuana. No attorney or family members were ever present during the removal process.

He was simply put on a bus to Tijuana. He had no money and could not even remember his family's phone number. He wandered the streets for three months, eating out of garbage cans and bathing in the Tijuana River while his terrified parents desperately searched for him. He was finally allowed to return to the United States after Customs and Border Protection agents learned that a warrant for his arrest had issued because he had missed meetings with his probation officer.

Pedro Guzman's specific experience is fortunately a rather rare scenario. But it is far from unique. Indeed, a nonprofit agency that serves detained immigrants in Arizona reported that it encountered forty to fifty detainees per month with potentially valid claims to U.S. citizenship, some 7 percent of the eight thousand detainees to whom it provided services in 2007.[94] If this ratio were true of the approximately three hundred thousand detainees throughout the country each year, it would exceed twenty thousand people. Although that number is highly unlikely, the cases discovered to date do indicate that such mistakes are far from unique.

It also appears that many thousands of noncitizen deportees ought to be in the United States with their families due to other kinds of mistakes. The full scope of this problem can never be accurately measured. But imagine even a 1 percent or 2 percent error rate (which would be an extremely positive accomplishment for the agencies involved.) Based on estimates of the annual number of removals from the United States, a 1 percent error rate would mean some eighty thousand to one hundred thousand mistakes just over the past few years, including refugees, asylum seekers, and many thousands of long-term legal residents. Part of the reason for such mistakes is the complexity of immigration and citizenship laws. But, as Pedro Guzman's case demonstrates, a fuller explanation demands systemic analysis.[95]

Many thousands of noncitizen deportees simply never should have been deported. Some gave up fighting their cases because they could not stand to remain in immigration detention. Many lacked immigration counsel, or they had inadequate counsel. As the Supreme Court recognized in 2010, many criminal defense lawyers had no awareness of possible immigration consequences and advised noncitizens very badly.[96] Still, in many such cases, there was no recourse, whether in criminal or in immigration court.[97] Further, thousands of noncitizens have been deported pursuant to legal interpretations that were later found by the Supreme Court to have been incorrect.[98] But those who may discover that they were wrongly deported face often insurmountable hurdles to reopening their cases or returning to the United States.[99]

In addition to all of this, we must consider the effects of deportation on U.S. families and communities, especially the children of the undocumented. More than 3 million such children are U.S. citizens. Tens of thousands of children have seen their families split or experienced the effective deportation of the entire family to countries "as foreign to them as they are to other American children."[100] The harm to a U.S. citizen child in these circumstances has been well described as "palpable and long-lasting."[101] However, as chart 1.3 shows, the number and percentage of children born to immigrants has been rising for decades.[102]

Negative effects of deportation have also been felt especially acutely in the countries to which deportees are sent.[103] To call such countries "home" for many of the deportees is at best a cruel joke. Many deportees know no one in the countries to which they are removed and do not even speak the native language. The United States, each year, expels hundreds of thousands of deracinated people who have no social networks or supports in the countries to which they are sent. Some countries, such as the Azores, El Salvador, and Ecuador, have devoted significant resources and thought to the reintegration of people whom they frequently call "migrants." The United States, however, provides scant resources or mechanisms for reacculturation or post-deportation support. Once these people are deported—no matter how long they have lived in the United States—they are someone else's responsibility.

In many countries, the treatment of deportees has been a serious human rights concern. In 2000, for example, the Haitian government imposed mandatory, indefinite detention on all criminal deportees arriving from the United States.[104] As U.S. courts have since recognized, "[t]he conditions of Haitian prisons are atrocious."[105] Prisoners and detainees "suffer from a lack of basic hygiene, malnutrition, poor quality health care, and, in some facilities, 24-hour confinement. Most prisons periodically suffered from lack of water, especially in the provinces. Many prisoners also suffered from diseases, including beriberi, AIDS, and tuberculosis.[106] The State Department also found a pattern of pervasive, brutal mistreatment including beating with fists, sticks, and belts, burning with cigarettes, choking, hooding, allegations of torture by electric shock, and withholding medical treatment.[107] But even this did not prevent deportations to Haiti. U.S. courts concluded that although the conditions in Haitian prisons

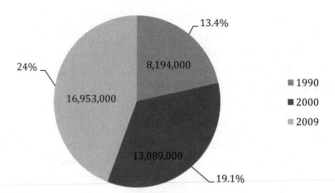

Chart 1.3 Children of Immigrants: Number and Percentage of Children under 18: 1990 to 2010.[108] Source: Migration Policy Institute, MPI Data Hub, available at: Hub http://www.migrationinfomation.org/data hub/charts/children2.shtml

were "atrocious,"[109] they did not rise to the level of torture required for relief under the Convention Against Torture.[110]

Finally, deportation has caused serious problems for receiving countries. First, there is the matter of lost remittances.[111] Worldwide, some 200 million people who reside in a country that is not their birthplace sent back to their native countries an estimated $305 billion in 2008.[112] For countries such as Mexico and Guatemala that have come to depend heavily on this monetary flow, the precipitous loss of remittances caused by deportation can be a financial catastrophe.[113] Ironically, such financial pressures tend to compel more migration, rendering deportation highly questionable as a border control mechanism. Deportation has also caused serious criminal law problems, especially in the Caribbean and Central America.[114] Though, as we shall see, one must be quite skeptical of such assertions, the problem is real, if complicated.[115] As one U.S. prosecutor argued, "We're sending back sophisticated criminals to unsophisticated, unindustrialized societies." The results of such a policy are predictable: "They overwhelm local authorities."[116] While many in the United States might view it as salutary that the criminals are now elsewhere, the reality is not so simple. Consider El Salvador. Since the late 1990s, the U.S. government has deported tens of thousands of noncitizens to El Salvador.[117] Many—probably most—of these deportees are young men, brought to the United States as infants and toddlers by refugee parents, fleeing the brutal civil wars of the early 1980s and their legacy.[118] Indeed, these were the cases with which I began my own career as an immigration lawyer. They often involved the most horrific tortures and the most compelling claims brought by innocents caught in the cross-currents. Tragically, many of the parents were unable to obtain U.S. citizenship for their children, in part because of the incredible complexity that surrounded their own legal situations for many years. Their children remained vulnerable to deportation. And, as they grew up, this potential vulnerability became real for many.[119] The reception that many of the Salvadoran deportees received in their "home" country was quite harsh. Fear of these "Americanized" young men and social prejudices impeded their ability to find jobs and to integrate into Salvadoran society. Vigilante violence targeted many deportees. Many "become victims before they can become victimizers." They are regarded as pariahs, hunted by vigilante squads, and some have been shot down within days of stepping off the planes from the United States.[120]

Even those who may remain unmoved by such stories should consider that these deportations have had other serious unintended consequences. The deportation of young men from the United States seems to have fueled a new stream of asylum seekers coming to the United States in part due to fear of persecution by U.S. deportees.[121] The "out of sight out of mind" model of deportation, in short, seems to have increased criminality abroad. In an era of transnational gangs, this has already led to serious negative domestic consequences.

Deportation can thus lead to strange ironies. In 2008, I traveled to Guatemala as part of my research into the effects of deportation. While there, I was told a remarkable story by Miguel Ugalde, an academic who has studied migration issues in Latin America for many years. As we drove through the chaotic streets of Guatemala City, Miguel pointed out the special airport where U.S. planes landed, loaded with deportees from the United States. "What happens to them when they arrive?" I asked. Miguel showed me a special center for returning "migrants" that was funded by the Guatemalan government. He explained that the migrants would be interviewed, given a bit of money (about enough for a bus ticket back to their village), and advised about job prospects in Guatemala. This last part struck me as strange, since I knew that so many of the migrants (and their families) had been compelled to incur great debt and to undertake the terrifying, difficult and often life-threatening journey north precisely because there were no jobs for them or their families in Guatemala. "What jobs are there for them here?" I wondered aloud. Miguel laughed and pointed out a high-rise building in the smoggy distance. "That," he said, "is where some of them, the English-speaking ones, can actually find pretty good jobs." It was a communications center where U.S.-based credit card companies routed phone calls from inquiring or complaining customers. Some deportees had lived long enough in the U.S. to have learned sufficiently fluent English to answer queries. The irony was stunning: many thousands of U.S. citizens have undoubtedly communicated their most personal and private credit card information to deportees who had been deemed unfit to remain with their families in the United States! Noting a similar phenomenon in El Salvador, Susan Bibler Coutin has reported how one U.S. caller to a credit card company—upon hearing an American accent as opposed, I suppose, to the expected Indian one—exclaimed: "Finally, I got an American! Where are you?" One can only imagine the absurd conversation that ensued.[122]

So, with due respect for the poignant complexities of our subject, let us take a hard, critical look at this strange U.S. deportation system. Let us examine its goals and its methods, its successes and its failures. Let us consider the real costs and consequences of deportation—both on its noncitizen targets and on ever-increasing numbers of U.S. citizens—in light of the best principles of U.S. legal doctrine and the deep norms of international human rights law. It is long past time for fresh thinking.

Notes

1. Fong Yue Ting v. United States, 149 U.S. 698, 759 (1893) (Field, J. dissenting).
2. James Anthony Froude, *Party Politics, in* 4 SHORT STUDIES ON GREAT SUBJECTS 322, 345 (Charles Scribner's Sons 1908) (1876).
3. This story is a composite, drawn from actual cases.

4. *But see Lopez v. Gonzales*, 549 U.S. 47 (2006) (an "aggravated felony" includes only conduct punishable as a felony under the *federal* Controlled Substances Act, regardless of whether state law classifies such conduct as a felony or a misdemeanor). We do not know exactly how many permanent residents like Marc were deported for such offenses pre-*Lopez*, but the number is likely in the hundreds, if not thousands.

5. U.S. Immigration and Customs Enforcement (ICE) is the largest investigative agency in the U.S. Department of Homeland Security (DHS). Formed in 2003 as part of the federal government's response to the 9/11 attacks, ICE's mission is "to protect the security of the American people and homeland by vigilantly enforcing the nation's immigration and customs laws."

6. *See* INA §§ 101(a)(43)(B), 236(c).

7. In a recent report about Cambodian deportees, of forty-eight returnees interviewed, only three knew the difference between a legal permanent resident and a U.S. citizen. *See* Walter Leitner International Human Rights Clinic, Returnee Integration Support Center, Deported Diaspora; *Removing Refugees: U.S. Deportation Policy and the Cambodian-American Community*, Spring 2010.

8. *See* Richard Chacon, *Imprisoned by Policy Convicts Deported by US Languish in Haitian Jails*, BOSTON GLOBE, October 19, 2000, at A1. *See also* ALTERNATIVE CHANCE/CHANS ALTE-NATIV, http://alternativechance.org/About-Alternative-Chance-Chans-Altenativ.

9. *See generally* DANIEL KANSTROOM, DEPORTATION NATION (Harvard University Press 2007).

10. *Id.*

11. FAMILY SECURITY MATTERS, http://www.familysecuritymatters.org/publications/id.4799/pub_detail.asp.

12. The editors of the website assert that "Americans remain unprotected from this unwanted invasion of unidentified people from across the world."

13. *See infra* chapter 4.

14. http://www.familysecuritymatters.org/authors/id.143/author_detail.asp

15. Anne Morrison Piehl & John J. DiIulio Jr., *Does Prison Pay? Revisited*, 13 BROOKINGS REVIEW (Winter 1995).

16. *See e.g.*, JOHN RAWLS, THE LAW OF PEOPLES 39 (Harvard University Press 1999) ("In the absence of a world-state, there *must* be boundaries of some kind.")

17. As Michael Walzer has put it, "The members of a political community have a collective right to shape the resident population. . . ." MICHAEL WALZER, SPHERES OF JUSTICE 52 (Oxford: Blackwell 1983).

18. *See, e.g.*, Christopher Wellman, *Immigration and Freedom of Association*, 119 ETHICS 109–41 (October 2008).

19. Walzer, *supra* note 17, at 62.

20. *Id.* at 62. *See also* DAVID MILLER, NATIONAL RESPONSIBILITY AND GLOBAL JUSTICE (Oxford University Press 2007).

21. MERRIAM-WEBSTER ONLINE THESAURUS, *available at* http://www.merriam-webster.com/

22. *See* JÜRGEN HABERMAS, BETWEEN FACTS AND NORMS (1996). As Habermas later put it, "informal public opinion-formation generates 'influence'; influence is transformed into 'communicative power' through the channels of political elections; and communicative power is again transformed into 'administrative power' through legislation. This influence, carried forward by communicative power, gives law its legitimacy, and thereby provides the political power of the state its binding force." Jürgen Habermas, *Three Normative Models of Democracy*, in 1(1) *Constellation* 8 (1994); *see also* Donald Kerwin, *The "Rule of Law" and US Immigration Policy*, 13(6) BENDER'S IMMIG. BULL. 328–31(Mar. 15, 2008).

23. As Jürgen Habermas has put it, human rights "belong structurally to a positive and coercive legal order which founds actionable individual legal claims." Jürgen Habermas, *Kant's Idea of Perpetual Peace: At Two Hundred Years' Historical Remove*, in THE INCLUSION OF THE OTHER: STUDIES IN POLITICAL THEORY 165–202 (Ciaran Cronin & Pablo De Greiff eds., MIT Press 1998), at 192.

24. *See* Matthew Gibney, *Precarious Residents: Migration Control, Membership and the Rights of Non-Citizens*, UNDP. Human Development Research Paper, 2009/10 at 32

25. U.S. Department of Homeland Security, Quadrennial Homeland Security Review Report: A Strategic Framework for a Secure Homeland, Washington, DC, Feb. 2010, at 27.

26. It also aims at "helping to eliminate the conditions that foster illegal immigration." *Id.*

27. *Id.*

28. According to Cecilia Muñoz, the White House Director of Intergovernmental Affairs, DHS and the Department of Justice (DOJ) will review the current deportation caseload "to clear out low-priority cases on a case-by-case basis and make more room to deport people who have been convicted of crimes or pose a security risk. And they will take steps to keep low-priority cases out of the deportation pipeline in the first place."

29. *See* THE WHITE HOUSE BLOG, *Immigration Update: Maximizing Public Safety and Better Focusing Resources,* August 18, 2011, *available at* http://www.whitehouse.gov/blog/2011/08/18/immigration-update-maximizing-public-safety-and-better-focusing-resources.

30. Brief for Respondent at 2, Carachuri-Rosendo v. Holder, No 09-60 (U.S. 2010).

31. Brief for Petitioner at 4–5, Carachuri-Rosendo v. Holder, No. 09-60 (U.S. 2010).

32. Kalina M. Brabeck, M. Brinton Lykes, & Rachel Hershberg, *Framing Immigration to and Deportation from the United States: Guatemalan and Salvadoran Families Make Meaning of Their Experiences*, in COMMUNITY WORK AND FAMILY 1–21 (2011).

33. David McFadden, *U.S. Deportees In Haiti Struggle With Post-Quake Conditions, available at* http://www.huffingtonpost.com/2011/03/01/us-deportees-haiti-earthquake_n_829781.html.

34. AP, *Deportees from US struggle in quake-hit Haiti*, March 1, 2011, *available at* http://www.cbsnews.com/stories/2011/03/01/ap/latinamerica/main20037756.shtml.

35. University of Miami, School of Law, *International Human Rights Commission Grants Miami Law Clinics' Emergency Request, Urging United States to Stop Deportations to Haiti*, Feb. 9, 2011 (quoting Rebecca Sharpless), *available at,* http://www.law.miami.edu/news.php?article=1786.

36. Essentially, proportionality demands a legitimate "fit" between the offense and the sanction, although the nature of the balancing process and the factors to be considered are inevitably somewhat contestable. *See generally* Daniel Kanstroom, *Deportation, Social Control, and Punishment: Some Thoughts About Why Hard Laws Make Bad Cases*, 113 HARV. L. REV. 1890–35 (June 2000); Daniel Kanstroom, *Deportation and Justice: A Constitutional Dialogue*, 61 B.C. L. REV. 771 (2000); DANIEL KANSTROOM, DEPORTATION NATION, *supra* note 9, at 244; Angela M. Banks, *Proportional Deportation*, 55 WAYNE L. REV. 1651, 1671–79 (2009) (proposing creation of rights-based category of relief from removal that would allow immigration judges to consider factors necessary to ensure due process—based proportionality); Juliet Stumpf, *Fitting Punishment*, 66 WASH. & LEE L. REV. 1683, 1732–40 (2009) (proposing a graduated system of sanctions for immigration violations); Michael J. Wishnie, *Proportionality: The Struggle for Balance in U.S. Immigration Policy*, 72 U. PITT. L. REV. (forthcoming 2011) (analyzing various types of proportionality review).

37. *See* Gerald L. Neuman, *The Extraterritorial Constitution After Boumediene v. Bush*, 82 S. CAL. L. REV. 259 (2009); Gerald L. Neuman, *The Habeas Corpus Suspension Clause After Boumediene v. Bush*, 110 COLUM. L. REV. 537 (2010).

38. Deportation is an example of how "globalization is taking place inside the national." *See, e.g.*, SASKIA SASSEN, TERRITORY, AUTHORITY, RIGHTS: FROM MEDIEVAL TO GLOBAL ASSEMBLAGES 1–2, 222–76; Cristina M. Rodriguez, *Immigration: The Citizenship Paradox in a Transnational Age*, 106 MICH. L. REV. 1111, 1117–19 (2006) (reviewing HIROSHI MOTOMURA, AMERICANS IN WAITING: THE LOST STORY OF IMMIGRATION AND CITIZENSHIP IN THE UNITED STATES (2007)); Susan B. Coutin, *Denationalization, Inclusion, and Exclusion: Negotiating the Boundaries of Belonging*, 7 IND. J. GLOBAL LEGAL STUD. 585 (2000).

39. RAINER BAUBÖCK & THOMAS FAIST, DIASPORA AND TRANSNATIONALISM: CONCEPTS, THEORIES AND METHODS 14 (2010).

40. Rogers Brubaker, *The 'Diaspora' Diaspora*, 28(1) ETHNIC & RACIAL STUD. 1 (Jan. 2005)

41. RAINER BAUBÖCK & THOMAS FAIST, DIASPORA AND TRANSNATIONALISM: CONCEPTS, THEORIES AND METHODS 12 (2010).

42. *See* Brubaker, *supra* note 40, at 3.

43. *See* Kim D. Butler, *Defining Diaspora, Refining a Discourse.* Diaspora: 10(2) A JOURNAL OF TRANSNATIONAL STUDIES 191 (2001); ROBIN COHEN, GLOBAL DIASPORAS: AN INTRO-DUCTION (1997); William Safran. *Diasporas in Modern Societies: Myths of Homeland and Return.* 1(1) DIASPORA: A JOURNAL OF TRANSNATIONAL STUDIES 83–84 (1991).

44. I am not the only one to use this nomenclature in this context. *See, e.g.,* DEPORTED DIAS-PORA, www.deporteddiaspora.org; Bryan Lonegan, *American Diaspora: The Deportation of Lawful Residents From the United States and the Destruction of Their Families,* 32 N.Y.U. REV. L & SOC. CHANGE 55 (2007). The current Wikipedia article entitled *Diaspora* lists thirty different uses of the term, ranging from "Armenian diaspora" to "Yugoslavs."

45. William Safan, *Diasporas in Modern Societies: Myths of Homeland and Return,* 1(1) DIAS-PORA: A JOURNAL OF TRANSNATIONAL STUDIES 83–99 (1991).

46. *Id.*; Brubaker, *supra* note 39, at 5. *Cf.* James Clifford, *Diasporas,* 9(3) CULTURAL ANTHRO-POLOGY 302–38 (Aug. 1994) (arguing that "de-centered, lateral connections may be as important as those formed around a teleology of origin/return.").

47. *See* Russell King & Anastasia Christou, *Diaspora, Migration and Transnationalism: Insights from the Study of Second-Generation "Returnees,"* in RAINER BAUBÖCK & THOMAS FAIST, DIASPORA AND TRANSNATIONALISM: CONCEPTS, THEORIES AND METHODS 173 (2010).

48. Brubaker, *supra* note 39, at 6.

49. *See, e.g.,* John A. Armstrong, *Mobilized and Proletarian Diasporas,* 70(2) AM. POL. SCI. REV. 393–408.

50. *Id.* On the other hand, however, some have emphasized "hybridity, fluidity, creolization and syncretisim," described by Stuart Hall as "a conception of 'identity' which lives with and through, not despite difference; by hybridity." Stuart Hall, *Cultural Identity and Dias-pora,* in IDENTITY: COMMUNITY, CULTURE, DIFFERENCE 222–37 (Jonathan Rutherford ed., 1990); Brubaker, *supra* note 39, at 6.

51. *See infra* Chapter 5.

52. One should not, of course, seek to impose "groupness" through definitional fiat. Brubaker, *supra* note 39, at 12–13.

53. Others might argue that the legal sanction in this case—deportation—fits the offense pass-ably well. The simple version of this argument tends to run something like this:

    1. U.S. legal residence and citizenship are precious things to which noncitizens have no claim of right;
    2. It is not unreasonable for the government to ask noncitizens not to commit crimes as a condition to obtaining such precious things;
    3. If they are convicted of crimes, noncitizens have thus consciously forfeited their claims to legal residence or citizenship.
    4. This is fair and just.

    A more sophisticated argument is that deportation is a symmetrical, proportional, and just and fair sanction for noncitizens who violate laws of entry.

54. *See* Lawrence Downes, *What Part of "Illegal" Don't You Understand,* N.Y. TIMES, Oct. 28, 2007, *available at* http://www.nytimes.com/2007/10/28/opinion/28sun4.html.

55. A proposed 2006 Arizona law would have criminalized, as a felony, "trespassing by illegal aliens." ArizonaproposedS.B.1157,http://www.azleg.state.az.us/legtext/47leg/2r/summary/s.1157jud_caucus-floor.doc.htm. The law sought to prohibit "a person who is not a citizen of the United States and who has improperly entered the United States, from entering into or being on any public or private land in Arizona." Indeed, in 2005, a New Hampshire police chief tried to use a state trespassing law to prosecute an undocumented worker whose car happened to break down on the side of the road. Josh Rogers, NHPR, *Illegal Alien Pleads Guilty to Trespass,* May 4, 2005. http://www.nhpr.org/node/8717. The chief's apparent theory was that the man had entered the country illegally and therefore was criminally trespassing in New Hampshire. Such extreme legal theories are typically struck down by judges, as was the New Hampshire prose-cution. The judge held that "[t]he criminal trespass charges against the defendants are unconsti-tutional attempts to regulate in the area of enforcement of immigration violations." *Judge Tells Police to Lay Off Immigration Enforcement,* WASH. TIMES, Aug. 12, 2005, *available at* http://www.washingtontimes.com/news/2005/aug/12/20050812-111318-7963r/

56. *Cf.* Jennifer M. Chacón, *Unsecured Borders: Immigration Restrictions, Crime Control and National Security*, 39 CONN. L. REV. 1827 (2007); Donald Kerwin & Margaret D. Stock, *National Security and Immigration Policy: Reclaiming Terms, Measuring Success, and Setting Priorities* 6 (2006), *available at* http://search.yahoo.com/r/_ylt=A0oG7nQMy_BO1hgAkcpXNyoA;_ylu=X3oDMTB2Z2owYnVoBHNlYwNzcgRwb3MDMQRjb2xvA2FjBDB4vA2FjMgR2dGlkA18yMDI-/SIG=131qpn8pr/EXP=1324432268/**http%3a//www.teachingterror.com/HS/National_Security_and_Immigration_Policy.pdf; Daniel Kanstroom, *Reaping the Harvest: The Long, Complicated, Crucial Rhetorical Struggle over Deportation*, 39 CONN. L. REV. 1911 (2007).

57. Examples of these methods include high-profile workplace raids during the Bush administration and stepped-up criminal removals during the Obama administration. *See* Spencer S. Hsu & Andrew Becker, *ICE Officials Set Quotas to Deport More Illegal Immigrants*, WASH. POST, Mar. 27, 2010, at A4, *available at* http://pqasb.pqarchiver.com/washingtonpost/access/1994698061.html?FMT=ABS&FMTS=ABS:FT&date=Mar+27%2C+2010&author=Spencer+S+Hsu%3BAndrew+Becker&pub=The+Washington+Post&edition=&startpage=A.4&desc=Immigration+officials+set+quotas+to+boost+deportation+numbers%3B+Focus+broadens+beyond+dangerous+criminals%3B+memo+draws+criticism

58. *But see* Joseph H. Carens, *Aliens and Citizens: The Case for Open Borders*, 49 REV. POL. 251 (1987); Joseph H. Carens, *Migration and Morality*, in FREE MOVEMENT (Brian Barry & Robert E. Goodin eds., 1992); Jacqueline Stevens, *Recreating the State*, 27(5) THIRD WORLD Q. 755–66 (2006); *See also* JACQUELINE STEVENS, STATES WITHOUT NATIONS: CITIZENSHIP FOR MORTALS (2009); JACQUELINE STEVENS, REPRODUCING THE STATE (1999). Stevens views the family as a legal fiction developed by nation-states to sustain artificial claims to naturalness. This allows hereditary relationships to work with rules of birthright citizenship (*jus sanguinis* or *jus soli*) to automatically ensure nation-states of stable "natural born" populations as it also justifies demanding loyalty. Stevens also argues that this regimes assuages male pregnancy and birth envy because pregnancy and birth guarantee women a connection to life beyond mortality that men lack. Men, she believes, have used gendered family law and violence, and the nation-state itself, to compensate for their fears of mortality.

59. *See* ZYGMUNT BAUMAN, SOCIETY UNDER SIEGE 54 (2002) ("A society is just in as far as it never stops criticizing the level of justice already achieved and [seeks] more justice and better justice." One can surely agree with Will Kymlicka that "territorial boundaries are a source of embarrassment for liberals of all stripes, and particularly for liberal egalitarians," without necessarily rejecting the entire nation-state enterprise. BOUNDARIES AND JUSTICE: DIVERSE ETHICAL PERSPECTIVES 249 (D. Miller & S. H. Hashmi eds., Princeton University Press 2001); *see also* ONORA O'NEILL, BOUNDS OF JUSTICE (Cambridge University Press 2001) (distinguishing approaches to justice based on rules versus those based on virtues such as care and community).

60. *See* Gerald L. Neuman, "Amnesty Should Be a Matter for Regret, Not a Bonus for Those Who Persevere," *The Case for Amnesty: A Forum on Immigration*, BOSTON REVIEW, May/June 2009, *available at* http://www.bostonreview.net/BR34.3/ndf_immigration.php.

61. For example, in 2010 Mexico had some 53 million people living in poverty, with almost 20 percent in extreme poverty. Many available jobs do not pay a wage capable of supporting a family. According to the Bank of Mexico, 95 percent of the eight hundred thousand jobs created in 2010 paid only $10 a day. Yet a gallon of milk in Tijuana or Juarez costs more than in the United States. *See* DAVID BACON, INSTITUTE FOR TRANSNATIONAL SOCIAL CHANGE–UCLA, BUILDING A CULTURE OF CROSS-BORDER SOLIDARITY (May 2011), *available at* http://www.cipamericas.org/wp-content/uploads/2011/05/culture-of-solidarity.pdf.

62. *See, e.g.*, PHILIP COLE, PHILOSOPHIES OF EXCLUSION (Edinburgh University Press 2000).

63. *See* CHANTAL MOUFFE, THE DEMOCRATIC PARADOX 39 (2000) (noting that in contrast to liberalism, the "democratic conception [of equality] requires the possibility of distinguishing who belongs to the demos and who is exterior to it; for that reason, it cannot exist without the necessary correlate of inequality." *See generally* Arash Abizadeh, *Democratic Theory and Border Coercion No Right to Unilaterally Control Your Own Borders*, 36 POL.

THEORY 37–65, at 46 (2008) (noting that "the act of constituting civic borders is always an exercise of power over both insiders and outsiders that intrinsically, by the very act of constituting the border, disenfranchises the outsiders over whom power is exercised. It is this *conceptual* feature of civic borders that confronts democratic theory with an externality problem).

64. MICHAEL WALZER, SPHERES OF JUSTICE 62 (1983).

65. *See, e.g.,* David Thronson, *Custody and Contradictions: Exploring Immigration Law as Federal Family Law in the Context of Child Custody,* 59 HASTINGS L. J. 3 (2008); David Thronson, *Choiceless Choices: Deportation and the Parent-Child Relationship,* 6 NEV. L.J. 1165–66 (2006); David Thronson, *Kids Will Be Kids? Reconsidering Conceptions of Children's Rights Underlying Immigration Law,* 63 OHIO ST. L.J. 979 (2002). *See also* Rainer Bauböck, "There Is a Mismatch between Citizens' Moral Intuitions and Their Political Views," *The Case for Amnesty: A Forum on Immigration,* BOSTON REVIEW, May/June 2009, *available at* http://www.bostonreview.net/BR34.3/ndf_immigration.php.

66. For an interesting argument that citizens should have standing in some cases, *see* Adam B. Cox, *Citizenship, Standing, and Immigration Law,* 92 CALIF. L. REV. 373 (2004).

67. *See generally* DANIEL KANSTROOM, DEPORTATION NATION, chs. 1–2.

68. *But see* discussion of *Padilla v. Kentucky,* 130 S. Ct. 1473 (2010) *infra.*

69. KAL RAUSTIALA, DOES THE CONSTITUTION FOLLOW THE FLAG? 5 (2009).

70. The 1996 changes in immigration law sought to bring this executive branch-controlled, largely rightless zone into the United States, by applying it to certain noncitizens: those who had not been "legally admitted." Thus, many millions of noncitizens are now deemed by *legal fiction* to not be here legally, although they are surely here physically. The courts have struggled to reconcile statutory non-presence with constitutional claims based on physical presence.

71. The same is true for such other governing principles of deportation law as finality. Though finality is surely a legitimate concern for a legal system that must process hundreds of thousands of complicated cases each year with very limited resources, it cannot be a rigid absolute.

72. It may include direct appellate review, *habeas corpus* review, and administrative motions to reopen. Direct review of deportation orders in the courts of appeals is now allowed from abroad. *See infra* Chapters 4–6.

73. For a fine, technical legal analysis of some of the issues presented herein, *see* Rachel E. Rosenbloom, *Remedies for the Wrongly Deported: Territoriality, Finality, and the Significance of Departure,* 33 U. HAW. L. REV. 139 (2011).

74. Also, some—operating at a still higher level of abstraction—might reason that the distinction between "immigrant-selecting" rules and other rules, such as those that deport long-term residents for minor crimes is "unhelpful and misleading." *See* Adam B. Cox, *Immigration Law's Organizing Principles Immigration Law's Organizing Principles,* 157 U. PA. L. REV. 341 (2008).

75. *Matter of Andres Armendarez-Mendez,* Int. Dec. 3626; 24 I. & N. Dec. 646 (BIA 2008).

76. *See* Paul Mishkin, *Foreword: The High Court, the Great Writ, and the Due Process of Time and Law,* 79 HARV. L. REV. 56, 100 (1965). *See* Rosenbloom, *supra* note 73, at 178.

77. As Justice Anthony Kennedy wrote in the Guantánamo case of *Boumediene v. Bush,* which held that the constitution protects even detainees who are not held on U.S. soil: "questions of extraterritoriality turn on objective factors and practical concerns, not formalism." Boumediene v. Bush, 553 U.S. 723, 764 (2008).

78. *See generally* DANIEL KANSTROOM, DEPORTATION NATION, *supra* note 9.

79. *See* The Antiterrorism and Effective Death Penalty Act of 1996 (AEDPA) Pub. L. No. 104–132, 110 Stat. 1214 (1996) (codified as amended in scattered sections of 8, 18, 22, 28, 40, 42 U.S.C.) (1999) and the Illegal Immigration Reform and Immigrant Responsibility Act of 1996 (IIRIRA) Pub. L. No. 104–208, Div. C, 110 Stat. 3009–3546 (1996) (codified as amended in scattered sections of 8, 18 U.S.C.) (1999).

80. From 2004 to 2010, over $100 billion has been spent on border control and enforcement. CHAD C. HADDAL, CONG. RESEARCH SERV., R41237, PEOPLE CROSSING BORDERS: AN ANALYSIS OF U.S. BORDER PROTECTION POLICIES (Mar. 2010), *available at* http://www.fas.org/sgp/crs/homesec/R41237.pdf. This figure combines appropriations from

FY2004–FY2010 to the four agencies with significant border protection functions—Customs and Border Protection (CBP), Immigration and Customs Enforcement (ICE), Transportation Security Administration (TSA), and the U.S. Coast Guard (USCG).

81. AILA questionnaire on file with author.

82. *See* ICE TOTAL REMOVALS THROUGH JULY 31, 2011, *available at* http://www.ice.gov/doclib/about/offices/ero/pdf/ero-removals.pdf. This figure includes both "removals" and "returns." Removal is defined by DHS as "the compulsory and confirmed movement of an inadmissible or deportable alien out of the United States based on an order of removal." Return is "the confirmed movement of an inadmissible or deportable alien out of the United States not based on an order of removal." *See* DHS Office of Immigration Statistics, *Immigration Enforcement Actions: 2010* (June 2011).

83. ICE, *A Day in the Life of ICE Enforcement and Removal Operations*, *available at* http://www.ice.gov/about/offices/enforcement-removal-operations/(last visited June 25, 2011).

84. *See generally* Foreign-Born Population of the United States Current Population Survey—March 2009, table 1.1, *available at* http://www.census.gov/population/www/socdemo/foreign/cps2009.html. *See also* BROOKINGS, *Immigrants in 2010 Metropolitan America: A Decade of Change* (interpreting ACS data to reach figure of 40 million), *available at* http://www.brookings.edu/papers/2011/1013_immigration_wilson_singer.aspx.

85. Pew Hispanic Center, Statistical Portrait of the Foreign-Born Population of the United States, 2009.

86. DHS, Office of Immigration Statistics, 2009 Yearbook of Immigration Statistics, table 25, *available at* http://www.dhs.gov/files/statistics/immigration.shtm.

87. Randall Monger & James Yankay, DHS, Office of Immigration Statistics, Annual Flow Report, U.S. Legal Permanent Residents, Mar. 2011, at 1.

88. Such as "VAWA applicants," "U and T visa holders," "Temporary Protected Status."

89. About half of these people are lawful permanent residents. Jeffrey Passel & D'Vera Cohn, *Trends in Unauthorized Immigration: Undocumented Inflow Now Trails Legal Inflow*, Pew Hispanic Center, Oct. 2, 2008; RUTH ELLEN WASEM, CONG. RESEARCH SERV., IMMIGRATION REFORM ISSUES IN THE 111TH CONGRESS, R40501, at 5 (Feb. 10, 2010); *see also* HIROSHI MOTOMURA, AMERICANS IN WAITING (2007).

90. CICERO, TUSCULAN DISPUTATIONS V.61, Loeb Classical Library, translated by J.E. King (1945).

91. *See* Jacqueline Stevens, *U.S. Government Unlawfully Detaining And Deporting U.S. Citizens As Aliens*,18 VA. J. SOC. POL'Y & L. 606 (2011).

92. This may happen:
    1. by mistake;
    2. due to increasingly fluid notions of denaturalization;
    3. by forcing family members, such as the U.S. citizen children of deportees, to choose (or have chosen for them) between U.S. residence and staying with their parents (i.e., de facto);
    4. by mechanisms of dubious legality related to the "war on terror."

93. *See* Stevens, *supra* note 91, at 613.

94. *Problems with ICE Interrogation, Detention and Removal Procedures: Hearing Before the Subcommittee on Immigration, Citizenship, Refugees, Border Security, and Int'l Law of the H. Comm. on the Judiciary*, 110th Cong. 1 (Feb. 13, 2008) (statement of Kara Hartzler, Esq., Florence Immigrant and Refugee Rights Project), *available at* http://judiciary.house.gov/hearings/pdf/Hartzler080213.pdf.

95. *See* Chapter 4.

96. *See* Padilla v. Kentucky, 130 S. Ct. 1473 (2010) (criminal defense attorneys have an obligation to inform their clients if a guilty plea carries a risk of deportation. "Our longstanding Sixth Amendment precedents, the seriousness of deportation as a consequence of a criminal plea, and the concomitant impact of deportation on families living lawfully in this country demand no less.").

97. Indeed, former Attorney General Mukasey once ruled that people in removal proceedings have no constitutional right to counsel, only a statutory "privilege" to retain counsel of their own choosing. Put simply, even if counsel was incompetent, fraudulent, asleep, or failed to appear, the AG held that such a hearing would not necessarily be "fundamentally unfair." Mr. Mukasey's

decision has since been overturned, but what of those who were deported while it was the law? *See* Matter of Compean, 24 I & N Dec. 710 (A.G. 2009) (overruling Matter of Lozada, 19 I & N Dec. 637 (BIA 1988) and Matter of Assaad, 23 I & N Dec. 553 (BIA 2003)).

98. This includes not only those whose offense should not have rendered them subject to deportation at all, but also many who were wrongly deprived of the right even to apply for discretionary relief to which they were entitled. *See, e.g.,* Lopez v. Gonzales, 549 U.S. 47 (2006) (an "aggravated felony" includes only conduct punishable as a felony under the *federal* Controlled Substances Act, regardless of whether state law classifies such conduct as a felony or a misdemeanor). *See* Kanstroom, *St. Cyr or Insincere: The Strange Quality of Supreme Court Victory,* 16 GEO. IMMIGRATION L. J. 413–64 (2002).

99. Reversal of a final removal order by a reviewing court may, under certain circumstances, permit the affected person to return, though the law is complex and the procedures remain unclear in such cases. *See* Trina Realmuto, American Immigration Law Foundation, Practice Advisory: Return to the United States after Prevailing on a Petition for Review (2007). Automatic "stays" of deportation during court appeals, which were a regular feature of the pre-1996 system, have been eliminated. Immigration Court and Board of Immigration Appeals delays have been a problem, but, as numerous recent studies have shown, they have been largely due to an under-resourced court system that has routinely been asked to exceed its capacity. *See, e.g.,* ABA Commission on Immigration, Arnold & Porter, *Reforming the Immigration System: Proposals to Promote Independence, Fairness, Efficiency, and Professionalism in the Adjudication of Removal Cases, available at* http://new.abanet.org/immigration/pages/default.aspx.

100. Dorsey & Whitney, *Severing a Lifeline: The Neglect of Citizen Children in America's Immigration Enforcement Policy, available at* www.dorsey.com/files/upload/DorseyProBono_SeveringLifeline_ReportOnly_web.pdf.

101. *Id.*

102. Family separation can be caused by the deportation system in many ways, including some that are not immediately apparent. For example, deportation proceedings may lead to the loss of custody of children in state courts. Encarnación Bail Romero, a Guatemalan woman, was one of 136 undocumented immigrants detained in a raid. A year and a half after she went to jail, a county court terminated Ms. Bail's rights to her child, Carlos, on grounds of abandonment. Carlos was adopted by a local couple. Judge David C. Dally of the Circuit Court in Jasper County favorably compared the adopting couple with Carlos's mother, who, he said, "had little to offer." Judge Dally wrote: "The only certainties in the biological mother's future, is that she will remain incarcerated until next year, and that she will be deported thereafter." Ginger Thompson, *After Losing Freedom, Some Immigrants Face Loss of Custody of Their Children,* N.Y. TIMES, April 22, 2009, *available at* http://www.nytimes.com/2009/04/23/us/23children.html?pagewanted=1&_r=1&emc=eta1.

103. *See, e.g.,* MICHAEL McBRIDE, THE EVOLUTION OF U.S. IMMIGRATION AND REFUGEE POLICY: PUBLIC OPINION, DOMESTIC POLITICS AND UNHCR 23 (1999).

104. Its ostensible goal was to provide a "warning" to the criminal deportees not to commit crimes in Haiti. *See generally* Bureau of Democracy, Human Rights, and Labor, U.S. Dep't of State, Country Report on Human Rights Practices—2002: Haiti (2003); Human Rights Watch, Haiti, in World Report 147 (2003); Resource Information Center, U.S. Citizenship and Immigration Services, Haiti: Information on Conditions in Haitian Prisons and Treatment of Criminal Deportees (2nd Response) (2002); Anne Fuller, Vera Institute of Justice, Prolonged Pretrial Detention in Haiti (2002).

105. Francois v. Ashcroft, 343 F. Supp. 2d 327, 329 (D.N.J. 2004), *vacated,* 488 F.3d 645 (3d Cir. 2006).

106. *Id.* (quoting Bureau of Democracy, Human Rights, and Labor, U.S. Dep't of State, *supra* note 104).

107. Police "almost never" were prosecuted for the abuse of detainees. Bureau of Democracy, Human Rights, and Labor, U.S. Dep't of State, *supra* note 104.

108. The chart includes only children who reside with at least one parent. The foreign-born population includes naturalized citizens, legal permanent residents, certain legal nonimmigrants (e.g., refugees and persons on student or work visas), and persons illegally residing

in the United States. Data from U.S. Census Bureau, American Community Survey 2008, and the 1990 and 2000 Decennial Censuses; Steven Ruggles, Matthew Sobek, Trent Alexander, Catherine A. Fitch, Ronald Goeken, Patricia Kelly Hall, Miriam King, and Chad Ronnander. Integrated Public Use Microdata Series: Version 4.0 [Machine-readable database]. Minneapolis, MN: Minnesota Population Center [producer and distributor], 2008. Available at http://usa.ipums.org/usa/.

109. *Francois*, 343 F. Supp. 2d at 329.

110. The Convention Against Torture and Other Cruel, Inhuman or Degrading Treatment or Punishment (CAT), G.A. Res. 39/46, U.N. Doc. A/RES/39/46 (Dec. 10, 1984). Article 3 of the Torture Convention mandates that signatory states shall not return a person to a country in which there is a substantial likelihood that he or she would be tortured. The Convention protects noncitizens from U.S. deportation via its incorporation into the Foreign Affairs Reform and Restructuring Act of 1998, Pub. L. No. 105–277, div. G, Title XXII, § 2242(b), 112 Stat. 2681–2822 (1998). CAT requests for asylum and withholding of removal need not involve claims of persecution on the basis of race, religion, nationality, membership in a particular social group, or political opinion because proof of torture, not simply persecution, is required. To obtain relief, an applicant must show that it is more likely than not that he would be tortured if returned to his home country. 8 C.F.R. § 208.16–18 (2007). And interpretive trends in CAT claims in the United States are toward increasingly restrictive interpretations. *See* Lori A. Nessel, *Forced to Choose: Torture, Family Reunification and United States Immigration Policy*, 78 Temple L. Rev. 897, 900 (2005) (suggesting that the narrow construction placed on CAT may be attributed to the view that the claimants are undesirable); Lori A. Nessel, *"Willful Blindness" to Gender-Based Violence Abroad: United States Interpretation of Article 3 of the United Nations Convention Against Torture*, 89 Minn. L. Rev. 71, 113 (2004).

111. *See* Dean Yang, *How Remittances Help Migrant Families*, Migration Information Source, Dec. 2004, www.migrationinformation.org/Feature/display.cfm?iD=270.

112. Uri Dadush & Lauren Falcao, *Crisis and the Diaspora Nation*, Int'l Econ. Bull., (June 17, 2009), http://carnegieendowment.org/publications/index.cfm?fa=view&id=23291&prog=zgp&proj=zie.

113. The Inter-American Development Bank estimates remittances as a percentage of national income: Haiti (26 percent), Guyana (24 percent), Jamaica (18.5 percent) and El Salvador (18 percent). Remittances to Mexico dropped by some $1 billion in 2008, then another 15.7 percent in 2009. Joel Millman, *Remittances to Mexico Fall More Than Forecast*, Wall St. J., Jan. 28, 2009, at A3; CBS News World, Associated Press, *Mexico Sees Record Drop in Remittances*, Jan. 27, 2010, http://www.cbsnews.com/stories/2010/01/27/world/main6148649.shtml. Remittances from the United States were Mexico's second largest source of foreign income after oil exports—totaling $21.2 billion in 2009, compared with $25.1 billion in 2008 Also, in 2008, remittances accounted for $4.3 billion or roughly 12 percent of Guatemala's GDP. Compare this to the $724 million that was spent by all foreign investors and the $646 million earned by its entire coffee crop. Ednar Segura, *Lack of U.S. Remittances Stagnates Guatemalan Economy* (April 6, 2009), http://www.allgov.com/ViewNews/Lack_of_US_Remittances_Stagnates_Guatemalan_Economy_90406.

114. *See generally* Margaret Taylor & T. Alexander Aleinikoff, Inter-American Dialogue, *Deportation of Criminal Aliens: A Geopolitical Perspective* 3 (1998).

115. Interpol estimated that murders in Honduras increased from 1,615 in 1995 to 9,241 after the first wave of U.S. criminal deportations. Honduran police argued that guns, drugs, and gangs brought by the deportees from the United States were largely responsible. *Id.*

116. *Id.*

117. Office of Immigration Statistics, *supra* note 87, at 172–73. Deportation courts completed more than one hundred thousand cases involving Salvadorans from 2005 to 2007 alone. *See* Office of Planning, Analysis, & Technology, U.S. Dep't of Justice, FY 2005-2008 Statistical Yearbooks at E1.

118. Nestor Rodríguez & Jacqueline Maria Hagan, *Fractured Families and Communities: Effects of Immigration Reform in Texas, Mexico, and El Salvador*, 2 Latino Studies 328, 344 (2004).

119. To be sure, some of these deportees have been convicted of serious crimes. But we must think more deeply about whether deportation is the appropriate solution to these sorts of societal problems. Are deportation and lifetime banishment an appropriate sentence for youthful (and in many cases minor) crimes?

120. *See* Randall Richard, *AP Investigation: 500,000 Criminal Deportees from America Wreak Havoc in Many Nations*, Oct. 26, 2003 [hereinafter 500K Criminal Deportees], *available at* http://www.threestrikes.org/ap_12.html. *See also*, Margaret Swedish, *Gang Violence Spreads through Central America*, CENTRAL AMERICA/MEXICO REPORT, Nov.–Dec. 2003.

121. *Id.*

122. Susan B. Coutin, *Confined Within: National Territories as Zones of Confinement*, POLITICAL GEOGRAPHY (2010), doi:10.1016/j.polgeo.2010.03.005; *see generally* SUSAN B. COUTIN, NATIONS OF EMIGRANTS: SHIFTING BOUNDARIES OF CITIZENSHIP IN EL SALVADOR AND THE UNITED STATES (2007).

2

The Goals of Deportation

Border Control, Social Control, or "Out of Sight Out of Mind"?

> There is more law in the end of a policeman's nightstick than in a decision of the Supreme Court.
> —New York Police Inspector Alexander S. Williams (1928)[1]

> A wrong committed by a republic is no less than a wrong done by an autocracy, nor is a mistake lessened by the character of the agency that commits it.
> —Charles S. Osborn (1920)[2]

Laws of exclusion and deportation are paradoxical in the United States. They may be understood both as the darker sides of the "nation of immigrants" ideal and, perhaps, as necessary prerequisites to it.[3] On the one hand, the immigration selection process—primarily implemented through laws of exclusion and then supplemented by certain types of deportation—serves to legitimate a relatively generous immigration policy. It seeks to assure current citizens and legal residents that newcomers will be admitted in certain categories and vetted. Of course, even these apparently rather simple functions are rendered complex as we consider the details of whom should be chosen and excluded, and how such tasks should be accomplished. The iconic inscription at the base of the Statue of Liberty welcomes

> [Y]our tired, your poor,
> Your huddled masses yearning to breathe free,
> The wretched refuse of your teeming shore.
> [and] . . . the homeless. . . .

But this welcome was largely fictional when it was written, when it was affixed to the statue, and indeed ever since.[4] Some have viewed this as a grand aspiration; others, more cynically, see it as a deep national hypocrisy: a disingenuous "tribute paid by vice to virtue."[5] The fact is that, as a matter of historical immigration policy, the "tired" (those who cannot work), the poor, and the homeless have long been excluded from the United States, not welcomed. And if the "yearning to breathe free" of the huddled masses involved socialism, anarchism, communism, or the like, then they, too, have been excluded. The U.S. open immigration ideal has long been strong and vital, but complicated.[6]

Still, it is no small thing that the current administration—and virtually all mainstream politicians—reaffirm our heritage as a "nation of immigrants."[7] This heritage, though its origins are contested and its content problematic, has deep and continuing importance.[8] Most importantly, it embodies a general (if idealized and qualified) acceptance of freedom of movement, societal openness, ethnic and racial diversity, and multiculturalism as social *desiderata*.[9] However one may view the exact nature and genuineness of the nation of immigrants ideal, to understand the goals of the U.S. deportation system one must surely take it into account. The questions, though abstract, are important: what components of that heritage do we wish to maintain? And does the current deportation system help or hinder us in this endeavor?

This apparently simple question—what are the goals of the deportation system?—is thus surprisingly hard to answer. Another reason for this difficulty is that deportation is essentially an enforcement system. Put simply, it has no independent goals, nor should it. Like the military, it is sometimes conceptualized as "a neutral instrument of the state."[10] As one immigration treatise put it: "[d]eportation, like exclusion, is an instrument of immigration policy, not a policy in itself; but . . . a means of implementing a policy of selecting those allowed to become and remain residents of the United States."[11] But there is an important distinction between what one might term justification neutrality and effect neutrality.[12] The deportation system, which may be neutral *in theory* as an instrument of other policies, has long been far from neutral in its effects. One must be particularly skeptical of the ostensibly narrow goals of a system the roots of which are so racially problematic and the effects of which are so harsh.[13] Whatever its legitimate goals may be, deportation has historically worked as a powerful and efficient government tool of discretionary social control and a key component of the national security state. It thus stands in peculiar equipoise with our relative openness to legal immigration, our legal system's general protections for the rights of noncitizens, and our grant of birthright citizenship to virtually all born on U.S. soil.[14]

What, then, is deportation? I would begin with a functional definition. By this, I mean simply that we consider deportation not by seeking some idealized essence of it, but by asking, first, what it does.[15] Basically, deportation is "the expulsion of noncitizens by a state through the (threatened or actual) use of force."[16] A leading U.S. immigration law treatise similarly describes it as "the

removal of a noncitizen who has entered the United States either legally or illegally."[17] This definition usefully differentiates two basic classes of deportees. But
it is still quite general. The more precise, technical definition is surprisingly elusive. Indeed, there is no single definition of deportation or, as it is technically
named, "removal" within the approximately five hundred-page Immigration
and Nationality Act that, along with hundreds of pages of regulations, governs
U.S. immigration law.[18]

One definition worth pondering, though, is that of "alien," a highly charged
and contentious term in public debate, especially when preceded by the adjec-
tive, "illegal." The statute defines "alien" negatively: "any person not a citizen or
national of the United States."[19] It then lists in rather exquisite detail various
"classes of deportable aliens." These are people who are "in and admitted to the
United States" and who "shall, upon the order of the Attorney General" be
"removed."[20] Of course, there are also many millions of noncitizens in the
United States who have never been legally admitted. They have crossed the
Rio Grande and the southern deserts or the Canadian woods on foot, arrived
in small boats, been smuggled in the trunks of cars, and so on. If they are
arrested by immigration agents, they too face removal.[21] It is at this point, I
suspect, that you may begin to appreciate why immigration law has been called
complex to the point where it would "cross the eyes of a Talmudic scholar"[22]
and an arena where "morsels of comprehension must be pried from mollusks
of jargon."[23]

So how might we define deportation (removal) with enough technical precision to have a meaningful discussion, with enough breadth to capture its many
features, but without creating an unwieldy number of crossed-eyes? I suggest the
following:

> Deportation is a major, complex law enforcement system that governs
> the lives of the many millions of noncitizens who live, study, travel, and
> work in this country. It may lead to arrest, incarceration, physical re-
> moval and subsequent exclusion from the United States.

As we proceed, this definition will be refined as we see how deportation actually
governs the lives of noncitizens. But, as a start, consider the size of the system: in
the last twenty-five years, the number of times an individual noncitizen has been
caught somewhere on U.S. soil and been subject to removal in one form or another has exceeded 25 *million*.[24] As noted, this includes many caught or near the
border.[25] However, the formal deportation system that is a main focus of this
book has also grown larger each year since the late 1990s, now handling well
over three hundred thousand cases per year (see chart 2.1).[26]

Type of Proceeding [minor miscellaneous categories omitted]

FiscalYear	2006	2007	2008	2009	2010
Deportation	3,648	4,030	4,185	3,592	3,597
Exclusion	385	453	436	379	315
Removal	302,906	272,824	285,419	321,729	318,435
Credible Fear	411	825	702	885	1,165
Reasonable Fear	78	131	172	241	398
Total	308,652	279,430	292,013	327,928	325,326

Chart 2.1 Immigration Court Proceedings. Source: Office of Planning, Analysis, & Technology, U.S. Dep't of Justice, FY 2010 Statistical Yearbook Figure 1, page B2 (2010) available at www.justice.gov/eoir/statspub/fy10syb.pdf

Both the numbers of deportations and spending on enforcement increased significantly in the first years of the Obama administration. Spending for U.S. Immigration and Customs Enforcement (ICE) and U.S. Customs and Border Protection (CBP) increased from fiscal year 2002, when it was almost $7.5 billion, to fiscal year 2010, when it exceeded $17 billion.[27]

The relationship between deportation and the evolving racial and ethnic characteristics of the noncitizen population is also a central fact that cannot be ignored. Though legal status is surely a relevant factor, there is a direct correlation between the rising deportation numbers since the mid-1990s and the size of the Mexican foreign-born population residing within the United States (see chart 2.2).

As noted, U.S. deportation has two basic forms that reflect somewhat different, if interrelated, goals. *Extended border control* seeks to remove those noncitizens who have evaded the rules that govern legal entry into the United States. *Post-entry social control* regulates the conduct of those who have been legally admitted (for example, as students, workers, or permanent residents) but who then engage in a wide variety of prohibited behaviors.[28] This distinction helps to illuminate various underlying functions of deportation in the United States. Apart from its obvious immigration control goals, deportation has long effectively regulated labor markets, controlled the movement of the poor, dovetailed with criminal law enforcement, challenged dissidents and labor organizers, and facilitated various amorphous "national security" initiatives. Such functions for deportation are, of course, not unique to the United States. As Barbara Roberts noted in a study of deportation in Canada: "Deportation helped to relieve employers, municipalities, and the state from the burdens of poverty, unemployment, and political unrest [and] helped to 'shovel out' some of their poor. . . ." In a rather disturbing but sadly accurate metaphorical turn, Roberts aptly captured the grim reality of what deportation ultimately may mean for a nation of immigrants: "Deportation was a necessary part of immigration, the equivalent of the sewage system of cities."[29]

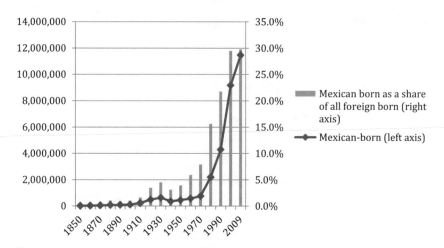

Chart 2.2 Mexican Foreign-Born Residing in the United States, 1850 to 2009. Source: Migration Policy Institute, http://www.migrationinformation.org/datahub/charts/fb-mexicans.cfm

The term "foreign born" refers to people residing in the United States who were not US citizens at birth. The foreign-born population thus includes naturalized citizens, lawful permanent residents (LPRs), certain legal nonimmigrants (e.g., persons on student or work visas), those admitted under refugee or asylee status, and persons illegally residing in the United States.

The most frequently articulated policy goals of deportation are thus linked, first, to the immigration law requirements of the border and the entry control regime.[30] More generally, and with more complex legitimacy claims, they may then relate to crime control, "national security" concerns, ideological controls, public health, foreign policy, labor market regulation, and other economic policies. The complexity of these goals and the potential for conflicts among them should not be underestimated. In its complaint challenging the Arizona immigration law, S.B. 1070, the Department of Justice wrote, for example, that "[i]n administering these laws, the federal agencies balance the complex—*and often competing*—objectives that animate federal immigration law and policy."[31] Politicians, however, tend to articulate these goals in exceptionally strong and blunt ways. Representative Steve King, for example, has referred to illegal immigration as "a slow-rolling, slow-motion terrorist attack on the United States costing us billions of dollars and, in fact, thousands of lives." As he continued, "we have an obligation to protect the American people, and that means seal and protect our borders."[32]

Another difficulty in assessing the goals of the deportation system thus derives from the fact that deportation involves many different government actors—legislative, executive/administrative, and judicial—whose goals may differ substantially. Even if we were to focus only on the Congress and the President, the goals have shifted significantly over time. The current deportation system is best understood within a long historical frame as it has grown slowly, incrementally, and reactively.[33] The current statutes have been crafted as much by accretion as by comprehensive revision. Take for example the current deportation rules pertaining to those who are convicted of "a crime involving moral turpitude."[34] This phrase derives from the 1917 Immigration Act that included a list of otherwise legal, resident aliens who were to be "taken into custody and deported."[35] Over the years, the "moral turpitude" term has been subject to a bewildering array of interpretations by immigration authorities and reviewing courts. At times, it has inspired frankly moralist discourse, such as, "[a] thief is a debased man; he has no moral character. . . ."[36] Judges have referred to "conduct which is inherently base, vile, or depraved, contrary to accepted rules of morality. . . ."[37] The term's open-ended quality has invited judicial flexibility. As one court held in 1929, "[w]e do not regard every violation of a prohibition law as a crime involving moral turpitude."[38] The original statutory moral turpitude language remains to this day, having withstood a "void for vagueness" challenge in 1951.[39] How can we assess the goals of such a law? It seems rather absurd to look to the Congress that enacted the 1917 statute. Even if we were to look to the last major revision of deportation law, which took place in 1996, we would be hard-pressed to find clear legislative goals relating to deportation for crimes involving moral turpitude. But it cannot be true that the goals of this law are unbounded discretion by the agency or the courts. Perhaps the best we can say is that the "crime involving moral turpitude" provision, like much of deportation law, is a *somewhat* open-ended mandate to deport *some* people who are convicted of *certain* types of crimes.[40] The system envisions an evolving, rather fluid conversation among various institutional actors: the Congress, the executive branch, agencies, federal judges, and, perhaps, state and local legislatures, state enforcement agencies, and state court judges.[41] Such definitional problems and institutional tensions highlight the (concededly amorphous) goal of legitimacy.[42]

But let us return to the basic question: what are the goals of the deportation system? The most obvious goal of the *extended border control* deportation system is to supplement border control. Though most Americans undoubtedly support this general goal, its substance, too, has changed considerably over time. In 1905, for example, the main focus was on the personal *qualities* of immigrants. In an era of largely open immigration policies for European immigrants, President Theodore Roosevelt sought

an increase in the stringency of laws to keep out insane, idiotic, epileptic and pauper immigrants. But this is by no means enough. Not

merely the anarchist, but every man of anarchistic tendencies, all violent and disorderly people, all people of bad character, the incompetent, the lazy, the vicious, and physically unfit, defective, or degenerate
should be kept out.[43]

Some of the provisions enacted in the following decades are still on the
books, but the primary focus of current *extended border control* deportation has
clearly shifted to the removal of undocumented—mostly Mexican and Central
American—noncitizens as part of a more complete border control strategy.[44] As
Mae Ngai has shown, the Quota Laws of the 1920s led to the creation of a large,
new category of people known as "illegal aliens."[45] It is this ill-defined group that
is still largely the focus of *extended border control* deportation. As Ngai put it, "the
notion of border control obscured the policy's unavoidable slippage into the
interior."[46]

It is, as we shall see, very hard to determine whether either border control as
such or "slippage into the interior" has actually worked. In 2006, Wayne Cornelius concluded that increased border enforcement since 1993 had not stopped
unauthorized migrants from entering the United States.[47] Indeed, it had likely
not even discouraged many. Neither the higher probability of being apprehended by the Border Patrol nor the sharply increased danger of clandestine
entry through deserts and mountainous terrain has much dissuaded potential
migrants from leaving home.[48] To be sure, increased border enforcement has
made clandestine border crossing increasingly expensive and risky. But an ironic
consequence has been to encourage undocumented people to remain in the
United States for longer periods and to settle permanently in this country in
much larger numbers. Cornelius argued persuasively that a border-enforcement-
only (or border-enforcement-first) approach to immigration control would only
produce more such unintended consequences and would not be an effective
deterrent to illegal entry.[49] Still, the specific, articulated goals of *extended border
control* deportation have remained clear: "consistent, comprehensive enforcement of the immigration law [would] reduce the number of new illegal arrivals and persuade a large share of illegals already here to give up and deport
themselves."[50]

As simple as such goals may appear, they imply rather distinct enforcement
models which, in turn, refine our understanding of the goals themselves. One
might envision two basic models that have been well described as (1) a metaphorical fortress and (2) an interdependence (or cooperation-based) model
that has been metaphorically termed a "complex organism."[51] The fortress model
seeks a secure physical perimeter. (Picture a walled-in city or a castle surrounded
by a moat.)[52] It implies guards who watch for outside dangers; although there
must of course also be a gate of some sort to permit economic and social activity

with outsiders. One can see the easy attraction of a fortress model in the context of such dangers as violence from Mexican drug cartels and concerns about foreign terrorists crossing the U.S. southern border.[53] However, fortress-type systems have many problems, ranging from the symbolic (they contradict the ideals of an open society and a nation of immigrants) to the pragmatic (they are static, unimaginative, and inevitably inspire criminal enterprises designed to circumvent their walls).[54]

Those who focus on increasing global interdependence and fluidity thus may suggest more nuanced models, such as that of a "complex organism."[55] This model envisions multiple interdependent systems and the flexibility to adjust to changes and trauma. Proponents of this model argue that we should not view the border in isolation or as a static front. Border threats are "dynamic, frequently decentralized, and respond to market forces, as well as terrorist opportunities, both at the border and in the interior."[56] Unlike the fortress model of a defended perimeter, the complex organism model envisions overlapping systems that work "to expel undesirable elements while facilitating the movements of desirable elements."[57] The basic virtue of the model is that it recognizes the interconnection between border systems, interior and foreign enforcement, and international cooperation.[58] This offers greater balance and distribution of the risk of failure throughout the "organism" rather than shifting it all to the border.[59] But it requires an effective, efficient, and, most important, a *just and fair* deportation system.

During the Bush administration—following the trauma of 9/11—there was a powerful reinvigoration of the fortress model, complete with a huge wall project along the southern border and a concomitant idea of the border as a zone of limited or no rights. Deportation also was used during this period as a powerful, flexible tool of enforcement for many purposes. Still, the basic U.S. border control goals have remained largely consistent for decades. The Border Patrol's 1994 Strategic Plan, for example, aimed to achieve "confidence in the integrity of the border."[60] As then President Clinton announced: "We will make it tougher for illegal aliens to get into the country."[61] Throughout the Clinton and George W. Bush administrations, spending increased dramatically on high-tech patrols, huge new walls, fences, radar, and increases in border patrol budgets.[62] An array of militaristic projects appeared with such names as Operation Blockade (quickly renamed Operation Hold the Line in response to criticism of the war-like metaphor) (El Paso 1993); Operation Gatekeeper (San Diego 1994); and Operation Safeguard (Arizona 1995).[63] The Department of Homeland Security spent more than $3.4 billion on border fencing alone, completing 640 of a planned 652 miles of fencing and vehicle barriers started during the Bush administration. A high-technology component of the border control plan, known as SBI*net*, budgeted $700 million for a "virtual" fence with some fifty camera and radio towers on a twenty-eight-mile region near Tucson and a thirty-mile stretch near Ajo, Arizona. It combined motion-detection sensors, remotely operated camera surveillance, ground-based radar, and unmanned aerial vehicles.[64] This was just a part of the broader Secure Borders Initiative (SBI), a multiyear plan designed to secure the nation's borders and to reduce illegal immigration.[65] The overall goals for SBI included securing and patrolling U.S. borders, expanding programs for detention and deportation, upgrading technology, and increasing worksite enforcement to target unauthorized workers.[66] All of this garnered great enthusiasm in some quarters and was pushed aggressively by then DHS Secretary Michael Chertoff.[67] As one report noted, the U.S. preoccupation with preventing another terrorist attack led to a "seemingly all-consuming pursuit of securing its borders by *all means available.*"[68]

Advanced, expensive border control technology was initially embraced by candidate Obama. In 2010, the White House released a statement affirming that one of the Administration's main goals was to "strengthen border control" and to "protect the integrity of our borders by investing in additional personnel, infrastructure, and technology on the border and at our ports of entry."[69] However, in March 2010, the SBI*net* project was ended by DHS Secretary Janet Napolitano, who said, "Not only do we have an obligation to secure our borders, we have a responsibility to do so in the most cost-effective way possible."[70] The goals of *extended border control* are thus always a mixture of the real and symbolic, the flamboyant and the subtle, the grandiose and the pragmatic.[71]

Consider ICE, the deportation enforcement agency. The ICE Strategic Plan contains a rather ambitious and bewildering hodgepodge of goals. One of its main goals is the prevention of terrorist attacks against the United States and the dismantling of "threats to homeland security" before they materialize.[72] But ICE also aims to control unlawful movement across the border—*in either direction*—of people, goods, and contraband, and to protect lawful commerce.[73] Moreover, ICE has such amorphous goals as the creation of a "culture of employer compliance";[74] the protection of the "integrity" of the immigration system;[75] and "greater efficiency in the removal process."[76] One particularly fascinating goal is to "Promote the Mission and Success of ICE." The language is largely that of marketing: "ICE will better define itself and promote its mission and success to the Department, public, media, Congress, community groups, and other law enforcement entities." In an almost charmingly optimistic vision, ICE hopes that young people interested in law enforcement careers will better come to understand "the unique and exciting mission of ICE."[77] Also, of course, ICE supports "Smart and Tough Interior Immigration Enforcement" through *extended border control* deportation.[78]

Of course, most of this is not new. In 1994, for example, a presidential commission urged "restoring credibility to the U.S. system of enforcement against illegal migration."[79] This frames what is perhaps the most difficult goals question: how should we reconcile border control and "restoring credibility" with high costs, collateral consequences, negative effects on bilateral international relationships, and the inevitable hard cases of extreme hardship that deportation might cause? Deportation law has long embodied a mix of answers: both strict rules and mediating discretionary provisions.[80] Since 1996, the balance has dramatically shifted toward strictness and away from ameliorative discretion, although, as noted, in 2010–2011, the Obama administration sought to use some of its discretionary power in more sophisticated and humane ways.[81]

Supporters of strict enforcement policies sometimes offer a utilitarian justification. Policy, they say, should not be made "on the basis of sentiment or emotion, nor should it deter us from the need to see that immigration laws are enforced." Indeed, some suggest "it becomes part of humanity's responsibility to make difficult decisions in order to secure the common good." The alternative would be "a false compassion that leads to tolerance of and a lack of enforcement against illegal migration." This, they conclude, is a "false type of generosity that often harms the very persons whom one might presume it would help."[82] This last point, of course, cannot be true for the actual beneficiaries of generosity themselves. However, as the argument runs, the goals of strict enforcement and generosity are, in the long run, consonant, because without credible enforcement, dangerous backlash is inevitable. This, I think, frames the ultimate *extended border control* debate well and forces us to understand the problem not as a clash of irreconcilable absolute positions, but as a more nuanced set of choices, a search for a balance. There are, of course, further considerations that must also be a part of the debate over enforcement goals. We should ask *why* are so many millions of people in this country illegally? Why do they endure such exploitation, uncertainty, family separation, and even physical danger? Clearly, even leaving aside refugee emergencies, neither border control nor deportation can solve all problems caused by inadequate admissions planning and ineffective bilateral or multilateral economic policies. The goals of *extended border control* deportation must therefore inevitably be partial and tentative; and systemic accomplishments, costs, and consequences will always be challenging. This, unfortunately, is another part of "illegal" that many do not sufficiently understand.

Let us turn now to the goals of *post-entry social control* deportation. These would seem easier to define than those of *extended border control*. This system is currently aimed mostly at criminal conduct within the United States, although it may also focus on various other types of conduct and associations. As I have described previously, *post-entry social control* deportation laws derive from what might be termed an "eternal probation" or an "eternal guest" model. The strongest version of this model would suggest that the millions of

noncitizens among us, including long-term lawful permanent residents, are
harbored subject to the whim of the government and may be deported for any
reason, whenever the government so desires. A constitutionally refined variant imposes at least some procedural limits on this power. Historically, however, U.S. courts have found precious few limits to the *post-entry social control*
deportation power. The basic idea has been that all noncitizens, whether legal
(in status) in status or undocumented, are subject to a flexible, ever-shifting—
even retroactive—regime of deportation.[83] Proponents of this form of deportation tend to focus on goals of safety and security concerns. Metaphors of
cleansing have long been common. The concern is not with the *quantity* of
immigrants, their legal status, or even with border control, but with noncitizens' post-entry *actions* and *qualities*.

Some such deportation initiatives have related to widely accepted human
rights goals. For example, alleged Nazi war criminals have been denaturalized
due to the efforts of the Office of Special Investigations in the Department of
Justice.[84] Following such denaturalizations (typically based on material mis-
representations during the immigration or naturalization process), many
former Nazis have faced deportation proceedings.[85] Such cases understand-
ably achieve wide popular support, are heavily publicized by the agencies
involved, and tend to inspire rather ringing prosecutorial rhetoric. John Demjanjuk, born in present-day Ukraine, had immigrated to the United States in
1952. He was first tried on allegations of participation in Nazi persecution in
a 1981 denaturalization hearing. The immigration judge found that Demjanjuk was a notorious gas chamber operator at the Treblinka extermination center known to prisoners as "Ivan the Terrible." Extradited in 1986 to Israel, he
was tried and convicted. However, the Israeli Supreme Court then found that
there was serious doubt about whether Demjanjuk was in fact "Ivan the Terrible," and he was released and returned to the United States in 1993. In 1999,
the Department of Justice started a second denaturalization case against
Demjanjuk, relying on newly discovered Nazi documents from the former
Soviet Union. This time, the district court found that Demjanjuk had actually worked at the Sobibor extermination center in Nazi-occupied Poland,
where some 250,000 Jewish men, women, and children were murdered.[86]
Following this second denaturalization, Demjanjuk was ordered removed
from the United States to either Ukraine, Germany, or Poland. He was finally
deported to Germany in 2009. John P. Torres of ICE eloquently supported the
goals of this type of deportation as well as the justice of this particular case:
"Millions have sought refuge from persecution in this country under liberty's
mantle. We will not suffer persecutors and mass murderers tarnishing her
image by staking such a claim for themselves." He continued to promise that
the U.S. government would prevent the "cynical exploitation of our nation's

immigration system by the worst of the worst" and noted that Demjanjuk's removal reaffirmed "our commitment to protection of the oppressed, not the oppressor."[87]

Clearly, such cases have the strongest legitimacy claims of any, and the Obama administration has continued to support them. A new Human Rights and Special Prosecutions (HRSP) section in the U.S. Justice Department pursues human rights violators under federal criminal statutes proscribing torture, war crimes, genocide, and recruitment or use of child soldiers.[88] It also enforces laws pertaining to visa fraud and unlawful procurement of naturalization and may work to revoke U.S. citizenship or other legal status.[89] Both HRSP and ICE proudly publicize such cases. A 2010 press release proclaimed: "Former Guatemalan Special Forces Soldier Sentenced to 10 Years in Prison for Making False Statements on Naturalization Forms Regarding 1982 Massacre of Guatemalan Villagers." The case involved Gilberto Jordan, a former Guatemalan special forces soldier who had lied about his participation in a horrific and brutal 1982 massacre at a Guatemalan village known as Dos Erres.[90] Assistant Attorney General Breuer connected the prosecution of Jordan to legitimate goals of deportation enforcement, such as stripping people of "ill-gotten U.S. citizenship" and preventing such people from making "this country their home."[91] ICE Director John Morton has promised to "continue to work tirelessly to ensure that human rights violators cannot seek safe haven in the United States."[92] ICE's website displays a list of such "Human Rights Violators."

But cases like Jordan's number in the dozens. It is much more garden-variety criminal conduct by noncitizens that has dominated *post-entry social control* deportation in recent years, with cases numbering in the hundreds of thousands. These cases, too, often inspire strong rhetoric. As former Senator D'Amato once flamboyantly put it, criminal aliens were "savaging our society."[93] Criminal deportation laws, many of which aim to relieve society of people who live in the United States legally, are thus justified as part of efforts to control crime in our communities. As we shall see, deportation law contains various mechanisms to achieve this cleansing goal, including expansive categories of deportation for "aggravated felonies," retroactive deportations for past crimes, mandatory detention, limited discretionary relief, and restrictions on judicial review of crime-based deportation cases.

We can see the apparent goals of crime-based, *post-entry social control* deportation in a major initiative called "Secure Communities."[94] The program's website described it early on as a "comprehensive strategy to improve and modernize the identification and removal of criminal aliens from the United States."[95] The Secure Communities program even had its own brochure, colored in a pleasant deep blue tone. With minimal bureaucratic lingo, it got right to the point, in large typeface:

Secure Communities
removes
dangerous criminals
from your community

Just to the right of this language, the brochure suggested that you could "**Report Suspicious Activity by calling 1-866-DHS-2-ICE.**" The program, strongly supported by the Obama administration as a "smart" deportation strategy, involves enhanced technological cooperation between state and local police and ICE. When an individual is booked into a jail, his or her fingerprints are checked against federal immigration-related databases to search for an individual's criminal and immigration history.[96]

How should we evaluate the goals of such programs? On first blush, deportation as a crime control strategy seems both legitimate and efficient. Aliens, one might say, have no absolute right to be here. And if serious "criminal aliens" are no longer here, they are no longer part of "our" crime problem.[97] So far, perhaps, so good. But life is not so simple. Following concerns about racial profiling, distraction of police resources, negative impacts on community policing strategies, and the deportation of noncriminal undocumented people and low-level offenders, the Secure Communities program has attracted furious, energetic responses from immigrants' rights organizations.[98] The governors of New York, Illinois, and Massachusetts rejected the program due to concerns about whether it was accomplishing its ostensible goals of deporting serious criminals.[99] As a result, ICE announced reforms, including expansion of the circumstances to be considered when officers decide whom to detain or deport.[100] Then, in August 2011, ICE announced that it would continue to operate the Secure Communities program even without agreements from the jurisdictions in which it operates.[101] Since one of the original goals of Secure Communities was to enhance cooperation between ICE and state and local authorities, this seemed to be a drastic revision of that aspiration. As with other deportation measures, this program's goals are a mix of the pragmatic and the political. Here, it seems that the Administration was willing to sacrifice some cooperation (and to override concerns about noncitizens now fearing to call local police when they are victims of crime) in order to show its commitment to tough immigration enforcement. But this, of course, calls into question whether the goal of *post-entry social control* deportation is really crime control in communities or something more complex.

Such questions about strategy and tactics, and long- versus short-term goals have long bedeviled the understanding of deportation and crime. As Voltaire once put it,

Not long ago one banished outside the sphere of jurisdiction a petty thief, a petty forger, a man guilty of an act of violence. The result was that he became a big robber, a forger on a big scale, and murderer within the sphere of another jurisdiction. It is as if we threw into our neighbours' fields the stones which incommode us in our own.[102]

Criminal deportees—even assuming that they have in fact been convicted of serious crimes—may no longer be "our" problem. But they are still *somebody's* problem. And the problem may get worse due to the effects of deportation itself. Simply dumping criminal deportees in, say, El Salvador, may well prove to be a penny-wise and pound-foolish approach to crime control. We will never know, of course, whether deportees might have been better off had they remained in the United States with family and some community constraints. But dumping them in El Salvador has made rehabilitation virtually inconceivable. In fact, as we shall see, it is not even clear that U.S. public safety has been enhanced in the long run. Still, such hard questions have concerned precious few U.S. policy makers in recent years.[103] There can be little doubt that "'[o]ut of sight, out of mind' perhaps best describes the traditional U.S. response" to the problems that U.S. deportees may cause in their receiving nations.[104] There are, indeed, few public policies less controversial than the removal of "criminal aliens."[105] The policy sustains tight bonds of solidarity among those (citizens, in particular, but also among many legally resident noncitizens) who share anger and indignation. Like criminal enforcement, it "brings together upright consciences and concentrates them."[106] It may also be seen to "send a message" not only domestically, but also abroad. As Edwin Grant put it in a remarkable 1925 article, *Scum from the Melting Pot*: "A systematic deportation not only eugenically cleanses America of a vicious element but the moral effect upon their native countries makes deportation . . . doubly worth while."[107] But this may also explain why such deportations also tend to overreach. As we shall see, for many years now, we have experienced dramatically stepped-up deportations of legal residents who have been convicted of crimes. Some such crimes are surely serious, but the majority, it appears, are drug possession and traffic offenses.[108] Tens of thousands of such deportees have been long-term legal residents.[109] A 2006 study found that some 70 percent of those charged as "aggravated felons" had lived in the United States for more than a decade. These charges are the most serious in terms of consequences, but very minor crimes, such as petit larceny and drug possession, have also been deemed aggravated felonies. The median length of residence prior to deportation was fourteen years.[110]

In sum, the goals of deportation have long been complex. In 1994, then New York City Mayor Rudy Giuliani, who had already established a strong law-and-order reputation, offered this rather nuanced view:

Some of the hardest-working and most productive people in this city are undocumented aliens. If you come here and you work hard and you happen to be in an undocumented status, you're one of the people who we want in this city. You're somebody that we want to protect, and we want you to get out from under what is often a life of being like a fugitive, which is really unfair.[111]

But those sorts of sentiments have, to say the least, not prevailed. Put simply, since major changes were implemented to the deportation system in 1996, millions of people, including many hundreds of thousands with legal immigration status, have been ordered to leave, and many are barred from ever returning. Let us now consider how this has been done and what its effects have been.

Notes

1. Quoted in HERBERT ASBURY, THE GANGS OF NEW YORK: AN INFORMAL HISTORY OF THE UNDERWORLD 1928, xviii (2008).
2. *Is Deportation the Cure?* 212 NORTH AMERICAN REV. 181 (Jan. 1920).
3. *See* DANIEL KANSTROOM, DEPORTATION NATION 21 (Harvard University Press 2007).
4. *Id.* at 33. *See also* JOHN HIGHAM, SEND THESE TO ME: IMMIGRANTS IN URBAN AMERICA 71–80 (rev. ed. 1984); Mark Gibney, *United States Immigration Policy and the "Huddled Masses" Myth*, 3 GEO. IMMIGR. L.J. 361 (1989) (contrasting the myth with then-current immigration policies); GERALD NEUMAN, STRANGERS TO THE CONSTITUTION: IMMIGRANTS, BORDERS, AND FUNDAMENTAL law 19 (1996) (viewing Lazarus's work as a "poetic fiction that the Statue of Liberty once welcomed the 'tired and poor' and the 'wretched refuse' of teeming shores.").
5. "L'hypocrisie est un hommage que le vice rend a la vertu" (*"Hypocrisy is the homage which vice renders to virtue"*), Francois Duc de la Rochefoucauld, *Maximes 218*, at 43 (Stuart D. Warner & Stephane Douard eds., 2001).
6. It is not, of course, completely unique to the United States. *See* Franca Iacovetta, *A Nation of Immigrants: Readings in Canadian History 1940s-1960s* (Paula Draper & Robert Ventresca eds., University of Toronto Press 1997); TIM DARE, AUSTRALIA: A NATION OF IMMIGRANTS (1988).
7. THE WHITE HOUSE, BUILDING A 21ST CENTURY IMMIGRATION SYSTEM 3 (MAY 2011), *available at* http://www.whitehouse.gov/sites/default/files/rss_viewer/immigration_blueprint.pdf.
8. *See generally* Donna R. Gabaccia, *Nations of Immigrants: Do Words Matter?*, 5(3) THE PLURALIST 5–31 (Fall 2010); Donna R. Gabaccia, *Response to Marilyn Fischer, Jose Jorge Mendoza, and Celia Bardwell-Jones*, THE PLURALIST 57–64 (Fall 2010) (describing the historical evolution of the phrase "nation of immigrants").
9. We can perhaps best appreciate the significance of this background norm by comparing it to countries in which it does not exist. As one commentator wrote of Germany in 1991, for example, "For Americans to understand the psychological underpinnings of the current debate among Germans on how to deal with immigration, it is necessary to realize that, unlike the multi-ethnic tapestry of the U.S., the nation-states of Europe have traditionally been ethnically homogenous." *See* Daniel Kanstroom, *Wer Sind Wir Wieder? Laws of Immigration, Citizenship, and Asylum in the Struggle for the Soul of the New Germany*, 18 YALE J. INT'L L. 155, 158 (Winter 1993) (quoting Kai Hailbronner).
10. This phrase was used by Admiral Mike Mullen, chairman of the Joint Chiefs of Staff, in an open letter written in May 2008: "The U.S. military must remain apolitical at all times," "It is and must always be a neutral instrument of the state, no matter which party holds sway."

Mullen to Troops: Stay out of Politics, INT'L HERALD TRIBUNE, May 27, 2008, *available at* http://www.military.com/news/article/mullen-to-troops-stay-out-of-politics.html?ESRC=eb. nl. It was more recently reiterated by Admiral Mullen in regard to the forced resignation of General Stanley McChrystal. *See* http://www.cbsnews.com/8301-503544_162-20008742-503544.html.

11. E.P. HUTCHINSON, LEGISLATIVE HISTORY OF AMERICAN IMMIGRATION POLICY 1798–1965, 443 (1981).

12. *See* GEORGE SHER, BEYOND NEUTRALITY: PERFECTIONISM AND POLITICS (1997); *see also* CHARLES E. LARMORE, PATTERNS OF MORAL COMPLEXITY 44 (1987); JOSEPH RAZ, THE MORALITY OF FREEDOM (1986), Will Kymlicka, *Liberal Individualism and Liberal Neutrality*, 99 ETHICS 883–905, at 883–84 (1989).

13. *See generally* KANSTROOM, DEPORTATION NATION, *supra* note 3.

14. *Id. See also* Linda S. Bosniak, *Membership. Equality, and the Difference That Alienage Makes,* 69 N.Y.U.L. REV. 1047 (1994).

15. *See, e.g.,* THE DEPORTATION REGIME (Nicholas De Genova & Nathalie Peutz eds., 2010).

16. Matthew Gibney, *Deportation*, in PETER CANE & JOANNE CONAGHAN, THE NEW OXFORD COMPANION TO LAW (Oxford University Press 2008). The article notes that "notwithstanding its different appellations, the practice of deportation remains a feature of all contemporary liberal democratic states." This is clearly true, though there is much about deportation that seems contradictory to many fundamental norms that otherwise sustain liberal states. http://www.oxfordreference.com.proxy.bc.edu/views/ENTRY.html?subview=Main&entry=t287. e608 (available to users only).

17. ALEINIKOFF, MARTIN, MOTOMURA & FULLERTON, IMMIGRATION AND CITIZENSHIP PROCESS AND POLICY 693 (6th ed. 2007).

18. The statute does have a "definitions" section for such important terms as "nonimmigrant" (a person who does not seek to live permanently in the United States). Other definitions explain legal terms of art. The term "child," for example, begins simply: "an unmarried person under twenty-one years of age" and then continues into a dizzying array of permutations, including legitimate children, adopted children, stepchildren, etc., each with its own complicated definitional rules. 8 U.S.C. § 1101(b). Some seem ridiculously circular and make one wonder how many tax dollars were spent researching *that* question. The term "Attorney General," for example, "means the Attorney General of the United States." 8 U.S.C. § 1101(a)(5). *But see* Pub. L. No. 107–296, § 471, 116 Stat. 2135, 2192, 2205 (Nov. 25, 2002), effective Feb. 23, 2003 (defining the term "Attorney General" in some situations to refer to the "Secretary of Homeland Security"). *See also* STEPHEN R. VINA, CONG, RESEARCH SERV., RL31997, AUTHORITY TO ENFORCE THE IMMIGRATION AND NATIONALITY ACT (INA) IN THE WAKE OF THE HOMELAND SECURITY ACT: LEGAL ISSUES (July 16, 2003).

19. 8 U.S.C. § 1101(a)(3).

20. 8 U.S.C. § 1227(a).

21. 8 U.S.C. § 1182. Many of those who have not been admitted have, of course, been here for decades. Still, the law treats them for some purposes as if they were still outside the borders of the United States, a problem that is explored in Chapter 5.

22. Cervantes v. Perryman, 954 F. Supp. 1257, 1260 (N.D. Ill. 1997).

23. Kwon v. Immigration & Naturalization Serv., 646 F.2d 909, 919 (5th Cir. 1981).

24. DHS, Office of Immigration Statistics, 2010 Yearbook of Immigration Statistics, tables 36 and 38, *available at* http://www.dhs.gov/files/statistics/publications/YrBk10En.shtm (this figure includes both forced removals and "returns," including voluntary departures).

25. *Id.*

26. According to the Executive Office for Immigration Review (EOIR), the total number of cases received for formal processing by immigration courts grew from 282,396 in 2001 to 368,848 in 2005 and then to 392,888 in FY 2010. Office of Planning, Analysis, & Technology, U.S. Dep't of Justice, FY 2010 Statistical Yearbook Figure 1, page B2 (2010). All of these cases involve people who face removal from U.S. soil by government action, though EOIR does not clearly disaggregate deportations from inadmissibility removal cases. Since April 1, 1997, all such proceedings have been called "removal." The total number of cases

(including some old "deportation" and "exclusion" cases) has risen from a total of some 237,000 in 2001 to over 325,000 in 2010. *Id.* at C3. ICE data differ somewhat from those reported by the DOJ Office of Planning, Analysis & Technology. *See* ICE TOTAL RE-MOVALS THROUGH JULY 31, 2011, *available at* http://www.ice.gov/doclib/about/offices/ero/pdf/ero-removals.pdf.

27. *See* Peter Slevin, *Deportation of Illegal Immigrants Increases under Obama Administration*, WASH. POST, July 26, 2010, *available at* http://www.washingtonpost.com/wp-dyn/content/article/2010/07/25/AR2010072501790.html.

28. *See generally* KANSTROOM, DEPORTATION NATION, *supra* note 3.

29. BARBARA ANN ROBERTS, WHENCE THEY CAME: DEPORTATION FROM CANADA 1900–1935, 3 (1988).

30. Of course, scholars such as Jacqueline Stevens, who profoundly question the very idea of the nation-state as currently constituted, would disagree with this legitimacy concession. Jacqueline Stevens, *Recreating the State*, 27(5) THIRD WORLD Q. 755–66 (2006); *See also* JACQUELINE STEVENS, STATES WITHOUT NATIONS: CITIZENSHIP FOR MORTALS (2009); JACQUELINE STEVENS, REPRODUCING THE STATE (1999)

31. Complaint ¶ 2, United States v. Arizona, Case No. 10-16645 (D. Ariz. filed July 6, 2010) (emphasis added), *available at* www.justice.gov/opa/documents/az-complaint.pdf.

32. Representative Steve King, *Comparing the Statistics—(House of Representatives—May 03, 2006)*, *available at* http://www.house.gov/apps/list/speech/ia05_king/sp_20060503_stats.html.

33. KANSTROOM, DEPORTATION NATION, *supra* note 3, at 6.

34. *See, e.g.,* 8 U.S.C. § 1227.

35. Act of February 5, 1917, ch. 29, 19, 39 Stat. 874, 889 (repealed 1952). The 1917 law did have some important ameliorative features. It recognized pardons as defenses to deportation and permitted a sentencing judge to override its provisions with a binding "recommendation" against deportation. The latter provision, the so-called JRAD, was repealed in 1990.

36. Tillinghast v. Edmead, 31 F.2d 81, 83 (1929).

37. Coykendall v. Skrmetta, 22 F.2d 120, 121 (5th Cir. 1927).

38. Iorio v. Day, 34 F.2d 920 (2d Cir. 1929). Modern judicial practice tends to involve more deference to the decisions of the Board of Immigration Appeals, which is part of the Department of Justice. *See, e.g.,* Michel v. INS, 206 F.3d 253, 263 (2d Cir. 2000) ("[W]e need only conclude that [the BIA's] interpretation is reasonable and that it considered the matter in a detailed and reasoned fashion.") (internal quotation omitted).

39. Jordan v. DeGeorge, 341 U.S. 223 (1951).

40. Immigration lawyers will note, too, that the term "conviction" is itself subject to statutory definition and administrative and judicial interpretation. *See* 8 U.S.C. § 1101(a)(43).

41. For example, Arizona's S.B. 1070, discussed above, requires police officers, "when practicable," to detain people they reasonably suspect are in the country without authorization and to verify their status with federal officials, unless doing so would hinder an investigation or emergency medical treatment. It also makes it a state misdemeanor to not carry immigration papers, and it permits people to sue local government or agencies if they believe federal or state immigration law is not being enforced.

42. As the Justice Department's complaint challenging the Arizona laws shows, it also involves complex questions of federal and state power. Complaint, ¶ 2. The main thrust of the federal legal challenge was not on racial profiling, discrimination, and the like, but on the argument that "[i]n our constitutional system, the federal government has preeminent authority to regulate immigration matters."

43. 40 CONG. REC. 101 (1906). Some of these suggestions were incorporated into the Immigration Act of 1907, 34 Stat. 898.

44. MAE NGAI, IMPOSSIBLE SUBJECTS: ILLEGAL ALIENS AND THE MAKING OF MODERN AMERICA (2004) [hereinafter Ngai, Impossible Subjects].

45. NGAI, IMPOSSIBLE SUBJECTS 56–89.

46. *Id.* at 57.

47. Wayne A. Cornelius, *Impacts of Border Enforcement on Unauthorized Mexican Migration to the United States* (Sept. 26, 2006), *available at* http://borderbattles.ssrc.org/Cornelius/.

48. *Id.*

49. *Id.*

50. MARK KRIKORIAN, CENTER FOR IMMIGRATION STUDIES, *Attrition and Enforcement*, http://www.cis.org/Attrition.

51. These metaphors were developed by CHAD C. HADDAL, CONG. RESEARCH SERV., R41237, PEOPLE CROSSING BORDERS: AN ANALYSIS OF U.S. BORDER PROTECTION POLICIES (Mar. 2010), *available at* http://www.fas.org/sgp/crs/homesec/R41237.pdf.

52. For a thoughtful discussion of how these systems interact see Adam B. Cox, *Immigration Law's Organizing Principles*, 157 U. PA. L. REV. 341 (2008).

53. *See, e.g.,* JENNIFER E. LAKE & KRISTIN M. FINKLEA, CONG. RESEARCH SERV., R41075, SOUTHWEST BORDER VIOLENCE: ISSUES IN IDENTIFYING AND MEASURING SPILLOVER VIOLENCE.

54. Some also note how fortresses tend to divide communities and local economies that rely on mobility. *See, e.g.,* Thomas Frank, *Tensions Rise with U.S.-Mexican Border Fence,* USA TODAY, Dec. 29, 2008, online edition, *available at* http://www.usatoday.com/news/nation/2008-12-28-fence-inside_N.htm.

55. *See* Colonel Gideon Netzer (Res.), Israel Defense Forces, *A Generic Model for Cooperative Border Security,* Sandia National Laboratories, SAND 98–0505/7, Albuquerque, NM, March 1999.

56. Haddal, *supra* note 51, at 8.

57. *Id.*

58. There are, of course, many risks to international cooperative relationships, too. Thus, the complex organism model envisions cooperative arrangements based on mutual economic and security interests that are "built on an underlying foundation of unilateral safeguards." Haddal, *supra* note 51, at 8.

59. As an Israeli military expert put it:

> Unilateral methods [of border security] rely on the use of military or police forces by the national government without regard to activities by the neighboring countries. Borders become fortified zones with observation posts, defensive positions, physical barriers, and heavily armed response forces. Unilateral actions have limits and disadvantages. Military based solutions to border security often have the undesirable effect of increasing tensions between two neighbors.... Confidence, the key factor in a stable relationship, becomes difficult to build. Netzer, *supra* note 55, at 6.

60. BORDER PATROL STRATEGIC PLAN 1994 AND BEYOND, 2.

61. PETER ANDREAS, BORDER GAMES: POLICING THE U.S.-MEXICO DIVIDE 87 (2000).

62. *Id.*

63. *Operation Rio Grande* in Texas used floodlights, watchtowers, video surveillance, and infrared sights along more than thirty miles of border. ANDREAS, *supra* note 61, at 106.

64. U.S. CUSTOMS AND BORDER PROTECTION, "SBI*net*: Securing US Borders" (fact sheet, September 2006), *available at* http://www.dhs.gov/xlibrary/assets/sbinetfactsheet.pdf.

65. Actually, SBI*net* replaced two previous efforts: the Integrated Surveillance Intelligence System (ISIS) and America's Shield Initiative (ASI). The ISIS program, established in 1998, sought to provide continuous monitoring of the borders. Due to contracting errors and lack of government oversight of the contract, ISIS was considered ineffective and was never completely installed. In June 2003, Customs and Border Protection (CBP) began developing ASI to integrate surveillance technology, communications, and visualization tools while maintaining and modernizing ISIS. In 2005, ISIS was formally subsumed under ASI, an integrated national web of border security with centralized command. ASI was created to strengthen U.S. ability to detect, intercept, and secure the borders against unauthorized immigrants, potential terrorists, weapons of mass destruction, illegal drugs, and other contraband. ASI also came to be seen as ineffective and wasteful. *See generally* Doris Meissner & Donald Kerwin, Migration Policy Institute, *DHS and Immigration: Taking Stock and Correcting Course,* February 2009, *available at* http://www.migrationpolicy.org/research/usimmigration.php.

66. Press Release, Dep't of Homeland Security, Fact Sheet: Secure Border Initiative (Nov. 2, 2005), http://www.dhs.gov/xnews/releases/press_release_0794.shtm.

67. But the system was plagued with problems and faced challenges from both the left and the right. In 2008, Republican Lamar Smith of Texas denounced the virtual fence as a failed "shortcut to border security" and asserted that "the administration's 'shortcut' turned out to be a dead end." Randall Mikkelsen, *U.S. Official Defends Problem-Plagued Border Fence*, REUTERS, Mar. 5, 2008, *available at* http://in.reuters.com/article/idINN0536848220080305.

68. Demetrios G. Papademetriou & Elizabeth Collett, Transatlantic Council on Migration, Migration Policy Institute, *A New Architecture for Border Management*, March 2011, at 8 (emphasis in original).

69. *See* http://www.whitehouse.gov/issues/immigration (last visited June 24, 2010).

70. Spencer S. Hsu, *Work to Cease on "Virtual Fence" Along U.S.-Mexico Border*, WASH. POST, Mar. 16, 2010, *available at* http://www.washingtonpost.com/wp-dyn/content/article/2010/03/16/AR2010031603573.html. In 2010, the Administration framed its policy as follows: "President Obama believes that our broken immigration system can only be fixed by putting politics aside and offering a complete solution that secures our border.... President Obama recognizes that an orderly, controlled border and an immigration system designed to meet our economic needs are important pillars of a healthy and robust economy." The President also aimed to "protect the integrity of our borders by investing in additional personnel, infrastructure, and technology on the border and at our ports of entry"; to "remove incentives to enter the country illegally by preventing employers from hiring undocumented workers and enforcing the law"; and "to promote economic development in Mexico to decrease the economic desperation that leads to illegal immigration." *See* http://www.whitehouse.gov/issues/immigration (last visited June 24, 2010), reprinted at http://usliberals.about.com/od/immigration/a/ObamaImmiPolicies.htm.

71. As ICE put it in its "Strategic Plan" for 2010–2014, "Our primary mission is to protect national security, public safety, and the integrity of our borders through the criminal and civil enforcement of Federal law governing border control, customs, trade, and immigration." Department of Homeland Security Immigration and Customs Enforcement (ICE) Strategic Plan FY 2010–2014, *available for download at* http://www.ice.gov/news/releases/1006/10 0630washingtondc.htm.

72. ICE also highlights the dangers posed by "transnational criminal and terrorist organizations" that attempt "to exploit lawful movement and transportation systems and to create alternative, illicit pathways through which people and illegal goods—narcotics, funds, and weaponry—can cross the border." It also includes: "investigating and removing suspected terrorists or their supporters; and preventing the export of weapons and sensitive technologies that could be used to harm the United States, its people, and its allies."

73. Priorities include (1) dismantling organized alien smuggling; (2) targeting drug trafficking organizations; (3) pursuing international money laundering and bulk cash smuggling; (4) countering international weapons trafficking; (5) targeting human trafficking and transnational sexual exploitation; and (6) invigorating intellectual property rights investigations to protect lawful commerce.

74. "ICE will use the following two-pronged strategy: (1) aggressive criminal and civil enforcement against those employers who knowingly violate the law; and (2) continued implementation of programs, such as E-Verify and ICE's IMAGE program, to help employers comply. Criminal investigations will increasingly focus on employers who abuse and exploit workers or otherwise engage in egregious conduct...."

75. "ICE will work closely with USCIS and the Department of State to identify, address, and prevent the many large-scale, organized frauds perpetrated on the government each year. In addition, ICE will pursue criminal cases against individuals who lie on applications, engage in fraud, and pose a threat to national security or public safety.... Also to protect the integrity of the immigration system, ICE will remove aliens who receive final orders, with a focus on convicted criminals and those who have most recently received orders. Similarly, ICE will begin to invest more resources to identify and remove aliens soon after they overstay non-immigrant visas."

76. "ICE will work to increase efficiency in every step of the removal process—from apprehension through removal—using the institutional removal program and other programs to reduce the duration of an alien's stay in ICE custody and increase compliance with final orders. Reducing transportation and removal costs is a critical aspect of efficiency. . . . ICE will work closely with the Department of State to improve the process for securing travel documents and country clearances. . . ."

77. As ICE is better understood through increased "outreach and branding," employees will feel increasingly "proud of the hours they dedicate to the work of ICE."

78. It mentions in particular the 2006 ending of the controversial "catch and release" policy at the U.S.-Mexican border region. Previously, most illegal border crossers from countries *other than Mexico* were released into the United States on their own recognizance pending a removal hearing. Many did not return for their hearings. Now, approximately 99 percent are being detained for deportation.

79. *See* U.S. Commission on Immigration Reform, U.S. Immigration Policy: Restoring Credibility 43–46 (1994).

80. The strong version of sovereignty that has governed deportation implicates Carl Schmitt's observation that the sovereign may also decide "the state of exception." CARL SCHMITT, POLITICAL THEOLOGY: FOUR CHAPTERS ON THE CONCEPT OF SOVEREIGNTY 5, 2d ed., (George Schwab trans., reprint MIT Press 1985) (1932). Schmitt, of course, was referring to a "state of emergency," but the ideas are related. *See* Austin Sarat, *At the Boundaries of Law: Executive Clemency, Sovereign Prerogative, and the Dilemma of American Legality*, in LEGAL BORDERLANDS: LAW AND THE CONSTRUCTION OF AMERICAN BORDERS 21 (Mary L. Dudziak & Leti Volpp eds. 2006).

81. *See supra*, Chapter 1.

82. Lamar Smith & Edward R. Grant, *Immigration Reform: Seeking the Right Reasons*, 28 ST. MARY'S L.J. 883, 893 (1997).

83. KANSTROOM, DEPORTATION NATION, *supra* note 3, at 6.

84. *See* http://www.mainjustice.com/2010/03/30/doj-creates-human-rights-and-special-prosecutions-section/.

85. *See, e.g.*, Press Release, Dep't of Justice, Former Nazi Death Camp guard John Demjanjuk Deported to Germany (May 12, 2009), *available at* http://www.ice.gov/news/releases/0905/090512washington.htm.

86. Demjanjuk had also served as an armed guard at the Majdanek concentration camp and extermination center and at Flossenbürg.

87. *Id.*

88. *See* http://www.justice.gov/criminal/hrsp/about/.

89. HRSP works closely with DHS and ICE, among other agencies. HRSP also, however, identifies one of its main priorities as "Protecting the Integrity of U.S. Borders." To this end, it investigates and prosecutes complex immigration offenses "that undermine the integrity of our nation's borders, particularly international criminal networks involved in smuggling of persons and trafficking in fraudulent travel and identification documents." *Id.*

90. According to court documents, a Guatemalan guerrilla group had ambushed a military convoy. In response, a patrol of approximately twenty Guatemalan special forces soldiers known as "Kaibiles," including Jordan, was deployed to search for the stolen rifles and find suspected guerrillas. According to court documents, Jordan and the special patrol entered Dos Erres, supported by a security perimeter around the village so that no one could escape. The members of the special patrol searched all of the houses for the missing weapons, forced the villagers from their homes, and separated the women and children from the men. Members of the special patrol then proceeded to systematically kill the men, women, and children at Dos Erres by, among other methods, hitting them on the head with a sledgehammer and then pushing them into the village well, according to information contained in court documents. Members of the special patrol also forcibly raped many of the women and girls at Dos Erres before killing them. Approximately 162 skeletal remains were later exhumed from the village well. At his plea hearing, Jordan admitted that he had participated in the massacre at Dos Erres. He also admitted that the first person he killed at Dos Erres was a baby, whom he had murdered by throwing in the well. *Id.*

91. *Id.*

92. *See* http://www.justice.gov/opa/pr/2010/September/10-crm-1042.html.

93. *D'Amato Says INS Fails to Protect City*, UPI, March 23, 1986, LEXIS News Library, Wires File.

94. *Julie Myers Wood Critiques ICE's Strategic Plan for Fiscal Years 2010–2014*, 2010 EMERGING ISSUES 5147, June 29, 2010, Matthew Bender.

95. The ostensible strategic goals of the program were:
    Identify aliens in law enforcement custody through modernized technology, continual data analysis, and timely information sharing;
    Prioritize enforcement action to apprehend and remove criminal aliens who pose the greatest threat to public safety; and
    Transform criminal alien immigration enforcement to efficiently identify, process, and remove criminal aliens from the United States.

96. If there is a database "hit," meaning a match to a record indicating an immigration violation, ICE and the local law enforcement authorities are automatically notified. In most cases, ICE will then issue a "detainer" against the jailed individual so that it will be notified before the noncitizen is released. According to ICE statistics, as of April 30, 2011, it had caught more than 77,000 immigrants convicted of crimes, including more than 28,000 convicted of "aggravated felony" (level 1) offenses. ICE, *Secure Communities: Get the Facts*, *available at* http://www.ice.gov/secure_communities/get-the-facts.htm The program operated in some 1,331 jurisdiction in 42 states.

97. One must, however, consider the long-term consequences of deporting parents of U.S.-citizen children who may remain behind. *See* Chapter 5, *infra.*

98. *See, e.g.,* National Immigration Forum, *Secure Communities*, *available at* www.immigrationforum.org/images/uploads/Secure_Communities.pdf (arguing that Secure Communities could lead to racial profiling, intimidate witnesses, cast too wide a net, have unclear priorities and insufficient accountability, and involve hidden costs); *see also* National Immigration Forum, *Secure Communities* (follow-up policy analysis July 6, 2011), *available at* www.immigrationforum.org/images/.../SecureCommunitiesPolicyAnalysis. pdf.

99. Julia Preston, *Immigration Program Is Rejected by 3d State*, N.Y. TIMES, June 7, 2011, at A13.

100. Tara Bahrampour, *ICE's Program Reforms to Protect Crime Victims, Witnesses*, WASH. POST, June 18, 2011, at A5 In June 2011, John Morton announced a series of changes including an admonition that "ICE officers, special agents, and attorneys should exercise all appropriate prosecutorial discretion to minimize any effect that immigration enforcement may have on the willingness and ability of victims, witnesses and plaintiffs to call police and pursue justice." Memorandum from John Morton for All Field Office Directors, All Special Agents in Charge, All Chief Counsel (June 17, 2011). ICE also crafted new training materials to educate communities about the program and the creation of an advisory committee to investigate how to deal with minor offenders, a complaint system, and quarterly statistical reviews. *See* Elise Foley, *Department Of Homeland Security to Reform Secure Communities Deportation Program*, HUFF POST, June 17, 2011 (last updated Aug. 17, 2011), http://www.huffingtonpost.com/2011/06/17/department-of-homeland-se_n_879611.html.

101. ICE rescinded Memoranda of Agreement with those jurisdictions that had signed them and announced that it would continue to operate Secure Communities regardless of the willingness of state and local jurisdictions to participate. Immigration Policy Center, Secure Communities: A Fact Sheet, *available at* http://www.immigrationpolicy.org/just-facts/secure-communities-fact-sheet.

102. Voltaire, *Banishment*, THE PHILOSOPHICAL DICTIONARY (selected and translated by H. I. Woolf 1924).

103. *See, e.g.,* Charles A. Radin, *A Homeland but Not Home: Young Cape Verdeans Face Grim Realities*, BOSTON GLOBE, Sept. 6, 1999, at A1 (describing the effects of deportations); Larry Rohter, *In U.S. Deportation Policy, A Pandora's Box*, N.Y. TIMES, Aug. 10, 1997, at A1 (describing the effects of deportation of Salvadoran gang members).

104. Margaret H. Taylor & T. Alexander Aleinikoff, *Deportation of Criminal Aliens: A Geopolitical Perspective*, § III.C (June 1998), *available at* http://www.thedialogue.org/PublicationFiles/

Deportation%20of%20criminal%20aliens%20a%20geopolitical%20perspective.pdf (also on file with the Harvard Law School Library).

105. Peter H. Schuck & John Williams, *Removing Criminal Aliens: The Pitfalls and Promises of Federalism*, 22 HARV. J. L. & PUB. POL'Y 367, 372 (1999).

106. EMILE DURKHEIM, THE DIVISION OF LABOR IN SOCIETY 102 (George Simpson trans., 1960).

107. Edwin E. Grant, *Scum from the Melting-Pot*, 30(6) AM. J. SOC. 641 (May 1925).

108. *See infra*, Chapters 3 and 4.

109. Though precise calculations are difficult given available statistics, we may roughly deduce these numbers from cases in which there were applications for discretionary relief apart from "defensive" asylum (such relief as cancellation of removal requires long-term residence, legal status, or both). The total number of such applications from FY06–FY10 was approximately 375,000 - 73,356 = 301,644 over five years. U.S. Department of Justice, Executive Office for Immigration Review, FY 2010 Statistical Yearbook, I-1, N-1. Another measure is "relief granted." Here, if one counts only those forms of relief that require long-term lawful permanent residence, actual grants by immigration judges totaled 21,449 over five years. *Id.* at R-1. This means that at least twice that number were in proceedings.

110. *See* 8 U.S.C. § 1101(a)(43) (2000). TRAC IMMIGRATION, HOW OFTEN IS THE AGGRAVATED FELONY STATUTE USED? (2006), http://trac.syr.edu/immigration/reports/158.

111. Deborah Sontag, *New York Officials Welcome Immigrants, Legal or Illegal*, N.Y. TIMES, June 10, 1994, at A1. *available at*: http://www.nytimes.com/1994/06/10/nyregion/new-york-officials-welcome-immigrants-legal-or-illegal.html.

3

The Major Methods of Deportation

They chase us like outlaws, like rustlers, like thieves.
—Woody Guthrie[1]

For some people, these are the equivalent of death penalty cases, and
we are conducting these cases in a traffic court setting.
—Immigration Judge Dana Marks[2]

As Supreme Court Justice Frank Murphy once noted, "few indeed have been the invasions upon essential liberties which have not been accompanied by pleas of urgent necessity advanced in good faith by responsible men."[3] In this spirit, this chapter examines the various methods of deportation used in the United States. In addition to considering how these methods connect to the system's goals, we will also ask whether essential liberties and other fundamental rights have been violated and, if so, whether such violations can be justified or corrected.

Some forms of deportation are relatively well-structured legal processes in which basic procedural rights are respected. The primary enforcement role is played by the Department of Homeland Security and its sub-agencies, Immigration and Customs Enforcement (ICE), which handles most interior enforcement, and U.S. Customs and Border Protection (CBP), which is responsible at the border and at ports of entry. CBP has a rather poetic Mission Statement, reading in part as follows: "We are the guardians of our Nation's borders, We are America's frontline."[4] Increased international mobility and a perception of greater threats from foreigners in an "age of risk" have inspired major changes to border control systems. As CPB's Mission Statement continues, "We safeguard America's homeland at and beyond our borders." The new architecture has information and technology as its centerpieces, with the aim of differentiating acceptable from potentially problematic travelers as far from the border as possible.[5] The goals of such systems are clear: to push out borders as far as possible through the extended use of detailed personal information, including biometrics. Such data may supplant nationality as a dominant means of screening. Though these new systems are quite effective in some regards, they also have significant costs and limita-tions.[6] In the United States, there has also been substantial recent thought about a comprehensive cross-agency border protection strategy that could operate both abroad and internally.[7] As DHS puts it, "[a] safe and secure homeland must mean more than preventing terrorist attacks. . . . It must also ensure that the liberties of all Americans are assured, privacy is protected, and . . . [that] travel, lawful immi-gration, trade, commerce, and exchange—are secured."[8] The balance tilts strongly toward government power and away from liberties when DHS acts abroad, espe-cially as to noncitizens who may be summarily denied visas or entry for undis-closed reasons. Further, at the physical border of the United States, as any traveler can attest, the discretionary power of government agents to question, search, and detain people is considerable.[9] The numbers are also huge. The agency reports that on a typical day in 2010, its agents processed 965,167 passengers and pedes-trians and 47,293 truck, rail, and sea containers. Further, on this single day, there were 1903 apprehensions for illegal entry, 11,435 pounds of seized narcotics, and 75 arrests of criminals at ports of entry.[10]

In the interior, however, the methods are rather different and agents' power is more constrained. Still, ICE agents are empowered, without a warrant, "to interrogate any alien or person believed to be an alien as to his right to be or to remain in the United States" and to arrest any "alien . . . in the United States," if they have "reason to believe" that the alien "is in the United States in violation of any such law or regulation."[11] They may also obtain warrants to arrest people whom they believe are subject to deportation, though this formal procedure is rarely used.[12]

Over the years, many procedures of deportation have been standardized. Most persons arrested for deportation are given a charging document (a "Notice to Appear") that lists their alleged violations of law. They then appear before immigration judges (employed by the Department of Justice) in hearings that must comply with some constitutional requirements of "fundamental fairness" and due process. The government, in virtually all cases, has the technical burden of proving at least that the arrestee is not a citizen (referred to as the burden of proving "alienage").[13] For the undocumented, that often is the end of the matter unless they fear persecution or torture. In cases involving otherwise legal resi-dents who face deportation due to post-entry conduct, the government must also prove by clear and convincing evidence that the person is "deportable."[14] Cases may be reviewed by an administrative Board of Immigration Appeals (BIA) and then, with limitations, by federal courts.[15]

Once a person is deported, a number of consequences follow. First, and most obviously, whatever immigration status the person had is now terminated. Sec-ond, even if a deportee were to become eligible for a new immigration status or even a temporary visa, removal will bar reentry for at least five years and, in many cases, forever. Further, illegal reentry following removal is a federal felony, with penalties of imprisonment that range from two to twenty years.[16]

Such procedures were designed to offer a "meaningful and fair hearing with a reasonable opportunity to be heard."[17] They reflect an evolutionary understanding of deportation that has developed since the late nineteenth century. As the Supreme Court has recognized, the fundamental due process protections of the Fifth Amendment "are universal in their application, to all persons within the territorial jurisdiction" of the United States.[18] This includes unlawful entrants;[19] and lawful permanent residents may receive heightened constitutional protection by virtue of their status and ties to the community.[20]

All of this is a major accomplishment, the product of centuries of vigorous advocacy and litigation.[21] But it is under constant pressure. In many ways, deportation has long been an anomalous system, largely exempt from important protections of the U.S. rule of law. Agents near the border may stop virtually anyone at virtually anytime for virtually any reason. And even during formal, interior deportations, deportees do not have the right to counsel (if a deportee cannot afford a lawyer she has no right to one and, in formal immigration court proceedings, some 60 percent are unrepresented).[22] Nor do deportees have the following rights: the right to bail (many thousands face mandatory detention every day, and more than 80 percent of those detained in formal proceedings lacked counsel);[23] the right to have illegally seized evidence suppressed (only if the agents' conduct was widespread or egregious); the right against *ex post facto* laws (a person can be deported for conduct that was not a deportable offense when it was done); the right to a jury trial; or the right against selective prosecution (being selected for deportation due to one's nationality, political opinion, etc.). Deportation hearings must be fundamentally fair, but this can be a very low standard. Even a finding that a court-appointed interpreter was incompetent will not necessarily invalidate a deportation hearing.[24] And judicial review of decisions by immigration judges is limited.[25]

Further, as we shall see, a bewildering array of new fast-track mechanisms with such names as "expedited removal" render much of the late twentieth- and early twenty-first-century story of deportation one of *deformalization* in which rights guaranteed since the late nineteenth century have been eliminated.

Attempts to rein in enforcement excesses and to develop more nuanced models have inspired polarized debate. In June 2011, ICE Director John Morton instructed officers, agents, and government attorneys to consider a wide range of factors before charging people with being in the country illegally or pursuing deportation cases. Special consideration, he said, is to be given to witnesses and victims of crimes, relatives of U.S. citizens and green card holders, military veterans, and college students brought to the United States as children, among others. Eleanor Pelta, then president of the American Immigration Lawyers

Association, called it "an example of smart enforcement of the immigration laws [that encourages] ICE agents to use their limited resources to pursue dangerous people who would do us harm, rather than harmless, innocent people . . . ."[26] But Chris Crane, president of the national ICE Council, took the opposite view: "This is a law enforcement nightmare," he said, "basically an out . . . for everyone illegally in the United States."[27]

Finally, a highly charged and legally questionable trend has sought to move immigration enforcement from federal authority to state and local governments. Reasonable minds may differ over the legality, wisdom, and propriety of some such initiatives.[28] Public debate, however, often lacks nuance. Proponents, such as Arizona's Russell Pearce, cite the federal government's alleged failure to uphold the "rule of law." As Pearce once put it: "I've always believed in the rule of law. We're a nation of laws."[29] Some use similar language to support a strategy called "attrition through enforcement" in which a variety of harsh—and often discriminatory—mechanisms are used to "encourage" the undocumented to leave the Untied States.[30] Such sentiments have garnered considerable support, but their connection to the rule of law seems tenuous, to say the least.

From 2006 to 2010, state legislators enacted more than five thousand immigration bills and some eight hundred state laws relating to immigration issues.[31] Arizona was an early leader, with a set of enforcement laws that are percolating through the federal legal system.[32] Alabama passed a 2011 law that requires police to check the status of anyone they suspect may be in the country illegally when stopped for another reason. The law also makes it a criminal offense to provide transport or housing to an illegal immigrant. Alabama state agents will check the citizenship of students, and any business that knowingly employs an illegal immigrant will be penalized.[33] Described by its sponsor as "a jobs-creation bill for Americans," its goal was reportedly to prevent "illegal immigrants from coming to Alabama and to prevent those who are here from putting down roots." Critics, however, have called it "outrageous and blatantly unconstitutional" and an invitation to discrimination.[34] One opponent said the law was "so oppressive that even Bull Connor himself would be impressed."[35]

Some states have gone further: enacting omnibus immigration laws, dealing with all sorts of school, employment, health, housing, benefits, and other enforcement issues.[36] Utah, for example, has enacted a comprehensive set of such laws. Chart 3.1 shows a breakdown of state legislation in 2010 and 2011.

Notwithstanding these state and local initiatives, the major mechanisms of deportation are still enforced directly by federal agents. Let us begin with two of the most iconic and controversial enforcement mechanisms: workplace and home raids.

	2010	2010	2011	2011
Main Sub-Topics	Number of Laws Enacted	Number of States	Number of Laws Enacted (Vetoed)	Number of States
Budgets	49	29	19 (2)	15
Education	17	11	20 (1)	11
Employment	27	20	27 (3)	18
Health	17	13	23 (2)	15
Human Traficking	8	8	5	5
ID/Driver's Licenses and Other Licenses	26	21	27	18
Law Enforcement	37	19	39 (5)	20
Miscellaneous	20	15	12 (1)	9
Omnibus/Multi-Issue Measures	2	1	6	5
Public Benefits	9	8	15 (1)	11
Voting	6	3	4	4
Total Enacted Laws	**218**	**43**	**197 (15)**	**42 (& PR)**
Resolutions	**138**	**27**	**109**	**26**
Total laws and resolutions passed/adopted by state legislatures	356	47	321	42 (& PR)
Vetoed by governors	10	2	15	8
Total enacted laws and adopted resolutions	**346**		**306**	

Chart 3.1 Laws and Resolutions on Immigration Passed by Legislatures in 2010 and 2011. Source: NCSL, Immigration Policy Report, 2011 Immigration-Related Laws and Resolutions in the States (Jan. 1-Dec.7, 2011) available at http://www.ncsl.org/default.aspx?TabId=23960#table1

Workplace Raids

Large, high-profile, and often rather brutal workplace raids on undocumented immigrants became a hallmark of the Bush administration in the aftermath of the failure of "comprehensive immigration reform" (CIR).[37] Though enforcement methods substantially changed in the Obama administration—from dramatic raids to more subtle modes of audits and more targeted workplace enforcement—the legacy of the workplace arrests that were so prominent through 2008 remain substantial, particularly for the deportees and their families.

The raids were initially aimed at specific industries, such as meatpacking. To many in the Administration, strong public support for the strategy undoubtedly seemed likely. However, from the very beginning, the stated purposes of the raids were often an odd mix of immigration-related and more amorphous goals. This indicated, perhaps, that political support was more fragile than it seemed. In 2006, for example, ICE trumpeted the arrest of more than 1,200 people for alleged immigration violations in a six-state raid on meat processing plants.[38] "This is not only a case about illegal immigration, which is bad enough," said then Homeland Security Secretary Michael Chertoff. "It's a case about identity theft and violation of the privacy rights and the economic rights of innocent Americans."

The raids and similar rhetorical strategies—some of which fantastically linked undocumented workers to all sorts of nefarious crimes—did garner public support for a time. However, due in large part to a series of aggressive, ham-handed workplace raids, support began to diminish. In one well-publicized debacle in

2007 in New Bedford, Massachusetts, a raid code-named "Operation United Front" mobilized ICE agents from around the country to arrest hundreds of noncitizen workers, almost all of whom were poor, indigenous Mayan peasants from Guatemala. These workers had been recruited to Massachusetts to engage in piecework stitching of leather bags and similar tasks.[39] The "uniting of the front" unfortunately did not apply to those arrested in the raid. Mothers were separated from babies, as were husbands from wives.[40] Many were summarily transferred to detention centers in Texas before lawyers could even meet with them.[41] Others were detained en masse on a military base. Community groups referred to it as "a humanitarian crisis."[42] Indeed, in an unusual reversal of the typical state/federal relationship in immigration matters, Massachusetts social workers were compelled to travel to Texas immigration detention facilities to ensure that the children of the detainees were receiving adequate care.[43] Interviews with those arrested detailed the brutal nature of the New Bedford raids. One woman described the scene at the airport when two immigration officers boarded the bus. Both officers had batons in their hand. One, standing near a trash can, said "if you don't behave well . . ." and then he kicked the trash can with great force implying to her that they would not hesitate to kick the deportees if they didn't do what they were told. She said that the officers yelled at them, "calling us 'shit' and telling us we were worthless."[44] The women were told that the ICE agents never wanted to see them in their country again. Such reports are disturbing to read under any circumstances. But they are especially so when we consider the backgrounds of these deportees, their history, and their traumas. When immigration officers would say things like "you're shit," or "you're worthless," said one deportee, it's almost impossible to disconnect these statements from the way people are treated in Guatemala, where soldiers and police are able to stop people on the street and demand information and to beat or even kill them with impunity.[45] Another deportee described the scene in graphic, chilling detail:

> Around me the armed officers were screaming very loudly. Among other things, I saw one man with a very bloody nose and a cut hand. I saw another individual named Susanna; she was dirty, as if she had been brutally dragged. She was crying. I remember feeling great fear, both for myself and my fellow workers. We were being treated like the worst criminals in the world.[46]

As such vignettes indicate, workplace raids were a problematic strategy for at least two reasons. First, rather than focusing on terrorism suspects or convicted criminals, their main goal was to find undocumented workers. As one man arrested in a workplace raid in Baltimore put it, echoing Woody Guthrie's famous ballad, *Deportee*, excerpted at the beginning of this chapter: "Instead of taking away people who are hurting the country or doing murders, they are taking away people who work hard and want this country to get ahead.... They chase us like animals and say they are doing it for the good of the country."[47] Second, the method itself is troubling: raids tend to be large militaristic exercises that often seem disproportionate to the threat posed by the often terrified workers. It was thus not surprising that eventually, large public demonstrations were organized against these and similar raids, and, in many quarters, sympathy for the deportees seemed to increase. The country was riven by fierce debates over the issue, sparked by controversies such as the waving of Mexican flags at pro-immigrant rallies and such high-profile deportees as Elvira Arellano, whose case clearly showed the deep tensions underlying this type of immigration enforcement. Ms. Arellano, a Mexican citizen, had first entered the United States without inspection in 1997. She was soon arrested and deported but later reentered the United States surreptitiously. She says she was compelled to do so by severe personal and economic hardship. She used a false Social Security number to get a job cleaning planes at Chicago's O'Hare International Airport and worked without incident for a few years. She later gave birth to a son in the United States (who therefore is a U.S. citizen).

Ms. Arellano was arrested in 2002 during a review of airport personnel after September 11, 2001, and was later convicted of working under the false Social Security number. She was ordered to surrender for deportation in August 2006, but sought refuge at Adalberto United Methodist Church in Chicago. While at the church, she became a high-profile symbol of the newly invigorated immigrant rights movement. In August 2006, flanked by civil rights activists, she said "I knew my church wouldn't abandon me in my moment of desperation.... I'm strong, I've learned from Rosa Parks—I'm not going to go to the back of the bus. The law is wrong." One year later, however, in August 2007, Ms. Arellano left the church and was soon arrested in downtown Los Angeles after speaking at a rally and attending a mass. Public opinion over her deportation was deeply divided. Some called it a belated, if perhaps harsh, step by the Bush administration to uphold the rule of law. Steven A. Camarota, of the Center for Immigration Studies, said "This woman knowingly violated the law and lived in the U.S. illegally. . . . She was deported, knowingly violated the law and came back." Others, such as Reverend Alexia Salvatierra, national coordinator of the Los Angeles-based New Sanctuary Movement, said that Ms. Arellano represents "families with U.S.-citizen children, with a long work record in this country, no criminal history, and who are part of the fabric of our country, who face the prospect of having parents ripped away from their kids." Mr. Camarota was unimpressed by such statements: "She does seem at times to have willingly used her son as a kind of prop. . . . We didn't, quote, 'separate the family.' She chose to do that."

Let us defer responding to this rather harsh sentiment for now and return to the summer of 2008. As prospects for CIR dimmed, the raids developed a more militaristic cast. Whatever its initial political purposes may have been, the raid regime seemed to have developed a momentum of its own. I recall vividly how immigration activists at the time would utter such refrains as "the dogs have been unleashed." Some young prosecutors became engaged in the enterprise with great energy and enthusiasm. They developed clever new methods and aimed them at another group of undocumented Guatemalan workers in a kosher meat-packing plant in Postville, Iowa.[48] The convergence of criminal law tactics with deportation became stronger. Following the arrest and prosecution of some three hundred undocumented workers, United States Attorney Matt M. Dummermuth proudly announced: "This is the greatest number of defendants ever to plead guilty and be sentenced in one day in the Northern District of Iowa." That day alone, seventy-seven defendants were sentenced to prison after they pled guilty to using a false identification document to obtain employment. In the end, many more received five months' imprisonment, three years' supervised release, and faced automatic removal from the United States following their prison sentences. Others were, of course, intimidated and confused by this prospect. The deportations thus proceeded with remarkable speed and efficiency. Prosecutors had created a new fast-track method of processing large numbers of deportees by combining tools from the criminal system with deportation.

However, their methods raised serious questions. An interpreter, Erik Camayd-Freixas, published a compelling account of the proceedings that caused many to wonder about the tactics and the effects of these raids. His job as an interpreter had been to explain the options to the arrested workers, along with a few overwhelmed court-appointed attorneys who represented the deportees. The explanation, to each individual client, involved three possibilities. If the client agreed to plead guilty to a charge of "knowingly using a false Social Security number," the government would withdraw a heavier charge of aggravated identity theft. The migrant would then serve five months in jail, be deported without a hearing, and be placed on "supervised release" for three years. A plea of not guilty could mean waiting in jail for six to eight months for a trial (because they were also facing deportation, the migrants were told that they had no right to bail). A loss at trial would mean a two-year minimum sentence, and quite possibly more. Even a victory at trial, however, would be followed by deportation. Many of those arrested were illiterate; some of the Mayans did not even speak Spanish well enough to understand what was happening to them. All were terrified. As Camayd-Freixas poignantly understated: "Some clients understood their options better than others." Most took the deal.

Postville was aptly called "a cold clinical experiment . . . [which] sought to criminalize immigrants on a mass scale." It was not enough to simply arrest and deport undocumented immigrants. They were also now to be sent home as con-victed felons.[49] Apart from humanitarian considerations, the legal process itself was troubling. Indeed, the Supreme Court ultimately rejected the criminal law theory used by the government in the Postville cases, though this came far too late for many of the deportees.[50]

Increasingly, the condemnation of such tactics and, more generally, of the regime of large workplace raids itself, prevailed. Many began to wonder whether the raids had had any significant positive effects. They had certainly "sent a message" of increased seriousness about interior enforcement. And they had deported a few thousand hapless workers. But what was the long-term strategy? Both major party presidential candidates in 2008 affirmed that deporting 12 to 15 million undocumented people was not realistically thinkable, let alone afford-able. One recalled Hannah Arendt's biting observation that "[i]t's true that you can't make an omelet without breaking a few eggs but you can break a great many eggs without making an omelet"[51] However, the abandonment of the raids strategy, as we shall see, led the Obama administration to choose more sophisti-cated and probably more effective "smart" mechanisms that have, in turn, resulted in a widespread perception that major workplace enforcement is not actually taking place. As with all law enforcement efforts, public perception may be as important as efficiency.

Home Raids

> Juan Williams: . . . When I see these immigration . . . people going in the middle of the night and breaking into people's homes and take away children from parents. . . . Parents get separated from children. . . .
> Sean Hannity: Why do we have laws if we are not going to enforce them? . . .
> Juan Williams: We also have unjust laws. . . . Slavery was an unjust law and when people were chasing slaves in the middle of the night you would have said it was wrong.
> Sean Hannity: It was, but that's not the same thing. I support immigration, but respect our laws! . . . And if you don't there are consequences. . . .[52]

Jimmy Slaughter and his wife Sheila were reportedly folding laundry one summer day in their Yuma, Arizona, home when he heard a knock at the door. He saw seven uniformed federal agents with bulletproof vests and guns standing outside the house. Slaughter, a retired Marine, opened the screen door and jovi-ally asked, "What's up, fellas?" Five of the armed agents suddenly walked into the house without asking permission. His wife, who asked if this was an episode of

Candid Camera, was ordered to stand in the middle of the living room. The agents, who were from ICE, began searching the house for a Hispanic woman. They had no court warrant. Slaughter, it turned out, was himself employed by U.S. Customs and Border Protection. The ICE agents had the wrong address. They soon left, but Slaughter's wife was so unnerved that she spent several days in an intensive care unit for hypertension. Slaughter brought a federal lawsuit against ICE.[53] This raid, though clearly an egregious error, was not an anomaly. It was simply one of the most obvious documented mistakes of an extremely controversial deportation enforcement method: home raids.

There is nothing inherently illegal or wrong with home raids as a law enforcement technique. Your home may be your castle for some purposes, but not for others, such as drug trafficking, bomb making, and the like. In the criminal realm, the boundaries of this tension are policed by Fourth Amendment constitutional norms and by the system of warrants that U.S. law has developed over more than two hundred years. When home raids are used as a tool of immigration enforcement, however, the tactic is much more problematic. First, the objects of such raids are rarely sought for criminal prosecution as such. Most are sought for civil violations of immigration laws. Some such violations may be significant, such as recidivist border crossing or absconding from a deportation hearing. But they are clearly not serious or violent crimes.[54] Second, many of the raids involved armed teams of ICE agents in predawn actions without warrants. In such cases, entries into homes require the informed consent of residents. But whether such consent was really given has been frequently contested.[55] Third, for reasons that are hard to explain, the information that ICE agents got before the raids was outdated or simply wrong in a nontrivial number of such cases. Fourth, most such immigration law violators do not live alone, and it is often hard for agents to disaggregate legitimate targets from others who may also lack legal status. As a result, many people have been caught in such raids, either accidentally or by design, who would not have been deemed legitimate targets of such tactics. Finally, the legal system does not apply the so-called "exclusionary rule" as vigorously in deportation cases as it does in criminal cases. Thus, evidence gathered in violation of Fourth Amendment norms may be used in a deportation hearing.[56] Federal agents, though trained to comply with Fourth Amendment norms, know that violations are much less likely to be proven in court in deportation cases than in criminal cases. In light of these factors, the home raid mechanism has, unsurprisingly, attracted particularly strong public scrutiny and criticism.[57]

One of the most compelling reports about this tactic was the moving account of a teenage girl, Mancha, reported by *The Nation*. One morning in 2006, Mancha came out of the shower. "My mother went out, and I was alone," she said. She was getting ready for school, getting dressed, when she heard a noise.

"I thought it was my mother coming back," she said in her "Tex-Mex Spanish-inflected Georgia accent." She said that some people were slamming car doors outside the trailer. She heard footsteps and then "a loud boom and then some-body screaming, asking if we were 'illegals,' 'Mexicans.'" Suddenly, men were standing in her living room holding guns. One man blocked the doorway. An-other grabbed a gun on his side. She described the scene in quintessential American teenage language: "I freaked out. 'Oh, my God!' I yelled." As more than twenty ICE agents surrounded the trailer, agents inside interrogated her. They asked her where her mother was; they wanted to know if her mother was Mexican and whether she had papers or a green card. They told her they were looking for "illegals."[58]

Apart from their basic intrusiveness and the fear caused by such raids, their collateral effects began to be a major concern as well.[59] On June 22, 2007, at around 6:00 a.m., ICE agents raided a trailer home park in Shakopee, Minnesota. The agents seized a married couple for suspected immigration violations. They didn't notice the couple's daughter, who was sleeping. Later that morning, the 7-year-old girl was found wandering alone, looking for her parents. Only when neighbors called the authorities did she learn what had happened to her parents.[60]

In the Obama administration, the incidence of home raids, like factory raids, has declined, though ICE teams continue to use raids to seek "absconders."

National Security Methods

Deportation has always been deeply intertwined with national security goals, rhetoric, and methods. The 1996 laws that dramatically stiffened the deporta-tion system were boosted by public reaction to the Oklahoma City bombing. Although by the time the legislation was enacted, the perpetrators were known to be white and U.S. citizens, early stories had reflected a very different sort of fear. Hours after the attacks, CNN reported that the FBI suspected that "[t]wo of the men involved, perhaps, are Middle Eastern men. One is 20 to 25. The other is 35 to 38. Both with dark hair and a beard, and they were both wearing blue pants, black shirts, and coats."[61] The *New York Daily News* published the fol-lowing the next day:

> News that the lethal Oklahoma City car bomb weighed about 1,200 pounds and was probably carried in a rented truck driven by Middle Eastern men immediately brought to mind the 1993 World Trade Cen-ter explosion. . . . [T]he FBI announced that agents are seeking three male suspects of Middle Eastern origin in the Oklahoma bombing. Two have dark hair and beards.[62]

On the same day, the *Dallas Morning News* reported that authorities in Oklahoma had issued a description of two suspects that was said to be "vague and ominous." The suspects were described as "Middle Eastern men with beards, one age 20 to 25, the other 35 to 38."[63]

Beyond such sadly common inflammatory misinformation, the debates over deportation as a tool of national security have remained remarkably consistent—from the Alien and Sedition Acts, through the Palmer Raids, the McCarthy era, the responses to the Oklahoma City bombing, and the 9/11 attacks.[64] By 2003, a common formulation was that the United States was a "nation of immigrants" engaged in a "war on terrorism."[65] Since much of the terrorist threat was seen to come from foreigners, the deep question was whether these two concepts could be consistently maintained. Since 2003, much of the balancing task has rested with the Department of Homeland Security (DHS)—an agency whose name, when originally chosen, was seen by some to have disturbing similarities to such terms as "fatherland," but to which Americans have now become inured. DHS has assumed full command of immigration enforcement (taken over—with no intended irony—from the Department of Justice) with a clearly dominant national security focus. In its view, homeland security means the intersection of "evolving threats and hazards" with traditional governmental and civic responsibilities for civil defense, emergency response, law enforcement, customs, border control, and immigration. However, the "overarching concept" of homeland security aims to break down long-standing "stovepipes of activity that may be exploited by those seeking to harm America."[66]

Of course, the first problem with using deportation in the service of this mission is to define its exact targets. The targets of *extended border control* or crime-based *post-entry social control* deportation are relatively easy to describe, at least in general. The former system, as we have seen, seen, aims at the undocumented and other violators of border control laws; the latter, is directed at those convicted of crimes defined with varying degrees of specificity. But who, exactly, should be deported as a threat to national security? The problem is a multifaceted one of definitional complexity, constitutional framing, and practical implementation. "National security" is about as elastic and potentially inflammatory a phrase as one could possibly conjure. It embeds a warm notion (security) within a malleable political theory (nationalism) as it responds implicitly to a threat from outsiders, strangers, aliens, etc. This is especially true in the context of deportation law.[67] As Jennifer Chacon has noted, "formulating immigration policy while gazing through a distorting lens of 'national security' perversely ensures that the law is ill-suited to achieve either national security or other immigration policy goals."[68] In this, she echoed Charles Evans Hughes, who, in 1922 as Secretary of State, wrote that on the "fundamental matter of national security . . . the instinct of self-preservation causes a quick response to any appeal on this score."[69] Hughes was not writing about deportation law as such, but he surely could have been. The great need, he wrote, is for "enlightenment ... with respect to what *really makes for national security*."[70] As the horrific 2011 attack on a summer youth camp in Norway illustrates, terror may come from within or nearby as much as it may come from without; and it may come from what Freud termed the "narcissism of minor differences"[71] as much as from the menacing stranger.

The constitutional and practical problems with national security deportation methods have long been recognized. As a prominent Federalist supporter of the 1798 Act Concerning Aliens (the first federal deportation law) said, "persons who come here with a view of overturning the government will not commit any overt act which shall bring them under the laws of the country."[72] The 1950 "Internal Security Act,"[73] among other provisions, authorized the exclusion and the retroactive deportation of Communists and members of other organizations considered to be dangerous to public safety.[74] In later debates over the comprehensive 1952 Immigration and Nationality Act, Senator Humphrey argued that the 1950 bill had embodied "the arbitrary procedures of the police state."[75] Though he too was "thoroughly in favor of deporting and excluding undesirable aliens,"[76] he argued for greater precision of focus. One should reject a model, he argued, that "unnecessarily [hurts] the innocent at the same time as it affects the guilty."[77] In the end though, the rhetoric of fear and national security triumphed, and major pieces of the current deportation regime were put into place. In the House, Representative John Rankin (D-Miss.)—well known as a nasty segregationist and an anti-Semite[78]—stated in 1952 that "[w]e have had too many questionable characters swarming into this country already, bringing ... communism, atheism, anarchy, infidelity...."[79] He suggested that rather than admitting more "of that ilk," the United States should begin to deport some who had already arrived in order to save the country from destruction at the hands of those he termed "the enemies within our gates."[80]

The Alien and Sedition Acts had solved the methods problem by giving the President unfettered discretion to deport any alien he deemed sufficiently dangerous to warrant the sanction. The ironically named 1798 "Aliens Friends Act"[81] stated that it would be lawful for the President "to order all such aliens as he shall judge dangerous to the peace and safety of the United States, or shall have reasonable grounds to suspect are concerned in any treasonable or secret machinations against the government thereof, to depart out of the territory of the United States." The method was simply the delivery of an order on the person or at the "usual abode" of the deportee. Much of the most powerful criticism against this law—by Jefferson, Madison, and others—focused on this excessive delegation of authority to the executive branch.[82]

In the early years of the twentieth century, Woodrow Wilson ominously warned of people "born under other flags but welcomed under our generous naturalization laws to the full freedom and opportunity of America, who have poured the poison of disloyalty into the very arteries of our national life. . . ." In 1915 he demanded that "[s]uch creatures of passion, disloyalty, and anarchy must be crushed out; . . . [and] the hand of our power should close over them at once."[83] Such sentiments continued to flourish after the war. Bombs had been sent through the mails to various well-known public figures including the Commissioner of Immigration, Supreme Court Justice Oliver W. Holmes, Jr., Attorney General Mitchell Palmer, John D. Rockefeller, and J.P. Morgan.[84] The government response revealed how, once again, the efficiency of deportation law had inspired the government to pass a new Alien Law in 1918[85] and now to use it "with relentless vigor" to deport hundreds of alleged anarchists, Bolsheviks, and other dissidents.[86] As Louis Post, the official charged with enforcing the deportation laws at that time, noted: "Whereas a citizen cannot be punished without substantial cause and after conviction at a judicial trial, an alien may be banished for frivolous causes and by autocratic 'administrative process.'"[87]

Nearly a century later, after September, 11 2001, thousands of people in the United States experienced interrogation, intimidation, arrest, and incarceration as the deportation system was used to achieve goals that had little, if anything, to do with immigration policy.[88] A general process of "securitization" dramatically eroded protections for the human rights of noncitizens.[89] Issues of security were commonly presented as "an existential threat, requiring emergency measures and justifying actions outside the normal bounds of political procedure."[90] Some sociologists and criminologists use the term "moral panic" to describe such discourse. It facilitates powerful, unusual state action against a social group or activity that is said to threaten the very "stability and well-being of society."[91] Consider how Representative Lamar Smith, a current champion of tough deportation laws, conflated immigrant crime and terrorism: "We should not give criminals who are not U.S. citizens more opportunities to further terrorize our communities."[92]

The deepest danger in such periods is that of targeting discrete, insular, (largely) politically powerless, ethnically, religiously or racially identified minority groups.[93] As David Cole has put it, "democratic society [optimally] strikes the balance between liberty and security in ways that impose the costs of security measures equally on all."[94] When the burden of security falls disproportionately on a particular group, the result is both "constitutionally and morally wrong."[95] The methods problems, essentially, is that of the blunt instrument. As one axiom from my youth in Brooklyn puts it: you don't kill a fly with a bazooka. This is not primarily out of concern for the individual fly.

Deportation law was a central part of the government's response to the September 11 attacks.[96] The USA PATRIOT Act authorized the Attorney General to incarcerate and detain noncitizens on the basis of suspicion alone if the government has "reasonable grounds to believe" that the individual may be a threat to national security. Such a person may be held for seven days pending the commencement of criminal or removal proceedings.[97] In October 2001, Attorney General John Ashcroft—with a similar formulation to that used by Representative Rankin in 1952—referred to an "enemy within our borders."[98] He then described his enforcement approach bluntly: "Let the terrorists among us be warned: If you overstay your visa—even by one day—we will arrest you. If you violate a local law, you will be put in jail and kept in custody as long as possible. . . ."[99] Unfortunately, but inevitably, many more people than the remarkably few, if any, "terrorists among us" were affected. Thousands were held in detention for technical violations[100] that were clearly pretextual.[101] Noncitizens encountered at the scene of the arrest of a person "of interest to the September 11 investigation" were detained "because the FBI wanted to be certain that no terrorist was inadvertently set free."[102] Mere allegations that a Muslim man had made "anti-American statements" resulted in his arrest for overstaying his visa. Though cleared of any terrorist links, the man languished in detention for more than four months before being deported.[103] While in such detention, a significant number of detainees were subjected to what a government report later described as "a pattern of physical and verbal abuse . . . by some correctional officers" as well as extremely restrictive conditions of confinement.[104]

Following 9/11, surveillance of noncitizens within the United States also dramatically increased. The government interviewed and required reports from thousands of men from countries where Al Qaeda was said to have a "terrorist presence or activity." No European country was on the list.[105] Failure to comply with the rules, or the discovery of even minor immigration violations while registering, could—and in thousands of cases did—result in arrest, detention, and deportation.[106] An estimated thirteen thousand of the Arab and Muslim men who voluntarily came forward to register with immigration authorities faced deportation proceedings, though almost none of them were linked in any way to terrorism.[107]

Zechariah Chafee, Jr., one of the most prominent critics of the Palmer Raids, noted many years ago that "[t]he life of a law is not in its words, but in its enforcement."[108] The most recent episode of national security deportation enforcement—like all of those that preceded it—raises the most profound questions about not only costs and benefits, but also the very nature of the enterprise itself. As federal Judge George W. Anderson of Boston once pointedly noted, "a mob is a mob" even if it is "comprised of government officials, following instructions from the Justice Department."[109]

Deformalized Deportations

As we survey the major methods of deportation, we must consider a recent trend of *deformalization*. This has been a major but largely untold story of deportation in recent years. New, informal, fast-track removal procedures represent a decisive historical turn away from the due-process-based understanding of deportation law that marked much of the twentieth century.[110] These new processes embody a wide range of mechanisms. Some are pure administrative processes, almost completely insulated from either appellate administrative review or judicial oversight. Others seek to render deportation a kind of bureaucratic afterthought. One of the signal features of the Postville, Iowa, deportations, for example, was the use of standardized form deportation agreements as part of the criminal plea process. Deportation thus became a rather automatic adjunct to the criminal process, lacking much consideration in its own right and lacking separate procedural protections.

Expedited removal, the largest of the informal deportation systems, was designed primarily to apply to people trying to enter the United States at border crossings or airports. But it could also apply to certain noncitizens inside the United States.[111] It is now used to deport noncitizens who are found within one hundred miles of the U.S. border and who cannot establish to the "satisfaction" of an immigration officer that they have been physically present in the United States for at least fourteen days. As a result, hundreds of thousands of deportees have never seen even an administrative immigration judge, let alone a federal judge. Some one hundred thousand people are deported per year who almost never have time to contact anyone, least of all a lawyer.

Another deformalized system, called *administrative removal*, applies to all noncitizens except for lawful permanent residents. It authorizes administrative immigration officials to completely avoid formal immigration court proceedings and to simply order people deported due to the conviction of an "aggravated felony."[112] As you consider this mechanism, recall that aggravated felonies often have included very minor offenses, and—strangely—even some misdemeanors. Administrative removal has become a fast, convenient, and efficient system.[113] Individuals are simply notified of the charges and are given ten days in which to respond to a DHS deportation and removal officer. Procedural safeguards are rather minimal.

Yet another such system, called *reinstatement of removal*[114] applies to one of the most vexing problems confronted by the U.S. deportation system: recidivist border crossers.[115] Deportees are barred from reentering the United States for periods ranging from five years to life, depending on a variety of factors. It has long been true that a deportee who reenters the United States without permission faces criminal prosecution. Indeed, the number of such prosecutions rose dramatically during the Obama administration.[116] However, prior to 1996, most recidivists were placed in deportation proceedings before an immigration judge. They had the opportunity to explain why a previous order was erroneous. They could also apply for certain forms of discretionary relief from deportation. Since 1997, however, a deported person who reenters the United States without authorization simply has the prior removal order "reinstated from its original date." Though there is some question as to how such orders are to be reviewed by federal judges, the basic model, with few exceptions, is that the original order may not be reopened or reviewed, and the noncitizen may not apply for any discretionary relief. A noncitizen may be removed under the prior order at any time after the reentry.[117] This system was challenged and upheld in a 2006 case before the U.S. Supreme Court.[118] While the main issue in the case was whether the reinstatement statute was retroactive, the Court's approach reinforced the divide between those few deportees who may still have formal procedural rights and those who, essentially, do not. But, as we shall see in the next chapter, the case left many fundamental questions unanswered.

Finally, we have a variety of plea bargaining-type deportation systems. Every year, untold thousands of deportees waive their procedural rights and sign *stipulated orders of removal*. Perhaps the most significant difference between these methods and criminal law plea bargaining is that deportees have no right to appointed counsel, and a distressingly high percentage of those who agree to stipulated removal have never even consulted with an attorney, let alone been represented. The number of stipulated orders has increased dramatically. In 2004, some five thousand stipulated orders were signed. By 2007, the number had increased—six-fold—to thirty thousand.[119] Immigration judges may approve such orders without even conducting hearings.[120] Although such waivers of rights are required to be "voluntary, knowing, and intelligent,"[121] there is no doubt that many deportees have signed such agreements without understanding either their rights or the consequences of signing. Lack of proper translation is often a problem, as are threats or deliberate misinformation given by deportation officers who may present the agreements as routine paperwork.[122] Moreover, unlike the criminal justice system, which contains various post-order safeguards, if a person is deported following a mistaken, misunderstood, or improvidently signed stipulated order of removal, it may be impossible to reopen the case from abroad.

Finally, *voluntary departure*, the most common form of deformalized removal, governs approximately 1 million cases per year. Voluntary departure has less draconian consequences than a removal order. It does not, for example, mandatorily bar the person from legally reentering the United States. In this sense, it offers a potentially reasonable deal. Still, most noncitizens who accept voluntary departure are unlikely to be permitted to return legally.

One can easily see the efficiency value in these sorts of deformalized proceedings. But many of them also involve important erosions of rights that are considered in later chapters.

"Force Multipliers"

As we have seen, deportation has long been primarily a responsibility of the federal government. In 1996, however, a new model of federal/state partnership was created by § 287(g) of the Immigration and Nationality Act. The law authorizes DHS to enter into agreements with state and local law enforcement agencies, thereby permitting their officers to perform immigration law enforcement functions, under the supervision of ICE officers. According to ICE, the cross-designation allows local and state officers the resources and latitude to pursue investigations "relating to violent crimes, human smuggling, gang/organized crime activity, sexual-related offenses, narcotics smuggling and money laundering." The participating entities are eligible for increased resources and support after signing a Memorandum of Agreement that outlines the authority to be designated.[123] The concept has always been controversial, facing criticism from both the right—on states' rights grounds—and the left—on civil liberties and human rights grounds. Indeed, the federal government did not enter into any § 287(g) agreements with state or local jurisdictions until after the 9/11 attacks. By 2006, however, increased interest in interior immigration enforcement at the state and local levels and more federal funding had spurred substantial growth in the program. Funding increased from $5 million per year in 2002 to around $68 million in 2006.[124] DHS came to describe the program as a valuable "force multiplier" and expanded it energetically.[125] By 2011, ICE had agreements with some sixty-nine law enforcement agencies in twenty-four states. It credits the program, since January 2006, with identifying more than 200,300 "potentially removable aliens" mostly at local jails. ICE has trained and certified more than 1,240 state and local officers to enforce immigration law.[126] As the following chart shows, the rise in such partnerships has been dramatic.

	2006	2007	2008	2009	Total
Individuals Identified for Removal	6,224	24,400	49,847	62,714	143,185
Fugitive Aliens (Absconders)	3	112	750	1,816	2,681
Previously Removed from US	482	3,547	6,433	7,952	18,414

Chart 3.2 287(g) Encounters and Removals. Source: Department of Homeland Security, Office of Inspector General, The Performance of 287(g) Agreements, OIG-10-63, March 2010 (data from ICE Office of State and Local Coordination) available at www.oig.dhs.gov/assets/Mgmt/OIG_10-63_Mar10.pdf

Operation Endgame: "Golden Measure" or Cautionary Tale?[127]

In June 2003, the Office of Detention and Removal (DRO) released a white paper the name of which was only the beginning of its striking attributes.[128] "Endgame" described the deportation authorities' strategic plan through 2010. The plan was posted on DRO's public website, but was then removed amid a firestorm of controversy. Before its removal, however, the ACLU managed to obtain a copy, and so the plan became widely known.[129] Then DRO Director Anthony S. Tangeman had glowingly described the plan as a "golden measure" of success, the aim of which was "the removal of all removable aliens." He explained that the endeavor was "to maintain the integrity of the immigration process and protect our homeland by ensuring that every alien who is ordered removed, and can be, departs the United States as quickly and effectively as practicable." The ultimate goal was "a 100% removal rate."[130]

The program was apparently motivated as much by a commitment to efficiency as by a belief in the necessity of strong enforcement tactics. Some of the impetus for *Endgame* came from a 1993 law, the Government Performance and Results Act (GPRA), which had sought to increase federal agency accountability by requiring agencies to set goals, measure their results, and make reports on their progress annually to Congress.[131] The concern was not just whether an agency was spending the correct amount of funds on programs. Rather, the law sought specific accountability: What kind of programs were supported by agencies' budgetary allocations? What did these programs actually accomplish? How could program success or failure be measured?[132] The law required agencies to develop mission statements, long-term strategic plans, and to set result-oriented goals with annual performance reviews. Each agency was given a report card.[133]

Still, there is no question that increased concerns about national security and enforcement also motivated the creators of *Endgame*. Adam Piceno, the primary author, recalled that GPRA became a "driving force" for the DRO. "If higher offices had a plan, then we wanted a plan," said Piceno.[134] This approach was supported by the Bush administration. DRO received exceptionally high scores, in great part because of *Endgame*.[135] DRO's leader, Anthony S. Tangeman, strongly supported such an extensive strategic plan. Tangeman was a former Coast Guard captain with prior Department of Defense (DOD) experience.[136] Prior to becoming DRO Director, Tangeman had been in charge of an experimental program in Hartford, Connecticut, designed to determine the effects of placing foreign nationals in custody immediately after receiving a final removal order, regardless of whether the immigration judge had ordered them removed or granted them voluntary departure.[137]

Those who worked at DRO understood the difficulty of the situation they faced. As Adam Piceno recalled:

> People [illegal immigrants] keep coming in and not as many people are leaving. . . . DRO removes illegals from the country and there are a lot of constraints on the ability to remove people. For just one [case]: arrest, detain, get travel documents. This requires a lot of intra-agency work, a lot of man power, work with states, transportation, escorts on the plane, and there are complications if the immigrant is criminal. All of these were the issues DRO was battling. Then [there were] administration changes, commission changes, and then 9/11 happened. . . .[138]

Nevertheless, the DRO personnel soldiered on. In September 2001, just days before September 11, Tangeman developed a Strategic Plan Working Group (SPWG).[139] Glenn Triveline, Field Office Director for DRO in Chicago, was one notable member of the group. Triveline later became known for his role in the prominent deportation case of Elvira Arellano, of whom he once said: "ICE has a sworn duty to ensure that our nation's immigration laws are applied fairly and without regard to a person's ability to generate public support."[140] Other SWPG members had backgrounds in the academic fields of strategic planning and organizational performance.[141]

Adam Piceno had been recruited to write the plan because of his strategic planning skills and education, despite his lack of immigration experience. He had never written anything like *Endgame* before.[142] Incredibly, Piceno's first day as a member of the working group was September 11, 2001.[143] Piceno based *Endgame* on a model for strategic plans that suggests that success requires a long-term strategy that can change and adapt to new circumstances, satisfy constituents, and guide leadership decision making.[144]

The group did not rely as much on scientific or empirical data as it did on anecdotal evidence from the field and DRO officers. It was Piceno who chose the name, *Endgame*, stunning many later critics who saw implicit connections to the phrase, "the Final Solution." Piceno, of course, had no desire whatsoever to be linked to national socialism. He says that the name was simply based on the idea that "in the end, the function of DRO was to remove everyone from the U.S. that could be removed."[145]

As published, *Endgame* was a model of utilitarian deterrence theory clothed in rather stunning bureaucratic optimism: not so much illustrative of the banality of evil, perhaps, as of the potential evil of banality. Its most basic idea was that a 100 percent removal rate would discourage foreign nationals from attempting to enter the United States illegally or from overstaying their authorized period of admission.[146] The Introduction to *Endgame* identifies "DRO

Stakeholders," i.e., those whose interests would be affected by *Endgame*.[147] These stakeholders are divided into internal "customers such as DHS enforcement agencies, USCIS, DRO employees, and the Office of General Counsel"—and "external" stakeholders such as "the alien," family members, attorneys, foreign governments, private sector groups like the American Immigration Lawyers Association, business owners, local enforcement agencies, and, most generally, the American government and "the American People." The introduction emphasizes that although *Endgame* was developed in consideration of every stakeholder, security was the highest priority. This, of course, resulted in a dramatically unequal balancing of stakeholder interests.[148]

Still, the *Endgame* report notes that "DRO must maintain cooperative relationships with each one of its stakeholders to ensure that enforcement operations are conducted as efficiently and professionally as possible and that all stakeholders' legitimate interests are addressed." A particularly earnest, if perhaps tragicomic passage states that the "alien" is a stakeholder even though "the alien will not necessarily perceive any benefit from DRO services." The "alien's" stake is not trivial, though. The "alien" is to be "provided with safe and secure confinement in detention facilities, as well as transportation from ports and points along the border to other detention facilities or his country of origin . . . in a professional manner." The "alien" is also entitled to be detained in "safe, secure and humane environments" and to be transported safely. The movement of deportees should be "fully coordinated with family, legal representative, and country of origin, whenever appropriate."[149]

The description of the actual endgame itself begins, remarkably, by citing with apparent approval the roundly discredited Alien and Sedition Acts of 1798. The paper notes that legislation since then has expanded the detention and removal operations and redefined the classes of aliens to be deported or excluded. "The basic mission," however, was said to have remained the same: "Remove all removable aliens."

The authors note that the Illegal Immigration Reform and Immigrant Responsibility Act (IIRIRA) of 1996 had expanded the number of crimes that made people subject to removal and required mandatory detention of those subject to removal on the basis of a criminal conviction, as well as certain categories of noncriminal deportees. As a result of these laws and others, DRO is now required "to detain and remove a much larger and more diverse population." Conflating the two forms of deportation, the report stated that the reason DRO aimed to increase its overall number of removals annually was "to thwart and deter continued growth in the illegal alien population." According to the report, moving toward a 100 percent rate of removal for all removable aliens would also would allow ICE to provide the level of immigration enforcement necessary "to keep America secure." *Endgame* contained a detailed list of ambitious milestones.

These include developing the capability to process removals at a rate equal to the number of removal orders issued and implementing controls to monitor and track some deportees without having to bring them into custody. *Endgame* also sought to eliminate the backlog of "fugitive aliens" present in the United States by 2012. This seemed a reasonable focus. However, "fugitive" meant not only absconders from final deportation orders, but also "any alien wanted by the DHS for a violation of status, order or law."[150]

Endgame was publicly available for a time on DRO's website, but it was removed after the publication of a *Boston Globe* op-ed written by the ACLU, entitled *Inhuman Raid Was Just One of Many*. The ACLU asserted that, *Endgame* "uses tactics similar to the ethnic cleansing we saw in the Balkans during the 1990s—lightning raids, mass arrests, packed detention centers, and mass deportations."[151] Some believe that the report was removed not only because of such charges, but also to avoid challenges made by lawyers that certain deportation raids were part of a large pattern and practice that warranted judicial intervention.

Given its thoroughness, logic, and Administration support one must ask why *Endgame* wasn't a successful model. Part of the answer is that it was too simplistic, too direct, and too utilitarian. It focused too much attention on the ultimate goal of deportation with insufficient attention to the inherently complex nature of the enterprise and its inescapable relationship to the nation of immigrants' ideal, civil and human rights, and the better conceptions of the rule of law. Thus, it may perhaps be best understood as a cautionary tale for all serious thought about deportation. One simply cannot be too simplistic or absolutist in this arena. Tensions are inevitable, and they must be accommodated with nuance and subtlety. There is no other option. Nevertheless, one should not be naïve. Within the deportation bureaucracy, especially in ICE, there are many people who believe that *Endgame* got it right.

Notes

1. Woody Guthrie, *Plane Wreck at Los Gatos (Deportee)* (TRO-Ludlow Music, Inc. 1961), *available at* http://www.woodyguthrie.org/Lyrics/Plane_Wreck_At_Los_Gatos.htm.
2. Jennifer Ludden, *Immigration Crackdown Overwhelms Judges*, NPR, Feb. 9, 2009, *available at* http://www.npr.org/templates/story/story.php?storyId=100420476.
3. Hirabayashi v. United States, 320 U.S. 81, 113 (1943) (Murphy, J., concurring).
4. *See* CPB Mission Statement and Core Values, (2/17/2009), *available at* http://www.cbp.gov/xp/cgov/about/mission/guardians.xml.
5. *Id., See also* Demetrios G. Papademetriou & Elizabeth Collett, *A New Architecture for Border Management*, MPI (Mar. 2011).
6. *Id.* at 2.
7. U.S. Department of Homeland Security, *Quadrennial Homeland Security Review Report: A Strategic Framework for a Secure Homeland*, vii. Washington, DC, Feb. 2010.

8. *Id.*

9. *See* CHAD C. HADDAL, PEOPLE CROSSING BORDERS: AN ANALYSIS OF U.S. BORDER PROTECTION POLICIES, CONG. RESEARCH SERV., R41237 (Mar. 2010), *available at* http://www.fas.org/sgp/crs/homesec/R41237.pdf.

10. *See On a Typical Day in Fiscal Year 2010, CBP. . . .* (Feb. 25, 2011) *available at* http://www.cbp.gov/xp/cgov/about/accomplish/typical_day_fy2010.xml.

11. INA § 287, 8 U.S.C. § 1357; *see also* 8 C.F.R. § 287.3.

12. *See* Chapter 4, *infra.*

13. 8 C.F.R. § 1240.8(c).

14. Decisions must be based upon "reasonable, substantial, and probative evidence." 8 U.S.C. § 1229a(3)(A).

15. The deportation (removal) becomes administratively "final" when upheld by the Board of Immigration Appeals or, if there is no administrative appeal, upon the expiration of the deadline for filing an appeal. *See* INA § 101(a)(47)(B), 8 U.S.C. § 1101(a)(47)(B) (2006); 8 C.F.R. §§ 1003.3, 1003.39 (2010). Cases may be appealed to the federal courts after this point, but there is no automatic stay or removal. Also, once a person who is subject to a removal order physically departs the United States, the order is deemed to have been executed. INA § 101(g), 8 U.S.C. § 1101(g) (2006), provides that "any alien ordered deported or removed . . . who has left the United States, shall be considered to have been deported or removed in pursuance of law, irrespective of the source from which the expenses of his transportation were defrayed or of the place to which he departed." *See also* Stone v. INS, 514 U.S. 386, 399 (1995); Mrvica v. Esperdy, 376 U.S. 560, 563–64 (1964).

16. *See* INA § 276(a), (b), 8 U.S.C. § 1326(a), (b) (2006).

17. *See* Landon v. Plasencia, 459 U.S. 21 (1982).

18. Yick Wo v. Hopkins, 118 U.S. 356, 369 (1886).

19. Referred to euphemistically as "aliens who have once passed through our gates." *See* Zadvydas v. Davis, 533 U.S. 678, 693 (2001) (quoting Shaugnessy v. Mezei, 345 U.S. 206, 212 (1953)) (even those who have so passed "illegally, may be expelled only after proceedings conforming to traditional standards of fairness encompassed in due process of law.").

20. As the Supreme Court held in 1982, "Once an alien gains admission to our country and begins to develop the ties that go with permanent residence, his constitutional status changes accordingly." Landon v. Plasencia, 459 U.S. 21, 32 (1982); *see also Zadvydas,* 593 U.S. at 694 (The nature of [due process] protection may vary depending upon status and circumstance); Johnson v. Eisentrager, 339 U.S. 763, 770–71 (1950) ("The alien, to whom the United States has been traditionally hospitable, has been accorded a generous and ascending scale of rights as he increases his identity with our society."); Bridges v. Wixon, 326 U.S. 135, 161 (1945) (Murphy, J., concurring) ("Once an alien lawfully enters and resides in this country he becomes invested with the rights guaranteed by the Constitution to all people within our borders.").

21. *See generally* DANIEL KANSTROOM, DEPORTATION NATION (Harvard University Press 2007).

22. Office of Planning, Analysis, & Technology, U.S. Dep't of Justice, FY 2010 Statistical Yearbook, figure 9, p. G1 (2010).

23. *See* NINA SIULC ET AL., VERA INST. FOR JUSTICE, *Improving Efficiency and Promoting Justice in the Immigration System: Lessons from the Legal Orientation Program 1* (2008), *available at* http://www.vera.org/download?file=1780/LOP%2BEvaluation_May2008.

24. *See* United States v. Leon-Leon, 35 F.3d 1428, 1431–32 (9th Cir. 1994) (failure to translate parts of hearing did not result in prejudice).

25. See Daniel Kanstroom, *The Better Part of Valor: The REAL ID Act, Discretion and the "Rule" of Immigration Law,* 51 N.Y. L. REV. 161 (2006).

26. AILA represents eleven thousand attorneys and law professors who practice and teach immigration law.

27. Susan Carroll, *New Rules Could Spare Some Immigrants from Deportation,* HOUSTON CHRON., June 20, 2011, *available at* http://www.chron.com/disp/story.mpl/metropolitan/7618722.html. AFGE National Council 118-ICE represents approximately 7,600 bargaining unit employees in the U.S. Immigration and Customs Enforcement.

28. *See* Clare Huntington, *The Constitutional Dimension of Immigration Federalism*, 61 VAND.
    L. REV. 787, 852–53 (2008) (arguing that state and local governments are not constitution-
    ally precluded from regulating immigration); Cristina M. Rodriguez, *The Significance of the
    Local in Immigration Regulation*, 106 MICH. L. REV. 567, 641–42 (2008) (arguing for better
    integrated federal-state-local immigration regulation); Peter H. Schuck & John Williams,
    Removing Criminal Aliens: The Pitfalls and Promises of Federalism, 22 HARV. J. L. & PUB.
    POL'Y 367, 458–63 (1999) (urging greater state cooperation with federal authorities con-
    cerning noncitizens who commit crimes); Peter J. Spiro, *The States and Immigration in an
    Era of Demi-Sovereignties*, 35 VA. J. INT'L L. 121, 121 (1994) (arguing, that, as a practical
    matter, immigration was even then "largely a state-level concern." *Cf.* Michael A. Olivas,
    Preempting Preemption: Foreign Affairs, State Rights, and Alienage Classifications, 35 VA. J.
    INT'L L. 217, 236 (1994) (arguing for federal preeminence); Michael J. Wishnie, *Labora-
    tories of Bigotry? Devolution of the Immigration Power, Equal Protection, and Federalism*, 76
    N.Y.U. L. REV. 493, 567 (2001) (arguing for exclusive federal authority in immigration law).
29. *Morning Edition: The Man Behind America's Toughest Immigration Laws* (NPR radio broad-
    cast Mar. 12, 2008).
30. *See, e.g.,* Mark Krikorian, *Downsizing Illegal Immigration: A Strategy of Attrition Through En-
    forcement*, CIS BACKGROUNDER, May 2005, at 1, *available at* http://www.cis.org/arti-
    cles/2005/back605.pdf (advocating mechanisms that deter the settlement of new illegals,
    increase deportations, and increase "number of illegals already here who give up and deport
    themselves"); Jessica M. Vaughan, *Attrition Through Enforcement: A Cost-Effective Strategy to
    Shrink the Illegal Population*, CIS BACKGROUNDER, Apr. 2006, at 1, *available at* http://
    www.cis.org/articles/2006/back406.pdf; *see also* Kris W. Kobach, *Attrition through Enforce-
    ment: A Rational Approach to Illegal Immigration*, 15 TULSA J. COMP. & INT'L L. 155, 156
    (2008) (describing various ways to encourage undocumented noncitizens to depart United
    States).
31. National Conference of State Legislatures, 2010 Immigration-Related Bills and Resolu-
    tions in the States.
32. The most controversial Arizona law, SB 1070, requires law enforcement to reasonably at-
    tempt to determine immigration status where reasonable suspicion of unlawful presence
    exists; allows state residents to sue state and local agencies for noncompliance; creates a
    state violation for failure to carry an alien registration document; establishes crimes in-
    volving trespassing by illegal aliens, stopping to hire, or soliciting work under specified cir-
    cumstances; and transporting, harboring or concealing unlawful aliens. *See generally*
    http://www.ncsl.org/default.aspx?tabid=20242.
33. *See* Julia Preston, *In Alabama, a Harsh Bill for Residents Here Illegally*, N.Y. TIMES, June 3,
    2011, *available at* http://www.nytimes.com/2011/06/04/us/04immig.html.
34. *Id.*
35. Wade Henderson, president and CEO of the Leadership Conference on Civil and Human
    Rights. *See* National Immigration Forum, *Alabama's New Anti-Immigrant Law is Radical
    Departure From American Values, Assault on Constitution*, June 9, 2011, *available at* http://
    www.immigrationforum.org/press/release-display/alabamas-new-anti-immigrant-law-is-
    radical-departure-from-american-values-a/.
36. In the first quarter of 2011 alone, more than 1500 such bills were introduced. NCSL, 2011
    Immigration-Related Laws, Bills and Resolutions in the States: January 1–March 31, 2011,
    available at http://www.ncsl.org/default.aspx?TabId=13114.
37. *See* U.S. Immigration and Customs Enforcement, *Worksite Enforcement Overview* April 30,
    2009 (highlighting worksite enforcement arrests in FY06-08), *available at* http://web.
    archive.org/web/20090507185612/http://www.ice.gov/pi/news/factsheets/worksite.
    htm.
38. Donna Leinwand, *Immigration Raid Linked to ID Theft, Chertoff Says*, USA TODAY, Dec. 31,
    2006, http://www.usatoday.com/news/nation/2006-12-13-immigration_x.htm.
39. Karen Lee Ziner, *Seeking Illegal Immigrants—Hundreds Nabbed in Raid*, PROVIDENCE J.,
    Mar. 7, 2007, at A-01, *available at* LEXIS, News Library, PRVJNL.
40. Carol Rose & Christopher Ott, *Inhumane Raid Was Just One of Many*, BOSTON GLOVE, Mar.
    26, 2007, at A9, *available at* LEXIS, News Library, BGLOBE File; Irene Sege, *"I Hope God*

Helps Us"—*For Barthila Solano, Future After New Bedford Raid is Precarious,* BOSTON GLOBE, Mar. 14, 2007, at C1, *available at* LEXIS, News Library, BGLOBE File.

41. Pam Belluck, *Lawyers Say U.S. Acted in Bad Faith After Immigrant Raid in Massachusetts,* N.Y. TIMES, Mar. 22, 2007, at A1, *available at* LEXIS, News Library, NYT File.

42. Karen Lee Ziner, *Factory Raid Sparks Crisis for Families—Concern Expressed for Children of Immigrants,* PROVIDENCE J., Mar. 8, 2007, at A-01, *available at* LEXIS, News Library, PRVJNL File.

43. Raja Mishra & Brian R. Ballou, *DSS to Check on Detainees Sent to Texas: Some Workers' Children May Lack Care, Officials Fear,* BOSTON GLOBE, Mar. 9, 2007, at A1, *available at* LEXIS, News Library, BGLOBE File.

44. Affidavit of B.L.G. Aguilar v. ICE, 510 F.3d 1 (1st Cir. 2007), Hearing on Motion for Temporary Restraining Order, Mar. 9, 2007, Appellants' Appendix, vol. 2, at 360 (reprinted in Gregoire Sauter, Case Study: *Aguilar v. ICE: Litigating Workplace Immigration Raids in the Twenty-First Century,* 14(7) BENDER'S IMMIGR. BULL. 9 (Apr. 1, 2009) (sworn statements taken by lawyers representing people who were arrested for deportation during Operation United Front, New Bedford, Massachusetts in 2007).

45. Affidavit of B.L.G., *id.*

46. Affidavit of K.G., Appendix, *supra* note 44, vol. 2, at 376.

47. Pamela Constable & N. C. Aizenman, *69 Immigrant Workers Held in Baltimore Area Raids,* WASH. POST, Mar. 30, 2007, at B1, *available at* LEXIS, News Library, WPOST File. American songwriter Woody Guthrie, as quoted above, had put it this way in 1948: "They chase us like outlaws, like rustlers, like thieves."

48. *See* Peter R. Moyers, *Butchering Statutes: The Postville Raid and the Misinterpretation of Federal Law,* 32(3) SEATTLE U. L. REV. 651 (2008).

49. David Leopold, *Postville, One Year Later,* AILA LEADERSHIP BLOG, May 11, 2009, *available at* http://ailaleadershipblog.org/2009/05/11/postville-one-year-later/.

50. Flores-Figueroa v. United States, 556 U.S. 646 (2009).

51. Hannah Arendt (quoted in THOMAS NAGEL, EQUALITY AND PARTIALITY 7 (Oxford University Press 1991)).

52. Video of FOX News Panel, including Juan Williams, MediaMatters.org, Mar. 18, 2009, http://mediamatters.org/mmtv/200903180035.

53. Edward Schumacher-Matos, *When Law Flies Out the Door,* WASH. POST, Aug. 1, 2009, at A15.

54. According to the Seton Hall Center for Social Justice, in January 2006, so-called "Fugitive Operations Teams" were each ordered by the Office of Detention and Removals Operations to meet a quota to find and arrest one thousand individuals per year who had outstanding deportation orders. This led to "an escalating pattern of pre-dawn raids of immigrant homes in at least 15 New Jersey towns. In these raids, Immigration and Customs Enforcement (ICE) agents entered immigrant homes in the early hours of the morning, without search warrants, using intimidation and—on occasion—force to gather and question everyone in the home. The ICE agents then arrest persons who cannot immediately prove legal residence. According to ICE statistics, of the 2,079 "fugitive" arrests that ICE made in New Jersey in 2005, 87 percent of those arrested had no criminal record. Individuals subjected to the home raids include children and adults who are U.S. citizens or Lawful Permanent Residents." *See* http://law.shu.edu/ProgramsCenters/PublicIntGovServ/CSJ/ICE-Raids.cfm.

55. *See* Cardozo Immigration Justice Clinic, *Constitution on ICE,* 2009 (describing tactics and suggesting a widespread national pattern of misconduct that involves:

- ICE agents illegally entering homes without legal authority—for example, physically pushing or breaking their way into private residences.
- ICE agents illegally seizing nontarget individuals during home raid operations—for example, seizing innocent people in their bedrooms without any basis.
- ICE agents illegally searching homes without legal authority—for example, breaking down locked doors inside homes.
- ICE agents illegally seizing individuals based solely on racial or ethnic appearance or on limited English proficiency.

56. INS v. Lopez-Mendoza, 468 U.S. 1032, 1033 (1984) (holding that the exclusionary rule generally does not apply in deportation hearings unless agents' conduct was widespread or egregious).

57. *See, e.g.*, Margot Mendleson, Shayna Strom, & Michale Wishnie, *Collateral Damage: An Examination of ICE's Fugitive Operations Program*, MPI (Feb. 2009) (describing problems in home raids in the context of the National Fugitive Operations Program [NFOP]).

58. Roberto Lovato, *Juan Crow in Georgia*, THE NATION, May 8, 2008, *available at* http://www. thenation.com/article/juan-crow-georgia.

59. A similar report came from Idaho in 2007. A family, which included U.S. citizens and legal permanent residents, said they were terrified by Immigration and Customs Enforcement agents who came to their home in the predawn hours along with sheriff's deputies. No one was arrested. But Dana Ayala, a U.S. citizen, described a chilling scene: "They pounded on my door so hard that my walls shook. My 19-year-old son opened the door to see what was happening, and six agents armed with guns, Tasers and flashlights pushed their way into my home." Terry Smith, *Immigration Agents Seize 20 Suspected Illegal Aliens*, IDAHO MOUNTAIN EXPRESS, Sept. 19, 2007, *available at* http://www.mtexpress.com/index2.php?ID=2005117099.

60. Statement of Senator Al Franken June 22, 2010, in support of Humane Enforcement and Legal Protections (HELP) for Separated Children Act (legislation designed "to keep kids safe, informed, and accounted for during Immigrations and Customs Enforcement (ICE) raids."), *available at* http://franken.senate.gov/?p=press_release&id=877.

61. *Description of Three Suspects Sought in Explosion*, CNN News, Apr. 19, 1995, 2:16 p.m. ET, Transcript # 635–11, *available at* http://www.lexisnexis.com/lawschool/research/default. aspx?ORIGINATION_CODE=00092&signoff=off.

62. Laurie C. Merrill, *Another Rented Van, Shades of WTC Hit*, NY DAILY NEWS, Apr. 20, 1995, at 27.

63. Todd J. Gillman, *Muslim Groups Fear Backlash; Mosques, Islamic Organizations Locally and Nationally Receive Threats*, DALLAS MORNING NEWS, Apr. 20, 1995, at 29A.

64. *See generally* Kanstroom, Deportation Nation, *supra* note 21, at 10, 46–136.

65. *See, e.g.*, Viet Dinh, *Life After 9/11: Issues Affecting the Courts and the Nation*, 51 KAN. L. REV. 219 (2003).

66. U.S. Department of Homeland Security, Quadrennial Homeland Security Review Report: A Strategic Framework for a Secure Homeland, Washington, DC, Feb. 2010.

67. *See* Daniel Kanstroom, *Reaping the Harvest: The Long, Complicated, Crucial Rhetorical Struggle over Deportation*, 39 CONN. L. REV. 1911, 1914 (2007).

68. Jennifer M. Chacón, Commentary, *Unsecured Borders: Immigration Restrictions, Crime Control and National Security*, 39 CONN. L. REV. 1827, 1831 (2007).

69. Charles E. Hughes, *Some Observations on the Conduct of Our Foreign Relations*, 16 AM. J. INT'L L. 365, 370 (1922).

70. *Id.* at 371 (emphasis added). As Hughes recognized: "In dealing with the problem of developing sound opinion, the fundamental consideration must always be that misinformation is the public's worst enemy, more potent for evil than all the conspiracies that are commonly feared." *Id.* at 366.

71. SIGMUND FREUD, CIVILIZATION AND ITS DISCONTENTS 60–63 (James Strachey trans., Norton 1961) (1930) (noting "the advantage which a comparatively small cultural group offers of allowing this instinct an outlet in the form of hostility against intruders is not to be despised. It is always possible to bind together a considerable number of people in love, so long as there are other people left over to receive the manifestations of their aggressiveness. I once discussed the phenomenon that is precisely communities with adjoining territories, and related to each other in other ways as well, who are engaged in constant feuds and in ridiculing each other—like the Spaniards and Portuguese, for instance, the North Germans and South Germans, the English and Scotch, and so on.").

72. JAMES MORTON SMITH, FREEDOM'S FETTERS: THE ALIEN AND SEDITION LAWS AND AMERICAN CIVIL LIBERTIES 64, n.2 (1956) (quoting DEBATES AND PROCEEDINGS IN THE CONGRESS OF THE UNITED STATES, 1789–1825, 5C, 2S (June 19, 1798) (1985–1986). Opponents of the bill highlighted their confidence in the "upright judges and vigilant magistrates" of the United States who could deal with any actual attempts at treason or sedition by either aliens or citizens under existing laws. See SMITH, FREEDOM'S FETTERS 63–64.

73. Internal Security Act, Pub. L. No. 81–831, 64 Stat. 987, 1006–1007 (1950); *see also* Patrick A. McCarran, *The Internal Security Act of 1950*, 12 U. PITT. L. REV. 481 (1951). *See generally* Charles Gordon, *The Immigration Process and National Security*, 24 TEMP. L.Q. 302 (1950–1951) (describing the Act).

74. The Internal Security Act also declared it unlawful to conspire to establish a totalitarian dictatorship, to conceal membership in the American Communist Party when seeking government employment, or to use a United States passport. President Truman vetoed it, saying that it "would betray our finest traditions" in its attempt to "curb the simple expression of opinion." Congress, however, overrode Truman's veto. President Harry S. Truman, Speech on the Veto of the McCarran Internal Security Act (Sept. 22, 1950), *available at* http://teachingamericanhistory.org/library/index.asp?document=859.

75. 98 CONG. REC. 2141 (1952) (joint statement by the sponsors of the Immigration and Nationality Act).

76. 98 CONG. REC. 5239 (1952).

77. *Id.*

78. *See* Kenneth Wayne Vickers, *John Rankin: Democrat and Demagogue* (1993) (M.A. Thesis, Mississippi State University); EMANUEL CELLAR, YOU NEVER LEAVE BROOKLYN (1953) (describing anti-Semitic attacks against him by Rankin).

79. 98 CONG. REC. 4320 (1952).

80. *Id.*

81. An Act Concerning Aliens; ch. 58, 1 Stat. 570. This law took effect on June 25, 1798, with a two-year expiration date.

82. KANSTROOM, DEPORTATION NATION, *supra* note 21, at 46–63.

83. MESSAGES AND PAPERS OF WOODROW WILSON 151 (Albert Shaw ed., 1924).

84. Attorney General A. Mitchell Palmer on charges made against Department of Justice by Louis F. Post and others, hearings before the committee on rules, House of Representatives, Washington, DC 1920) 157–58.

85. The Immigration Act of 1918 (ch. 186, 40 Stat. 1012) was enacted on October 16, 1918. It greatly expanded the definition of those subject to deportation on political grounds.

86. ZECHARIAH CHAFEE, JR., FREEDOM OF SPEECH 229 (1920).

87. LOUIS F. POST, THE DEPORTATIONS DELIRIUM OF THE NINETEEN-TWENTIES 34 (1923).

88. KANSTROOM, DEPORTATION NATION, *supra* note 21, at 8–20.

89. *See, e.g.,* BARRY BUZAN ET AL., SECURITY: A NEW FRAMEWORK FOR ANALYSIS 23–29, 121–22 (1998).

90. *Id.* at 23–24; *see also* H. Richard Friman, Politics, Migrants and Security: The Erosion of Protection in the Name of Order, Paper Prepared for Presentation at the Fairfield University Symposium: Migration Studies and Jesuit Identity: Forging a Path Forward, (June 8–12, 2005) (draft paper on file with author).

91. GARY W. POTTER & VICTOR E. KAPPELER, CONSTRUCTING CRIME: PERSPECTIVES ON MAKING NEWS AND SOCIAL PROBLEMS 7 (1998); *see also* Erich Goode & Nachman Ben-Yehuda, *Moral Panics: Culture, Politics, and Social Construction*, 20 ANN. REV. SOC. 149, 149–71 (1994).

92. *Prepared Statement of Honorable Lamar Smith Chairman Before The House Judiciary Committee Subcommittee on Immigration and Claims Subject—Detention of Criminal Aliens and Additional New Border Patrol Agents*, FED. NEWS SERVICE, February 25, 1999, at In the News, *available at* LEXIS, News Library, FEDNEW File.

93. Kanstroom, *Reaping the Harvest*, *supra* note 67, at 1918.

94. DAVID COLE, ENEMY ALIENS: DOUBLE STANDARDS AND CONSTITUTIONAL FREEDOMS IN THE WAR ON TERRORISM 5 (2003).

95. *Id.* at 7.

96. *See generally* KANSTROOM, DEPORTATION NATION, *supra* note 21, at 8–10.

97. Act of 2001, Pub. L. No. 107–156, 115 Stat. 272 (2001) § 412.

98. Quoted in *The September 11 Detainees: A Review of the Treatment of Aliens Held on Immigration Charges in Connection with the Investigation of the September 11 Attacks*, Office of the Inspector General April 2003 [hereinafter OIG Report], at 12.

99. *Id.*

100. OIG Report at 13.
101. Also, some 762 persons, about whom there was at least some specific suspicion, were held by INS in a scattered network of federal, local, and private detention facilities throughout the country. Their detention was a direct result of the so-called "Penttbom" investigation, led by the FBI. *Id.* at 1–2.
102. Indeed, even if the FBI could not determine whether it had an interest in a particular immigration detainee, the person was treated as "of interest." *Id.* at 16. Detainees were subjected to a "hold until cleared by the FBI" policy which resulted in an average length of time from arrest to clearance of eighty days, with considerable numbers of people being held for more than six months. *Id.* at 46. The largest number of "interest" detainees came from Pakistan, Egypt, Turkey, Jordan, and Yemen. But more than twenty countries' nationals were ultimately included. *Id.* at 21.
103. *Id.* at 64.
104. *Id.* at 142.
105. Registration and Monitoring of Certain Nonimmigrants. 67 Fed. Reg. 40,581. The rule became final on August 12, 2002, effective September 11, 2002. 67 Fed. Reg. 52,584. Men over the age of 16 years from the following countries were required to register: Iran, Iraq, Libya, Sudan, Syria, Afghanistan, Algeria, Bahrain, Eritrea, Lebanon, Morocco, North Korea, Oman, Qatar, Somalia, Tunisia, United Arab Emirates, Yemen, Pakistan, and Saudi Arabia. The registration process, divided into three distinct waves, affected tens of thousands of noncitizens within the United States.
106. INS confirmed this practice in a subsequent memo, which stated that "officers conducting these interviews may discover information which leads them to suspect that specific aliens on the list are unlawfully present or in violation of their immigration status." *See* Memorandum from Michael A. Pearson, INS Executive Associate Commissioner (Nov. 23, 2001). *See generally* Kevin R. Johnson, *The End of "Civil Rights" as We Know It?: Immigration and Civil Rights in the New Millennium,* 49 UCLA L. Rev. 1481, 1481–1511 (2002).
107. Diane Cardwell, *Threats and Responses: The Immigrants; Muslims Face Deportation, But Say U.S. Is Their Home,* N.Y. Times, June 13, 2003, at A22.
108. Zechariah Chafee, Jr., Freedom of Speech 231 (1920).
109. Morton Keller, Regulating a New Society: Public Policy and Social Change in America 1900–1933, 103; *see also* Lewis S. Gannett, *A Yankee Verdict: Judge Anderson's Decision,* 111 The Nation 7 (July 3, 1920).
110. *See* Kanstroom, Deportation Nation, *supra* note 21.
111. 8 U.S.C. § 1225(b)(1)(A)(iii)(II) (applying to those who have not been admitted or paroled and who have not "affirmatively shown, to the satisfaction of an immigration officer, that [they have] been physically present in the United States continuously" for the prior two years).
112. INA § 238(b), 8 U.S.C. § 1228(b).
113. Fifty-five percent of those removed in 2006 on the basis of an aggravated felony conviction were processed through administrative removal. *New Data on the Processing of Aggravated Felons,* Transactional Records Access Clearinghouse (TRAC), Syracuse University (2007), *available at* http://trac.syr.edu/immigration/reports/175/.
114. Former INA § 242(f) applied to persons who were deported (not "excluded") for certain criminal convictions, failing to register or falsification of documents, or security- or terrorist-related grounds and subsequently reentered the country illegally.
115. The development of "unlawful presence" bars is another such mechanism.
116. *See* TRAC Immigration, *Illegal Reentry Becomes Top Criminal Charge* (June 10, 2011), *available at* http://trac.syr.edu/immigration/reports/251/.
117. 8 U.S.C. § 1231(a)(5). There are some technical exceptions to the no relief rule that are beyond the scope of this work. Also, the regulations provide "[i]f the alien wishes to make a statement, the officer shall allow the alien to do so and shall consider whether the alien's statement warrants reconsideration of the determination." 8 C.F.R. § 241.8(a)(3). Judicial review may be available to challenge some aspects of a reinstatement order. *See e.g.,* Arevalo v. Ashcroft, 344 F.3d 1, 9 (1st Cir. 2003) (allowing application for adjustment of status to proceed and rejecting retroactive application of reinstatement statute); *cf.* Delgado

v. Mukasey, 516 F.3d 65, 66–74 (2d Cir. 2008) (denying adjustment of status). *See generally* Trina Realmuto, *Reinstatement of Removal*, Legal Action Center Practice Advisory, Apr. 23, 2008, *available at* http://www.legalactioncenter.org/practice-advisories/reinstatement-removal.

118. Fernandez-Vargas v. Gonzales, 548 U.S. 30 (2006).

119. *Backgrounder: Stipulated Removal*, by Jayashri Srikantiah, Stanford Immigrants' Rights Clinic, and Karen Tumlin, National Immigration Law Center, based on data obtained through a Freedom of Information Act (FOIA) request submitted to the Executive Office of Immigration Review by Stanford Immigrants' Rights Clinic, National Lawyers Guild-San Francisco Bay Area, National Immigration Law Center, and ACLU of Southern California. *Available at* http://www.law.stanford.edu/program/clinics/immigrantsrights/pressrelease/Stipulated_removal_backgrounder.pdf.

120. 8 C.F.R. § 1003.25(b).

121. *Id.*

122. *See* "Language Barriers May Lead Immigrants to Waive Right to Hearing Before Deportation," National Immigration Justice Center (June 3, 2008), http://www.immigrantjustice.org/press_releases/new-data-suggests-language-barriers-lead-immigrants-waive-right-hearing-deportation.

123. It also establishes a supervisory structure and a complaint process governing officer conduct. The agreement must be signed by the ICE Assistant Secretary and the governor, a senior political entity, or the head of the local agency before trained local officers are authorized to enforce immigration law. *See* http://www.ice.gov/news/library/factsheets/287g.htm.

124. OIG Report, table 1.

125. OIG Report, p. 5.

126. *Id.*

127. I am particularly grateful to Mariah Rutherford-Olds for her meticulous research about Operation Endgame.

128. The DRO was established on March 1, 2003, as one of the four law enforcement divisions within ICE. Its blanket mission is to "[p]romote the public safety and national security by ensuring the departure from the United States of all removable aliens through the fair and effective enforcement of the nation's immigration laws." DRO defines its chief responsibility as "to identify, apprehend and remove illegal aliens from the United States." ICE Office of Detention and Removal, http://web.archive.org/web/20090826025207/http://www.ice.gov/pi/dro/.

129. U.S. Dep't of Homeland Security, Immigration & Customs Enforcement, *Endgame: Office of Detention and Removal Strategic Plan, 2003–2012* [hereinafter *Endgame*], *available at* http://wayback.archive.org/web/*/http://www.aclum.org/pdf/endgame.pdf.

130. Anthony S. Tangeman, Memorandum of Introduction to Endgame. *Id.*

131. Pub. L. 103–162 (1993); *see* Walter Groszyk, "Implementation of the Government Performance Results Act of 1993" (1995), *available at* http://govinfo.library.unt.edu/npr/library/omb/gpra.html.

132. *Id. See also* John Mercer—*GPRA & Performance Management*, http://www.john-mercer.com/gpra.htm.

133. Grades were based on a mix of factors including the mission statement, goals and objectives, stakeholder consultation, program evaluation, coordination of functions, and strategies for achieving objectives. Further motivation for *Endgame* came from President George W. Bush's Program Assessment Rating Tool (PART) program, implemented by the Office of Management and Budget (OMB) in 2002. Dep't of Justice, FY 2006 Performance and Accountability Report: PART: OMB's Program Assessment Rating Tool, IV-14 (2006), *available at* http://www.justice.gov/ag/annualreports/pr2006/P4/p14.pdf.

134. Telephone Interview with Adam X. Piceno, Chief of Strategic Planning Unit, DHS, Immigration and Customs Enforcement conducted by Mariah Rutherford-Olds (Mar. 26, 2010) (transcript on file with author).

135. Interview with Adam X. Piceno, *id.* Indeed, the agency received a 100 percent score on the strategic planning component, along with an overall rating of "Moderately Effective," and a

total weighted score of 81 percent. *See* U.S. Dep't of Homeland Security, Dep't of Homeland Security Annual Performance Report Fiscal Years 2008–2010: Appendix C—Summary Findings of Program Evaluations 3 (2010), *available at* http://www.dhs.gov/xlibrary/assets/cfo_aprappc_fy2008.pdf. In comparison, ICE's Federal Protective Service (reviewed in 2007) and ICE's Office of Investigations (reviewed in 2004) received only an overall rating of "Adequate," and had total weighted scores of 52 percent and 63 percent, respectively. *Id.*

136. Interview with Adam X. Piceno, *supra* note 134.

137. The underlying principle of this project would ultimately become a component of *Endgame*. AILA/BICE Committee Meeting, "ICE Liaison Minutes (11/12/03),"AILA InfoNet Doc. No. 03120243 (posted Dec. 2, 2003), *available at* http://www.uslawnet.com/library/ice_liaison_minutes_111203.htm.

138. Interview with Adam X. Piceno, *supra* note 134.

139. *Id.* Sam Roudebush, a former DRO/ICE officer, drafted a charter convening a work group to draft a strategic plan for DRO. The SPWG ultimately consisted of over thirty men and women, including officers from DRO headquarters and from other ICE enforcement programs.

140. ABC Local News, WLS-TV Chicago, IL, *Arellano: Fight for Immigration Reform Not Over*, Aug. 20, 2007, http://abclocal.go.com/wls/story?section=news/local&id=5584566 (last visited Apr. 28, 2010).

141. Others came from military backgrounds, including the Naval Postgraduate School in Monterey, CA, the U.S. Air Force Air Command and Staff College, and Naval Air Systems Command. Several SPWG members also had postgraduate degrees in business or business administration. Some had moved up within the ranks of different government agencies. See *Endgame Office of Detention and Removal Strategic Plan, 2003–2012, supra* note 129, at G-9 (my research assistant searched listed names using online search engines, such as www.google.com or www.bing.com, to determine background academic and biographic information on social networking websites, e.g., Facebook and LinkedIn, for several SPWG members). *See, e.g.,* Jay Fadgen, http://www.bentoni.com/fqcg/team_jay.html (last visited Apr. 28, 2010); interview with Adam X. Piceno, *supra* note 134; Baldrige National Quality Program—About Us, http://www.nist.gov/baldrige/about/index.cfm (last visited Apr. 28, 2010). Strategic planning as an academic field may be defined as "a disciplined effort to produce fundamental decisions and actions that shape and guide what an organization (or other entity) is, what it does, and why it does it. . . ." JOHN M. BRYSON, STRATEGIC PLANNING FOR PUBLIC AND NONPROFIT ORGANIZATIONS: A GUIDE TO STRENGTHENING AND SUSTAINING ORGANIZATIONAL ACHIEVEMENT, at x (Jossey-Bass Publishers 1995).

142. Interview with Adam X. Piceno, *supra* note 134.

143. Following this dramatic start date, the SPWG met regularly for some eighteen months. *Id.*

144. Bryson, *supra* note 141, at ix. Most of *Endgame* directly corresponds to the method set out in Bryson's book, which identifies the key steps of strategic planning: (1) initiating and agreeing on a strategic planning process; (2) clarifying organizational mandates and mission; (3) assessing the environment to identify strengths, weaknesses, opportunities, and threats (SWOT); (4) identifying strategic issues facing the agency or organization; (5) formulating and then adopting strategies and plans to manage the issues; (6) establishing an organizational vision for the future; (9) implementing the strategies and plans; and (7) reassessing and revising the strategic plan as time goes on.

145. Interview with Adam X. Piceno, *supra* note 134.

146. See *Endgame Office of Detention and Removal Strategic Plan, 2003–2012, supra* note 129, at 1–4. *Endgame* also suggested the use of "nontraditional" detention methods in conjunction with traditional ones. For instance, the report proposed an electronic monitoring system to track immigrants released from custody prior to the issue of a final order of removal. *Endgame* also propounded using family shelters and halfway houses to compensate for the shortage of detention space. By integrating such nontraditional and traditional detention methods, "DRO hope[d] to increase the number of immigrants who . . . appear[ed] before immigration hearings by 10 percent until the 100 percent goal [was] reached."

147. *Id.* at 1–4.

148. *Id.*

149. *Id.*

150. *Endgame*, Glossary, G-3.

151. ACLU of Massachusetts, "Endgame" Documents: Before and After (2007), http://wayback.archive.org/web/*/http://www.aclum.org/pdf/endgame.pdf. Jamie E. Zuieback, from ICE, responded to the ACLU op-ed with a strenuous column entitled "Immigration op-ed a new ACLU low," published on March 31, 2007: "As director of public affairs for US Immigration and Customs Enforcement, I know what actually happened March 6 in New Bedford: Careful planning resulted in a successful worksite operation to enforce immigration laws. Our agency took extraordinary steps, in concert with Massachusetts social-service and law-enforcement agencies, to help ensure that no child was, at any point, without proper care. Immigration hearings, legal representation, and interpreters were all provided. Rather than report this, the authors opted for unsubstantiated rumors and cheap sensationalism. Their irresponsible, offensive comparison of our work to that of mass-murderer Slobodan Milosevic brought the ACLU's credibility to a new low. The men and women of ICE are professionals who handle their duties seriously and with compassion. While we hope for comprehensive immigration reform, the issues at stake won't be resolved by continued misuse of the national press. And if Rose and Ott need a lesson in the repulsive truth of ethnic cleansing, I am happy to buy them tickets to the Holocaust Museum here in Washington."

4

Accomplishments and Problems: Does Deportation Work Within the Rule of Law?

> I don't think they play at all fairly, . . . they don't seem to have any rules in particular: at least, if there are[,] no-body attends to them—and you've no idea how confusing it is. . . .[1]

We can now begin to assess the deportation system by relating its goals (to the extent we have been able to determine them) to what has actually been done by deportation authorities in recent years. This chapter will first consider the system's achievements and then some of its major problems.

Accomplishments

> CBP explained *increases* in apprehensions made at checkpoints in some border sectors to improved CBP operations and *decreases* in apprehensions in other sectors to the deterrent effects of improved CBP technologies and increased staffing. Clearly, a measure that reflects successful performance whether it rises or falls has limited value as a management tool.
>
> —RAND Report (2011)[2]

At the outset, we must again accept that *extended border control* deportation can never fully control illegal immigration.[3] That has never been its goal, and, as the *Endgame* debacle demonstrates, even to aim for such an outcome would be politically divisive, logistically impossible without unacceptable costs to basic rights, and prohibitively expensive. Indeed, the estimated cost would exceed the entire annual budget for the Department of Homeland Security.[4] If one adds to this the cost of deporting all those otherwise legal noncitizens (students, workers, permanent residents, refugees, asylees, etc.) who may have violated an immigration law, the practical problems with such a program are clear. And, of course, such a massive enforcement system would also amount to a police state for noncitizens, their families, and anyone who might look like a noncitizen. It would mark the definitive rejection not just of the "nation of immigrants" ideal, but of the open society as well. Moreover, its gains would likely be temporary unless the border were somehow completely sealed and all future visitors, students, workers, and immigrants were somehow pervasively watched and tracked at all times. As two former INS commissioners have pointed out, only some five thousand visas are available for low-skilled workers. However, through 2008, the unauthorized population grew annually by about five hundred thousand mostly low-skilled workers. Put most simply, there is a powerful disjuncture between the demands of the U.S. labor market and immigration admissions policies. Indeed, the tightening of border controls has actually exacerbated the problem of undocumented workers. It is precisely because our borders are more secure that those who are here illegally feel they must stay: reentry is increasingly legally perilous and physically dangerous.[5]

Thus, in practical terms, (i.e., leaving aside political and symbolic considerations) *extended border control* deportation is like using fingers to plug holes in a rapidly leaking dike. Or, more accurately, it is like using one's hands to scoop up some of the water that has already seeped through. It shows a certain concern, but its real effects on the flow are minimal. This form of deportation has done "little to reduce illegal inflows and much to drive the illegals into an underclass that degrades them and offends our moral sensibilities."[6] This view has become a virtual consensus in American politics: *this form of deportation simply is not working.*[7]

In fairness, this broad critique may be too strenuous, especially for a section entitled "Accomplishments." After all, there can be little doubt that *extended border control* deportation—by removing many hundreds of thousands of people per year—has surely accomplished *something*. But it is quite difficult, perhaps impossible, to measure the system's accomplishments. This is no less true of such "attrition through enforcement" strategies as denials of public assistance or drivers' licenses, and health care restrictions.[8] The effects of enforcement are exceedingly difficult to measure.[9] Indeed, a growing body of evidence suggests that such factors as expanding economic and educational opportunities, rising border crime and shrinking families are suppressing illegal immigration from Mexico at least as much as economic slowdowns or immigrant crackdowns in the United States.[10] Part of the explanation may also be positive effects from the opposite of strict enforcement. There has reportedly been a significant recent expansion of *legal* immigration from Mexico, apparently aided by American consular officials. Mexicans who have become American citizens have legally brought in 64 percent more immediate relatives, 220,500 from 2006 through 2010, compared with the previous five years. Tourist visas are also being granted at significantly higher rates, and American farmers have legally hired 75 percent more temporary workers since 2006, according to the *New York Times* report. Edward McKeon, who was in charge of U.S. consular affairs in Mexico, said that easier visa policies would prevent people from giving up and going illegally, including those with prior illegal stays in the United States. As he put it, "If people are trying to do the right thing, we need to send the signal that we'll reward them."[11]

A 2010 study by the Pew Hispanic Center illustrates the difficulty of measuring the effects of enforcement as such.[12] The report found that the annual inflow of unauthorized immigrants to the United States was nearly two-thirds smaller in the March 2007 to March 2009 period than it had been from March 2000 to March 2005—a rather stunning decline. However, the report also conceded that the data do not explain *why* these changes occurred. There had been major shifts in the level of immigration enforcement and in enforcement strategies. But the U.S. economy had also entered a major recession late in 2007, just as border enforcement was increasing. Economic and demographic conditions in sending countries—especially Mexico—and strategies employed by potential migrants had also changed.[13] Indeed, the report indicates that the recent decrease in the unauthorized population was especially notable along the nation's Southeast coast and in its Mountain West, which, in general, are not areas that correlate especially strongly with increased *extended border control* deportation. Moreover, the report notes that nearly half of unauthorized immigrants living in the country in 2009—47 percent, or 5.2 million people—arrived in 2000 or later, during years of rather strenuous deportation activity. The editors of the *New York Times*, after reading the Pew study, suggested a sensible understanding of the decline. Harsher enforcement, they believed, probably had something to do with it. But so did the recession. And while the total undocumented population had fallen somewhat, to about 11 million, there was no exodus. "They are not flooding in as much, but they are not flooding out."[14]

Perhaps we can measure the accomplishments of the system in other ways, though. The Customs and Border Patrol agency regularly cites apprehensions data as its measure of effectiveness. Thus, the agency claimed success in 2007–2009 due to a *decrease* in the number of apprehensions.[15] Clearly, such data do not prove cause and effect. But DHS Secretary Chertoff proudly cited these data in congressional testimony,[16] even as he appropriately conceded that "enforcement alone is not enough to address our immigration challenges." So long as the "opportunity for higher wages and a better life draws people across the border illegally or encourages them to remain here illegally," he noted, the "battle" would be difficult.[17] The whole enterprise, in short, is inevitably incremental and extremely difficult to assess. As then head of ICE, Julie Myers once admitted: "Do I think we have solved this problem? No. Do I think we are starting to make an impact? I think we're starting to."[18] This, however, was in 2008, after more than a dozen years of stepped-up enforcement.

Some have sought more creative, if oblique, ways to measure the impact of border control systems. For example, researchers determined that the average fee paid to smugglers ("coyotes") increased from $978 in 1995 to $2,124 in 2006, which might, at least in part, be a reflection of enforcement impact.[19] Measurements of declining remittances also might provide a rough metric.[20] But such measures are hard to correlate with enforcement by deportation in particular.

Perhaps most strangely, though, DHS has also cited an *increase* in violence against Border Patrol officers as a sign that enforcement is working. Such violence was reportedly up 31 percent in FY 2007.[21] How the agency can positively cite these data while also heralding decreasing numbers of arrests at the border is a bit mysterious.

In any case, as noted, researchers do agree that there has been a notable decline in the undocumented population since 2008. But few count this as a success for *extended border control* enforcement. As one study noted: "The estimated decline of the illegal population is at least seven times larger than the number of illegal aliens removed by the government in the last 10 months, so most of the decline is due to illegal immigrants leaving the country on their own."[22] This could, of course, be due in part to the fear of deportation, but others have concluded that it is more likely due to many other factors, such as unemployment.[23]

The particular measuring problem for this form of deportation is thus both obvious and inescapable: we can measure the number of deportees, of course, but it will never be clear what this tells us about effectiveness. One might of course say that the millions of people who were deported in recent years would have supplemented the current undocumented population had the deportation system not been in place. But even this seemingly logical analysis is problematic. We know that many undocumented workers (not to mention their children) reenter the United States after removal or voluntary departure. Many of the deformalization initiatives discussed earlier, such as *reinstatement of removal*, were designed to enhance the efficiency of *extended border control* deportation and to process recidivists quickly.[24] As the director of ICE Field Legal Operations put it in a 2005 interview, the idea is, "Look, if you got removed (deported) and you came back . . . we're not going to give you another whole

new proceeding."[25] The government asserted in 2005 that reinstatement of removal had accounted for about ninety-eight thousand removals in the prior
three years, some 40 percent of all removals in the United States.[26] But this, of
course, indicates a failure of border control as much as a success of *extended
border control* deportation.

So what are we to make of this? We know that perfect control of the U.S. border seems to be impossible at or near any cost we are willing to pay. Indeed, it
may simply be impossible at any cost. We can therefore frame certain inevitable
features of *extended border control* deportation:

1. It is an expensive and growing enforcement system with second-order goals
   derived from a very imperfect border control system;
2. Its goals are a complex mix of the practical and the rhetorical/symbolic;
3. It can never be fully effective, and it is very difficult, perhaps impossible, to
   measure its effectiveness accurately.

None of these conclusions necessarily argue powerfully in favor of the abolition
of all such deportations. However, we should bear in mind this difficulty in
framing goals and accomplishments as we move to consideration of an array of
systemic problems, due process and federal/state preemption concerns, and significant collateral effects on individuals, families, and communities in the United
States and internationally.

Now let us consider the accomplishments of *post-entry social control* criminal deportations. As we have seen, an energetic focus on deportation of "criminal aliens" has marked both the George W. Bush and the Obama
administrations. The obvious metric for success in such an endeavor would
seem to be lower crime rates, generally, or at least crime rates involving noncitizen perpetrators. Also, like *extended border control*, crime-based deportation
has more subtle goals: some pragmatic, some symbolic, some rhetorical, and
some, for lack of a better term, perhaps a bit circular. In January 2008, for example, Julie L. Myers, then head of ICE, announced that her agency expected
to identify and start to deport more than two hundred thousand immigrants
who were convicted criminals serving time in prisons and jails across the
country.[27] The number continued a rather dramatic increase seen in recent
years. What was particularly interesting was one of the justifications for this
new campaign: *to help federal and state prisons reduce the costs of housing immigrants.*[28] This stepped-up deportation regime thus seemed partly motivated
not so much by crime control concerns as by complaints voiced by cities,
counties, and states frustrated by having to pay for the detention of noncitizens convicted of crimes.

The first questions we should ask of crime control-type deportation are the most simple ones: at whom is the deportation system aimed, and does it actually work to reduce serious crime? As with other areas of deportation law and policy, we are sorely in need of more empirical research. But what we do know is troubling. First, we should note that *post-entry social deportation*, like other forms of crime-related law enforcement, is largely focused on the young. This is a very large population, and, as we have seen, it is also well-entrenched and acculturated in the United States. In 2008, the number of young adults in the United States (aged 18 to 34) either foreign-born or of foreign parentage exceeded 20 million.[29]

As we have seen, the numbers of criminal deportations are on the rise. Of the nearly four hundred thousand people formally deported in the fiscal year that ended in September 2010, about half were deported because of crime, or at least listed as criminals in government databases (the record keeping is imperfect). Still, criminal deportation was a signal feature of the "smart enforcement" strategy of the early Obama administration. But at whom was criminal deportation aimed? The majority of criminal deportees in 2010 had committed drug-related crimes, some 45,003.[30] The data also show that 27,635 had been arrested for drunken driving, more than double the 10,851 deported after drunken driving arrests in the last full year of the Bush administration. In 2010, 13,028 were deported after being arrested on less serious traffic law violations, nearly three times the 4,527 traffic offenders deported two years earlier.[31]

Similar realities were found by a 2009 Human Rights Watch study of the effectiveness of such *post-entry social control* deportations.[32] The researchers' conclusions were striking. First, *the vast majority of all such deportees were deported for a nonviolent offense.* Across all immigration status categories, "more than two-thirds of those for whom we have crime data were deported for a nonviolent crime."[33] Of course, nonviolent crime is still crime. But to evaluate crime-fighting priorities and methods, the seriousness of the targeted offenses surely matters.

Moreover, illegally present noncitizens were more likely to have been deported for a violent or potentially violent offense and less likely to have been deported for a nonviolent offense than legally present noncitizens. The researchers thus suggested an interesting strategy: that enforcement resources should perhaps be focused upon persons in the United States in an undocumented or illegal status, *who were also* involved in serious, violent criminal offenses. Although the data kept by ICE in this regard were woefully inadequate, the Human Rights Watch researchers were able to draw a troubling conclusion about the government's current focus: in those cases in which adequate records were kept, 77 *percent of "legally present" noncitizens deported for crime were deported for nonviolent offenses.*[34]

A potentially positive accomplishment of crime-based deportation would be a reduction in criminal recidivism. If the already-deportable population consists of people who are more likely than others to commit crimes or to reoffend repeatedly, then deportation seems reasonable. A 2008 RAND Corporation study, however, found that this hypothesis was not sustained.[35] The study determined that deportable immigrants released from the Los Angeles County jail system were no more likely to be rearrested than similar nondeportable immigrants released during the same period. As one researcher noted: "Our findings run counter to the notion that illegal immigrants are more likely than other immigrants to cycle in and out of the local criminal justice system."[36]

Nor have studies shown that noncitizens in general are more likely to commit crimes than are citizens. Indeed, in 2006, a group of sociologists sent a powerful shot across the bow to those who had supported harsh *post-entry social control* deportation by asserting general notions of immigrant criminality.[37] The researchers noted that mainstream theories of crime and incarceration routinely predict higher rates for young adult males from ethnic minority groups with lower educational backgrounds. Since these are characteristics that are already found in a greater proportion of the foreign-born population than of the native-born, one might naturally expect immigrants to have higher incarceration rates than native-born citizens. However, using census data to measure the institutionalization rates of immigrants and natives and focusing on males aged 18 to 39, the researchers came to quite surprising conclusions: the data showed that the conventional hypotheses were simply unfounded.[38] In fact, the incarceration rate of the U.S.-born was *four times* the rate of the foreign-born. The foreign-born rate was half the rate for non-Hispanic white natives, and thirteen times less than the 11.6 percent incarceration rate for native black men.[39]

Another intriguing finding was that the extraordinarily low incarceration rates among immigrants rise rapidly by the second generation. The data suggested that "the process of 'Americanization' leads to downward mobility and greater risks of involvement with the criminal justice system among a small but significant segment of this population." After further data analysis, the researchers came to a startling conclusion: *"For every group without exception, the longer immigrants had resided in the United States, the higher were their incarceration rates."*[40]

These conclusions, though perhaps counterintuitive, were consistent with other recent studies.[41] Sociologist Robert J. Sampson and colleagues, for example, concluded that Latin American immigrants are less violent and less likely to commit crimes than the second and third generations. This was true even when the immigrants lived in dense communities with high rates of poverty. Indeed, foreign-born immigrants were 45 percent less likely to commit violent crimes than were third-generation Americans. Second-generation immigrants were 22 percent less likely.[42] Studies of homicides in three high-immigration border cities (San Diego, El Paso, and Miami), and of drug violence in Miami and San Diego, reached similar conclusions.[43] In yet another study, published in 2007, Rubén Rumbaut and Walter Ewing examined three decades of census data to determine the incarceration rates of various ethnic and nationality groups. Their goal was to determine relative criminality. The key finding of the study was that U.S.-born men aged 18 to 39 (who comprise the vast majority of the prison population) were five times more likely than foreign-born men to be imprisoned for criminal activity. The researchers also noted that in general, U.S. crime rates have declined as immigration has increased, a phenomenon that has also been true in cities with large immigrant populations such as Los Angeles, New York, Chicago, and Miami.

In short, these researchers have highlighted a "paradox of assimilation." Assimilation often involves the acquisition by immigrants and their descendants of English-language proficiency, higher levels of education, job skills, and other attributes that improve their chances of success. However, immigrants' health status—and that of their children—worsens the longer they live in the United States and with increasing acculturation. The children and grandchildren of many immigrants—as well as many immigrants themselves—become subject to economic and social forces, such as higher rates of family disintegration and drug and alcohol addiction, that increase the likelihood of criminal behavior.[44] Such conclusions are particularly important as we try to assess the justifications for deportations of large numbers of young people from certain communities. For example, between 1996 and 2006, as many as fifty thousand Dominicans were deported from the United States.[45] One can view this phenomenon as a negative variant of what has been called by Alejandro Portes and Min Zhou "segmented assimilation."[46] As they note, the process of growing up American "oscillates between smooth acceptance and traumatic confrontation."[47] For many of today's deportees, the path was more traumatic than smooth. This has been due in large part to the changed structure of economic opportunities as well as to race. The white descendants of European immigrants could assimilate largely by deciding to "embrace American ways." Though one must be extremely wary of racial stereotyping in such analyses, it does seem correct that this option has been much more problematic for "the black, Asian, and mestizo children of today's immigrants."[48] Assimilation may not be into the "mainstream culture" but into the "values and norms of the inner city."[49] *Post-entry social control* deportation renders this an extremely perilous path. Basically, as Jock Young has framed it, such deportations amount to a "bulimic society," where "massive cultural inclusion is accompanied by systematic structural exclusion. . . . it absorbs and it rejects."[50]

The more one digs into the historical attempt to justify *post-entry social control* deportation as a crime control measure, the more one finds that supporting data have often been lacking. As Rumbaut, et al. noted in their 2006 study, the Industrial Commission of 1901, the [Dillingham] Immigration Commission of 1911, and the [Wickersham] National Commission on Law Observance and Enforcement of 1931 each had sought to measure how immigration resulted in increases in crime. Instead "each found lower levels of criminal involvement among the foreign born but higher levels among their native-born counterparts." The disturbing conclusion is clear: "If there was an 'immigrant crime problem' it was not found among the immigrants, but among their U.S.-born sons."[51] Lest one draw the conclusion that this argues in favor of preventing immigration in order to prevent such procreation, remember that the rates among these sons are no higher—and may be lower—than the native-born population in general. In any event, whatever one may think of such a problem, it is obvious that its solution is not deportation.

Problems within the Deportation System

An Abjuration, which is a Deportation for ever into a foreign Land, was antiently with us, a civil Death.

—John Ayliffe (1726)[52]

As we have seen, the specificity with which one may articulate the goals of the U.S. deportation system ranges from the relatively clear goals of *extended border control* to the more amorphous aspirations of *post-entry social control*. In both subsystems, however, measurement of accomplishments is challenging. Let us now consider some systemic problems of the deportation system. Some of these are structural or bureaucratic and subject to managerial improvement.[53] Others are more inherently related to the deep rule of law concerns that are examined in Chapters 6 and 7.

Detention and Transfer: Navigating the "American Gulag"

One of the major consequences of the 1996 changes to U.S. deportation law has been a massive and unprecedented increase in the detention of noncitizens for deportation.[54] Detention, which had been largely abolished by INS in

1954, except for those who were likely to abscond or who were deemed dangerous to national security or public safety, has gradually come to be a defining characteristic of the immigration enforcement system.[55] As Mark Dow noted in his 2004 book, *American Gulag*, enforcement procedures that had long "tended to be casual," became increasingly "brutal."[56] In fact, detention came to be seen as a tool with more utility than simply to guarantee appearance at hearings. It was also thought useful as a deterrent—first to Haitian refugees during the Reagan administration, then, with the increasingly militaristic approach to the southern border, to many others. Indeed, the Reagan administration also developed a "contingency plan" to detain hundreds of thousands of undocumented aliens in the event of a national emergency, along with "alien activists."[57]

A variety of factors have coalesced to create the current massive detention scheme. Enforcement focus has increasingly turned to "criminal aliens," and increased fears over asylum-seekers—such as some 286 smuggled Chinese noncitizens in the famous Golden Venture incident of 1993—are major background reasons. Also, in the 1990s, there was increased concern about absconders from deportation proceedings who were granted bond and then failed to show up for their hearings or for deportation.[58] Detention has now become the norm for hundreds of thousands of people annually. The 1996 immigration laws expanded mandatory detention during removal proceedings for individuals convicted of certain crimes. The events of September 11, 2001, and the subsequent emphasis on border security and immigration law enforcement, along with the broader detention powers authorized by the USA PATRIOT Act, have also played a major role in normalizing the idea of broad detention,[59] as has the expanded use of expedited removal. Finally, increased state and local enforcement and privatization have sustained and enhanced the detention system. In the former case, this is largely due to "force multiplier" strategies and overlapping detention mandates. In the latter, one must also consider the effect of profit motives in large, new, privately run facilities.[60]

The cumulative results have been dramatic. ICE has come to operate the largest detention and supervised release program in the country.[61] The average daily population of detained noncitizens has exploded, from approximately 5,500 in 1994 to 19,500 in 2001, and to over 30,000 by the end of 2009.[62] On September 1, 2009, ICE had 31,075 aliens in detention at more than three hundred facilities throughout the United States and its territories, with an additional 19,169 people in supervised "Alternative to Detention programs."[63] In 2010, ICE detained over 360,000 people.[64]

The majority of detainees are held in facilities near where they were arrested. However, ostensibly due to "detention shortages" in California and the mid-Atlantic and Northeast states, large numbers of people have been summarily transferred to areas where there are "surplus beds." The profound problems caused by such transfers are discussed below. Detention also became a growth enterprise for both private companies and a few counties, which received substantial federal funding to run ICE operations.[65] As of 2011, for example, the Corrections Corporation of America (CCA) received about 40 percent of its business from the federal government, including Immigration and Customs Enforcement (ICE) and the Federal Bureau of Prisons (BOP).[66] Human rights activists have raised concerns about BOP directors, who have overseen the transfer of millions of dollars in contracts to the CCA, leaving government and then taking lucrative positions with CCA.[67]

Quality control at these facilities has long been a major concern. Although the Bush administration purported to know little about such problems, behind the scenes, deaths in private facilities generated thousands of pages of government documents, secret investigative reports, and a pattern of officials working to stymie outside inquiry.[68] In 2010, the *New York Times* reported that nine deaths had occurred at the CCA's prison facility in Eloy, Arizona, more than any other immigration contract prison facility in the country.[69] Government officials had in fact long been aware of such problems, but little was done. Nina Bernstein described the tragic case of one detainee at Eloy, Emmanuel Owusu. Mr. Owusu, a barber, had arrived from Ghana on a student visa in 1972. He had been a U.S. legal permanent resident for thirty-three years, mostly in Chicago. He was arrested by ICE in 2006 because of a 1979 conviction for misdemeanor battery and retail theft. Even the Phoenix ICE field office director was struck by the case: "Convicted in 1979? That's a long time ago." Nevertheless, a government report on his death referred to a "lengthy" criminal history ranging from 1977 to 1998. It did not note that this lengthy history, which had ended more than a decade earlier, consisted mostly of shoplifting offenses. By the time he was arrested, Mr. Owusu was 62 years old and a diabetic with high blood pressure. He was incarcerated at Eloy for two years while he fought deportation. He died of a heart ailment weeks after his last appeal was dismissed.[70]

Local facilities, commonly run by counties, have also long been problematic. About half of the detained population of potential deportees—nearly two hundred thousand people per year—have been held in a vast array of more than two hundred county jails throughout the country. These facilities frequently also house county prisoners and other criminal detainees. In November 2000, INS published a Detention Operations Manual which contained Detention Standards.[71] However, they were only "guidelines" for the county jails and prisons that incarcerated some 80 percent of detained noncitizens at the time.[72] The standards were not binding and were in most cases virtually unenforceable.[73] Some of the worst reported abuses regarding mistreatment and lack of medical care took place in these unregulated facilities. Why do counties want to house noncitizen detainees? The answer is simple: money.

Mark Dow quotes a Pennsylvania county commissioner who said, "We tried like the dickens to get some of the Chinese . . . but it didn't pan out. . . . If no immigrants are secured, some layoffs may be inevitable."[74]

Serious problems have also long been cited in regular ICE facilities.[75] The failure to care for health needs of those living with HIV/AIDS is a major concern.[76] And, as Mr. Owusu's case exemplified, a disturbing number of people have died in or shortly after leaving ICE custody.[77] ICE has argued that the death rate for individuals in its custody has declined and compares favorably to that of the U.S. prison population.[78] However, such comparisons are problematic given the comparatively short periods of time that the average person remains in ICE custody.[79]

Human rights reports have concluded that sexual abuse is a long-standing issue throughout the entire ICE detention system.[80] A letter sent by a detainee described the more general medical problems faced by women in ICE custody.

> Medical care that is provided to us is very minimal and general. . . . If you do not speak English, you cannot fuss, the only thing you can do is go to bed & suffer. . . . We have no privacy when our health record is being discussed. . . . When we've complained to the nurses, we get ridiculed with replies like: "You should have made better choices. . . . ICE is not here to make you feel comfortable. . . . [O]ur hands are [tied]. . . . Well, we can't do much you're getting deported anyway. . . . [L]earn English before you cross the border. . . . *Mi casa no es su casa.*" . . . Our living situation is degrading and inhuman. . . .[81]

Since many immigration detainees are "criminal aliens," one might assume a certain level of dangerousness among them. This, however, turns out not to be true. Indeed, the government's own figures estimate that the majority of the population is characterized as "low custody, or having a low propensity for violence." Only about 11 percent had committed violent crimes.[82] Nevertheless, two-thirds are subject to mandatory detention with no right to bail under the law.[83]

Though the metaphor of the Soviet *gulag* used by some to describe the ICE detention system is surely strained, the frequent transfer of detainees to remote locations gives it a certain bite. Imagine what this is like for families. One day, your husband, wife, parent, or child is simply gone. You frantically search for them in hospitals, with local police, or even in the morgue. If you are lucky, perhaps you get a call from them. But noncitizens arrested by ICE can be held in any of the hundreds of facilities around the country. In my experience, many detainees have not even known where they are when they call. Detainees from Massachusetts, for example, have found themselves suddenly held in Batavia,

New York, Oakdale, Louisiana, or Texas. Reasons for transfers are almost never given, nor, frequently is prior notice to families or to attorneys, who often learn of such transfers long after the fact. Though ICE generally explains that such transfers are due to lack of local bed space, the system's apparent arbitrariness and lack of transparency have long raised suspicions that it is also used tactically to facilitate deportations.

Some have also alleged that transfers punish those who complain about conditions of detention. An ACLU report cited a group of detainees who had written to the *Boston Globe* alleging that they had been forced to submit to a strip search in front of other detainees.[84] After the story appeared, two of the detainees were quickly transferred, after having spent months in their prior facility without incident. Cellmates of one of the transferred persons said that his bed remained empty for weeks after his departure. A detained person who was picked up by his neck and slammed against the wall by a guard in Boston was transferred to a jail in Vermont where an ICE agent told him that he had been sent there "to cool things off." Another Boston detainee protested her detention because she believed her habeas corpus petition had been granted. She wrote a letter to the sheriff and was soon moved to York, Pennsylvania. She said an ICE agent told her that she was being moved so she would stop speaking out. According to the report, and according to many stories I have personally heard over the years, "troublemakers get transferred." It is of course hard to assess the validity of such complaints. But neither ICE's history of self-investigation nor the system's opacity has inspired great trust or confidence.[85]

While travelling in Guatemala in 2008, I was called to a meeting of distraught women in Chimaltenango. They were the mothers, wives, and girlfriends of men who had been arrested in the Postville raids. Tearfully, one after another, they begged us to help with a simple task: to find the men. We reassured them that, unlike their worst fears based on the history of Guatemala, the men would not be "disappeared" in the U.S. detention system. And yet it was hard to explain to them that we could not easily find out where they were, in whose custody, under what conditions, and with what prospects for release. For many years, one of the most frustrating and frightening aspects of ICE detention has been this inability of family members and lawyers even to learn the exact location of particular detainees. There was no comprehensive, accurate, and current list of all of the facilities in the country where ICE detained people, let alone a way to track a particular person. ICE's system for tracking detainees lacked real-time data about the location of detainees in transit. As one report described, "after an initial arrest, the ICE Boston Field Office has no information for the first few days. Days after a transfer, the . . . computers continue to show that the person is at the facility they have just left, even though that facility's records reflect that the person was picked up by ICE."[86]

Critiques of the deportation detention system have forced some reforms. The government has begun to experiment with a variety of "Alternatives to Detention" programs (ATDs).[87] In fall 2009, ICE implemented a series of other important detention reforms.[88] The agency created the Office of Detention Policy and Planning—as well as an independent Office of Detention Oversight—aiming for greater federal oversight, more specific attention to detainee care, and the design of a better overall civil detention system.[89] Most important, ICE has announced the launch of a public, Internet-based tool designed to assist family members, attorneys, and others in "locating detained aliens in ICE custody."[90] This is potentially a major improvement, the adequacy of which remains to be seen. The system, in short, has been improved during the Obama administration, but major problems remain.

Despite such reform efforts, detention and transfers continue to have real consequences on the outcome of cases. Lack of notice of hearings remains a significant problem. One deportee has described how he had missed the ninety-day window to keep his appeal alive, even as the Supreme Court took up the very same issue, because he did not receive notice of a denied appeal. "They don't give you a chance," he said. "They move you around to try to lose you." Another put it in more graphic terms: "I think I got railroaded," he said by telephone from remote detention, about 150 miles southeast of Naples, Florida. "I'm in hell here."[91] Many detainees, deprived of contact with family, friends, or even their lawyers, simply give in to despair and give up, even though they may have viable defenses. One attorney sharply described the system in 2010 as "a war of attrition."[92]

The Agencies

There has long been a societal consensus that the U.S. immigration system is broken. However, as one policy analyst has noted, this consensus erodes as soon as discussion turns to reform.[93] Still, dating back to its earliest days, immigration agencies have had severe reputation problems, not only due to inefficiency, but also because of brutality and corruption. When Frances Perkins took over immigration enforcement during the Roosevelt administration (even before there was an "INS"), her very first official act was to eliminate "case fixing and terrorization of aliens," one infamous component of which had been the extortion of money from legal immigrants on threat of deportation.[94] In the 1970s and 1980s, a series of critical GAO reports focused continual negative attention on INS.[95] The 1981 Select Commission Report referred to the agency as "beleaguered."[96] Indeed, few, if any, governmental programs have been subject to the sort of sustained criticism that has been leveled against the U.S. immigration and deportation systems. Despite this rather negative consensus, in my personal experience there are many able, intelligent, decent, and compassionate people who toil in these trenches every day. Much of the critique they have faced derives from the impossible tensions of the job. For many years, the former INS was famously torn between its enforcement and its "service" missions. Many years ago, I recall hearing Alan C. Nelson, former INS Commissioner, say, rather amiably, if implausibly: "We are called the Immigration and Naturalization *Service* for a reason. Service is part of our name." Unfortunately, the reputation of INS, to put it mildly, was never primarily one of "service." Part of the reason for this was the agency's mixed mandate—it adjudicated such matters as green card and citizenship applications while at the same time overseeing the growing deportation system. The lines between those functions were often blurry. Similarly, the somewhat separate realm of immigration courts endured significant growing pains as challenges were made to a system in which adjudicators lacked the independence of today's immigration judges and, by and large, they did not command much respect.[97] As one participant in the evolution described his colleagues: "their predecessors labored in an uncertain and unrewarding environment" that problematically combined the function of prosecutor and judge.[98] Justice Robert Jackson, reviewing this system against the backdrop of the Administrative Procedure Act,[99] described the deportation hearing as "a perfect exemplification" of practices that had been "unanimously condemned."[100]

Things have improved since then, but major problems remain. In 1983, the newly created Executive Office for Immigration Review aimed to create greater independence among immigration judges. The importance of this formalization should not be underestimated, as it has led to standard rules of procedure and a sense of professionalism.[101] Still, as one judge wrote more than two decades ago, the system still faces "crushing caseloads," and "an ever-increasing complexity of issues" with insufficient resources.[102]

These agency problems worsened with the passage of the 1986 Immigration Reform and Control Act (IRCA), which simultaneously tasked INS with administering a major legalization program and with ratcheting up enforcement. Many again began to criticize the mixed functions within the agency.[103] In 1989, a highly publicized government audit described the agency as riddled with mismanagement. It cited missing documents, massive backlogs of cases, and failures to conduct background checks on applicants for citizenship. INS officials were unable to find more than twenty-three thousand certificates of citizenship and naturalization that, if stolen, could be sold for as much as $115 million. Huge adjudication backlogs had grown from 325,000 at the beginning of fiscal year 1987 to 408,000 by the end of 1988. INS Commissioner Alan C. Nelson reacted angrily to the report, calling it "an accumulation of a lot of picky stuff." He said it did not represent the overall performance of the agency.[104] In a strenuous effort to keep his job, Nelson later called the audit "totally incorrect and an outrageous misrepresentation of facts."[105] But he was fired soon thereafter.

By 1997, the U.S. Commission on Immigration Reform described INS as an agency "suffering from conflicting priorities and mission overload, whose enforcement and service missions were incompatible."[106] The Commission recommended a complete reorganization of the immigration system and the dismantling of INS.[107]

The end of INS came in the wake of 9/11, with the passage of the Homeland Security Act of 2002, which nested deportation within the newly created Department of Homeland Security (DHS).[108] Beyond the strongly increased emphasis on national security that justified this move, some also thought that bifurcating the enforcement mandate from "services" (i.e., adjudications of applications for status, naturalization, and the like) would result in greater efficiency.[109] However, in 2004, the U.S. Government Accountability Office reported that many of the problems that had bedeviled the former INS continued in DHS.[110] A 2004 report by the Heritage Foundation offered a biting and gloomy assessment: "in consolidating responsibility for border, immigration, and transportation security, DHS actually increased the number of involved agencies to eight and created additional problems that now need solving."[111] In March 2005, Representative Christopher Cox, then Chairman of the House Committee on Homeland Security, confirmed that questions remained about "whether DHS has organized itself and is managing its immigration enforcement and border security resources in the most efficient, sensible, and effective manner."[112]

Formal adjudications (immigration courts), which remain within the Department of Justice, have also continued to face withering critique. The American Bar Association Immigration Commission, of which I was a member, undertook a comprehensive analysis of deportation adjudications in 2009–2010.[113] The Commission's mandate was to approach the project without preconceived notions or conclusions and to seek information and views from all sources and sides.[114] On the whole, the study concluded, government policies and procedures had failed to ensure due process for noncitizens and had decreased "confidence and trust in the adjudication system."[115] Among the study's specific findings were that DHS policies and procedures had contributed to "an exploding caseload that has overwhelmed the removal adjudication system." Immigration courts simply had too few immigration judges and support staff for the workload.[116] Moreover, there were significant disparities in the rates at which immigration judges granted favorable decisions, even among judges on the same court and for cases involving nationals from the same country.[117] These problems were compounded by the fact that more than half of the noncitizens in removal proceedings, and 84 percent of the detained ones, lacked legal representation. This substantially affected the prospects of fair adjudication and called into question the fairness of "a convoluted and complicated process . . . ."[118]

Overzealousness by Government Prosecutors

The ideals of fair adjudication are not only the responsibility of judges. One of the most frequent complaints raised by those who represent noncitizens is the overzealousness and tunnel vision exhibited by many government prosecutors. Such complaints are to some degree to be expected, given the adversarial system, the high stakes in deportation cases, and the potential harshness of the law. But in recent years, an increasing number of judges have also been struck by this phenomenon. Consider the case of Jinyu Kang, an ethnic Korean citizen of China who fled a Chinese arrest warrant for giving food and shelter to Korean refugees. Others named in the same warrant and caught by the Chinese police had described beatings, suffocation, electric shocks, sleep deprivation, and other forms of torture to get them to disclose details about the human rights group to which they all belonged.[119] Ms. Kang was still ordered deported. An immigration judge had granted her protection under the Convention against Torture. But the government's lawyers appealed, and the BIA overturned the judge's decision. After reviewing the case, however, the Court of Appeals for the Third Circuit reversed the deportation order, going on to state that it was "disappointing, even shocking" that the government had failed to acknowledge that the evidence was not only strongly in Ms. Kang's favor, but, indeed, also compelled the conclusion that she would likely be tortured. Calling the government's position "inexplicable," the judges said that both the BIA and the government lawyers had ignored overwhelming evidence.[120]

The United States Court of Appeals for the Fourth Circuit highlighted a government mix-up in which a Chinese father who had provided detailed evidence to support his account of his wife's forced abortion and the threat of sterilization had been denied asylum based on vague material from someone else's file. Even after the mistake was revealed, the government argued that the decision should be upheld anyway.[121]

As Judge Marjorie O. Rendell wrote in the *Kang* case, the adversarial system may permit such advocacy by private parties. But "when the United States appears before us, it is duty-bound to 'cut square corners' and seek justice rather than victory." Such critique, though harsh, highlights the critical importance of judicial oversight over immigration deportation decisions and, more specifically, the need for effective supervision over the Office of Immigration Litigation.[122]

We will consider in later chapters, however, how many deportees have already suffered the consequences of such overzealous government advocacy.

Mistakes

Men feared witches and burnt women.[123]

At 5:00 a.m. on a spring morning on Long Island, a 12-year-old girl was suddenly awakened by loud banging on the front door and the shouts of strangers inside her family's home. The girl, Erica Leon, later said she thought the house was on fire. But suddenly, her bedroom door burst open and armed men in blue bullet-proof vests pushed in, demanding to know if she was hiding someone. They rushed to the next room where her 4-year-old brother was asleep with their mother, pulling off the covers as they shouted and demanded information. Only later did the family learn that these were federal immigration agents hunting for Erica's long-gone father, who was ordered deported four years earlier after divorcing Erica's mother. The household into which the deportation agents had stormed contained only innocent American citizens.[124]

The U.S. deportation system—like any large, complex administrative system—inevitably makes mistakes. The reasons include the complexity of the law, overzealous agents and prosecutors, lack of appointed counsel (and, sadly, often ineffective retained counsel), detentions, transfers, and inadequate judicial resources. To assess such mistakes, we might usefully divide them into two broad categories, which I will call—with apologies for oversimplification—*bureaucratic* and *forensic*. The former are the type of mistakes made by those who do the day-to-day work of the agencies that implement immigration and deportation law. Some minor mistakes are unlikely to have serious consequences and may be fairly easily remedied if they come to light. Common examples of relatively minor *bureaucratic* mistakes include inadvertent discrepancies of names and the misfiling of documents. Others, such as incorrectly targeted home raids, sending notices to incorrect addresses, and the like, are potentially much more serious. Indeed, there are specific regulations and an extensive body of administrative and judicial precedent dealing with the problem of so-called *in absentia* deportations that may result from improper notice of a hearing.[125]

Forensic mistakes are, however, inherently more serious because they involve incorrect decisions undertaken by those who have been given legal authority to act decisively in the public sphere. By forensic, I mean to invoke the word's original etymology from the Latin *forensis* (public) and *forum*.[126] Common mistakes of the forensic type include misunderstandings of legal status in expedited removal or formal deportation proceedings, factual errors about a non-citizen's personal history or criminal record, and incorrect interpretations of law by government lawyers or immigration judges. They may also include enforcement errors, such as illegal arrests, and procedural errors, such as failure to properly advise deportees of their rights. Finally, the forensic category includes an array of more subtle but highly important errors relating to the exercise of discretion at various levels of the deportation system.

It is impossible to assess with precision how often mistakes of either type are made. And yet what we do know is troubling. To evaluate the seriousness of the mistake problem in the U.S. deportation system, we must consider not only the number of mistakes, as best we can determine it, but also *how* and *why* mistakes have been made, *by whom*, and *with what consequences*. The last point is especially important in light of the fact that post-departure motions to reopen—which are often the only means by which a deportee might challenge a mistake—remain frequently unavailable.

Let us start with the most egregious possible error: the deportation of a U.S. citizen. Deportation law, by its very nature, technically only applies to "aliens"— i.e., people who are not citizens or nationals of the United States.[127] Put simply, U.S. citizens may not be arrested or detained by DHS and certainly may not be deported. In an early formulation of this basic premise, proof of "alienage" was called "a jurisdictional fact."[128] Indeed, it was in a case enunciating this principle that Justice Brandeis wrote that deportation may result "in loss of both property and life; or of all that makes life worth living."[129]

Still, wrongful deportations of U.S. citizens have occurred with distressing frequency.[130] As we have seen, the Florence Immigration and Refugee Rights Project, encountered some forty to fifty detainees *per month* who presented what they deemed potentially valid claims to U.S. citizenship.[131] The government response to such cases has frequently been one of denial. Gary Mead, ICE Deputy Director for Detention and Removal, testified at a 2008 congressional hearing that cases such as that of Pedro Guzman, the cognitively disabled citizen described in Chapter 1, are unique. Mead stated that ICE officers are "ever mindful of their sworn duty to protect the rights of all individuals to the best of their abilities." He asserted that ICE officers interview hundreds of thousands of individuals annually to determine citizenship and immigration status "with the utmost professionalism and respect for individual rights."[132] But California Democratic Congresswoman Zoe Lofgren has called Guzman the "poster child" for an epidemic of detention and deportation of U.S. citizens. Kara Hartzler, from the Florence Project, testified that deportation of U.S. citizens was not happening "monthly, or weekly, but every day." Jacqueline Stevens, a political scientist, called fifteen private immigration attorneys whose names appeared on a Justice Department list of pro bono attorneys in Los Angeles and asked whether they had clients in the past three years who were U.S. citizens held in ICE detention for at least one month. Seven of them called her back, each describing one to four clients who met these criteria. Using these accounts, and those from attorneys at nonprofit immigration clinics, Stevens has documented more than 160 cases from across the country of U.S. citizens who have already been found through legal processes to have been wrongly detained or deported.[133] ICE has not kept records on such case, and numbers are difficult to verify. However, Stevens estimates that 1 percent of detained noncitizens have been eventually found to be U.S. citizens through the immigration adjudication process (after having been wrongly arrested and detained) and that another .05 percent were physically removed from the United States.[134] If these astonishing estimates are right, then ICE, since 2003, may have held some twenty thousand U.S. citizens in detention facilities and deported thousands.[135]

How can we explain such apparently bizarre phenomena? We should note at the outset that the error rate is comparable to that found in the criminal justice system, estimated at 1 to 2 percent.[136] But that is a system with appointed counsel and juries. Partly, the mistaken deportations of citizens illustrate legitimate problems of proof and of the complexity of immigration and citizenship laws. The Fourteenth Amendment guarantees that "all persons born . . . in the United States . . . are citizens of the United States." But the United States has no national birth certificate system and no central registry of native-born citizens. Thus, many U.S. citizens may have difficulty proving their citizenship unless they can retrieve a birth certificate issued by the state in which they were born. In 2006, the NYU Brennan Center concluded that as many as 13 million U.S. citizens may not have ready access to documents establishing their citizenship.[137] Moreover, the Immigration and Nationality Act confers citizenship at birth to those born in Puerto Rico, the U.S. Virgin Islands, and Guam, and to some people born in the Republic of Panama and the Canal Zone. In all such cases, similar problems of proof may arise.[138] Other citizenship laws are even more complicated. A person born abroad to a U.S. citizen parent may or may not be a U.S. citizen, depending upon a dizzying array of factors. Some adopted children may gain citizenship automatically; others do not. Stevens tells an illustrative, if Dickensian, tale of "Robert," who was born in Mexico in 1970, orphaned at age 4, adopted at age 8 by a U.S. citizen uncle, granted legal permanent resident status at age 13, at which point he seems to have automatically acquired U.S. citizenship by law. Unfortunately, though, due to a combination of immigration agency stubbornness and perhaps bad lawyering, Robert found himself not only deported but also convicted and incarcerated for three years for falsely impersonating a U.S. citizen before finally being informed by a government agent: "Congratulations! You've been a U.S. citizen since 1983."[139]

But complexity alone does not excuse many of these mistakes. Another U.S. citizen deportee, Diane Williams, who was born in Louisiana, said that she was given a Final Administrative Removal Order and told to sign it: "They didn't read nothing to me. They just told me to sign." Threatened with years of jail time to be followed by deportation, her reason for signing was simple: "I was scared."[140]

The tale of Mark Lyttle is particularly disturbing.[141] Lyttle, a U.S. citizen born in Salisbury, North Carolina, was deported in December 2008. According to his mother, an occupational therapy assistant who raised Mark and his three special needs siblings after adopting them, Mark was supposed to have been released from criminal custody after serving most of a one hundred-day sentence for a misdemeanor. Instead, a woman from ICE told him that his real name was Jose Thomas, that he was Mexican, and that he was going to be sent to Mexico. Mark said,

> *The prison gave me my release papers and the next thing I know, I'm in a white minivan and they drive me all the way to Raleigh. Then after that they fly me [to a detention center] and I stayed there for a month. They were calling me Jose Thomas. They were trying to say that's my real name. I told them my name is Mark Daniel Lyttle, I was born in North Carolina. . . . My mother's Jeanne Lyttle, here's my social security number, my brother's in the army, please call someone!*

He told this to several ICE agents and then to Immigration Judge William Cassidy, who nevertheless ordered him removed. He repeated it to the U.S. Border Patrol in Texas after he was forcibly sent to Mexico. "No one checked," he said, "No one believed me."

At all levels of the system, government agents have explanations for why such things can happen, amid the mass volume and frequent chaos of deportation proceedings. But Mark's mother asks simple, poignant questions that demand answers: "Why didn't they look up his fingerprints, his social security number, why didn't they follow through on anything?" Indeed, Mark's case also illustrates why procedural protections are often ineffective in the context of detention and deportation. Mark could have appealed the judge's order to the Board of Immigration Appeals and then to federal court. Why didn't he do so? He said, "I was going to appeal until I found out that it would be six months to two years before I'd have a chance, and even if I did that, they still wouldn't believe me."

After his deportation, Mark, who does not speak Spanish, reportedly headed south, wandering around Mexico, penniless and without food for two weeks until missionaries gave him shelter and fed him. Some two months later, Mark encountered Mexican police who confiscated the only identity document he had, his deportation order, and put him on a bus to Honduras. When he couldn't produce a passport for the border guards in Honduras, they drove him to San Pedro and left him in a jail "with robbers and killers." After more than a month in the Honduran jail, Honduran immigration officials sent Mark to Guatemala, where he finally found the U.S. embassy. When officials there spoke with his brother, they were convinced he was a U.S. citizen. The embassy staff bought him a hamburger at the McDonald's across the street. Finally, he was returned to the United States. His mother, Jeanne, an immigrant from Ireland, said that she loves this country so much that she cries every time she hears *The Star Spangled Banner*. And yet, the story of her son's illegal deportation "tears my heart to pieces." She asks, "How many others are out there we don't know about who are stuck places?"[142] Only ICE can possibly know; and, as Jacqueline Stevens notes, the system is marked by the absence of both accountability and transparency.[143]

Deporting the Disabled

Noncitizens with mental disabilities[144] have long suffered some of the most tragic consequences in the U.S. deportation system. Deportation courts must regularly deal with "a hidden population of immigrants who are particularly vulnerable": individuals with mental disabilities ranging from trauma as a result of persecution to depression caused by detention, and from intellectual deficits to profound mental illness.[145] Although the system contains some vague procedural protections, courts have even permitted institutionalized, mentally disabled noncitizens to be deported. As one court rather coldly put it, the Immigration and Naturalization Act "contemplates that deportation proceedings may be had against mental incompetents."[146] The numbers are far from trivial. In 2008, DHS estimated that as many as 18,929 immigration detainees suffered from "serious mental illness." Others have estimated much higher numbers—as high as fifty-seven thousand detainees in 2008.[147]

Meaningful safeguards are lacking for people with mental disabilities facing possible deportation from the United States. Major recognized problems include no right to appointed counsel; inflexible detention policies; lack of substantive or operative guidance for attorneys and judges; and inadequately coordinated care and social services to aid detainees while in custody and upon release.[148] Immigration courts have no clear standards for fair hearings for people with mental disabilities, other than a general mandate that the U.S. Attorney General must provide "safeguards" for individuals who cannot participate in proceedings by reason of their "mental incompetency."[149] The problems are shocking and severe. According to one report, some deportees did not understand what the judge asked them in court (one individual did not even know what a judge was). Others were delusional or experienced hallucinations or could not read or write, tell time, name their birthplace, or say what day it was. Still others apparently did not understand the concept of deportation at all, tragically asking to be deported to New York or to Louisiana.[150] Particularly in asylum cases, the problems can be overwhelming. As one psychologist put it, "How does a person with paranoid schizophrenia explain a credible fear of returning when they also are having de-lusional or irrational thoughts?"[151] Immigration judges have described them-selves as "overwhelmed" and the cases as "truly emotionally exhausting."[152] As one judge noted, "there is not enough guidance out there on what to do."[153] The Executive Office for Immigration Review (EOIR) has recently added a short section on mental incompetence to its *Immigration Judge Benchbook*, suggesting certain "best practices," including that judges use direct, simple sentences, build a very good record, and consider appropriate and necessary actions such as attempting to recruit representation or granting necessary continuances to secure representation, though the judges are reminded of the importance of de-ciding detainee cases expeditiously. Although the *Benchbook* suggests that termi-nation of a case might be appropriate, it notes that the BIA "has not upheld a case that terminated proceedings based on a theory that the respondent was so incompetent as to render the proceedings unfair."[154] Further, researchers have found that in many cases, the ICE attorney prosecuting the case did not inform the judge when a noncitizen facing deportation had a diagnosed or suspected mental disability—even when one had been previously adjudged by a criminal court. In other cases, ICE attorneys refused or neglected to perform competency evaluations and to supply information from evaluations to the court—even when the court ordered them to do so.[155]

Put simply, our deportation system "fails—and further marginalizes—this vulnerable population."[156] The labyrinthian system that we have permitted to flourish permits unnecessary detentions, arbitrary transfers away from family and medical support communities, insufficient mental health care, disorga-nized medical records systems, denials of basic protections, and, ultimately, removal from the United States of individuals "with little concern for their safety and well-being."[157] A *New York Times* story described the plight of an unrepresented, mentally ill Chinese deportee in a court where the "fundamen-tal fairness" owed to deportees by law seemed to be tragically lacking. The judge asked the woman's name twice, and she answered twice, "Xiu Ping Jiang." But the judge became frustrated because she had answered his question before the court interpreter had translated it into Mandarin. The woman had already been in detention for a year and, according to her family, her mental condition had deteriorated. Her sister worried that she would commit suicide while in detention and that she had been too ill even to recognize her. The immigration judge pressed on: "Ma'am, we're going to do this one more time, and then I'm going to treat you as though you were not here." The judge threat-ened to issue an order of deportation that would say she had failed to show up. The woman, a waitress with no criminal record, no lawyer, and a history of attempted suicide, replied, "Sir, I not—cannot go home" to China. Her family said she had fled in 1995 after being forcibly sterilized at age 20. She told the judge, "If I die, I die America." The judge responded. "The respondent, after proper notice, has failed to appear." The woman said, "I'm going to die now," as an order deporting her to China was entered into the record and she was sent back to immigration detention.[158] Luckily, Ms. Jiang later received excellent pro bono legal representation and was ultimately granted asylum.[159] Still, in response to the reporting of this story, a spokeswoman for EOIR offered a tragic assessment of the state of the law: there are no rules for determining competency in deportation proceedings and thus no way to ensure representation for a mentally ill person facing deportation. As there is no right to appointed counsel, even those already declared incompetent often must proceed without counsel and alone.[160]

Detentions and transfers are especially severe problems.[161] As one lawyer put it, "more and more people with mental illness are being put into the detention system. And sometimes these people disappear."[162] Consider the case of a 50-year-old legal permanent resident with schizophrenia who had lived in New York City since 1974. In November 2009, a New York criminal court had declared him incompetent to stand trial on a trespassing charge and sentenced him to serve ninety days in a mental institution. But he was summarily transferred to a detention center in South Texas, where he faced a deportation proceeding without counsel. All of this happened so quickly and so secretly that even his family and lawyer did not know about it until after it was completed. After receiving no medication for weeks, he was deported to the Dominican Republic. His mother, described as "devastated," said "he will die out there on the streets." As his sister, a U.S. citizen, plaintively asked, "If we have a law system and the law system has declared that you are incompetent and should be taken to a mental hospital, why are you taken to Texas to be deported?" Even those who are released from detention can face life-threatening problems due to inadequate supervision. The Post-Deportation Human Rights Project that I direct became aware of a mentally disabled refugee from Southeast Asia who was wrongly taken into custody in Providence, Rhode Island, sent to Texas, then abruptly released without notice at a rural gas station at 11:00 p.m.

Problems with Expedited Removal

As we have seen, expedited removal was designed primarily to allow the government a free hand to deal with "noncitizens who indisputably have no authorization to be admitted to the United States."[163] When it was first implemented in 1997, the Department of Justice (DOJ) said removal would only be applied to "arriving aliens" at ports of entry. Even there it raised serious concerns, especially for refugees and asylum seekers.[164] A major report by the bipartisan United

States Commission of International Religious Freedom[165] found a pattern of worrisome conduct, including the failure to ask questions designed to elicit information about possible claims for asylum; the expeditious removal of people who had a "credible fear of persecution"; and numerous factual and legal errors. Indeed, two experts estimated that in its first decade of use, the expedited removal process wrongly denied entry to some twenty thousand genuine asylum seekers.[166]

DOJ recognized that applying expedited removal to noncitizens already present in the United States would involve more complex determinations of fact and would be more difficult to manage.[167] However, DHS has incrementally expanded expedited removal to include noncitizens who have arrived "by sea" without being admitted or paroled and also to include noncitizens caught within one hundred air miles of the U.S. border, who are present in the United States without being admitted or paroled and who cannot prove to the satisfaction of an immigration officer that they have been physically present in the United States continuously for the fourteen-day period immediately preceding the date of apprehension. When a noncitizen is arrested in this vast swath of the United States, the officer will try to determine whether he or she has a legal right to be in the country. The individual has the burden of proof.[168]

The system is growing exponentially. The number of expedited removal orders increased by approximately 122.4 percent between fiscal year 2004 and fiscal year 2008.[169] Some courts are beginning to recognize problems with this fast-track system, but many cases appear to be more in the mode of hand-wringing than intervention. As the Seventh Circuit Court of Appeals worried about the airport version of expedited removal:

> The troubling reality of the expedited removal procedure is that [an] officer can create the . . . charge by deciding to convert the person's status from a non-immigrant with valid papers to an intending immigrant without the proper papers, and then that same officer, free from the risk of judicial oversight, can confirm his or her suspicions of the person's intentions and find the person guilty of that charge.[170]

The procedures are almost completely opaque, discretionary, and insulated. As the court continued:

> The entire process—from the initial decision to convert the person's status to removal—can happen without any check on whether the person understood the proceedings, had an interpreter, or enjoyed any other safeguards.[171]

The court recognized that this procedure is "fraught with risk of arbitrary, mistaken, or discriminatory behavior" (imagine that a particular rogue officer decides that enough visitors from Africa have already entered the United States). Nevertheless, due to jurisdictional limitations, the court could not even consider whether the expedited removal procedure had been properly invoked.[172]

Problems with "Force Multipliers"

In response to the increasing use of such "force multipliers" as § 287(g) agreements and Secure Communities, immigrants rights groups have long voiced concerns about allegations of racial profiling, inadequate supervision and oversight, harsh collateral effects on families and communities, and more.[173] Such concerns were validated in March 2010 when the Office of the Inspector General (OIG) conducted a review of the § 287(g) program.[174] The OIG report noted major problems, including instances in which ICE and participating law enforcement agencies "were not operating in compliance with the terms of the agreements," failed to focus on serious criminals, and failed to adequately protect civil rights and civil liberties. The Report stated that ICE needed to thoroughly revise the program.[175] ICE was clearly stung by the highly critical report and stated that it had already fundamentally reformed the § 287(g) program, "strengthening public safety and ensuring consistency in immigration enforcement across the country by prioritizing the arrest and detention of criminal aliens." However, many concerns still remain, particularly over the management of the program, its oversight of state and local actors, and its focus on low-level offenders.[176]

Similar concerns have emerged about the Secure Communities Program. It has become increasingly clear that Secure Communities has led to deportations of very minor offenders. In Boston, for example, an 18-year-old Brazilian woman named Lizandra DeMoura was arrested for traffic violations and driving without a license. She was then held in jail overnight, taken to court in the morning, and turned over to immigration agents who "hauled her away in chains" for deportation to Brazil.[177] DeMoura, who has spent most of her life in the United States, echoed the experience of many deportees: "I feel like an animal."[178]

Supporters of force multiplier programs focus on serious criminals, such as a violent Jamaican gang member who was deported from Boston in 2009 and an undocumented Guatemalan man who committed a rape in 2008. But problems with Secure Communities may derive from overly broad legal deportation categories. The category of "level 1" offenders, at whom the Secure Communities program is primarily aimed, includes noncitizens convicted of "aggravated felonies" or two or more crimes each punishable by more than one year. But, as we have seen, the aggravated felony category may include many relatively minor offenses, such as simple assault and drug possession offenses. As Lizandra DeMoura's lawyer, a former immigration judge put it: "The problem is they don't seem to be getting the right people."[179]

Deportation, as it has expanded, can be tempting even for private entities. In a particularly troubling phenomenon, U.S. hospitals have in effect deported noncitizen patients who were ineligible for long-term care under Medicaid. Luis Alberto Jiménez, an undocumented noncitizen, was severely injured while working as a gardener in Stuart, Florida. He suffered devastating injuries, including a severe traumatic brain injury, in a car crash with "a drunken Floridian." After being treated at a community hospital, Mr. Jiménez was involuntarily sent back to Guatemala.[180] He received no medical care or medication—"just Alka-Seltzer and prayer" as he lived, isolated in a wheelchair, cared for by his elderly mother. His condition, according to a reporter, has deteriorated, with routine violent seizures, falls, convulsions, a loud gurgling, the vomiting of blood, and, finally, a collapse into unconsciousness.[181] Nevertheless, in 2009, a Florida jury concluded that the hospital did not act unreasonably when it chartered a plane and repatriated the severely brain-injured patient against the will of his guardian.[182] His lawyer was "stunned," and the president of the hospital, though gratified by the verdict, noted that "our political leadership" had failed to address the challenges facing hospitals that provide uncompensated health care to undocumented noncitizens.[183]

Two years later, however, a young man from Mexico faced the same fate. Quelino Ojeda Jiménez, an undocumented worker, fell from a roof and lost the ability to speak, breathe, or move most parts of his body. Just before Christmas, he was taken from the hospital, loaded onto an air ambulance, and flown to Oaxaca, Mexico.[184] "They threw him out like he was a piece of garbage," said a disability rights advocate. The 20-year-old man was sent to a Mexican hospital that was reportedly so resource-poor that it had to reuse filters for the breathing machine needed to keep the quadriplegic alive. The U.S. hospital where Jiménez had been treated, named "Advocate Christ," said it regretted the way this process flowed and the "steps that were taken." The hospital said it had spent about $650,000 on Ojeda's medical care and another $60,000 to transport him to Mexico after several private long-term care facilities had refused to take him as a patient. The hospital said it had "saved his life and brought him to a stable condition." But when it became clear that he would need lifetime care, the hospital frantically searched for options, found none in the United States, and then sent Mr. Jiménez to Mexico.[185]

"Doubly Wary": The Supreme Court Corrects Deportation Law

As we have seen, the harshness and rigidity of the 1996 changes to deportation law have long been seen as problematic by courts, lawyers, scholars, activists, and even some of the legislators who enacted them. After a few years, the

Supreme Court began to take challenges to the regime seriously. In the 2001 case of *INS v. St. Cyr*,[186] the Court rejected apparent jurisdictional limitations and held that certain discretionary waivers of deportation (so-called § 212(c) waivers) remained available to noncitizens.[187] Later, the Court set limits on the length of time a person could be detained following a deportation order when deportation was physically accomplished by the government.[188]

It took longer for the Court to consider the overzealousness of government deportation lawyers as to the relationship between certain types of criminal offenses and the most severe category of deportation: the so-called "aggravated felony." Eventually, however, more than a decade after the 1996 laws had substantially hardened the deportation regime, the Supreme Court decided a series of cases involving drunk driving and drug possession. These cases revealed not only the tortuous complexities of *post-entry social control* deportation but also important questions about how deportation laws ought to be interpreted. They now also prompt the question whether thousands of wrongly deported people should have the right to return.

The first such case involved a Haitian immigrant named Josue Leocal who had entered the United States from Haiti in August 1980 at the age of 24. He married a U.S. citizen and had four children, all of whom were U.S. citizens. In December 1987, Mr. Leocal became a lawful permanent resident and had applied for naturalization in March 1997.[189]

On January 7, 2000, Mr. Leocal was arrested following a car accident in which two individuals were injured. He pled guilty to two counts of driving under the influence of alcohol (DUI) and causing serious bodily injury.[190] A few months later, Mr. Leocal was charged as being removable for having committed an aggravated felony.[191] INS had deemed his DUI to be a "crime of violence," a major sub-category within the aggravated felony definition. On October 16, 2001, an immigration judge ordered Mr. Leocal to be deported to Haiti.[192]

In November 2002, while his appeal was pending, INS removed Mr. Leocal to Haiti without notice to his legal counsel of record.[193] Two years later, however, in an opinion for a unanimous Court, written by then Chief Justice William Rehnquist, the Court held that the Mr. Leocal's DUI conviction had not been a valid basis for deportation because his conviction was not a "crime of violence."

It is easy to miss the legal significance of this in the esoterica and technicalities of a legal case. But the point could not be clearer: *the government was not just a little bit wrong; in the eyes of the Supreme Court this was not even a close question.*[194] Mr. Leocal eventually was able to return to the United States and be reunited with his family.[195] But what about all the people who were deported pursuant to the government's now rejected legal theory? As we have seen, the numbers are not trivial. As early as 1998, the *Los Angeles Times* noted that more than five hundred immigrants, most of them legal permanent U.S. residents, had been rounded up for deportation in the lustily named "Operation Last Call."[196] Following Mr. Leocal's victory, the *New York Times* noted that "there was no estimate . . . of the number of people who might be affected," but more than seventy-nine thousand immigrants had been deported in the previous year as "criminal aliens," more than eight thousand of whom were legal permanent residents.[197] No formal mechanism exists to process their possible claims to return.

A similar situation faced those deported due to drug possession. Jose Antonio Lopez first came to the United States in 1985, to San Diego, California, from Mexico. He worked on farms growing tomatoes, grapes, and grapefruit. In 1990 he gained lawful permanent residence.[198] In 1994, he married Maria Delaluz with whom he had two children, both citizens of the United States. Lopez eventually opened two businesses: a taco stand in Sioux Falls, South Dakota, and then a grocery store.[199]

However, in 1997 he was arrested, and he admitted telling another person where to find drugs. Ultimately, he pled guilty to aiding and abetting possession of cocaine, though he maintained that he had never possessed cocaine himself. Under federal law, a first offense for cocaine possession is a misdemeanor.[200] Under South Dakota law, however, possession of cocaine is a felony, punishable by up to five years in prison.[201] Moreover, South Dakota law treats "aiders and abettors" the same as principals.

Lopez was sentenced to five years' imprisonment, but was released after fifteen months. Indeed, he was granted a rare early release from parole for good behavior, which his parole officer stated is "something that does not happen often in South Dakota." His parole officer described him as "one of the best parolees [he had] ever had."

Still, INS instituted removal proceedings against Lopez, alleging that his aiding and abetting conviction was a drug crime and also an aggravated felony.[202] Lopez conceded that his conviction was a controlled substance violation and that he was subject to deportation, but he denied the aggravated felony charge. The difference was significant. A person facing deportation for a controlled substance violation may apply to the immigration judge for discretionary "cancellation of removal."[203] An aggravated felon is barred from all such discretionary relief. The immigration judge granted Lopez's application. While his case was pending, however, the BIA changed its long-standing position on whether state law felony drug convictions are aggravated felonies. The immigration judge *then* held that Lopez's single conviction was an aggravated felony, denied his application for cancellation of removal, and ordered him deported.[204]

The Supreme Court took the case on April 3, 2006. As in *Leocal*, the decision was not a close one. The Court held, rather simply, that an "aggravated felony" must be a felony under federal law, regardless of how state law classifies it.[205] As

Justice Souter said: "There are a few things wrong with [the government's] argument, the first being its *incoherence with any commonsense conception of 'illicit trafficking,' the term ultimately being defined.*"[206] Reading the statute the government's
way, said the Court, "would often turn simple possession into trafficking, just
what the English language tells us not to expect, and that result makes us very
wary of the Government's position." The decision against the government was 8
to 1, with only Justice Clarence Thomas dissenting.

The final case is perhaps the most compelling as it raises fundamental issues
of proportionality. Jose Angel Carachuri-Rosendo had lived legally in the
United States since he entered the country in 1993 at the age of 5. He was convicted of two misdemeanors: marijuana possession and a single tablet of Xanax
without a prescription. This added up to an "aggravated felony" in the opinion
of DHS and the lower court. Carachuri, said the prosecutors, had committed a
"drug trafficking crime."[207] Of course, he had not actually trafficked any drugs.
No matter, argued the government. Their logic was seemingly precise: the term
"drug trafficking" technically includes "any felony *punishable* under the Controlled Substances Act [CSA]."[208] Under the CSA, in turn, a second federal
misdemeanor possession offense may be punished as a felony under certain circumstances.[209] Carachuri had two misdemeanor possessions therefore, they
concluded, his second conviction was an aggravated felony. But wait, his lawyers
replied, Carachuri had no federal convictions at all! He had only been convicted
of *state* misdemeanors in Texas. No matter. The federal government's rejoinder
was that Carachuri's second state conviction *could have been* punished as a
felony under the CSA *if* he had he been prosecuted in federal court. Therefore,
they concluded, he had committed a "drug trafficking crime."[210] In 2006, he was
thus deported to Mexico as an aggravated felon for two minor state misdemeanor drug offenses. (As we have seen, he was far from the only person
deported in this way.)

During the oral argument of his case before the Supreme Court, the Justices
were naturally struck by the harshness of the government's position. "Here we
are talking about two crimes," said Justice Ginsburg, "One is a small amount of
marijuana. He gets 20 days in jail. The other is a pill that I never heard of, a Xan-
something, and he gets what, 10 days in jail for that." Describing the result sought
by the government as "absurd," she sought to apply a bit of common sense:

> If you could just present this scenario to an intelligent person who
> didn't go to law school, that you are not only going to remove him from
> this country, but say, "Never, ever darken our doors again" because of
> one marijuana cigarette and one Xan-something pill—it, it just seems
> to me that if there is a way of reading the statute that would not lead to
> that absurd result, you would want to read the statute. . . .

But U.S. Attorney Nicole A. Saharsky gave no ground: "What controls is Congress' judgment," she asserted. "And Congress has taken a hard line over the past 20 years on criminal aliens, particularly recidivist criminal aliens."

The Court again disagreed. This time it was a unanimous decision written by Justice Stevens.[211] As it had done in the *Lopez* case, the Court, in effect, reprimanded the government lawyers and mandated a "commonsense conception" of statutory terms.[212] Trafficking, the Court reasoned, means some sort of commercial dealing. And "[c]ommerce . . . was no part of" possessing a single tablet of Xanax. A felony, said the Court, is a serious crime that is usually punishable by imprisonment for more than one year or by death. An aggravated offense is one that is made worse by such aspects as violence, the presence of a deadly weapon, or the intent to commit another crime. Here, there had only been a ten-day sentence for the unauthorized possession of a trivial amount of a prescription drug. The government was arguing for a result that "the English language tells us not to expect." Thus, in a stinging rebuke, the Court was "very wary of the Government's position."[213] In fact, in a formulation that, to the best of my knowledge has never been used before by the Supreme Court, the Justices said they were *"doubly wary."*[214]

Post-departure Motions to Reopen: Is There a Way Home?

The *Leocal, Lopez,* and *Carachuri* cases were extremely important for the individuals involved and for future potential deportees. They were also an important check on an overly zealous and legally dubious prosecution strategies. But what about all the others who had been deported in the years before the Supreme Court clarified the law? For most noncitizens, for most practical purposes, deportation is the end point of the U.S. legal system. Indeed, post-departure legal impediments are as great for the long-term legal resident with U.S. citizen family as for the undocumented worker caught near the border immediately after entering illegally. The reasons are a mix of history and legal doctrine. In the modern deportation system, since the early twentieth century, departure from the United States had long barred judicial review. Once a person was gone—either forcibly deported or voluntarily departed during proceedings—the possibility of *both* administrative and judicial review ended. Under that system, there was an obvious concern that a wrongful deportation could never be remedied. Therefore, to protect the rights of deportees, an automatic "stay of deportation" took effect upon the filing of a direct appeal to the Board of Immigration Appeals, or after that to the federal courts. This meant that so long as such a direct appeal was pending, the deportee could remain in the United States.

There was also a well-developed, discretionary system of intermediary motions to "reopen" or to "reconsider" to which the deportation agencies had to respond. These motions could redress factual or legal mistakes and could also safeguard against unusually unjust outcomes. The basic idea of such motions was to give noncitizens "a means to provide new information relevant to their cases to the immigration authorities."[215] Used as early as 1916,[216] they have been governed by detailed regulations for more than half a century.[217] They have always been somewhat controversial—straddling the lines between efficiency and justice; between law and discretion; and between finality and potentially unlimited review.[218] As the BIA once put it, a motion to reopen is "a disfavored process that imposes a heavy burden on the moving party to show that reopening is warranted."[219] The Board highlights finality and predictability as important legal principles, while supporting the "strong public interest in bringing litigation to a close as promptly as is consistent with the interest in giving the adversaries a fair opportunity to develop and present their respective cases."[220]

The relationship between territorial presence and such motions has long been problematic. A "departure bar" was first imposed in 1952 by a regulation that barred motions filed by "a person who is the subject of deportation proceedings subsequent to his departure from the United States." Any departure from the United States (voluntary or compelled) would constitute an automatic withdrawal of such motion.[221] The BIA has long construed the departure bar rule as a rather absolute, jurisdictional limitation.[222]

But the backdrop against which the departure bar operates has changed considerably over the years. As noted, the law prohibited courts from reviewing deportation orders if the deportee had departed from the United States after issuance of the administrative order.[223] The harshness of this system was mitigated by "stays of deportation." Essentially, people could litigate their cases fully before being physically removed.[224] In 1990, however, Congress expressed a renewed concern about alleged abuses of motions to reopen (and automatic stays of deportation) to delay deportations.[225] The Attorney General was directed to conduct a study of such motions and to place limits on the time limits for, and the permissible number of, motions. Surprisingly, the 1991 Attorney General's report found that there was in fact no abuse of motions to reopen.[226] Still, the Department of Justice set a number limit (one) and a time limit (ninety days) on most such motions.[227]

Then, in 1996, along with other changes to deportation law, motions to reopen were transformed from a (subsidiary) regulatory device into a statutory form.[228] The statute now clearly states that an "alien may file one motion to reopen proceedings under this section."[229] One might assume from this language that even a deported noncitizen would be allowed to file one motion. However, many federal statutes are implemented by regulations.[230] And therein lies the rub. Despite the 1996 statutory language allowing one motion, the regulations—essentially the same as the prior ones—state that a motion to reopen or a motion to reconsider "shall not be made by or on behalf of a person who is the subject of exclusion, deportation, or removal proceedings subsequent to his or her departure from the United States." Any departure occurring after the filing of a motion "shall constitute a withdrawal of such motion."[231] Of course, though the regulation is the same, the system is quite different: there are no more automatic stays. Deportees routinely are physically removed quickly, often before they can file motions or, worse, after they have filed but before the motions have been adjudicated.

Put simply, what this means for many deportees is that there *is no consideration of their motions after they have departed the United States*, whether the departure was voluntary or forced by the government. As a result, factual and legal mistakes are ignored and not remedied. One can certainly appreciate the expediency of such post-deportation limitations. It saves the immigration courts considerable time and trouble. The change from automatic stays to faster deportation may even have a certain humane aspect, at least if the alternative to deportation is long incarceration in the United States. For some, it might be better to be at liberty abroad than to be detained in ICE custody in the United States. For many, however, the short filing period (now just thirty days) is impossible to meet. And surely it is hard to justify allowing the government to preclude consideration of a motion by quickly deporting the person who filed it.

The most obvious legal peculiarity with all of this is that the regulation that bars post-departure motions *preceded* the 1996 changes to the statute. In other words, the regulatory post-departure bar could not have been designed to implement the new statutory scheme. In fact, it seems to contradict it. The statute was designed to move post-deportation law outside of U.S. territory. The regulations make presence on U.S. soil the crucial determinant of whether one may seek review or not. How can we explain this?

The Board of Immigration Appeals offered its analysis in a 2008 decision involving Andres Armendarez-Mendez, whose deportation was due to a conviction for possessing cocaine with intent to distribute, allegedly an aggravated felony.[232] During his initial proceedings before the immigration judge, Armendarez had requested a discretionary waiver of deportation,[233] but the immigration judge denied that request because the law at that time did not allow such relief, though challenges to that rule were percolating through the legal system.[234] So Armendarez was physically removed from the United States in 2000.

Soon thereafter, however, the Supreme Court decided that people like Armendarez *did* have the right to apply for discretionary relief from deportation.[235] The government had been wrong. A special set of rules for such motions was designed by the Department of Justice. A time limit was set,[236] and, like other motions, the government said that motions could not be filed at all by noncitizens who were outside the United States or who had illegally reentered the country after removal.[237] Armendarez, who had already been deported, thus asked for *sua sponte* reopening.[238] (Immigration judges and the BIA have general power, *sua sponte* (i.e., on their own) to reopen or reconsider any case in which they have made a decision "at any time."[239]) The Board, however, declined to do so.[240] Its ruling was not discretionary, but a bright-line, jurisdictional one: "Removed aliens have, by virtue of their departure, literally *passed beyond our aid*." The Board also defended its adherence to the departure bar because the "burdens" associated with the adjudication of motions to reopen and reconsider on behalf of deported or departed aliens "would greatly outweigh any advantages this system might render."[241] Of course, Mr. Armendarez did not see it this way.[242] The Board's decision meant that, although his claim might well have been correct and just, he simply had no remedy.

The deep question, then, is how one ought to evaluate this. Is deportation, as the BIA also put it, a "transformative event that fundamentally alters the alien's posture under the law"?[243] What does it mean to say that—even for long-term lawful permanent residents with U.S. families—the consequence of a deportee's removal is, "not just physical absence from the country, but also a nullification of legal status, which leaves him in no better position after departure than any other alien who is outside the territory of the United States"?[244] We shall soon consider these questions in greater depth.[245] At this point, let us simply note that the agency's approach means that many mistakes have gone and will go undiscovered, let alone rectified.[246]

Reentry

Illegal reentry after removal is a federal felony for which a person may face up to twenty years in prison.[247] The law's harshness reflects an obvious attempt to increase the efficacy of deportation and to combat recidivism. For some deportees, the risk nevertheless seems worth taking. Some such cases raise a complex legal problem: what are the rights of such people if their prior deportation order had somehow violated due process? Can they challenge that prior order in subsequent proceedings, or is it simply "water under the bridge"? In the 1987 case of *United States v. Mendoza-Lopez*, the Supreme Court held that those who are *criminally* prosecuted in such cases did have due process rights to reconsideration of the underlying deportation order.[248] The government had argued that there were "absolutely no due process limitations to the enforcement of [the criminal statute]."[249] The Court, however, held that to impose a criminal penalty for reentry, regardless of how violative of rights the first deportation proceeding may have been, would violate the constitution.[250] The Court noted that this would not necessarily delay a second deportation.[251] But this raises an obvious question: if, in fact, the prior proceeding had been so deeply flawed as to implicate due process, can it legitimately form the basis for a "redeportation"?[252] Put another way, does the noncitizen have the right to treat the prior proceeding as a nullity? If so, the noncitizen might still be subject to removal, but there might be various available defenses and forms of discretionary relief.

The Supreme Court has not, to date, decided whether a redeportation can legitimately be based upon an unconstitutional prior order. The issue, however, was implicit, if not presented directly, in a case involving the fast-track removal mechanism known as *Reinstatement of Removal.* As we have seen, this deformalized removal tool provides that a deported person who reenters the United States without authorization will simply have the prior removal order "reinstated from its original date." Crafted in the McCarthy era as part of the 1950 Internal Security Act, it was originally recognized as an unusual provision to be aimed only at certain serious criminal deportees and those deported as anarchists or "subversives."[253] For others, the ordinary deportation rules applied. In 1952, with the passage of the Immigration and Nationality Act, Congress retained the reinstatement law, again aiming only at certain specified reentrants.[254] The law was also interpreted with a certain amount of flexibility. The BIA, for example, held that if the basis for the prior deportation order were removed, say by a dismissal of the underlying criminal charge that had been the basis for the original deportation, then the use of the fast-track reinstatement procedure might be improper.[255]

The current statute, passed in 1996, adopted the model of the earlier reinstatement of removal laws but took a much harsher line: it applies to *all* "illegal" reentrants (not just those deported for certain reasons), and it states that that no discretionary relief is to be available. With few exceptions,[256] the government has argued that the original order may not be reopened or reviewed and the noncitizen may not apply for any relief from deportation.[257] Indeed, the regulations provide for deportation by order of an immigration agent—not an immigration judge.[258] This system was challenged in the 2006 Supreme Court case of *Fernandez-Vargas v. Gonzales.*[259]

The central issue in the case was whether the statute applies to those who entered before the 1996 law and whether it retroactively affects any right of, or imposes any impermissible burden on, a reentrant. But on a deeper level, the case involved still more fundamental questions: what rights do deportees possess after a final order? How much does or should it matter whether they are *here* or *there* or whether they have illegally reentered?

Humberto Fernandez-Vargas, a citizen of Mexico, came to the United States in the 1970s. He was deported for immigration violations but then reentered, apparently, more than once. His last border crossing was in 1982. He was arrested more than two decades later, in November 2003, after having started a trucking business, married, and fathered a son in the United States. The government sought to reinstate his old deportation order. (He was arrested because he had affirmatively applied for legal permanent resident status through a family-based visa petition filed by his wife. When he applied to adjust his status, the filings apparently tipped off the authorities to his illegal presence.)

The Court adopted an apparently simple approach: unlawful reentry after a deportation order and remaining in the United States after reentry are "continuing violations," so actually the law was not being applied retroactively.[260] I say that this theory is "apparently" simple because it actually masks some complexity, which one can perhaps understand best by focusing on the word "violations." In other areas of immigration law, the question of whether unlawful presence is a continuing *crime* has split many judges and many commentators over many years.[261] Some say that the crime was the act of reentry itself, not the subsequent staying in the United States to work, to be with family, etc. Crimes normally requires specific acts, and mere presence, some say, is not such an act. In this context, it is not entirely clear whether the Court's denomination of unlawful presence as a "violation" is meant as a kind of moral point (i.e., "he knew he was violating the law, and therefore he should not complain about facing the consequences") or as a more technical component of the Court's retroactivity analysis, implying that presence is a criminal violation.[262] Still, there is no question that Mr. Fernandez-Vargas did not have legal status in the United States. The Court concluded that the reinstatement law applied not because Mr. Fernandez-Vargas reentered in 1982 or at any other particular time, but "because he chose to remain after the new statute became effective."[263] Though it seems extremely unlikely that this man actually had any idea of this subtle and complicated change to the law in 1996, the Court did not pause on that point.

Another background idea was that the subsequent deportation, unlike criminal prosecution, was not meant to "penalize an alien for the reentry." Rather it was meant to enforce the prior order due to the conduct of remaining in the country after entry.[264] The Court's tone hardened when it noted that this was a violation that "the alien himself could end at any time by voluntarily leaving the country." It was therefore "the alien's choice to continue his illegal presence . . . that subjects him to the new and less generous legal regime, not a past act that he is helpless to undo up to the moment the Government finds him out."[265]

But note, again, how one may frame such cases very differently. Justice Stevens' dissent demonstrated a completely different understanding of the law, as was apparent from his first sentences. He noted that Mr. Fernandez-Vargas, in the more than twenty years since he reentered, had worked as a truck driver, owned a trucking business, fathered a child, and eventually married the child's mother, a United States citizen. He further pointed out that the laws in place at the time of his entry and for the first fifteen years of his residence here "would have rewarded this behavior, allowing him to seek discretionary relief from deportation on the basis of his continued presence in and strong ties to the United States."[266]

This sort of reasoning has long vied with stricter views in deportation legal history. Justice Stevens' approach is redolent of some of the concerns that had animated the Court's 1982 decision in *Plyler v. Doe* in which the Court held that the state of Texas could not deny public education to undocumented children. In Stevens' view of unlawful presence, "those involved in enforcement today must be allowed to defer to equities created in the past by decisions not to enforce immigration law." The concern is not only about those "equities" them-selves (e.g., marriage, children, business), but also about the noncitizen's right to some form of ameliorative discretion to temper rigid enforcement of harsh, complicated, shifting laws.[267]

So where does this leave us? Unfortunately, the post-deportation system is in a state of some confusion. Once a deportation order is "final" a deportee who discovers errors of fact or law (or perhaps new facts that were not available before, or perhaps a change in the law) may file a single motion to reopen subject to strict time limits. But if the government executes the deportation order (or if the deportee leaves voluntarily), then this right may be taken away by the post-departure regulations.

On the other hand, if a deportee reenters the United States and is criminally prosecuted for that reentry, he may challenge the original order on due process grounds as a defense to that criminal prosecution. But even a "due process-defective" deportation order may permit redeportation. Most possibilities of discretionary relief will be unavailable to the noncitizen in that setting, even if he had been available previously and even if he was wrongly denied. In Chapters 6 and 7 we will consider more deeply the logic, justice, and fairness of this system. But as attention has begun to focus on it, some judges, including Justices of the Supreme Court, have clearly been troubled. In a more recent Supreme Court case, for example, Justice Ginsburg asked whether an illegal reentry meant that the petitioner had truly lost any hope of applying for cancellation of removal or any other discretionary relief from deportation. The government lawyer stated that a removal by "reinstatement" left open an argument that if "the initial re-moval order wasn't good because cancellation should have been granted, that also carries through to the reinstatement." The Justices were mightily confused by this as, I fear, some readers may be. But this reflects the confused state of the law:

JUSTICE SCALIA: I—I—I'm not sure I understand what you are saying. You are saying that his reentry was not illegal because his removal was il-legal? Is that what you are saying?

MR. SRINIVASAN: No, it's not that his reentry was not illegal. It's that when he was then again removed, the way that that was accomplished was by reinstatement of the original removal order.

JUSTICE SCALIA: I see.

MR. SRINIVASAN: And so if the original removal order would have been extinguished by a grant of the cancellation order, then that carries forward to the reinstatement of the original removal—removal order as well.

JUSTICE KENNEDY: But does it make the—the second unlawful entry now lawful?

MR. SRINIVASAN: It doesn't make—

JUSTICE KENNEDY: I thought—I thought—it's a separate offense to enter, to reenter improperly, and—and that stays no matter, isn't that correct, regardless of the correctness of the prior removal order?

MR. SRINIVASAN: It does, Justice Kennedy—

JUSTICE KENNEDY: Or am I wrong?

MR. SRINIVASAN: —but I think—I think the way that gets taken into account is it would be one of the discretionary considerations that the Attorney General could take into account in determining whether to grant discretionary relief in the same way that the original conviction for drug possession could be taken into account.[268]

The basic thrust of this interchange—as confirmed by the Court's ultimate decision in the case—is that if, somehow, a noncitizen can challenge his *first removal order* on the grounds that he was improperly denied the possibility even to apply for discretionary relief, then that right to apply for such relief continues even if he later reenters the country illegally and is placed in reinstatement of removal.[269] As such, it is a bit of a breach in the more rigid model of the *Fernandez-Vargas* case and perhaps an implicit recognition by the Court that post-deportation law as a whole requires considerably more careful thought. The next chapters will endeavor to do this.

Notes

1. LEWIS CARROLL, ALICE'S ADVENTURES IN WONDERLAND (1865), reprinted in THE COMPLETE WORKS OF LEWIS CARROLL 81–86 (Barnes & Noble Books 2001) (internal quotation omitted).
2. Andrew R. Morral, Henry H. Willis, & Peter Brownell, *Measuring Illegal Border Crossing Between Ports of Entry, An Assessment of Four Promising Methods*, RAND OP-328 (2011).

3. *See* Demetrios G. Papademetriou and Elizabeth Collett, Transatlantic Council on Migration, Migration Policy Institute, *A New Architecture for Border Management*, March 2011.

4. One earlier study had concluded that it would cost the American taxpayer between $206 billion and $230 billion over five years to deport the population of "illegal aliens" in the United States. Rajeev Goyle & David A. Jaeger, Center for American Progress, *Deporting the Undocumented: A Cost Assessment* (July 2005).

5. Doris Meissner & James W. Ziglar, *Why the U.S. Had to Challenge Arizona on Immigration*, Washington Post, July 22, 2010, at A19, *available at* http://www.washingtonpost.com/wp-dyn/content/article/2010/07/21/AR2010072104559.html.

6. Jagdish Bhagwati, *Getting Policy Wrong*, Boston Rev., Oct./Nov. 1998, *available at* http://bostonreview.net/BR23.5/Bhagwati.html.

7. Responding to the federal lawsuit filed by the Department of Justice against Arizona's immigration enforcement law, Governor Jan Brewer wrote: "As a direct result of failed and inconsistent federal enforcement, Arizona is under attack from violent Mexican drug and immigrant smuggling cartels." Press Release, Statement by Governor Jan Brewer (July 6, 2010), *available at* http://www.azgovernor.gov/dms/upload/PR_070610_StatementGovBrewer.pdf.

8. *See* Stephen H. Legomsky, *Immigration, Federalism, and the Welfare State*, 42 UCLA L. Rev. 1453, 1460 (1995) (noting undocumented immigrants' ineligibility for federal and state benefit programs); Janet M. Calvo, *The Consequences of Restricted Health Care Access for Immigrants: Lessons from Medicaid and SCHIP*, 17 Annals Health L. 175, 175–77 (2008) (arguing that health care access reform should include provisions for noncitizens). The REAL ID Act, Pub. L. 109–113, 119 Stat. 313 (2005) (codified at 49 U.S.C. § 30301) mandates that states require proof of lawful status before issuing driver's licenses; *see* Kevin R. Johnson, *Driver's Licenses and Undocumented Immigrants: The Future of Civil Rights Law?* 5 Nev. L.J. 213, 239 (2004) (arguing denial of drivers' licenses to undocumented immigrants denies them important societal membership rights); Margaret D. Stock, *Driver Licenses and National Security: Myths and Reality*, 10 Bender's Immigr. Bull. 422, 422 (2005) (arguing denying drivers' licenses to undocumented immigrants jeopardizes national security).

9. *Compare* Steven A. Camarota & Karen Jensenius, *Homeward Bound: Recent Immigration Enforcement and the Decline in the Illegal Alien Population*, CIS Backgrounder, July 2008, at 2, *available at* http://cis.org/articles/2008/back808.pdf (suggesting that the fall in the size of the likely illegal population was caused by enforcement rather than deterioration in the economy), *with* Immigration Policy Ctr., American Immigration Law Found., *Attrition through Recession: CIS Report Marred by Inaccuracies, Contradictions, and Wishful Thinking* 2–3 (2008), *available at* http://www.immigrationpolicy.org/just-facts/attrition-through-recession-cis-report-marred-inaccuracies-contradictions-and-wishful-thi (citing data from Federal Reserve Bank of St. Louis that show that undocumented immigrants responded to changing conditions in industries in which they work).

10. Damien Cave, *Better Lives for Mexicans Cut Allure of Going North*, N.Y. Times, July 6, 2011, at 1.

11. *Id.*

12. *See* Jeffrey S. Passel & D'Vera Cohn, *U.S. Unauthorized Immigration Flows Are Down Sharply Since Mid-Decade*, Pew Hispanic Center, Sept. 1, 2010, *available at* http://pewresearch.org/pubs/1714/annual-inflow-unauthorized-immigrants-united-states-decline.

13. *Id.*

14. *Border News*, N.Y. Times, Sept. 5, 2010, at WK7, *available at* http://www.nytimes.com/2010/09/05/opinion/05sun2.html?_r=1&ref=opinion.

15. Apprehensions in FY 2007 dropped 20 percent at the southern border from the FY 2006 numbers. Decreases continued an additional 17 percent in FY 2008. Press Release, Customs and Border Patrol, CBP Border Patrol Announces Fiscal Year 2008 Achievements El Centro Sector (Oct. 15, 2008), *available at* http://www.cbp.gov/xp/cgov/newsroom/news_releases/archives/2008_news_releases/2008_fiscal/10152008_2.xml.

16. *Secretary Chertoff Cites Border Security Progress During House Testimony, Statement for the Record, The Honorable Michael Chertoff, Secretary, United States Department of Homeland Security Before the United States House of Representatives Committee on Homeland Security*, July 17, 2008; *available at* http://www.cbp.gov/xp/cgov/newsroom/congressional_test/chertoff_testimony.xml.

17. *Id.*

18. Quoted in Julia Preston, *U.S. to Speed Deportation of Criminals in Jail*, N.Y. TIMES, Jan. 15, 2008, *available at* http://www.nytimes.com/2008/01/15/us/15immig.html?_r=1&pagewanted=all.

19. *See* Olivia García, Jezmín Fuentes, Jonathan Andres Hicken, & Jessica Sisco, *Illegal Migration and US Immigration Policy: All Eyes on the Border*, in FOUR GENERATIONS OF NORTEÑOS: NEW RESEARCH FROM THE CRADLE OF MEXICAN MIGRATION (Wayne A. Cornelius, David Fitzgerald, & Scott Borger eds., San Diego Center for Comparative Immigration Studies 2007).

20. Indeed, Secretary Chertoff also cited such data favorably, noting that the *Financial Times* had reported that, following nearly a decade of double-digit increases, remittances reported to the Bank of Mexico fell to $7.3 billion in the first four months of 2008, 2.4 percent less than in the equivalent period in the prior year. He endorsed the article's conclusion that "it . . . appears that the laws to crack down on illegal workers are having an impact." Chertoff Statement, July 18, 2008, *supra* note 16.

21. *Id.*

22. Steven A. Camarota & Karen Jensenius, *Homeward Bound: Recent Immigration Enforcement and the Decline in the Illegal Alien Population*, Center for Immigration Studies, July 2008, http://www.cis.org/trends_and_enforcement.

23. *See* Jeffrey Passel & D'Vera Cohn, *U.S. Unauthorized Immigration Flows Are Down Sharply Since Mid-Decade*, Pew Hispanic Center, Sept. 1, 2010, *available at* http://pewresearch.org/pubs/1714/annual-inflow-unauthorized-immigrants-united-states-decline. *See also* data at Mexican Migration Project, Jorge Durand Arp-Nisen & Douglas S. Massey, *available at* http://mmp.opr.princeton.edu/results/results-en.aspx.

24. 8 U.S.C. §1231(a)(5) states: "If the Attorney General finds that an alien has reentered the United States illegally after having been removed or having departed voluntarily, under an order of removal, the prior order of removal is reinstated from its original date and is not subject to being reopened or reviewed, the alien is not eligible and may not apply for any relief under this chapter, and the alien shall be removed under the prior order at any time after the reentry." Under the relevant regulation interpreting the statute, an alien subject to reinstatement "has no right to a hearing before an immigration judge." 8 C.F.R. § 241.8(a).

25. William Odencrantz, quoted in Brock N. Meeks, *A Twist in the Battle Against Illegal Immigrants: Feds Confront Court Decision That Allows Previously Deported to Remain*, MSNBC, Nov. 3, 2005, http://www.msnbc.msn.com/id/9911793/.

26. *See* Trina Realmuto, *Reinstatement of Removal*, AILF Practice Advisory, July 11, 2006, *available at* http://www.lexisnexis.com/Community/immigration-law/cfs-filesystemfile.ashx/__key/CommunityServer.Components.SiteFiles/ImmigrationLawPDFs/05041866.pdf (citing statistics provided by the government in its rehearing petition (at 3–4) in *Morales-Izquierdo v. Ashcroft*, 388 F.3d 1299 (9th Cir. 2004), *reh'g en banc granted and decision withdrawn sub nom. Morales-Izquierdo v. Gonzales*, 423 F.3d 118 (Sept. 12, 2005), *en banc proceedings stayed*, 432 F.3d 1112 (Jan. 5, 2006).

27. Julia Preston, *U.S. to Speed Deportation of Criminals in Jail*, N.Y. TIMES, Jan. 15, 2008, *available at* http://www.nytimes.com/2008/01/15/us/15immig.html?_r=1&pagewanted=all.

28. The big increase in deportations was placing "a significant burden" on ICE's detention centers, said Myers, and on the airplanes used by the agency to fly deportees back to "their home countries." Ms. Myers also said ICE would work with states to devise parole programs allowing immigrants imprisoned for nonviolent crimes to reduce their prison time if they agreed to be deported immediately upon release.

29. Rubén G. Rumbaut & Golnaz Komaie, *Immigration and Adult Transitions, The Future of Children*, 20(1) TRANSITION TO ADULTHOOD 43–66 (Spring 2010).

30. *Id.*

31. Suzanne Gamboa, Associated Press, *Traffic Crime, Drunken Driving Deportations Way Up*, July 22, 2011, *available at* http://abcnews.go.com/Politics/wireStory?id=14131888.

32. Human Rights Watch, Forced Apart (By the Numbers) 2009, *available at* http://www.hrw.org/en/reports/2009/04/15/forced-apart-numbers.
I worked with the drafters of this Report.

33. *Id.* 70.5 percent were deported for a nonviolent offense and 29.5 percent were deported for a violent or potentially violent offense.

34. *Id. See* figure 4 and appendix E. More specifically, for lawful permanent residents—some 49 percent of the "legally present" category and some 87,844 individuals—the vast majority had no crime data kept by ICE. Still, data related to 4,453 showed that the large majority of lawful permanent residents, some 68 percent, were deported from the United States for nonviolent offenses.

35. Laura J. Hickman & Marika J. Suttorp, *Are Deportable Aliens a Unique Threat to Public Safety? Comparing the Recidivism of Deportable and Nondeportable Aliens.* 7(1) CRIMINOLOGY & PUB. POL'Y 59–82, published online Feb. 19, 2008. The study excluded immigrants who were sent from Los Angeles jails to state prisons or were transferred to the custody of immigration officials.

36. Quoted at http://www.rand.org/publications/randreview/issues/spring2008/news.html.

37. Rubén G. Rumbaut et al., Migration Policy Institute, *Debunking the Myth of Immigrant Criminality: Imprisonment Among First-and Second-Generation Young Men* (2006); available at: http://www.migrationinformation.org/Feature/display.cfm?id=403.

38. The data were from the 5 percent Public Use Microsample (PUMS) of the 2000 census.

39. *Id.*, table 1.

40. *Id.*, table 3.

41. *See, e.g.,* Kristin F. Butcher & Anne Morrison Piehl, *Why Are Immigrants' Incarceration Rates So Low? Evidence on Selective Immigration, Deterrence, and Deportation,* FRB Chicago, Working Paper No. 2005-19 (2005); Kristin F. Butcher & Anne Morrison Piehl, *Recent Immigrants: Unexpected Implications for Crime and Incarceration,* Nat'l Bureau of Econ. Research, Working Paper No. 6067 (1997); *see also* John Hagan & Alberto Palloni, *Sociological Criminology and the Mythology of Hispanic Immigration and Crime,* 46 SOCIAL PROBLEMS 617–32 (1999).

42. *See* Robert J. Sampson, Jeffrey D. Morenoff, & Stephen Raudenbush, *Social Anatomy of Racial and Ethnic Disparities in Violence,* 95 AM. J. PUB. HEALTH 224, 224–32 (2005); Robert J. Sampson, *Open Doors Don't Invite Criminals,* N.Y. TIMES, Mar. 11, 2006, at A27.

43. Martínez, Jr., Ramiro, Matthew T. Lee, & Amie L. Nielsen. *Segmented Assimilation, Local Context and Determinants of Drug Violence in Miami and San Diego: Does Ethnicity and Immigration Matter?,* 38(1) INT'L MIGRATION REV. 131–57 (2004).

44. Rubén G. Rumbaut & Walter A. Ewing, *The Myth of Immigrant Criminality and the Paradox of Assimilation: Incarceration Rates among Native and Foreign-Born Men* (May 23, 2007) *available at* http://borderbattles.ssrc.org/Rumbault_Ewing/printable.html.

45. David G. Brotherton & Luis Barrios, BANISHED TO THE HOMELAND: DOMINICAN DEPORTEES AND THEIR STORIES OF EXILE (2011).

46. A. Portes & M. Zhou, *The Segmented Assimilation and its Variants,* 530 ANNALS OF THE AM. ACAD. POLITICAL & SOC. SCI. 74–96 (1993); R.G. Rumbaut, *Assimilation and Its Discontents: Ironies and Paradoxes,* in THE HANDBOOK OF INTERNATIONAL MIGRATION: THE AMERICAN EXPERIENCE 172–95 (C. Hirschman, P. Kasinitz & J. DeWind, eds., Russell Sage Foundation 1999).

47. Portes & Zhou, *supra* note 46, at 76.

48. *Id.*

49. *Id.* at 81.

50. Jock Young, *Crossing the Borderline: Globalisation and Social Exclusion: The Sociology of Vindictiveness and the Criminology of Transgression* ch. 3, in GANGS IN THE GLOBAL CITY (John M. Hagedorn ed., 2007), *available at* http://www.malcolmread.co.uk/JockYoung/crossing.htm. J. YOUNG, THE VERTIGO OF LATE MODERNITY 32 (Sage Publications 2007).

51. Rumbaut et al., *supra* note 37.

52. John Ayliffe, *Parergon juris canonici Anglicani, Or a Commentary by Way of Supplement to the Canons and Constitutions of the Church of England* 15 (Kessinger Publishing 2008) (1726) (quoted in OED, Deportation, 2d ed., 1989).

53. *See generally Problems with ICE Interrogation, Detention, and Removal Procedures: Hearing Before the Subcomm. on Immigration, Citizenship, Refugees, Border Security and Int'l Law of the H. Comm. on the Judiciary,* 110th Cong. (2008), *available at* http://judiciary.house.gov/hearings/printers/110th/40742.PDF.

54. ICE does not have authority to detain aliens for criminal violations, but it does have authority, pursuant to the Immigration and Nationality Act, to detain aliens during the removal process.

55. *See* Text of Attorney General's Talk to New Citizens, N.Y. TIMES 14 (Nov. 12, 1954).

56. MARK DOW, AMERICAN GULAG: INSIDE U.S. IMMIGRATION PRISONS 7 (2004).

57. *Id.*

58. *See, e.g.,* Demore v. Kim, 538 U.S. 510, 519 (2003) (citing congressional concerns about absconders in the 1990s).

59. USA PATRIOT Act, Pub. L. 107–156, Title IV, § 412(a), 115 Stat. 350 (2001).

60. *See* THE INFLUENCE OF THE PRIVATE PRISON INDUSTRY IN IMMIGRATION DETENTION, DETENTION WATCH NETWORK (2011), *available at* www.detentionwatchnetwork.org/privateprisons.

61. Dora Schriro, Director of the Office of Detention Policy and Planning, U.S. Immigration & Customs Enforcement "Immigration Detention Overview and Recommendations" (Oct. 6, 2009), *available at* http://www.ice.gov/doclib/about/offices/odpp/pdf/ice-detention-rpt.pdf. About half of all detainees were held in twenty-one facilities, including seven Service Processing Centers (SPC) owned by ICE and operated by the private sector; seven "dedicated Contract Detention Facilities" (CDF) owned and operated by the private sector; and seven "dedicated" county jail facilities, with which ICE maintains "intergovernmental agency service agreements" (IGSA).

62. THE HISTORY OF IMMIGRANT DETENTION IN THE U.S., DETENTION WATCH NETWORK, *available at* http://www.detentionwatchnetwork.org/node/2381.

63. *Id.* The average length of detention was thirty days, and 95 percent of detainees were held no longer than four months. However, about 2,100 people are detained by ICE for a year or more, most typically as they contest their deportation cases or because ICE is unable to deport them for other reasons. There are legal limits to such detentions. *See* Zadvydas v. Davis, 533 U.S. 678 (2001).

64. OFFICE OF IMMIGRATION STATISTICS ANNUAL REPORT, ENFORCEMENT ACTIONS: 2010, at 4 (June 2010).

65. *See* Sarnata Reynolds, *Immigration Detention: The Golden Goose for Private Prisons,* June 10, 2011, *available at* http://blog.amnestyusa.org/iar/immigration-detention-the-golden-goose-for-private-prisons/.

66. The three largest corporations with stakes in immigration detention today are Corrections Corporations of America (CCA), the GEO Group, Inc., and the Management and Training Corporation (MTC). In 2010, CCA and GEO reported annual revenues of 1.69 billion and 1.17 billion respectively, but because neither the corporations nor ICE make the necessary data publicly available, it is so far not possible to determine what percentage of these profits are attributable to ICE contracts. *See* PRIVATE PRISON INDUSTRY, DETENTION WATCH NETWORK, *supra* note 62.

67. *See* Reynolds, *supra* note 65.

68. Nina Bernstein, *Officials Hid Truth of Immigrant Deaths in Jail,* N.Y. TIMES, Jan. 9, 2010, *available at* http://www.nytimes.com/2010/01/10/us/10detain.html?pagewanted=1& ref=correctionscorporationofamerica%29.

69. *Id.*

70. *Id.*

71. *See* Sunita Patel & Tom Jawtez, *Conditions of Confinement in Immigration Detention Facilities,* ACLU briefing (citing *INS News Release-INS to Adopt New Detention Standards* (Nov. 13, 2000)), *available at* www.aclu.org/pdfs/prison/unsr_briefing_materials.pdf. The Detention Standards apply to Service Processing Centers (SPCs), Contract Detention Facilities (CDFs), and Intergovernmental Service Agreement (IGSA) facilities holding detainees for more than seventy-two hours.

72. As the Detention Operations Manual puts it, "IGSA facilities may find such procedures useful as guidelines"; *see also* Spenser S. Hsu & Sylvia Moreno, *Border Policy's Success Strains Resources: Tent City in Texas Among Immigrant Holding Sites Drawing Criticism,* WASH. POST, Feb. 2, 2007.

73. *See* Petition for Rule-Making to Promulgate Regulations Governing Detention Standards for Immigration Detainees (Jan. 25, 2007), *available at* http://www.nationalimmigrationproject. org/legalresources/Immigration%20Enforcement%20and%20Raids/Detention%20Standards%20Litigation/Detention%20Standards%20Petition%20for%20Rulemaking%20-%20 2009.pdf.

74. Dow, *supra* note 56, at 10.

75. *See, e.g.*, Human Rights First, *In Liberty's Shadow-US Detention of Asylum Seekers in the Era of Homeland Security*, 2004; *available at* http://www.humanrightsfirst.org/2004/04/23/in-libertys-shadow-u-s-detention-of-asylum-seekers-in-the-era-of-homeland-security/; UNHCR, "*Alternatives to Detention of Asylum Seekers and Refugees*," April 2006, *available at* http://www. unhcr.org/refworld/docid/4472e8b84.html. HRF, "*The Detention of Asylum Seekers in the United States: Arbitrary under the ICCPR*" (background briefing), January 2007, *available at* http://www.humanrightsfirst.org/our-work/refugee-protection/archive/detention-of-asylum-seekers-in-the-u-s-%E2%80%93-archive/; NILC and ACLU Foundation of Southern California, United Nations Special Rapporteur on the Human Rights of Migrants, *U.S. Immigration Detention System: Substandard Conditions of Confinement and Ineffective Oversight*, May 3, 2007, *available at* http://www.nilc.org/immlawpolicy/arrestdet/UNspecialrapporteur_presentation_2007-05-03.pdf; Women's Commission for Refugee Women and Children and The Lutheran Immigration and Refugee Service, *Locking Up Family Values: The Detention of Immigrant Families*, February 2007, *available at* http://womensrefugeecommission.org/docs/famdeten.pdf; Amnesty International USA, *Unaccompanied Children in Immigration Detention*, June 2003, *available at* http://www.detentionwatchnetwork.org/ node/286; ACLU, *Conditions of Confinement in Immigrant Detention Facilities*, June 2007, *available at* www.aclu.org/pdfs/prison/unsr_briefing_materials.pdf.

76. A 2007 Human Rights Watch Report found that ICE failed to consistently deliver medication, conduct lab tests on time, prevent infections, provide access to specialty care, and ensure the confidentiality of medical care. Human Rights Watch, *Chronic Indifference: HIV/ AIDS Services for Immigrants Detained by the United States* (Dec. 2007), http://hrw.org/ reports/2007/us1207/.

77. *See generally* Dana Priest & Amy Goldstein, *System of Neglect*, WASH. POST, May 11, 2008, http://www.washingtonpost.com/wp-srv/nation/specials/immigration/cwc_d1p1. html; Nina Bernstein, *Ill and in Pain, Detainee Dies in U.S. Hands*, N.Y. TIMES, Aug. 12, 2008, http://www.nytimes.com/2008/08/13/nyregion/13detain.html?pagewanted=all; Nick Miroff, *ICE Facility Detainee's Death Stirs Questions*, WASH. POST, Feb. 1, 2009, http://www. washingtonpost.com/wp-dyn/content/story/2009/01/31/ST2009013101877.html.

78. A 2008 Report by the Office of Inspector General for the Department of Homeland Security reported that between January 1, 2005, and May 31, 2007, thirty-three immigration detainees had died in custody. However, the government had only investigated two of those deaths in detail. Department of Homeland Security Office of the Inspector General, *ICE Policies Related to Detainee Deaths and the Oversight of Immigration Detention Facilities*, *available at* http://www.oig.dhs.gov/assets/Mgmt/OIG_08-52_Jun08.pdf.

79. *See, e.g.*, Homer D. Venters, M.D., Testimony before the House Judiciary Committee's Subcommittee on Immigration, Citizenship, Refugees, Border Security, and International Law, Statement on Immigration Detainee Health Care, June 4, 2008, http://judiciary.house. gov/hearings/pdf/Venters080604.pdf.

80. *See* letter to Janet Napolitano from ACLU, et al., June 29, 2010, *available at* http://www.aclu. org/immigrants-rights/letter-dhs-regarding-sexual-assault-detention-facilities.*See also* Carol Lloyd, *Hanky-Panky or Sexual Assault?*, Salon.com, May 31, 2007, http://www.salon. com/2007/05/31/hutto/; *Former ICE Officer Pleads Guilty*, FIAC, Apr. 3, 2008, *available at* http://www.fiacfla.org/printable.php?id=105; Mary Flood, *Ex-Prison Guard Admits to Fondling Immigrant Women*, HOUSTON CHRON., Sept. 24, 2009; Suzanna Gamboa, *ICE Investigating Alleged Officer Sex Assault of Detainees*, ASSOCIATED PRESS, June 1, 2010; Susan Carroll, *ICE to Make Detention Centers More Humane*, HOUSTON CHRON., June 8, 2010.

81. Letter from "The Female Detainees," Pinal County Jail, Florence, Arizona, to Christina Powers, Attorney, Florence Immigrant and Refugee Rights Project, January 2008 (reprinted

in Human Rights Watch, *Detained and Dismissed: Women's Struggles to Obtain Health Care in United States Immigration Detention*, Mar. 17, 2009), *available at* http://www.hrw.org/en/reports/2009/03/16/detained-and-dismissed. As the Report stated: "Unfortunately, the system for providing health care to detained immigrants is perilously flawed, putting the lives and well-being of more and more people at risk each year." HRW, *Detained and Dismissed, supra* at 2, 10. Due to a series of exposés about substandard conditions in ICE detention facilities, Congress included language in its FY 2009 appropriations bill that requires ICE to discontinue use of any facility with less than satisfactory ratings for two consecutive years.

82. *Id.*

83. ICE supposedly distinguishes between "noncriminal aliens," "nonviolent criminal aliens," and "violent criminal aliens." In practice, however, a recent government report conceded the fact—long known by many involved in the system—that "'non-criminal aliens' and 'non-violent criminal aliens' are frequently housed together, as are 'non-violent criminal aliens' and 'violent criminal aliens.'" *Id.* at 17.

84. ACLU of Massachusetts, *Detention and Deportation in the Age of ICE, available at* http://www.aclum.org/ice/.

85. In 2007 alone, ICE spent more than $10 million to transfer nearly 19,400 detainees. HRW, *Detained and Dismissed, supra* note 81, at 24.

86. *Id.* at 25.

87. In 2008, Congress directed ICE to develop a plan for the nationwide implementation of an ATD program.

88. *See* http://web.archive.org/web/20100527084653/http://www.ice.gov/dro/detention-reform/.

89. *Id.*

90. The Online Detainee Locator System (ODLS), located on ICE's public website (www.ice.gov), provides users with information on the location of the detention facility where a particular individual is being held, a phone number to the facility, and contact information for the ICE Enforcement and Removal Office in the region where the facility is located. A brochure explaining how to use the ODLS is also available on the website in the following languages: English, Spanish, French, Mandarin, Vietnamese, Portuguese, Russian, Arabic, and Somali.

91. Nina Bernstein, *For Those Deported, Court Rulings Come Too Late*, N.Y. TIMES, July 20, 2010, *available at* http://www.nytimes.com/2010/07/21/nyregion/21deport.html?_r=1&ref=todayspaper.

92. HRW, *Detained and Dismissed, supra* note 81 at 26.

93. RUTH ELLEN WASEM, IMMIGRATION REFORM ISSUES IN THE 111TH CONGRESS, CONG. RESEARCH SERV., 7-5700, R40501, CRS-5 (Feb. 10, 2010), *available at* http://www.docstoc.com/docs/41257146/Immigration-Reform-Issues-in-the-111th-Congress.

94. LILLIAN HOMLEN MOHR & FRANCES PERKINS, THAT WOMAN IN FDR's CABINET 132 (1979).

95. U.S. GOV'T ACCOUNTABILITY OFFICE, B-125051 NEED FOR IMPROVEMENT OF MANAGEMENT ACTIVITIES OF THE IMMIGRATION AND NATURALIZATION SERVICE (Aug. 14, 1973); GAO, GGD-76-101, IMMIGRATION—NEED TO REASSESS U.S. IMMIGRATION POLICY (Oct. 19, 1976); GAO, GGD-81-4, PROSPECTS DIM FOR EFFECTIVELY ENFORCING U.S. IMMIGRATION LAWS (Nov. 5, 1980); ADP Acquisitions: Immigration and Naturalization Service Should Terminate Its Contract and Recompete (1986) (cited in WASEM, *supra* note 93, at CRS-4).

96. SELECT COMM'N ON IMMIGRATION & REFUGEE POL'Y, U.S. IMMIGRATION POLICY AND THE NATIONAL INTEREST, iii (1981).

97. The adjudicators were long known as "special inquiry officers" in the immigration statute until finally being recognized as "immigration judges" in 1973 regulations and, finally, by statute in 1996. *See* 8 C.F.R. § 1.1(l); 8 U.S.C. § 1101(b)(4); Sidney B. Ravitz, *From Wong Yang Sun to Black Robes*, 65 INTERPRETER RELEASES 453 (1988).

98. *Id.*

99. Pub. L. No. 404, 60 Stat. 237, 5 U.S.C. § 1001 et seq.

100. Wong Yang Sung v. McGrath, 339 U.S. 33, 45 (1950).

101. *See* 48 Fed. Reg. 8056 (effective Feb. 15, 1983).

102. Ravitz, *supra* note 97.

103. *See* Jeffrey Juffras, The Rand Corporation & The Urban Institute Joint Program for Research on Immigration Policy, *Impact of the Immigration Reform and Control Act on the Immigration and Naturalization Service* (1991); Daniel Kanstroom, *Hello Darkness: Involuntary Testimony and Silence as Evidence in Deportation Proceedings*, 4 Geo. Immig L. J. 599 (1990); Daniel Kanstroom, *Judicial Review of Amnesty Denials: Must Aliens Bet Their Lives to Get into Court?* 25 Harv. C.R.-C.L. L. Rev. 53 (1990).

104. Lee May, *Mismanagement Rampant in INS, Audit Says*, L.A. Times, Mar. 3, 1989, *available at* http://articles.latimes.com/1989-03-03/news/mn-272_1_ins-officials.

105. Lee May & Ronald J. Ostrow, *Head of INS Organizes Effort to Keep His Job: Nelson Denounces Scathing Audit of His Agency, Lobbies Congress and White House, Shows Film*, L.A. Times, Mar. 16, 1989, *available at* http://articles.latimes.com/1989-03-16/news/mn-2165_1_white-house.

106. U.S. Commission on Immigration Reform, Report to Congress, *Becoming an American: Immigration and Immigrant Policy*, Washington, DC: Government Printing Office, 1997; *see also* Wasem, *supra* note 93, at CRS-4.

107. *Becoming an American, supra* note 106, at appendix B.

108. Pub. L. 107-296, 116 Stat. 2135 (2002).

109. *See* David A. Martin, *Immigration Policy and the Homeland Security Act Reorganization: An Early Agenda for Practical Improvements*, Migration Policy Institute, April 2–003, No.1 (reprinted at 80 Interpreter Releases 601 (2003)).

110. U.S. Gov't Accountability Office, GAO-05-81, Management Challenges Remain in Transforming Immigration Programs (2004).

111. James Jay Carafano & David Heyman, Heritage Foundation, *DHS 2.0: Rethinking the Homeland Security Department* (Dec. 2004).

112. He also wondered whether the distinction between the interior enforcement activities of ICE and the border security functions of CBP were "artificial constructs that contribute to needless administrative overlaps, programmatic turf battles, mission gaps, and sometimes dangerous operational conflicts." House Committee on Homeland Security, Hearing on "CBP and ICE: Does the Current Organizational Structure Best Serve U.S. Homeland Security Interests?" Statement of Hon. Christopher Cox, Mar. 9, 2005.

113. The study was primarily researched by the law firm of Arnold & Porter.

114. ABA Commission on Immigration, Arnold & Porter, Reforming the Immigration System: Proposals to Promote Independence, Fairness, Efficiency, and Professionalism in the Adjudication of Removal Cases (2010), *available at* http://www.americanbar.org/content/dam/aba/publications/commission_on_immigration/coi_complete_full_report.authcheckdam.pdf.

115. *Id.* at ES-6.

116. *Id.*, at 1-65. In 2008, immigration judges completed an average of 1,243 proceedings per judge and issued an average of 1,014 decisions per judge.

117. *Id.*

118. *Id.*

119. Nina Bernstein, *U.S. Court Orders Safety, Not Deportation, for Woman Facing Torture*, N.Y. Times, July 16, 2010, A20, *available at* http://www.nytimes.com/2010/07/16/nyregion/16torture.html.

120. Another panel of judges similarly chided the government for a "manifestly incorrect" argument that the court had no jurisdiction to consider the case of an impoverished legal immigrant who had been ordered deported without being told that free legal help might be available. *Id.* (citing Leslie v. Attorney General of United States, 611 F.3d 171, 178–80 (3d Cir. 2010)). Further, the Court noted, "the government's failure to assist the court in evaluating the specifics of [the *pro se*] petitioner's argument [which] required the court to conduct a special, searching analysis of petitioner's contentions before, during and after oral argument."

121. Jian Tao Lin v. Holder, 611 F.3d 228, 235 (4th Cir. 2010).

122. In 2009, Juan Osuna, a well-respected attorney who was Acting Chair of the BIA, was appointed to be the Deputy Assistant Attorney General for the Office of Immigration Litigation in the Civil Division of the Department of Justice.

123. Whitney v. California, 274 U.S. 357, 376 (1927) (Brandeis, J., concurring).

124. Nina Bernstein, *U.S. Raid on an Immigrant Household Deepens Anger and Mistrust*, N.Y. TIMES, Apr. 10, 2007, at B1, *available at* http://www.nytimes.com/2007/04/10/nyregion/10suffolk.html.

125. Beth Werlin, *Rescinding an In Absentia Order of Removal*, AILF PRACTICE ADVISORY (Sept. 21, 2004), *available at* http://www.scribd.com/doc/35892549/AILF-on-in-Absentia-7C79E5CB2220E.

126. OXFORD ENGLISH DICTIONARY, 2d ed. (1989).

127. INA § 101(a)(3); 8 USC 1101(a)(3).

128. *See* U.S. *ex rel* Bilokumsky v. Tod, 263 U.S. 149, 153 (1923) ("[A]lienage is a jurisdictional fact, and . . . an order of deportation must be predicated on that finding 'of fact'"); Woodby v. INS, 385 U.S. 276 (1966).

129. Ng Fung Ho v. White, 259 U.S. 276, 284 (1922).

130. *See, e.g.*, Perez v United States, No. 1:05-CV-1294 (LEK), 2006 WL 2355868 (N.D.N.Y. Aug. 15, 2006). *See, e.g.*, Andrew Becker & Patrick J. McDonnell, *U.S. Citizens Caught Up in Immigration Sweeps*, L.A. TIMES, Apr. 9, 2009, at A1, *available at* http://articles.latimes.com/2009/apr/09/nation/na-citizen9 (describing citizens placed in ICE custody due to mistaken beliefs about their citizenship status); Tyche Hendricks, *Citizens Wrongly Held by ICE Sue U.S.*, S.F. CHRON., July 28, 2009, at A1 (reporting that hundreds of U.S. citizens have been detained and, in some cases, deported by U.S. Immigration and Customs Enforcement).

131. *Problems with ICE Interrogation, Detention and Removal Procedures: Hearing Before the Subcomm. on Immigration, Citizenship, Refugees, Border Security, and Int'l Law of the H. Comm. on the Judiciary*, 110th Cong. 1 (2008) (statement of Kara Hartzler, Esq., Florence Immigrant and Refugee Rights Project) *available at* http://judiciary.house.gov/hearings/pdf/Hartzler080213.pdf.

132. *Problems with ICE Interrogation, Detention and Removal Procedures: Hearing Before the Subcomm. on Immigration, Citizenship, Refugees, Border Security and International Law* (Feb. 13, 2008) (statement of Gary E. Mead Deputy Director, Office of Detention and Removal Operations, U.S. Immigration and Customs Enforcement Department of Homeland Security), *available at* http://judiciary.house.gov/hearings/pdf/Mead080213.pdf.

133. Jacqueline Stevens, *U.S. Government Unlawfully Detaining and Deporting U.S. Citizens as Aliens*, 18(3) VA. J. SOC. POL'Y & L. 606, 620 (2011).

134. *Id.*

135. *Id.* at 630; *see also* Jacqueline Stevens, *Thin Ice*, THE NATION, June 23, 2008, *available at* http://www.thenation.com/article/thin-ice. *See also* Stevens, *supra* note 133, at 608.

136. Robert Ramsey & James Frank, *Wrongful Conviction: Perceptions of Criminal Justice Professionals Regarding the Frequency of Wrongful Conviction and the Extent of System Errors*, 53 CRIME & DELINQ. 436 (2007). *See also* Stevens, *supra* note 133, at 632 n.88.

137. CITIZENS WITHOUT PROOF: A SURVEY OF AMERICANS' POSSESSION OF DOCUMENTARY PROOF OF CITIZENSHIP AND PHOTO IDENTIFICATION, BRENNAN CENTER FOR JUSTICE 2 (Nov. 2006), *available at* http://www.brennancenter.org/page/-/d/download_file_39242.pdf.

138. INA §§ 302–303, 306–307, 8 U.S.C. §§ 1402–1403, 1406–1407.

139. Stevens, *Thin Ice, supra* note 135.

140. *See* Robert Zullo, *Despite Citizenship Claims, Woman Shipped to Honduras*, DAILY COMET, June 14, 2009, http://www.dailycomet.com/article/20090614/ARTICLES/906141011.

141. Jacqueline Stevens, *U.S. Kidnaps Mark Lyttle, Leaves Him Stateless in Mexico, Honduras, Nicaragua, Guatemala*, April 24, 2009, http://stateswithoutnations.blogspot.com/2009/04/us-kidnaps-mark-lyttle-leaves-him.html; Stevens, *supra* note 133, at 674–77; *see also* Kristin Collins, *N.C. Native Wrongly Deported to Mexico*, CHARLOTTE OBSERVER, Aug. 30, 2009, *available at* http://www.charlotteobserver.com/local/story/917007.html.

142. Stevens, *Thin Ice supra* note 135.

143. Stevens, *supra* note 133, at 674–77.

144. In this context, I am using the term "mental disability" quite generally to include severe mental illnesses such as depression, schizophrenia, and post-traumatic stress disorder, as well as such vaguely defined intellectual disabilities as "mental retardation."

145. Texas Appleseed Foundation, *Justice for Immigration's Hidden Population, Protecting the Rights of Persons with Mental Disabilities in the Immigration Court and Detention System,* Mar. 20, 2010, *available at* http://www.texasappleseed.net/index.php?option=com_conte nt&view=category&layout=blog&id=26&Itemid=268. Maunica Sthanki, then a staff attorney for the Boston College Post-Deportation Human Rights Project, of which the author is a director, was on the Advisory Committee for this Report.

146. Nee Hao Wong v. INS, 550 F.2d 521 (9th Cir. 1977) (citing 8 C.F.R.§ 242.11 (1976), which provided: "When it is impracticable for the respondent to be present at the hearing because of mental incompetency, the guardian, near relative, or friend who was served a copy of the order to show cause shall be permitted to appear on behalf of the respondent. If such a person cannot reasonably be found or fails or refuses to appear, the custodian of the respondent shall be requested to appear on behalf of the respondent.").

147. Human Rights Watch & Am. Civil Liberties Union, *Deportation by Default: Mental Disability, Unfair Hearings, and Indefinite Detention in the US Immigration System* 16–17 (2010), *available at* http://www.aclu.org/human-rights/deportation-default-mental-disability-unfair-hearings-and-indefinite-detention-us-immig. Others cite a much higher figure of 15 percent of the detained immigrant population on any given day, which would have been approximately fifty-seven thousand people in 2008. *Id.* (citing Dana Priest & Amy Goldstein, *Suicides Point to Gaps in Treatment,* WASH. POST, May 13, 2008, at A1).

148. *See generally* HRW and ACLU, *Deportation by Default, supra* note 147.

149. 8 U.S.C. § 1229a(b)(3).

150. HRW and ACLU, *Deportation by Default, supra* note 147, Summary.

151. *Id.* at 25 (quoting Dr. Judy Eidelson, psychologist, Philadelphia, PA, Feb. 16, 2010).

152. *Id.* at 47.

153. *Id.* at 43.

154. *See* EXEC. OFFICE FOR IMMIGRATION REVIEW, DEP'T OF JUSTICE, MENTAL HEALTH ISSUES, IMMIGRATION JUDGE BENCHBOOK, *available at* http://www.justice.gov/eoir/vll/ benchbook/tools/MHI/index.html. *But see* Alice Clapman, *Crossing the Border: The Future of Immigration Law and Its Impact on Lawyers: Hearing Difficult Voices: The Due-Process Rights of Mentally Disabled Individuals in Removal Proceedings,* 45 NEW ENG. L. REV. 373, 383–84 (2011) (describing actions taken by the BIA in unpublished, nonprecedential decisions).

155. HRW and ACLU, *Deportation by Default, supra* note 147 at 6.

156. Texas Appleseed Foundation, *Justice for Immigration's Hidden Population, supra* note 145, at 1.

157. *Id.*

158. Nina S. Bernstein, *Mentally Ill and in Immigration Limbo,* N.Y. TIMES, May 3, 2009, *available at* http://www.nytimes.com/2009/05/04/nyregion/04immigrant.html?_r=1&fta=y.

159. Telephone conversation with Theodore Cox, July 15, 2010. *See also* Nina Bernstein, *Judges Grants Asylum to Chinese Immigrant,* May 17, 2010; *available at* http://cityroom.blogs.nytimes. com/2010/05/17/judge-grants-asylum-to-chinese-immigrant/?scp=2&sq=%22Nina%20 Bernstein%22%20and%20Jiang&st=cse. Had she been physically deported, such a motion would have been considerably more difficult, perhaps impossible.

160. *Id.*

161. ICE says that "in cases where ICE is required by law to detain certain aliens with serious medical and mental health issues, we work to ensure the person receives sound, appropriate and timely care." But the detention and transfer policies of the deportation system are clearly a major structural problem in such cases. As Ann Baddour, who directed the study, stated, "When you take a mentally ill person from New York to rural Texas, you're basically setting them up for almost certain deportation." Nina Bernstein, *Disabled Immigration Detainees Face Deportation,* N.Y TIMES, Mar. 30, 2010, at A18, *available at* http://www.nytimes. com/2010/03/30/us/30immig.html.

162. *Id.*
163. *See, e.g.,* H.R. Rep. No. 104-828, at 215 (1996); H.R. Rep. No. 104-469(I), at 12, 107, 118–25 (1996).
164. *See* Michele R. Pistone & John J. Hoeffner, *Rules Are Made to Be Broken: How the Process of Expedited Removal Fails Asylum Seekers,* 20 Geo. Immigr. L. J. 167 (2006).
165. *See generally* U.S. Comm'n on Int'l Religious Freedom, *Report on Asylum Seekers in Expedited Removal,* Feb. 8, 2005, *available at* http://www.uscirf.gov/index.php?option=com_content&task=view&id=1892.
166. Pistone & Hoeffner, *supra* note 164, at 203.
167. 62 Fed. Reg. 10312, 10313–10314 (Mar. 6, 1997) (codified as amended at 8 C.F.R. § 235.3(b)).
168. *See* Blas Nuñez-Neto et al., Cong. Research Serv., RL33097, Border Security: Apprehensions of "Other than Mexican" Aliens (2005); 69 Fed. Reg. 48,877, 48,880 (Aug. 11, 2004).
169. The ratio of expedited removals to the number of removal proceedings received by the immigration courts increased from approximately 20.4 percent in fiscal year 2004 to approximately 39.8 percent in fiscal year 2008. ABA Immigration Commission, Reforming the Immigration System 1–41.
170. Khan v. Holder, 597 F.3d 360, 364 (2010).
171. *Id.*
172. *Id.*
173. *See, e.g.,* A. Elena Lacayo, The Impact of Section 287(G) of the Immigration and Nationality Act on the Latino Community, 21 NCLR Issue Brief (2010), *available at* http://www.nclr.org/images/uploads/publications/287gReportFinal.pdf; *see also* Melissa Keaney & Joan Friedland, Nat'l Immigration Law Ctr., *Overview of the Key ICE ACCESS Programs: 287(g), the Criminal Alien Program, and Secure Communities* (Nov. 2009), www.nilc.org/immlawpolicy/LocalLaw/ice-access-2009-11-05.pdf; Deborah M. Weissman, Rebecca C. Headen, & Katherine Lewis Parker, ACLU, The Policies and Politics of Local Immigration Enforcement Laws: 287(g) Program in North Carolina 17 (2009), *available at* http://www.law.unc.edu/documents/clinicalprograms/287gpolicyreview.pdf.
174. *The Performance of 287(g) Agreements,* OIG-10-63, Dep't of Homeland Security Office of Inspector General (Mar. 2010), *available at* http://www.trac.syr.edu/immigration/library/P4485.pdf [hereinafter OIG report].
175. Indeed, the OIG offered thirty-three specific recommendations to strengthen management controls and improve oversight.
176. *See, e.g., The Performance of 287(g) Agreements Report Update,* OIG-10-124, http://www.oig.dhs.gov/assets/Mgmt/OIG_10-124_Sep10.pdf. Elizabeth Mauldin, National Immigration Law Center, DHS Office of Inspector General Report, *ICE Reforms Fail to Solve Fundamental 287(g) Problems* (Apr. 2010).
177. Maria Sachetti, *Traffic Cases Settled, but Deportations Loom,* Boston Globe, July 3, 2011, at A1.
178. *Id.*
179. *Id.* at A11.
180. The hospital leased an air ambulance for $30,000 and "forcibly returned him to his home country," as one hospital administrator described it.
181. Deborah Sontag, *Immigrants Facing Deportation by U.S. Hospitals,* Aug. 3, 2008; *available at* http://www.nytimes.com/2008/08/03/us/03deport.html?_r=1.
182. What is perhaps most stunning about this verdict is the fact that the (all white) jury had been specifically instructed by the judge that a Florida appeals court decision had found as "a matter of law" that Jiménez, had been unlawfully detained and deprived of his liberty. Still, the jury found that the hospital had not committed false imprisonment and was not liable for damages. Montejo v. Martin Mem'l Med. Ctr., Inc., 874 So. 2d 654, 656 (Fla. Dist. Ct. App. 2004). This legal victory did not permit Mr. Jiménez to return to the United States, however. *See* 8 U.S.C. § 1182(a)(9)(B)(i)(II) (2006) (barring admission of alien who has been unlawfully present in the United States for one year or more, and who seeks admission within ten years of the date of such alien's departure or removal from the United States).

183. Deborah Sontag, *Jury Rules for Hospital That Deported Patient*, NY Times, July 27, 2009, *available at* http://www.nytimes.com/2009/07/28/us/28deport.html.

184. Judith Graham, Becky Schlikerman, & Abel Uribe, *Undocumented Worker Who Became Quadriplegic Is Moved to Mexico Against His Will*, Chicago Tribune, Feb. 6, 2001, *available at* http://articles.chicagotribune.com/2011-02-06/news/ct-met-quadriplegic-immigrant-deporte20110206_1_advocate-health-care-ojeda-mexican-hospital.

185. According to a recent report from the American Medical Association's Council on Ethical and Judicial Affairs, hospitals are legally required to discharge all patients to "appropriate facilities" where they can receive adequate follow-up care. This is also an ethical obligation for physicians. *See also* Kendra Stead, Note: *Critical Condition: Using Asylum Law to Contest Forced Medical Repatriation of Undocumented Immigrants*, 104 Nw. L. Rev. 307 (2010).

186. INS v. St. Cyr, 533 U.S. 289 (2001); INS v. Calcano-Martinez, 533. U.S. 348 (2001). The Court's reasoning was contained in *St. Cyr*.

187. *See* Daniel Kanstroom, *St. Cyr or Insincere: The Strange Quality of Supreme Court Victory*, 16 Geo. Immigr. L. J. 413–64 (2002).

188. Zadvydas v. Davis, 533 U.S. 678, 693 (2001). *But see* Demore v. Kim, 538 U.S. 510 (2003) (upholding the regime of mandatory detention during deportation proceedings).

189. *See* Brief for Petitioner at 2–6, Leocal v. Ashcroft, No. 03-583 (U.S. May 10, 2004).

190. Although Mr. Leocal had no prior criminal record, the circuit court for Dade County sentenced him to two and a half years in prison on the first count and two and a half years of probation on the second. Mr. Leocal served more than two years of his sentence, during which time he completed a ten-month course of treatment for alcohol abuse.

191. INA § 101(a)(43)(F), 8 U.S.C. § 1101(a)(43)(F) (2002). Congress first made conviction of an "aggravated felony" grounds for deportation in 1988, and it defined the term to include offenses such as murder, drug trafficking crimes, and firearm trafficking offenses. See Anti-Drug Abuse Act of 1988, §§ 7342, 7344, 102 Stat. 4469, 4470. Since then, Congress has frequently amended and broadened the definition. *See, e.g.*, Antiterrorism and Effective Death Penalty Act of 1996, § 440(e), 110 Stat. 1277 (adding a number of offenses to § 101(a)(43) of the INA); Illegal Immigration Reform and Immigrant Responsibility Act of 1996 (IIRIRA), § 321, 110 Stat. 3009–627 (same). The inclusion of a "crime of violence" as an aggravated felony came in 1990. *See* Immigration Act of 1990, § 501, 104 Stat 5048.

192. The immigration judge ruled that Mr. Leocal was ineligible for various forms of discretionary relief. The BIA affirmed the immigration judge's decision and dismissed the appeal.

193. In June 2003, without oral argument, the court of appeals dismissed the petition for review. The court held that it lacked jurisdiction over Mr. Leocal's case under the 1996 IIRIRA, which limits judicial review of removal orders. Illegal Immigration Reform and Immigrant Responsibility Act of 1996, Pub. L. No. 104–208, 110 Stat. 3009 (Sept. 30, 1996). The Eleventh Circuit also rejected the argument that the court was not bound to follow prior Eleventh Circuit precedent because the Court of Appeals in the earlier case had simply deferred to and affirmed the Board's position as reasonable, and the BIA had now changed its interpretation.

194. As Justice Rehnquist put it:

> [W]e cannot forget that we ultimately are determining the meaning of the term "crime of violence." The ordinary meaning of this term, combined with [the statute's] emphasis on the use of physical force against another person (or the risk of having to use such force in committing a crime), suggests a category of violent, active crimes that cannot be said naturally to include DUI offenses. *Leocal v. Ashcroft*, 543 U.S. 1, 11 (U.S. 2004).

195. The law has now been clarified. Some serious DUI offenses still will result in deportation as aggravated felonies, particularly those where a person was injured. *See* Maria-Teresa Davenport, *Deportation and Driving: Felony DUI and Reckless Driving as Crimes of Violence following Leocal v. Ashcroft*, 96 J. Crime L. & Criminology 849, 849–75 (2006).

196. *INS Set to Deport 500 for Drunken Driving*, L.A. Times, Sept. 4, 1998, *available at* http://articles.latimes.com/1998/sep/04/news/mn-19458.

197. Linda Greenhouse, *Justices Rule Drunken Driving Cannot Mean Automatic Deportation of Immigrants*, N.Y. TIMES, Nov. 10, 2004, at A17.

198. 8 U.S.C. § 1160.

199. Brief for Petitioner at 10–12, Lopez v. Gonzales, No. 05-547 (U.S. June 19, 2006).

200. *See* 21 U.S.C. § 844(a).

201. S.D. Codified Laws §§ 22-42-5, 22-6-1 (1997).

202. *See* 8 U.S.C. §§ 1227(a)(2)(B)(i), 1227(a)(2)(A)(iii).

203. INA § 240A.

204. The BIA affirmed, as did the Eighth Circuit Court of Appeals, which held that "the plain language of the INA, and of the other statutes . . . states that any drug conviction that would qualify as a felony under either state or federal law is an aggravated felony."

205. The government had argued that despite it being a federal misdemeanor, the fact that a particular state had decided to classify a drug possession offense as a felony would turn it into a federal aggravated felony. Lopez v. Gonzales, 549 U.S. 47 (2006).

206. *Lopez*, 549 U.S. at 53 (emphasis added).

207. 8 U.S.C. § 1101(a)(43)(B).

208. 18 U.S.C. § 924(c)(2) (emphasis added).

209. 21 U.S.C. § 844(a); 18 U.S.C. § 3559(a) (defining a felony as any offense punishable by more than one year in prison).

210. Even the BIA found this argument to be strained at best. But it felt bound by the law of the Fifth Circuit which, as we have seen, is where thousands of deportees from around the country are routinely transferred.

211. Justices Scalia and Thomas concurred.

212. Carachuri-Rosendo v. Holder, 130 S. Ct. 2577, 2579 (2010) (citing *Lopez*, 549 U. S. at 53).

213. 549 U. S. at 54.

214. *Carachuri-Rosendo*, 130 S. Ct. at 2585.

215. *See* CHARLES GORDON, STANLEY MAILMAN, & STEPHEN YALE-LOEHR, IMMIGRATION LAW AND PROCEDURE § 3.05[7][a] (2004).

216. *See, e.g.*, Chew Hoy Quong v. White, 244 F. 749, 749 (9th Cir. 1917) (application to reopen to explain discrepancies in testimony); *Ex parte* Chan Shee, 236 F. 579 (N.D. Cal. 1916) (application to the Immigration Bureau to reopen for proof of marriage).

217. *See, e.g.*, Regulations Governing Departmental Organization and Authority, 5 Fed. Reg. 3502, 3504 (Sept. 4, 1940) (codified at 8 C.F.R. § 90.9); New Regulations Governing the Arrest and Deportation of Aliens, 6 Fed. Reg. 68, 71–72 (Jan. 4, 1941); Board of Immigration Appeals: Power; and Reopening or Reconsideration of Cases, 27 Fed. Reg. 96, 96–97 (Jan. 5, 1962) (promulgating the original § 3.2 reopening provision upon which the current motion to reopen regulation is based. GORDON ET AL., *supra* note 215; *see also* Achacoso-Sanchez v. INS, 779 F.2d 1260, 1264 (7th Cir. 1985).

218. *See* Daniel Kanstroom, *Surrounding the Hole in the Doughnut: Discretion and Deference in U.S. Immigration Law*, 71 TUL. L. REV. 703–818 (1997).

219. *In re* Abreu, 2009 BIA LEXIS 12, at *14–15 (B.I.A. 2009) (citing INS v. Doherty, 502 U.S. 314, 323 (1992); *INS v. Abudu*, 485 U.S. 94, 107 (1988)).

220. *In re* Abreu, 2009 BIA LEXIS, at *15 (citing *Abudu*, 485 U.S. at 107).

221. Immigration and Nationality Regulations, 17 Fed. Reg. 11,469, 11,475 (Dec. 19, 1952) (codified at 8 C.F.R. § 6.2).

222. *See* G-y B-, 6 I. & N. Dec. 159, 159–60 (B.I.A. 1954); G-N-C-, 22 I. & N. Dec. 281, 288 (B.I.A. 1998); Okoh, 20 I. & N. Dec. 864, 864–65 (B.I.A. 1994); Estrada, 17 I. & N. Dec. 187, 188 (B.I.A. 1979), *rev'd on other grounds*, Estrada-Rosales v. INS, 645 F.2d 819 (9th Cir. 1981); Palma, 14 I. & N. Dec. 486, 487 (B.I.A. 1973); *accord* Yih-HsiungWang, 17 I. & N. Dec. 565 (B.I.A. 1980).

223. *See* Act of September 26, 1961, Pub. L. No. 87-301, § 5(a), 75 Stat. 650, 651 (codified at § 106(c) of the Act, 8 U.S.C. § 1105a(c) (1964)).

224. *See* Daniel Kanstroom, *Marcello v. Bonds: The Story Behind the Longest, Most Expensive, and Most Futile Deportation Case in U.S. History*, in IMMIGRATION STORIES (Foundation Press 2005).

225. Pub. L. 649, § 545; 104 Stat. 4978, 5066.

226. Attorney General's Report to Congress on Consolidation of Requests for Relief from Deportation. *See* 68 Interpreter Releases 907, 908 (July 22, 1991).
227. Executive Office for Immigration Review; Motions and Appeals in Immigration Proceedings, 61 Fed. Reg. 18,900, 18,905 (Apr. 29, 1996).
228. 8 U.S.C. § 1229a(c)(6)(A) (1996). The ninety-day time limit does not apply in asylum cases involving changed circumstances. *See* 8 U.S.C. § 1229a(c)(6)(C)(ii).
229. 8 U.S.C. § 1229a(c)(7)(A).
230. 8 C.F.R. § 3.2(c) (1997), recodified as 8 C.F.R. § 1003.2(c) (2004).
231. 8 C.F.R. § 1003.2(d); similar language appears in 8 C.F.R. §§ 1003.4, 1003.23(b).
232. Matter of Andres Armendarez-Mendez 3626; 24 I. & N. Dec. 646 (B.I.A. 2008).
233. 8 U.S.C. § 1182(c) (1994).
234. *See* Matter of Soriano 21 I. & N. Dec. 516, 533–40 (B.I.A. 1996; A.G. 1997).
235. *See* INS v. St. Cyr, 533 U.S. 289 (2001).
236. 8 C.F.R. § 1003.44(h) (2006).
237. 8 C.F.R. § 1003.44(k) (2006).
238. The idea of *sua sponte* power is worth considering a bit further. *Sua sponte*, in Latin, means "on its own will or motion." Its typical usage describes a spontaneous act by a judge without prompting from a party to a legal action. *See, e.g.,* Carlisle v. United States, 517 U.S. 416 (1996) (district court could not order a judgment of acquittal *sua sponte* when motion was late filed). The earliest reported U.S. usage of the phrase by the U.S. Supreme Court was in 1839, regarding an action taken by a clerk. "The clerk thought it his official duty, sua sponte, to make the proper entries in his minutes of the proceedings; but on application to the judge was refused permission." *Ex parte* Whitney, 38 U.S. 404 (1839). The term is sometimes used in a negative sense regarding a court's ability to determine its own lack of jurisdiction. *See, e.g.,* Lange v. Jones, 32 Va. 192 (1834) ("objection for want of jurisdiction may be taken for the first time in the appellate court, and may be enforced by the court *sua sponte* though not raised by the pleadings, nor suggested by counsel."). This usage was famously undertaken by Justice Curtis in his dissent in the *Dred Scott* case:

> The course of the court is, where no motion is made by either party, on its own motion, to reverse such a judgment for want of jurisdiction, not only in cases where it is shown, negatively, by a plea to the jurisdiction, that jurisdiction does not exist, but even where it does not appear, affirmatively, that it does exist. . . . I consider, therefore, that when there was a plea to the jurisdiction of the Circuit Court in a case brought here by a writ of error, the first duty of this court is, *sua sponte*, if not moved to it by either party, to examine the sufficiency of that plea; and thus to take care that neither the Circuit Court nor this court shall use the judicial power of the United States in a case to which the Constitution and laws of the United States have not extended that power.

Scott v. Sandford, 60 U.S. 393, 567 (1857) (Curtis, J., dissenting).
239. 8 C.F.R. §§ 1003.23(b)(1), § 1003.2. The immigration judge may reopen only if jurisdiction has not vested with the Board.
240. This was a rather unusual decision because in the administrative setting, this term *sua sponte* has long had rather positive connotations, as a discretionary power to entertain unusual claims. The Board has thus long recognized that it can exercise its discretion, *sua sponte*, to reconsider or reopen a case even if a party's motion fails to comply with procedural requirements. Unsurprisingly, the BIA exercises its *sua sponte* authority "sparingly." It is not seen as a general remedy for hardships, but as an extraordinary remedy reserved for truly exceptional situations. *In re* G-D-, 22 I. & N. Dec. 1132, 1133–34 (B.I.A. 1999); Motions and Appeals in Immigration Proceedings, 61 Fed. Reg. 18,900, 18,902 (1996) ("Section 3.2(a) of the rule provides a mechanism that allows the Board to reopen or reconsider *sua sponte* and provides a procedural vehicle for the consideration of cases with exceptional circumstances."). For example, a change was made in 1996 to statutory asylum law that protected people who feared coercive population-control measures. Many previously ineligible asylum seekers from China were suddenly eligible, but their motions would have been technically barred

due to time or number limitations. For five years following this change in law, the Board, *sua sponte*, reopened such asylum cases. The point is that the power exists, and the decision whether to use it is a deeply discretionary one that ought to consider a wide variety of factors.

241. Inspection and Expedited Removal of Aliens; Detention and Removal of Aliens; Conduct of Removal Proceedings; Asylum Procedures, 62 Fed. Reg. 10,312, 10,321 (Mar. 6, 1997) (Supp. Information).

242. The AG also expressed confidence that "the immigration judge's discretionary authority to stay the deportation or removal of an alien who has filed a motion to reopen or reconsider will safeguard an alien from being inappropriately deported before he is heard on his motion to reopen or motion to reconsider." This confidence, of course, has nothing to do with those who have already been deported before they discover the mistakes in their cases. *Id.* at 10,321

243. *Id.*

244. *Id.*

245. *See infra*, Chapters 6 and 7.

246. The Board may be slowly recognizing the seriousness and complexity of this problem. *See* Matter of Bulnes-Nolasco, 25 I. & N. Dec. 57 (B.I.A. 2009) (improper notice may permit reopening).

247. Section 276(a) and (b). One of the signal features of the early Obama administration was a dramatic increase in such prosecutions.

248. United States v. Mendoza-Lopez, 481 U.S. 828, 837 (1987).

249. Transcript of Oral Argument at 10, United States v. Mendoza-Lopez, *supra* note 248.

250. *Mendoza-Lopez*, 481 U.S. at 837. The Court declined "to enumerate which procedural errors are so fundamental that they may functionally deprive the alien of judicial review, requiring that the result of the hearing in which they took place not be used to support a criminal conviction." (The petitioners in the case had alleged that they were improperly denied the opportunity to apply for discretionary relief from deportation, but the Supreme Court focused on the fact that they had also waived appeals. *Id.* at 840.)

251. *Id.* at 839.

252. Congress has clarified that an individual who is prosecuted for illegal reentry may challenge the validity of the underlying order only under certain circumstances: if the "alien" exhausted any administrative remedies that may have been available to seek relief against the order; the deportation proceedings at which the order was issued improperly deprived the alien of the opportunity for judicial review; and the entry of the order was "fundamentally unfair." 8 U.S.C. § 1326(d). The interpretation of these protections has varied considerably among the circuit courts of appeals. For example, the failure of an immigration judge to inform a deportee of the possibility of discretionary relief or of appellate rights may render proceedings "fundamentally unfair." United States v. Sosa, 387 F.3d 131 (2d Cir.2004); United States v. Ubaldo-Figueroa, 364 F.3d 1042, 1050 (9th Cir. 2004) (quoting United States v. Muro-Inclan, 249 F.3d 1180, 1183 (9th Cir.2001)). Other courts, however, have differed, finding such relief to be a "matter of discretion" as opposed to a liberty or property interest protected by due process norms. *See, e.g.,* United States v. Wilson, 316 F.3d 506 (4th Cir. 2003); United States v. Lopez-Ortiz, 313 F.3d 225 (5th Cir. 2002); United States v. Aguirre-Tello, 353 F.3d 1199 (10th Cir. 2004) (en banc).

253. Section 23(d) provides: "Should any alien subject to the provisions of subsection (c) unlawfully return to the United States after having been released for departure or deported pursuant to this section, the previous warrant of deportation against him shall be considered as reinstated from its original date of issuance." Internal Security Act of 1950, § 23(c) and (d), 64 Stat. 1012, 8 U.S.C. § 156(d) (1946 ed., Supp. V); *see also* Internal Security Act of 1950, § 23(c) for a list of those to whom the law applied.

254. "Should the Attorney General find that any alien has unlawfully reentered the United States after having previously departed or been deported pursuant to an order of deportation, whether before or after the date of enactment of this Act [June 27, 1952], on any ground described . . . in subsection (e) . . ., the previous order of deportation shall be deemed to be reinstated from its original date and such alien shall be deported under such previous order at any time subsequent to such reentry." INA § 242(f), 66 Stat. 212; 8 U.S.C. § 1252(f) (1994 ed.).

255. Matter of C—8 I & N Dec. 276 (B.I.A. 1959).

256. The following noncitizens are not subject to reinstatement of removal:

     1. Applicants for adjustment of status under INA § 245A covered by certain class action lawsuits. *See* Legal Immigration Family Equity Act (LIFE Act), § 1104(g), Pub. L. No. 106-555, 114 Stat. 2763 (2000); Catholic Soc. Servs., Inc. v. Meese, 813 F.2d 1500 (9th Cir. 1987); League of United Latin Am. Citizens v. INS, 1988 U.S. Dist. LEXIS 12599 (C. D. Cal. 1988), *vacated sub nom.* Reno v. Catholic Social Services, Inc., 509 U.S. 43 (1993); Zambrano v. INS, 972 F.2d 1122 (9th Cir.1992), *vacated sub nom.* INS v. Zambrano, 509 U.S. 918 (1993).
     2. Nicaraguans and Cuban applicants for adjustment under § 202 of the Nicaraguan Adjustment and Central American Relief Act of 1997 (NACARA). LIFE § 1505(a)(1), codified in NACARA § 202(a)(2), 8 C.F.R. § 241.8(d).
     3. Salvadoran, Guatemalan, and Eastern European applicants under NACARA § 203. LIFE § 1505(c).
     4. Haitian applicants for adjustment under the Haitian Refugee Immigration Fairness Act of 1998 (HRIFA). LIFE § 1505(b)(1) codified in HRIFA §902(a)(2), 8 C.F.R. § 241.8(d).

257. 8 U.S.C. § 1231(a)(5). There are some technical exceptions to the no-relief rule that are beyond the scope of this work. Also, the regulations provide "[i]f the alien wishes to make a statement, the officer shall allow the alien to do so and shall consider whether the alien's statement warrants reconsideration of the determination." 8 C.F.R. § 241.8(a)(3). Judicial review is generally available for the reinstatement order, but this may well occur after the individual has been removed. *See, e.g.,* Arevalo v. Ashcroft, 344 F.3d 1, 9 (1st Cir. 2003); Delgado v. Mukasey, 516 F.3d 65, 67 (2d Cir. 2008). *See generally* Trina Realmuto, *Reinstatement of Removal*, Legal Action Center Practice Advisory, Apr. 23, 2008, *available at* http://www.legalactioncenter.org/practice-advisories/reinstatement-removal.

258. *See* 8 C.F.R. § 241.8 (2008).

259. 548 U.S. 30 (2006).

260. 548 U.S. at 42–44.

261. *See, e.g.,* Daniel Kanstroom, *Criminalizing the Undocumented: Ironic Boundaries of the Post-September 11th "Pale of Law,"* 29 N.C. J. Int'l L. & Com. Reg., 639–70 (2004).

262. Statutes are disfavored as retroactive when their application "would impair rights a party possessed when he acted, increase a party's liability for past conduct, or impose new duties with respect to transactions already completed." Landgraf v. USI Film Prods., 511 U.S. 244, 280 (1994). Accordingly, it has become "a rule of general application" that "a statute shall not be given retroactive effect unless such construction is required by explicit language or by necessary implication." United States v. St. Louis, S. F. & T. Ry. Co., 270 U.S. 1, 3 (1926) (opinion for the Court by Brandeis, J.). This is what is sometimes called a clear statement methodology. Courts will first look to "whether Congress has expressly prescribed the statute's proper reach," *Landgraf,* 511 U.S. at 280, and in the absence of a clear indication, courts will then ask whether applying the statute to the person objecting would have a retroactive consequence in the disfavored sense of "affecting substantive rights, liabilities, or duties [on the basis of] conduct arising before [its] enactment," *Landgraf,* 511 U.S. at 278. If the answer is yes, the presumption against retroactivity leads to a construction of the statute as inapplicable to the event or act in question owing to the "absen[ce of] a clear indication from Congress that it intended such a result." INS v. St. Cyr, 533 U.S. 289, 316 (2001); Fernandez-Vargas v. Gonzales, 548 U.S. 30, 37–38 (2006).

263. Moreover, according to the Court, the law's effective date, which was some six months after its passage, gave Fernandez-Vargas "an ample warning of the coming change in the law, but [he] chose to remain until the old regime expired and [the new law] took its place." 548 U.S. at 43. IIRIRA became law on September 30, 1996, but it became effective and enforceable only on "the first day of the first month beginning more than 180 days after" IIRIRA's enactment, that is, April 1, 1997. § 309(a), 110 Stat. 3009–3625.

264. Fernandez-Vargas v. Gonzales, 548 U.S. at 44.

265. *Id.*

266. *Id.* at 47 (Stevens, J. dissenting)

267. Hiroshi Motomura, *Immigration Outside the Law*, 108 COLUM. L. REV. 2037. 2067–68 (2008).

268. Carachuri-Rosendo v. Holder, (transcript of oral argument), *available at* http://www.oyez.org/cases/2000-2009/2009/2009_09_60.

269. The technical key seems to be that Mr. Carachuri had filed a direct appeal—which had continued to wend its way through the legal system even as he was removed—had reentered, had been reinstated, and had been removed again. But what if he had not filed his appeal in a timely way? What if he had simply remained abroad and then tried to file a motion to reopen? What about all the other people in reinstatement who have strong arguments that their original deportation orders were defective?

5

The Effects of Deportation in the United States and in the New Diaspora

The Challenge to "All That Makes Life Worthwhile"

What shall we do with these Americans—and they are Americans by virtue of their birth here—when we deport their parents? Shall we build a lot of new orphanages? Find adoptive parents for them? Deny their citizenship and ship them back, too? We all know we aren't going to find and deport so many millions and suffer the dislocation and agonizing moral dilemmas that such an impossible task would engender. So let's be honest about that, shall we?

—Senator John McCain (2006)[1]

I entered the United States as an infant, made my mistakes as a juvenile and was punished for those mistakes as a young adult. And as I now embrace life as a reformed, tax-paying civilian, the actions of my past still haunt me with what my fate might be. I can only implore mercy from a system in which I trust forgiveness and second chances still exist.

—Chally Dang, *written from ICE detention while facing deportation*[2]

Among the most poignant and compelling stories one hears in deportation cases are those that describe the effects on individuals, families, and, indeed, on entire communities. In one sense, of course, this is inevitable, obvious, and perhaps even a goal of deportation. But the more one hears such stories, the more one is struck by the extent of these collateral consequences and their frequently disproportionate harshness. When judges, politicians, reporters, and scholars write about deportation as a sanction that may deprive a "man and his family of all that makes life worthwhile," this is what they are thinking of.[3]

Let us begin with family separation and the *de facto* deportations of U.S. citizen children. It is not my particular purpose in this book to reify or idealize the modern family. It can of course be a site of oppression, negotiation, and struggle, as well as what it should be: an institution of love, stability, support, positive values transmission, and intergenerational continuity.[4] Its very definition is a question of considerable current debate and evolution, particularly in the realm of U.S. immigration law.[5] Moreover, global inequality, migration, and deportation have long been recognized as causes of radical shifts in family structures and as particular burdens for women.[6]

It is nevertheless especially striking how the protections given by law to the family are absent from much deportation law.[7] In general, the U.S. legal system is strongly protective of marriage and family. The Supreme Court has long recognized a fundamental right "to marry, establish a home and bring up children."[8] The Court has referred to marriage as one of the "basic civil rights of man, fundamental to our very existence and survival."[9] The freedom of personal choice in the matter of marriage and family life is one of the most well-respected liberties protected by the Due Process Clause of the Fourteenth Amendment.[10] Moreover, though the system is surely not without its problems, U.S. immigration *entry* laws still rely heavily on family relationships to grant hundreds of thousands of immigrant visas annually. However, for many deportees, one of the cruelest aspects of their plight is the complete disregard by the legal system of their family ties. This is an approach that contradicts norms of state laws, other federal laws, and international human rights law, for which a basic proposition is that the family is "the natural and fundamental group unit of society" and therefore entitled to protection.[11]

The hard fact is that the separation of families has been one of the most compelling consequences of the increase in deportations since the 1996 changes in the law. Deportation laws devastate families in the United States as they separate U.S. citizen children from their parents and spouses from each other, and disrupt the fabric of American communities.[12] Deep disregard about such consequences is built most fundamentally into the *post-entry social control* deportation system, in which certain types of criminal convictions have resulted in virtually automatic deportation, with no consideration of hardship, rehabilitation, or effects on family.

One can see this clearly in certain *post-entry social control* deportations aimed a drunk drivers. David Balderrama was 68 years old and a grandfather.[13] He was born in Mexico. Together with his wife, Marina, and infant daughter, Lucy, he had crossed the border into Texas more than four decades earlier, in 1956. They became legal permanent residents. The Balderramas had seven more children, all born in the United States. David Jr. served in the Army's 82d Airborne Division. George became the owner of a sheet metal company. Patsy worked in a hospital. Joe was a sheet metal worker, like his father. Peter was a produce manager in a grocery store. Mario worked for the state natural resources department. All had graduated from high school. Maritza, the youngest, went on to college and was studying for a master's degree.

For years, David had worked in a sheet metal factory by day, fixed houses by night, and paid his taxes promptly every year, and then he retired to spend time with his family. But he also got behind the wheel of his pickup truck after drinking beer with his relatives and some union buddies. There is no question that he had a serious problem. In fact, the police caught him driving drunk three times, and he received his punishment in the criminal justice system. But then, on September 3, 1998, armed INS agents showed up at Balderrama's home and told him he would be deported to Mexico––not because of any problem with his immigration status, but because of his three crimes. He was one of more than five hundred people, most of them Mexican laborers, who were rounded up in Texas in one frenzied month pursuant to an INS operation jauntily named "Operation Last Call."

In support of the operation, INS had enlisted the support of community groups such as Mothers Against Drunk Driving. Dale Chavez, from the MADD chapter in El Paso, offered a rather chilling justification: "If someone is deported, his family still has the opportunity to get together, even if it's in another land," she said. "But if he kills somebody, then the victim's family can only get together at the graveyard." Of course, no one supports drunk driving; but David Balderrama had not killed anyone.

Operation Last Call was criticized as being overinclusive as well as betraying a class bias (it did not focus on the well-to-do who drank and drive) and being racist. Many, including Balderrama's youngest son, Mario, were also concerned about disproportionality: "Drinking and driving is a serious offense, but you can't compare it to murder, rape, or drug dealing."[14] Moreover, it seemed like double-punishment. Balderrama's attorney noted that deportation punished those who had already paid fines and gone through court-ordered rehabilitation programs."[15] Others focused on the consequences of deportation for families: "If [my child's father] is deported, who is going to pay those bills?"[16] David's wife, Marina sat inside their house, surrounded by photos of her twenty-two grandchildren and one great-grandchild. As she pondered David's impending deportation, she said, "I have diabetes and sometimes I have to go to the emergency room. Who is going to take me?"[17]

Such deportations frequently turn hearings in immigration courts into tragic spectacles. Family members and friends simply cannot believe that the system lacks all possibility of mercy or consideration of effects on close family members. David C. Brotherton and Luis Barrios have described a particularly poignant—but all too typical—deportation hearing in New York of a Dominican man who had lived and worked legally for twenty-seven years in Manhattan.[18] The hearing took place at the Eastern Correction facility in Ulster County, New York, which they describe as a "fortress-like maximum security prison . . . impressive in its colossal symbolic might peering over the Catskills like some

hungry ogre." Some twenty-one family members came to testify in support of
the deportee, Mr. Delgado. Mr. Delgado's father offered his sense of the unfairness of the proceedings: "He never should have pleaded guilty. . . . [T]he
lawyers said . . . he would only do 3 years. He never said anything about being
deported." As the father continued, the unfairness began to seem much deeper:

> My son didn't do anything. He's a good boy. He's always lived with his
> mother and father. How can they do this to us? All he wanted to do was
> play baseball. When he couldn't play anymore he started to drink. He
> started to get depressed. . . . Oh God, Oh Maria, we are good religious
> people; we go to church. He was raised a good boy. Why this?

The deportee's mother said that she was an old woman and had terrible blood
pressure. "I cannot take the stress. My heart, my heart can't take it. I love my son.
I don't want to see him taken away. He's my baby, my son, I can't stand it. I can't."

For the U.S. deportation system, however, all of this is essentially irrelevant
background noise. Mr. Delgado, while drunk, had allegedly gotten into a fight.
Although there was apparently no weapon involved, this would still be a "crime
of violence" and—because of the sentence he received—an "aggravated felony."
His defenses were minimal and highly unlikely to succeed. His fears of mistreatment by the Dominican police did not rise to the level of torture. As the judge
put it: "I have no doubt the country we are sending [him] to is a bad place. I have
no doubt that the deportees do not wish to go there and that life will be difficult
for them. I have no doubt that for some of them it will lead to serious harm." But,
under the law of the United States, those concerns were basically irrelevant. The
judge even described a deportation he had ordered of a man with full-blown
AIDS in which he had agreed that the man should not be sent back. But the
Board of Immigration Appeals had disagreed and sent him to what the judge
said was almost certain death. As the judge sadly intoned: "That . . . is the law of
this land."

Still, Mr. Delgado's family tried, with desperate futility, to appeal to the judge's
heart. His father testified that the Dominican Republic is a place "where the
police kill people for nothing, absolutely nothing." Soon, the father began to vis-
ibly shake as the other people in the room howled in tears. A guard distributed
tissues to an audience that could not control its grief. The judge, however, was
mostly annoyed at Mr. Delgado's lawyer. The judge asked pointedly, "was all this
necessary? Did you have to put the father through this? . . . Why are you putting
this family through this?"

The mother's testimony was tragically similar. "Nothing good can come of
this," she said. "I know he will face terrible things, I know this. My country will
harm him, I know this. . . . I can't bear to think about it. I don't want to talk about

it. I don't want to think about this evil." Suddenly, she raised her hands into the air to pray, "Oh God, oh Jesus, oh Maria, I pray to you release my son from this trial. Oh Judge, please forgive my son. . . . Allow him to come back to his mother and father. . . . What use is this to take him away from us and his children. Please, please I beg you. . . ." Even one of the guards, "a bulky African-American man," started to cry.

But forgiveness was not part of the law for Mr. Delgado. And family did not matter. The judge knew the law all too well and instructed the lawyer harshly: "Please don't let's go through this again. It is not helping your case. It is not helping Mr. Delgado." In the end, the judge stated his ruling with banal simplicity: "I see nothing that alters the opinion of the court that Mr. Delgado will be deported . . . to his homeland after completing his sentence."

But there was still more. The judge allowed Mr. Delagdo to address the court. He expressed simple despair: "I agreed to plea for something I didn't do. . . . I don't need to be torn away from everything I love. This is my life here. I've been here since I was a kid. This is all I know . . . . What am I gonna do there? Where am I gonna live? How am I gonna see my children again? Where is the justice in all of this?" Rather than attempting to answer such questions, the judge could not resist asking an obvious question: "Why, Mr. Delgado, didn't you become a citizen like your sisters? Why?" The answer was stunningly simple: "Because I can't read or write, judge. I knew if I took the test I wouldn't be able to write down all those names of the states. . . . I got a scholarship to a college when I was a kid, somewhere in Oklahoma, to play baseball, but they never taught me to read or write. It's as simple as that." As David Brotherton notes, the whole hearing seemed to be little more than "an exercise in different levels of humiliation."[19]

Such stories are neither unique nor even rare. Hearings much like this have likely occurred tens, if not hundreds, of thousands of times since the 1990s. I have personally participated in some. The deportation and detention systems place families "in crisis" from the moment a family member is arrested and incarcerated. The numbers of people involved are simply staggering. Some 33 million native-born citizens have at least one foreign-born parent.[20] Further, among the estimated 12 million undocumented people in the United States, more than 1.5 million are children.[21] In 2009, Human Rights Watch estimated that over 1 million family members have been forcibly separated by deportation.[22] Unfortunately, we may never know the full effects of our recent deportation delirium on long-term residents because the government has failed to keep comprehensive, accurate data on deportations from the United States.[23] Such data are especially important because the losses are felt acutely throughout U.S. communities: "shops close, entrepreneurs lose their business partners, tax revenues are lost, and, most tragically, U.S. citizens and lawful permanent residents are forced to confront life without their fathers, mothers, children, husbands, or wives."[24] The family may lose a breadwinner; those left behind may face eviction; and the family suffers emotionally from having a loved one in detention, often thousands of miles away.[25] Then comes permanent separation. There are obviously rather stark contradictions between the best practices of family law and children's rights versus deportation law.[26] This is a disturbing two-way problem: immigration law enforcement goals compromise family integrity, and family integrity often can only be achieved through the violation of immigration laws.[27]

The effects of deportation are especially hard on families with preexisting difficulties. Yvonne Johnson, a Jamaican-American woman in her 60s, faced a terrible ordeal due to the deportation of her son, Christopher, 40, who suffers from bipolar disorder and schizophrenia. After spending more than half of his life in prison or juvenile detention, Christopher was deported. He has almost no memory of a Jamaican childhood, and, at the time his story was reported, he was sleeping in a temporary shelter for deportees in Kingston. His mother went deep into debt wiring him money, while struggling to keep her house from sliding into foreclosure.[28] Another Jamaican deportee, also separated from his family and community in the United States, simply and eloquently summed up the feeling of many others: "It's all kind of heartbreaking, you know."[29]

Family separations have particularly devastated Cambodian refugees who managed to survive the "killing fields" of Pol Pot's Khmer Rouge regime from 1975 to 1978.[30] Thousands of their children, many of whom came to the United States as infants, have faced deportation to a land about which they may know nothing beyond horror stories. The *New York Times* reported the case of Loeun Lun, who had escaped from the Khmer Rouge as a baby and was brought to the United States. Years later, he fired a gun in a shopping mall as he fled a group of teens who he thought were attacking him.[31] Convicted of assault, he served eleven months in prison. After this, he lived a model life, marrying, starting a family, and working steadily. He decided to apply for citizenship and a couple of years later innocently walked into an INS office to inquire about his case after a two-year delay. Arrested on the spot for deportation, separated from his wife and children, he was sent to Cambodia in 2003, after more than two decades in the United States, nearly his entire life. Under the law, he may be banished from the United States forever, permanently separated from his elderly mother, his wife, and his two young daughters.[32]

Family members who are left behind in the United States also frequently face great hardship as a consequence of their relatives' deportation. This ironically reflects the strong tendency of the children of immigrants to help support their families. A recent study of 1.5[33] and second-generation middle-class Mexican young adults in the Los Angeles area found three common patterns of "giving back" to their immigrant families: providing total financial support to their parents or younger siblings, or both; becoming the "safety net" for their parents, siblings, and relatives during times of hardship; and providing regular financial support to supplement their parents' incomes.[34] The authors found that about one-fifth of the respondents fully supported their immigrant parents. Maria, a second-generation entrepreneur with two young children, described how she supported her mother: "I pay her rent, I give her money, I take her to the doctors, I buy her prescriptions." The most common form of such giving back by the children of immigrants was monthly supplemental income to their parents. Half of the respondents in this study gave their parents between $200 and $1,000 every month for household expenses in addition to translating documents, drafting letters, making phone calls, and accompanying them to work-related and medical appointments.[35]

Deportation has two distinct types of effects on children. On the one hand, parental deportation can be devastating for children (many of whom are U.S. citizens) who remain in the United States. Such children often must grow up in a family broken by deportation or must move in with other relatives or friends if they wish to remain in the States. In addition, there is the less well-known phenomenon of children who are, in effect, *de facto* deported along with their parents. These children, though they may retain U.S. nationality, often grow up in substantially worse situations, with significantly diminished life prospects than they would have had in the United States. As we have seen, U.S. law generally does not require any sort of balancing of harms in such cases. The "best interests of the child" are, in fact, merely an afterthought—if a thought at all—in many deportation proceedings.[36] In one particularly troubling case, the Seventh Circuit Court of Appeals affirmed the removal order of a lawful permanent resident mother who had argued that her 9-year-old citizen daughters would be subject to genital mutilation in Nigeria. Rather than keeping the family together, the best the court could do was report to state social service authorities that the mother had said that she would take her children with her back to Nigeria, where they might well be subject to harm.[37] The implication was that a good mother would leave the child behind.

These are hard stories, but they reflect pervasive phenomena. In 2007, the Urban Institute estimated that for every two adults apprehended in a raid, at least one child was affected.[38] The Department of Homeland Security (DHS) Inspector General's Office concluded that over 108,000 undocumented parents of U.S. citizen children were removed from the United States between 1997 and 2007.[39] A 2010 study determined that from 1997 to 2007, nearly 88,000 U.S. citizen children were negatively affected by the deportation of an legal permanent resident (LPR) parent. More than one-third of these children were under the age of five at the time of the parent's deportation.[40]

The voices of deportees and their families poignantly describe their fate, though they are not frequently heard. In a 2008 study, with which I was involved, a nuanced set of questions revealed how Guatemalan and Salvadoran noncitizens in New England perceived deportation.[41] The initial findings, while perhaps not surprising, were compelling.[42] Adults described their experiences of deportation in three contexts:

1. *a historical context* that included multiple threats to their families;
2. *a social context* in which deportation's impact extended far beyond the deported individual to encompass her/his family and community; and,
3. *a transnational* context in which deportation affected family members both in the United States and in their country of origin.

They all identified not only poverty, but also both poverty and violence in their countries of origin as forces that motivated them to migrate to the United States.[43] Migrants described a search for economic opportunity as well as one for safety. They first recounted the difficult decisions to migrate within their national borders where possible (to *fincas* or cities) and then beyond them (to Mexico or the United States). Migration itself inevitably resulted in family members, especially parents and children, being separated. This produced feelings of isolation, loneliness, and sadness. Families described various ways in which they worked hard to maintain communication and connection with loved ones "*allá.*" (back there). Many discussed the emotional pain of migration-related separation, and those who had children "*allá*" and "*acá*" (there and here) experienced what one participant described as "a heart divided."

All of this was powerful enough, but the study also revealed particularly harsh aspects of how deportees understand deportation. Participants described how recent shifts in attitudes, practices, and policies toward immigrants in the United States have profoundly affected their families. Fourteen families (78 percent) described the experience and/or threat of detention and deportation as a threat to "keeping the family together." Eight parents (44 percent) reported that actual or threatened deportation-related separation had already definitely affected the well-being of their children. Negative effects on children identified by their parents included: academic problems, sadness, crying, sleep and appetite disturbance, insecurity about the future, worry, fear, nightmares, speech difficulties, withdrawing, and increased tantrums.

Parents also reported that they, too, were emotionally affected. This, in turn, affected their interactions with their children and the children's development. Parents described their own sadness, loss of energy, hopelessness, crying, anxiety, lost sleep, weight loss and gain, anger, fear, distrust, nightmares, and worry. They talked about what it was like to live every day in a constant state of vulnerability and insecurity.

Perhaps most strikingly, the participating families clearly linked the current threats to their families posed by deportation to a history of repressive practices that have threatened them for generations. They recounted the bitter irony of having fought so hard to reunite after the separation due to migration, only to face once again being torn apart. They also noted similarities between their current environment in the United States—one that includes fear, silence, anxiety, and suspicion—to the climate in their countries of origin during *la violencia*. One participant even described deportation as "the second war."

Such research helps those of us who are not directly affected by deportation to understand how uncertainty, fear, and mistrust permeate the current environment in which noncitizens live, work, and raise children. It expands our understanding of the dramatic negative effects for individuals, families, and the community. But government responses have been minimal, and, as noted, the deportation laws do not much respect family unity. In the aftermath of a series of raids that affected hundreds of children in 2007, ICE promulgated some new "humanitarian" policies for enforcement actions.[44] New guidelines mandate screening and expedited release of pregnant women, nursing mothers, and parents who are the sole caretakers of minor children, as well as alternatives to detention programs for arrestees who do not pose a threat or flight risk. ICE agents must now also coordinate with other federal and local social service agencies to determine humanitarian needs of those arrested.[45] In some situations, these guidelines seem to have lessened the duration of parent-child separations and, occasionally, have prevented separation entirely.[46] But all of this, of course, addresses only the harmful effects of the *process* of deportation raids and arrests, not the ultimate family trauma and separation caused by deportation itself. Though some progress has been made on that front as a matter of prosecutorial discretion, this has been a controversial and in many respects marginal enterprise to date.

The effects of deportation on children and families have clearly moved some judges. Some—seeing no legitimate alternative—have dutifully rendered their decisions and then bemoaned the consequences. A typical formulation might begin: "While the court is not unmoved by the plight . . . ." Other cases may contain a plea to the Congress or the executive to recalibrate the laws or to exercise some sort of ameliorative discretion. Judge Harry Pregerson of the Ninth Circuit Court of Appeals, for example, dissented in some sixty unpublished dispositions in which he noted that ordering the deportation of a noncitizen parent in effect would result in the effective deportation of a U.S. child. In a published dissent to a decision deporting the parents of four U.S. citizen children, Judge Pregerson wrote: "I pray that soon the good men and women in our Congress will ameliorate the plight of families like the [petitioners] and give us humane laws that will not cause the disintegration of such families."[47] As we shall see, however, some judges have been still more strenuous in attempting to interpret deportation laws in the most humane ways possible, though in many cases such actions test the outer bounds of their judicial role and of legal legitimacy.

So how should we assess the effects of deportation? We have long known, of course, that international migration often causes family separation and distortions of various kinds.[48] It may also later lead to family re-formation, as migrants develop new family ties. Countless generations of voluntary migrants—from Ireland to China, from Palestine to Poland, from Ethiopia to Vietnam—have endured the poignant pain mixed with hope attendant to the departure of a loved one seeking a better life. But deportation—especially of the types practiced in the United States recently—adds a harsh and involuntary complication to such separation. As we have seen, U.S. deportation law is increasingly aimed at long-term residents, and it then bars reentry (for some, for life). A deportation order often means never seeing one's children grow up, not being able to care for one's parents, or not being able to be with a spouse.[49]

Finally, we should consider an array of other effects of deportation. First, there is the question of monetary cost. As we have seen, the system as it exists costs billions of dollars annually. In March 2010, researchers attempted to assess the costs of "mass deportation."[50] They estimated the total cost to American taxpayers for the mass deportation of all undocumented noncitizens to be $285 billion. A federal dragnet to arrest some 11 million undocumented immigrants in the United States over five years would cost about $200 billion. Annual recurring border and interior enforcement costs would be at least another $17 billion annually (in 2008 dollars) just to maintain the status quo at the border and in the interior, or a total of nearly $85 billion over five years. To be sure, some might be willing to spend such a large amount of money to achieve the ultimate goals of *extended entry border control* deportation and to eliminate the undocumented from our midst. But think of the positive programs on which such sums could also be spent. Further, deportation cost estimates must include not only direct costs, but also the costs of family separation, the increased physical and mental health consequences caused by family separation, and the likelihood that children in such families will have greater difficulty in school, more trauma, and perhaps even a greater likelihood of criminal behavior in their future. Indeed, the alternative strategy—legalization and the creation of more flexible immigration channels—could significantly *expand* the economy by a cumulative $1.5 trillion in gross domestic product over ten years through increased consumer spending, higher tax receipts, and other related factors.[51] The deportation approach, by contrast, could drain some $2.5 trillion over ten years from the U.S. economy, a $4 trillion swing in GDP.[52] Obviously, all of this is somewhat speculative. But a proper audit of the accomplishments and effects of deportation requires at least the attempt.

Consider, too, the effect of such a massive deportation regime on other aspects of our legal system and culture. How, exactly, would the removal of more than 11 million undocumented people be accomplished? How many people would leave the country voluntarily in response to a massive government crackdown? How many would have to be forcibly arrested? The integration of millions of these individuals in the United States suggests that the number who would leave voluntarily would be small. A 2010 study noted that only about 0.9 million—or about 8 percent—of the estimated 10.8 million undocumented residents arrived in the United States between 2005 and 2008. The rest arrived earlier and were thus deeply integrated. "Many work multiple jobs, actively engage with their faith congregations, and have children and spouses who are U.S. citizens."[53] Full enforcement would require approximately 8.64 million separate arrests, detentions, legal proceedings, and, finally, transportation out of the country of such people.[54] All of this, of course, is hypothetical and highly unlikely in the current political climate, as was *Operation Endgame* (see Chapter 3). But we should look at the *existing* system through a similar lens and ask whether it is really worth the monetary, social, and other costs. When viewed not as a *fait accompli*, but as a massive social experiment, one might well wonder about the balance between harm and demonstrable good done by a system that was rigidly designed and has been poorly planned and badly administered.[55]

Human Rights, Crime Control and National Security in the New Diaspora

Proponents of *post-entry social control* deportation often cite the removal of serious social problems or, as some put it, "bad people" as one of its main virtues. This position has garnered strong political support and inspired moralistic discourse since the founding of the republic to the young J. Edgar Hoover and early twentieth-century sociologists advocating the skimming of the "scum from the melting pot," to the present calls for removal of gang members and drug dealers.[56] There may of course be some wisdom in this—nobody wants gangs or drug dealers in their communities. This is why banishment had had such a long pedigree. The modern prison, too, is often similarly used as a "warehouse" to store undesirables away from law-abiding communities. This seems to many a sensible strategy—until the inmates are inevitably released, often lacking job skills, rehabilitation, or counseling.[57] Deportation may at first blush seem a less problematic strategy: the insulating effects of borders and distance seem more protective even than prisons. And many deportees, as we have seen, will never be able to return legally to the United States.

But as we examine it closely, the wisdom of *post-entry social control* deportation becomes considerably less clear. First, as we have seen, the deportation laws have cut a very wide swath through the population of noncitizens convicted of crimes. The vast majority of criminal deportees have been relatively minor offenders, and sociological research has shown that crime is not particularly caused by immigrants so much as it is caused by living in the United States. Crime rates among first generation immigrants are quite low—even lower than those for U.S. citizens (see studies cited in Chapter 4).

Let us turn first to how deportation actually affects the deportees themselves, a problem that raises serious questions about the proportionality of the sanction. The human rights abuses often endured by deportees should shock the consciences of people in both the sending and the receiving countries. These include incarceration under terrible conditions, deracination, alienation, profound social ostracism, and outright torture. Apart from the concern we ought to have about deportees as human beings, the role of the U.S. government in such matters raises very powerful questions that have largely gone unconsidered and unaddressed by the U.S. legal system.

Following this inquiry, we will consider, more pragmatically, the actual effects of deportation on the countries and communities to which the deportees are sent. Emerging research indicates that these consequences have been profoundly negative in many places, both in terms of economics and crime rates. Whatever one may think of the reliance by developing countries upon remittances, the sudden shock caused by stepped-up deportations is certainly a crude mechanism to effect change.[58]

Finally, we must think about a complex and worrisome effect of decades of deportation: the creation of a large, world-wide, American *diaspora* of deportees. From Cambodia to Ecuador, from the Azores to Brazil, from Haiti to Pakistan, we find tens, if not hundreds, of thousands of English-speaking, U.S.-acculturated deportees. It is difficult, perhaps impossible, to assess perfectly the human rights, national security, economic, and foreign policy aspects of this unplanned state of affairs. But the fact that it was unplanned and that its possible consequences have been largely ignored to date surely is both unwise and inexcusable.

Human Rights Abuses Faced by Deportees

The more one studies the fate of deportees, the more deeply one becomes concerned about severe human rights abuses. To be sure, some governments, such as in the Azores, Guatemala, and Ecuador, have developed agencies to greet and reintegrate deportees. Ironically, these agencies sometimes style themselves "Migration Agencies" even as they welcome back people whom they also consider their own. But, over the years, the human rights abuses suffered by deportees in many places amount to a worldwide scandal for which the United States must be considered at least partially responsible.

For many deportees, the process begins when they are arrested for committing a crime and after a long incarceration in a U.S. prison cell. Most will be escorted by federal marshals, often in handcuffs and sometimes in leg shackles, too, to an airport for the trip "home." Some have been forcibly medicated; others simply suffer silently through the inevitable dread and anxiety. As one deportee put it, "I had never felt a fear like I felt when they deported me."[59] Another said, "I felt like I had been kidnapped and left in Santo Domingo to waste."[60] Many remain in restraints throughout the flight and often are not permitted to use lavatories, which, for some, leads to embarrassing urination in their clothes. Stories of the anxiety and humiliation of deportation are remarkably consistent across cultures. Jane Lopacka, a mental health professional in Phnom Penh who works with U.S. deportees, described new arrivals as "pretty desperate people, very lonely, and traumatized."[61]

What they encounter when they reach their destinations varies tremendously. Some describe beatings by the police upon arrival;[62] and many others describe various humiliating rituals that make it clear to them that the police have their eyes on them from the start. Some of the worst reported abuses have been in Haiti. Consider the case of Kervence Video Carry, a Haitian man with minor criminal convictions who was deported to Haiti, imprisoned, returned to the United States for his appeal, and then finally redeported to Haiti. Carry's case offers a painfully clear look at the horrors that have awaited many deportees.[63] As his lawyers described in their brief to the Eleventh Circuit Court of Appeals, uniformed Haitian officials, armed with automatic weapons and clubs, boarded the airplane as the deportees arrived.[64] They called out the names of the deportees, removed their handcuffs and tied their hands with plastic rope. Mr. Carry was then taken to a jail and locked in a cell measuring approximately ten by twelve feet together with thirteen other deportees. The cell was filthy and completely bare: no mattresses, chairs, beds, washbasins, or toilets. The only source of light and ventilation was a small hole in the wall. After sundown, the cell was completely dark. Because of overcrowding, the detainees had to sleep sitting up. They were provided with plastic bags in which to urinate and defecate. Sometimes these bags remained uncollected for several days at a time and overflowed onto the floor of the cell. The detainees were then forced to urinate on the floor of the cell. If it rained during the day, they would be attacked by swarms of mosquitoes at night. The cell was full of vermin including roaches, rats, mice, and lizards. Detainees who got sick vomited all over the floor of the cell.

The detainees were only let out of the cell for five minutes every two to three days. They were given two minutes to defecate into a hole in the ground and three minutes to wash themselves with collected rain water. They were provided no food, water, or medical attention. Mr. Carry was forced to beg other detainees for juice and water. On the second day after he arrived, he drank rain water from the courtyard and became violently ill after a few hours with vomiting, uncontrollable diarrhea, and a fever. The skin on his feet became severely infected from the filth he was forced to step in. When Mr. Carry requested medical attention, guards mockingly told him, "You gotta be halfway dying . . . before they take you . . . to see a doctor." He witnessed a detainee dying of AIDS. This person was barely able to move or even talk and was vomiting profusely. He was given no medical attention and was left to die in the cell.

Mr. Carry also witnessed guards and police officers beating detainees frequently. One detainee was clubbed on the head by a police officer. He had a big gash on his forehead and was bleeding on the concrete floor of the cell. He was not given any medical attention. At night Mr. Carry would hear the screams of inmates being beaten and tortured. He was held for weeks in such conditions. Others have reportedly been held for as long as ten months.[65] Still, a U.S. court concluded that although the conditions in Haitian prisons were "atrocious,"[66] they did not rise to the level of torture required for relief under the Convention Against Torture (CAT).[67] Thus, deportation to these conditions continued apace, with full knowledge U.S. authorities.[68]

Severe human rights problems, though extreme in Haiti, are certainly not unique to that country. Nor are they only caused by government confinement of deportees. A recent newspaper story about a deportee in El Salvador began like a Raymond Chandler novel: "One man is dead, shot in the mouth . . . presumably for speaking ill of a gang. Another man lives in hiding . . . hoping his former gang will not mete out a similar punishment to him."[69] Both men, it turned out, had once fled to the United States, where they had sought asylum, based on their fear of harm from the street gangs in El Salvador. Both men had been deported, like thousands of others, simply swept away pursuant to contemporary deportation laws. "Good riddance," said our legal system to these swarthy, often-tattooed, "wretched refuse."

Such cases force us to consider the often deadly consequences of deportation. In the case of the murdered man from El Salvador—Benito Zaldívar—the Board of Immigration Appeals knew that he had "indicated that the gang members threatened to hurt his family if he did not join." But this was apparently not a specific enough threat for the BIA, which held that "neither the respondent nor anyone in his family has ever been harmed" and then ordered him deported. Mr. Zaldívar was murdered two months later.[70]

Perhaps it is unfair, with the clarity of hindsight, to blame the immigration judge or the BIA. But, as we learn more about these cases, they appear increasingly common and predictable. As a boy, Mr. Zaldívar was left with grandparents in La Libertad, a town on the coast of El Salvador, when his parents came in 1994 to work in the United States. He said the Mara-18 gang (which was formed by Hispanic immigrants in Los Angeles in the 1980s and had established a presence in Central America when its members were deported from the United States to their native countries) had started trying to recruit him when he was not yet a teenager. The gang was more forceful with him than with his friends. He thought it was because the gang members knew he didn't have a big family to take care of him. Then his grandmother died. In 2003, when he was 15, Mr. Zaldívar decided he could no longer safely resist the gang, and he fled El Salvador to join his parents, legal residents with temporary status, living in Carthage, Missouri. His parents could not obtain a legal visa for him, and Mr. Zaldívar was caught by border agents when he tried to cross into the United States. This was when he applied for asylum and was permitted to rejoin his parents. "I'm going to high school in Carthage," he informed the court, "and I feel safe for the first time in my life."[71]

Eight weeks after he was denied asylum and was deported, a white van pulled alongside Mr. Zaldívar as he rode his bicycle through La Libertad. Witnesses saw a Mara-18 gunman shoot him in the face, in apparent revenge for speaking against the gang. Mr. Zaldívar's father said his daughter had persuaded him not to return for his son's funeral. "It left me with an empty place .... But she said the gangs could blow me away, too."[72]

According to the United Nations Development Program, Central America is, in general, the most violent region of the world, apart from war zones.[73] This is primarily due to violence from criminal gangs. Still, in 2008, the BIA, though recognizing that "gang violence and crime in El Salvador appear to be widespread," maintained substantial legal hurdles for asylum seekers fleeing gangs.[74] As one expert put it: "Requirements have been imposed that make no sense in terms of prior jurisprudence and are impossible to interpret."[75] Indeed, a well-known conservative, Judge Richard A. Posner of the United States Court of Appeals for the Seventh Circuit, referred to the Board's standards as "illogical" and "perverse."[76] And still, in El Salvador, thousands of deportees remain in a situation where, as one put it, "There are gangs everywhere here. . . . [W]hen you leave [them], even your best friend will murder you."[77] Most tragically, the gangs are often the only social group available to deportees.

To local police, it often matters little whether deportees are actually gang members or not. In El Salvador, as in many countries, deportees have become scapegoats for worsening crime and other societal problems. They are widely treated as gang members, which leads to societal stigmatization and abuses by the police.[78] Indeed, even the then-President of El Salvador, Antonio Saca, once referred to deportees coming from the United States as "extremely dangerous people that have to be watched."[79] The Director of the National Civil Police described deportees as "a problem for public security."[80] All of this exposes deportees to abuse and persecution, such as being targets for pervasive rights abuses committed by police, starting from the moment they arrive at the airport in San Salvador.[81] Cases have been reported of newly arrived deportees being detained and arrested for pretextual reasons. The National Human Rights Ombudsman, Beatrice Alamanni de Carrillo, said that following deportees' registration at the airport, "When a crime is committed, one of these people will be detained."[82] Deportees in Salvadoran society have thus been well described as "victims of a cycle that seems to leave them with few options."[83]

The situation is often worst for those who had migrated from El Salvador as children.[84] A 2008 study focused on deportees who had lived for long periods in the United States (on average fourteen years), many of whom were deported for criminal conduct. The study found that the age at which a person migrated is a primary predictor of educational attainment, language proficiency, gang involvement, and reason for deportation: the younger, the better. It was also, however, predictive of reintegration problems following deportation. The deportees who had emigrated as children and who had formed the deepest U.S. ties suffered the most. Deportees had migrated with their families during the Salvadoran civil war in the 1980s. Many were now fluent in English. Indeed, some could not speak Spanish. All were well adapted to American norms, including, unfortunately, Los Angeles gang culture. For them, deportation was an especially harsh and often confusing sanction. Many had seen their lives as a process of "becoming American." In fact, one had not even known he was Salvadoran until he found himself in deportation proceedings.[85] All had "left family members and other loved ones behind."[86]

After deportation, these young people experience stigmatization more intensely than those who had migrated as adults.[87] Deportees who had formed the deepest connections to U.S. society "consistently stated that they are identifiable by how they walk . . . their English- and Mexican-influenced accents, lighter color skin, style of dress, and visible tattoos."[88] They report that the general Salvadoran public "gives them dirty looks, refuses to sit next to them on the bus . . . ." They also said they were regularly strip-searched and detained by police officers and vigilantes posing at police.[89]

Throughout the new American diaspora, the suffering experienced by U.S. deportees is deep, multifaceted, and pervasive. Julianne Hing has eloquently described the plight of a Jamaican deportee, Calvin James, 45, who in 2004 was sent to Kingston, Jamaica, a place he had not seen since the age of 12.[90] Detained upon his arrival, in the standard practice of the police, he was thoroughly interrogated—"Do you have family you will be contacting? What address will you be staying at? What are your local relatives' names?" But James, like so many others, had no one to call. Things soon got worse: he landed in Spanish Town, which he described as "like a battle zone." He said, "that's where they leave you. A foreigner don't make it past a night on those streets."

Eventually, James found a distant relative living in the countryside town of Rosemount, on the northwestern coast of Jamaica. He went to live with her, but life was very difficult. Like most Americans, he had taken running water and electricity for granted, but Rosemount had neither. He had to walk half a mile up and down a mountain to bring water to the two-room house. He and his aunt were practically strangers to each other. He had no job prospects and no source of income. A coordinator with a resettlement group that helps connect deportees with family, jobs, and housing found James's story to be typical. Many deportees are men of his age who had left Jamaica as children. She offers them hard advice: "You have to unlearn to relearn. Let go of your past. Dr. Wendel Abel, a professor of psychiatry noted that "Deportees arrive, and they are homeless, effectively stateless, and without family." Another psychiatrist offered a demoralizing portrait of the typical Jamaican deportee: "You don't know what to eat; you don't know where to sleep." She said that almost 100 percent of deportees deal with depression and anxiety.[91] In addition to these tangible hardships, deportees in Jamaica, as elsewhere, face powerful social stigma. As Bernard Headley, a professor of criminology, put it: "You were supposed to go abroad and send home remittances, but now you come back here a worthless deportee." Nancy Anderson, the director of the Independent Jamaican Council of Human Rights, offered a still bleaker assessment: "The word 'deportee' is a bad word. Even used cars that break down on the road, you say, 'It's a deportee.'"[92] James, luckier than many, was finally able to find a job. He had hoped to save money and to send for his partner and their son someday. But such a goal began to seem very unlikely as he realized that—even working sixteen hours a day—with a take-home pay averaging $75 a week—he would never accumulate what his family would need to make the move to Jamaica.[93]

Similar stories of ostracism and hardship are told by deportees around the world.[94] In Cambodia, the deportees are "little more than tourists, dependent on maps to find their way around." Many have no language skills and are unable to communicate with other Cambodians. They are treated like outsiders. As of mid-2010, at least six Cambodian deportees have reportedly committed suicide.[95] In the Dominican Republic, it is said that native Dominicans can "spot a deportee from afar," as they are revealed by their dress, their walk, their language. This marks them—perhaps for life—as outsiders. They have been well described as "the Other of the Other."[96]

Effects of Deportation on the Countries to Which Deportees are Sent

Even if we were to ignore the powerful normative policy concerns about deportation—domestically and abroad—we would see problems with deportation as a crime control strategy. As many have noted, the deportation of criminals is problematic in terms of its effects on the countries to which deportees are sent. Charles S. Osborne, the former governor of Michigan, put it this way nearly a century ago:

> What right have we to dump on anybody anywhere a contagion, intellectual, or social, or physical, or moral.... Suppose that the Asiatic cholera had broken out here. ... [W]ould we try to cure it by shipping it back to Asia where it could most illy be dealt with and where it would continue to germinate and form a world menace until the cause were eradicated?[97]

Such questions about the efficacy and consequences of deportation are even more worthy of serious consideration now.

The effects of deportation are difficult enough to measure in the United States and still harder to quantify abroad. However, a growing body of research has documented serious problems of increased crime and economic disruption related to U.S. deportees. The basic causes of such problems might seem fairly obvious. But they must be considered with great care, as dangerous stereotypes abound, and the potential for scapegoating is quite real.

There is no doubt that the presence of large, displaced populations can lead to increased criminality, especially—as is the case with U.S. deportation—when that population includes many young men without roots, jobs, families or language skills. This observation does not contradict the fact that, as we have seen, there is no direct link between immigration and crime in the United States. The main difference, it seems, is that between an energetic, optimistic, enterprising, and situated immigrant community, versus a dispirited, deracinated, demoralized deportation cohort. The crime problems caused by deportation, moreover, are not necessarily confined to the countries of deportation. A U.N. study has noted how "diaspora networks" of marginalized populations can form the basis of transnational organized crime.[98] Unfortunately, the crime problem has been exacerbated by "zero tolerance" enforcement-focused government policies known in Central America as *mano dura* (iron fist). The general conclusion among researchers is that these policies have been "both ineffective and counterproductive."[99] According to a U.N. report, under these circumstances, a heavy hand is not what is needed. Rather, "the hand must be applied with finesse, and all the resources of government, not just the security sector, must be applied strategically." What is needed is a thoughtful, cross-disciplinary strategy for crime prevention.[100]

Deportees—especially criminal deportees—can certainly be a very heavy burden for small Central American states, with rates of underemployment that have averaged approximately 65 percent and with severely strained law enforcement and judicial capacity.[101] The quick solutions to the crime problems posed by deportees have led to deprivations of civil liberties and overcrowded prisons. But these methods do not solve the problems. Violent crime in Central America is still a major social fact, and increasingly sophisticated criminal ties between Central America and the United States have also "exacerbated the United States' illegal immigration problems."[102] Many factors explain the crime and violence plaguing, for example, El Salvador.[103] Of critical importance were political and social consequences of the country's brutal twelve-year civil war. These must in turn be understood in light of centuries of repressive authoritarian rule in the service of a small elite, wide class stratification, weak democratic institutions, persistent political polarization, corruption, an ineffective judicial system, and high levels of poverty and unemployment.[104]

Even a cursory look at recent history demonstrates the poignant complexity of the effects of large numbers of deportees in such a country. By 2007, an estimated 750,000 people were internally displaced, and another 1 million had left the country (about 20 percent of the population), mostly headed for the United States. What was originally a "symptom of crisis" in El Salvador became a key source of economic support for those left behind. Incomes earned in the United States and transferred home had become the country's largest foreign exchange earner, equal to 16 percent of GDP in 2005.[105] This, of course, is not unique to El Salvador.[106] As I have personally observed in Guatemala and Ecuador—and as many studies elsewhere have confirmed—the sudden drop in such remittances has caused massive economic disruptions with which governments struggle to cope. Some of this, of course, has been caused by the economic downturns in 2008–2009; but deportations have also played a major role.

The basic story is similar for many groups, though the particular neighborhoods and specific cultural details obviously vary. In the case of El Salvador, the standard account is that through the 1980s and 1990s, large numbers of Salvadoran immigrants settled in the United States, mostly in Southern California, where Spanish is widely spoken. Many stayed in historically Hispanic neighborhoods, such as the Los Angeles Rampart district, which were, unfortunately, relatively poor and rather crime-ridden. The migrants and, more significantly, their children were often victimized by existing gangs. Largely in self-defense and in imitation of the model they experienced, they formed the *Mara Salvatrucha* gang, which eventually metastasized into a major, violent criminal enterprise, sucking in new recruits and expanding internationally.[107] Many of the gang's early members had fought in the Salvadoran civil war, and others were hardened by the bloodshed they had seen. As one commentator put it, "most of the founding gang members were intimately familiar with violence."[108] However, the streets of Los Angeles "served as a 'finishing school' for the members of MS-13 as they learned quickly the importance of organization and violence to survive."[109]

Within a decade, MS-13 (the rival gang of Mara-18, discussed above in the case of Benito Zaldívar) had become one of the largest and most violent gangs in Southern California.[110]

Deported Salvadoran gang members were then forcibly returned to a country afflicted by poverty, corruption and chaos, The result, exactly as Voltaire and Governor Osborne would have predicted, was not reduced crime but the *exact opposite*: a huge, violent, worldwide gang, estimated by the FBI in 2007 to have had 10,000 members in forty-two states, with an additional 50,000 members living in El Salvador, Guatemala, Honduras, and Mexico.[111] As we have seen, many U.S. members of this group were deported back to El Salvador during the late 1990s for a host of different reasons, some because of criminal convictions, and others because of their association or suspected association with the gang. In El Salvador, they reorganized, re-armed, and brought with them a hard-edged, violent gang culture they had learned in the United States. They thus presented unprecedented, powerful challenges for El Salvador's police and society, resulting not only in the *mano dura* policies described above, but also in considerable social ostracism and isolation. Similar stories can be told about flows of people from and to Honduras and Guatemala as well as Haiti, the Dominican Republic, Jamaica, and Cape Verde. In 2005, the Guatemalan police asserted that half of the deportees they saw were gang members, a conclusion doubted by others, but difficult to prove one way or the other.[112] Of course, as many would respond, these gang members and convicted criminals must bear personal responsibility for their conduct. We cannot simply excuse them as suffering from "a social disease" or say, as Bernstein and Sondheim once put it, "*I'm depraved on account I'm deprived.*"[113] But our recognition of the personal culpability of many of these young people should not obscure the clear fact that they have now been rendered a dangerously—sometimes tragically—deracinated, largely inassimilable, permanently "foreign" population in their countries of birth. The question, in short, is not about culpability—remember, too, that nearly all of criminal deportees have *already served their sentences* through the criminal justice system—it is about wise, fair, and mature social policy.

Further, causation is a major question. How much responsibility should the United States bear for criminalizing these young men, if indeed that is what has happened? Since, as we have seen, many of the deportees were removed for minor crimes, is it not logical to ask whether it was the *fact of deportation itself* that may have hardened their criminal tendencies and forced them into deeper associations with gangs that they might well have outgrown had they been permitted to live more normal lives with their families and communities in the United States? Further research on all such questions is crucial, but there can be little doubt that the criminal deportation system might actually be responsible for some of the rising crime rates that have afflicted the countries to which deportees have been sent.

Some of the most vigorous debates and best research about these phenomena have taken place in Jamaica. For years, Jamaica has received more criminal deportees than any other country in the Western Hemisphere. These have included deportees from the United Kingdom and Canada, as well as from the United States. Jamaica has also witnessed dramatic increases murder rates in the first few years of the twenty-first century. Were the deportees to blame? One can understand the Jamaican government's hypotheses in this direction. Indeed, the United States deported over 200 convicted murderers and 128 sex offenders to Jamaica between 2001 and 2004. On the other hand, however, some 81 percent of criminal deportees were for nonviolent offenses, and murder has traditionally had a low recidivism rate, so the statistics are not conclusive. Researchers have struggled to answer these questions. Bernard Headley, a professor of criminology at the University of the West Indies, examined some five thousand records of criminals deported from the United States between 1997 and 2003. He found that the mean age of entry to the United States was 23 years and that the majority of deportees (62 percent) were 31 years or older (the average age was 35) when they arrived back in Jamaica. Under normal circumstances, men of this age are rather unlikely to reoffend, especially with street violence.[114] Indeed, in 2006, the Minister of National Security, Peter Phillips, announced to the Jamaican House of Representatives that a government study had reached a remarkable conclusion: deportees *were in fact no more likely than the general population to be convicted of a crime.* About one in eighteen deportees had been convicted in Jamaica, compared to one in seventeen in the general population.[115]

Ultimately, of course, the best way to answer the question of deportees and crime would be to maintain careful statistics. Early attempts at such studies undertaken by Barbados and Trinidad and Tobago have also tended to exonerate deportees. Of 332 criminal deportees returned to Barbados between 1994 and 2000, only 43 (13 percent) had been charged with a criminal offense at the time of the study, mostly for burglary or drug-related offenses. In Trinidad and Tobago, of the 565 deportees received between 1999 and 2001 only 83 (15 percent) had been charged with a crime, of whom almost half (47 percent) had been charged with larceny or drug offenses. These reoffense rates are reportedly much lower than among local criminals.[116] Further research on the composition of the prison population in Jamaica has similarly indicated that deportees are less likely to be convicted than the average Jamaican.[117]

So what is to be done? Though garnering relatively little attention in the United States,[118] the problems caused by deportation and other forms of "return migration" have become important international issues. In 2002, for example, a "Reintegration Fund" was created by the International Organization for Migration (IOM) to provide financial support to returnees. The aim was "to facilitate a sustainable return to the country of origin." The stories of its support for returned migrants range from the charming to the bizarre, but all show at least a continuing sense of responsibility for those who were forced to leave.[119] Many governments and NGOs have also begun to develop programs to help deportees. For example, the Returnee Integration Support Center works to help the integration into Cambodian society of people who were admitted to the United States as refugees and deported back to Cambodia. The organization provides assistance with documentation, employment, housing, and referral services "in order to support returnees who seek assistance in becoming independent and productive members of society."[120]

Deportation of a long-term resident, with its forced separation from family, "is a kind of mourning experience. There is disappointment, and the missing, and shame and embarrassment, and it can be hard for love to find a way through all of these hurts."[121] Deportees describe themselves as like "bags of garbage thrown into a trash heap."[122] In my experience with many deportees over the years, the sadness never seems to go away; the hope of a possible return—a flickering, ephemeral evanescence—mixes with guilt and shame and haunts deportees for the rest of their lives. As one Dominican deportee put it, "I just want to be a father for my daughter, and I think she deserves it. . . . She's my only child, and she deserves it, and she wants to be a doctor, and I can't do it from here."[123] His sentiments were echoed by a father in Cambodia, deported away from his two sons, aged 10 and 13. "I paid for what I did. It shouldn't take me away from those I love."[124]

Of course, such concerns are not new, though the numbers have risen astronomically. A 1953 Presidential Commission on Immigration & Naturalization issued a powerful report entitled, "Whom We Shall Welcome," a phrase that was taken from George Washington's speech to Irish immigrants in 1783. Yet some of the Commission's most critical findings involved not whom we would welcome but whom we should deport. The Commission concluded that the criminal deportation laws of that era should be reformed. As the Commission noted in the case of three particular deportees:

> Each of the aliens is a product of our society. Their formative years were spent in the United States, which is the only home they have ever known. The countries of their origin which they left—in two cases during infancy, in another, at the age of 5 years—certainly are not responsible for their criminal ways. . . . If such a person offends against our laws, he should be punished *in the same manner as other citizens and residents of the United States* and should not be subject to banishment from this country.[125]

In subsequent years some of the Commission's suggestions for ameliorative discretion and proportionality were adopted by the Congress and by administrative practice. But since 1996, many of these practices have been abandoned in favor of harsh, automatic deportations. It may be impossible—though I do not believe it is completely impossible—to undo the harm caused by our recent deportation delirium, but surely it is possible to recognize it and to begin to craft more nuanced and humane systems. How might this be done? In the next chapter, we will grapple with problems of legitimacy and the rule of law and consider whether legal solutions may be found in the aftermath of our deportation frenzy.

Notes

1. U.S. Senate floor debate, Mar. 30, 2006, http://mccain.senate.gov/public/index. cfm?FuseAction=PressOffice.Speeches&ContentRecord_id=ce7596a1-0670-40f0-b054-e5c3650c02dd&Region_id=&Issue_id=cc583bcb-bd9b-45b2-8a8e-180567714118.
2. Michael Matza, *200 March in Philly to Protest Deportation of Four Cambodians,* PHILADELPHIA INQUIRER, Jan. 18, 2011, *available at* http://articles.philly.com/2011-01-18/ news/27034660_1_protest-deportation-khmer-rouge-cambodian-men.
3. Harisiades v. Shaughnessy, 342 U.S. 580, 600 (1952) (Douglas, J., dissenting).
4. *See* Evelyn Nakano Glenn, *The Social Construction and Institutionalization of Gender and Race: An Integrative Framework,* in REVISIONING GENDER 3, 5 (Myra Marx Ferree et al. eds., 1999).
5. *See generally* BRIAN POWELL ET AL., COUNTED OUT: SAME-SEX RELATIONS AND AMERICANS' DEFINITION OF FAMILY (2010).
6. *See, e.g.,* Rhacel Salazar Parrenas, *Transnational Mothering: A Source of Gender Conflicts in the Family,* 88 N.C. L. REV. 1825, 1854–55 (2010); Leah Schmalzbauer, *Disruptions, Dislocations, and Inequalities: Transnational Latino/a Families Surviving the Global Economy,* 88 N.C. L. REV. 1857, 1869–72 (2010).
7. *See* BILL ONG HING, DEPORTING OUR SOULS: VALUES MORALITY AND IMMIGRATION POLICY 58–64 (2006) (discussing the "rise and fall" of the 212(c) waiver); *see also* Nancy Morawetz, *Rethinking Retroactive Deportation Laws and the Due Process Clause,* 73 N.Y.U. L. REV. 97, 110–11 (1998).
8. Meyer v. Nebraska, 262 U.S. 390, 399 (1923).
9. Loving v. Virginia, 388 U.S. 1, 12 (1967) (quoting Skinner v. Oklahoma, 316 U.S. 535, 541 (1942)).
10. Moore v. East Cleveland, 431 U.S. 494, 499 (1977) (quoting Cleveland Bd. of Educ. v. LaFleur, 414 U.S. 632, 639–40 (1974)).
11. Universal Declaration of Human Rights, Article 16, G.A. Res. 217A, at 71, U.N. GAOR, 3d Sess., 1st. plen. mtg., U.N. Doc A/810 (Dec. 12, 1948). *See also* International Covenant on Civil and Political Rights, G.A. Res. 2200A (XXI), art. 23(1), at 52, U.N. Doc. A/6316 (Mar. 23, 1976); Organization of American States, American Convention on Human Rights, art. 17(1), Nov. 22, 1969, O.A.S.T.S No. 36, 1144 U.N.T.S. 123.
12. Alison Parker & Daniel Kanstroom, *United States: Time to Rethink the Deportation of Long-Time Legal Non-Citizen Residents Who Commit Low-Level Offenses* (Sept. 24, 2006), *available at* http://hrw.org/english/docs/2006/09/25/usdom14258.htm.
13. David L. Marcus, *Three Times and Out; Some Face Deportation for Repeat Drunken Driving,* BOSTON GLOBE, Oct. 14, 1998, at A1.
14. Mario also noted: "My dad hasn't hurt anybody and he has never been involved in any kind of accident." Another of his sons, Joe, 36, said: "The federal government is picking and choosing when to apply the law. . . . What they're doing seems to us to be based on race and who has political power." *Id.*
15. Frank Trejo, *2 Groups Defend DWI Deportations—INS, MADD Say Effort Necessary; Critics Call Actions Anti-Immigrant,* DALLAS MORNING NEWS, Sept. 4, 1998, at 33A.

16. *Id.*

17. Marcus, *supra* note 13.

18. DAVID C. BROTHERTON & LUIS BARRIOS, BANISHED TO THE HOMELAND: DOMINICAN DEPORTEES AND THEIR STORIES OF EXILE 164–76 (Columbia University Press 2011).

19. *Id.* at 176.

20. Thus, one in five people in the United States is either a first- or second-generation U.S. resident. U.S. Census Bureau, *Nation's Foreign-Born Population Nears 37 Million, More Than One in Five People in the U.S. are First or Second Generation* (Oct. 19, 2010), *available at* http://www.census.gov/newsroom/releases/archives/foreignborn_population/cb10-159.html. *See also* Foreign-Born Population of the United States Current Population Survey—March 2009, *available at* http://www.census.gov/population/www/socdemo/foreign/cps2009.html.

21. U.S. Census Bureau, *Nation's Foreign-Born Population supra* note 20.

22. HUMAN RIGHTS WATCH, *Forced Apart (By the Numbers)*, table 1 (Apr. 15, 2009), *available at*, http://www.hrw.org/en/reports/2009/04/15/forced-apart-numbers-0.

23. *Id.,* Overview. Indeed, Human Rights Watch showed that ICE has kept records for only 10.7 percent of noncitizens who were legally in the United States prior to their deportation.

24. *Id.*

25. Nancy Morawetz, *Understanding The Impact Of The 1996 Deportation Laws And The Limited Scope Of Proposed Reforms*, 113 HARV. L. REV. 1936, 1954 (2000).

26. David Thronson, *Choiceless Choices: Deportation and Parent-Child Relationship*, 6 NEV. L. REV. 1165 (2006).

27. Thronson, *Choiceless Choices, supra* note 26, at 1165; *see also* Jennifer M. Chacon, *Loving Across Borders: Immigration Law and the Limits of Loving*, 2007 WISC. L. REV. 345, 357–58 (2007).

28. Julianne Hing, Seth Wessler, & Jorge Rivas, *Torn Apart by Deportation*, COLORLINES (Oct. 22, 2009), *available at* http://www.colorlines.com/archives/2009/10/torn_apart_by_deportation.html.

29. *Id.*

30. *See* BILL ONG HING, DEPORTING OUR SOULS, *supra* note 7.

31. *See* Deborah Sontag, *In a Homeland Far from Home*, N.Y. TIMES, Nov. 16, 2003 *available at*, http://www.nytimes.com/2003/11/16/magazine/in-a-homeland-far-from-home.html?pagewanted=all.

32. *Id.*

33. The phrase "1.5 generation" refers to those brought to the United States as young children.

34. Rubén G. Rumbaut & Golnaz Komaie, *The Future of Children*, 20(1) TRANSITION TO ADULTHOOD 43 (Spring 2010), http://www.jstor.org/stable/27795059 (citing Jody Agius Vallejo and Jennifer Lee, *Brown Picket Fences: The Immigrant Narrative and "Giving Back" among the Mexican-Origin Middle Class*, 9 ETHNICITIES 5 (2009)).

35. Perhaps most importantly, those who grew up poor (but were not poor now) were more likely to "give back" to their parents, relatives, and the co-ethnic community. Jody Agius Vallejo & Jennifer Lee, *Brown Picket Fences: The Immigrant Narrative and "Giving Back" among the Mexican-Origin Middle Class*, 9 ETHNICITIES 5 (2009).

36. *See* Peter Margulies, *Children, Parents, and Asylum*, 15 GEO. IMMIGR. L.J. 289, 301–02 (2001) (discussing necessity for independent representation for minors in immigration proceedings).

37. Olowo v. Ashcroft, 368 F.3d 692, 695 (7th Cir. 2004); *see* Thronson, *Choiceless Choices, supra* note 26.

38. R. Capps, & R. Castaneda, PAYING THE PRICE: THE IMPACT OF IMMIGRATION RAIDS ON AMERICA'S CHILDREN (Urban Institute for the National Council of La Raza 2007).

39. OFFICE OF THE INSPECTOR GENERAL—DEPARTMENT OF HOMELAND SECURITY, REMOVALS INVOLVING ILLEGAL ALIEN PARENTS OF UNITED STATES CITIZEN CHILDREN (2009).

40. IN THE CHILD'S BEST INTEREST? THE CONSEQUENCES OF LOSING A LAWFUL IMMIGRANT PARENT TO DEPORTATION, (U.C.–Berkeley School of Law & U.C.–Davis, School of Law 2010).

41. Between February and July 2008, lawyers and social science researchers from the Center for Human Rights and International Justice (CHRIJ) at Boston College collaborated with two immigrant rights community organizations, Centro Presente and Organización Maya K'iche, in a "participatory action research project." One of the project's aims was to document the experiences related to migration and deportation of a group of Guatemalans and Salvadorans living in Rhode Island and Massachusetts. Additional goals were to identifying challenges and resources among participating families, and to strengthen leadership capacity and advocacy with and for immigrants in New England. *See* Kalina Brabeck, Brinton Lykes, & Rachel Hershberg, *Framing Immigration to and Deportation from the United States: Guatemalan and Salvadoran Families Make Meaning of Their Experiences*, 14 COMMUNITY, WORK AND FAMILY, 275–96 (2011).

42. The project involved an initial series of meetings to build on existing relationships, discuss concerns, identify common goals, and design a means of studying the impact of deportation. Community leaders identified potential families for participation on the basis of the following qualities: (1) their ability to strengthen the organization's leadership, (2) their having been directly or indirectly affected by detention or deportation, and (3) their having children who were living with them in the United States. Throughout the project, meetings were held between university researchers and community organizations to share understandings and concerns that emerged from the process and to identify action steps.

43. Fifteen families (83 percent) cited poverty as the main reason for migrating to the United States. Nine families (50 percent) spontaneously discussed the fear, silence, and displacement of family that took place during *la violencia* (the violent years). Eight families (44 percent) reported the murder of an immediate family member during the years of armed conflict in their countries of origin. Four participants (22 percent) described decisions to migrate to the United States as related to loss of family, security, land, and community that followed from *la violencia*.

44. The guidelines at first applied only to actions that involved more than 150 arrests. They were later applied to operations as small as 25 arrests. ICE Release, "Guidelines for Identifying Humanitarian Needs among Administrative Arrestees" (Nov. 2007).

45. *See* Wendy Cervantes, Yali Lincroft, & Ken Borelli, *Caught Between Systems: The Intersection of Immigration and Child Welfare Policies*, May 21, 2010, *available at* http://www.firstfocus.net/library/reports/caught-between-systems-the-intersection-of-immigration-and-child-welfare-policies.

46. *See generally* A. Chaudry, R. Capps, J.M. Pedroza, R.M. Castaneda, R. Santos, & M. Scott, FACING OUR FUTURE: CHILDREN IN THE AFTERMATH OF IMMIGRATION ENFORCEMENT (The Urban Institute 2010).

47. Memije v. Gonzales, 481 F.3d 1163, 1165 (9th Cir. 2007) (Pregerson, J., dissenting) (citing Cabrera-Alvarez v. Gonzales, 423 F.3d 1006, 1015 (9th Cir.2005) (Pregerson, J., dissenting)).

48. Jacqueline Hagan, Karl Eschbach, & Nestor Rodriguez, *U.S. Deportation Policy, Family Separation, and Circular Migration*, 4(1) INT'L MIGRATION REV. 64, 76 (Spring 2008); Jacqueline Hagan, Brianna Castro, & Nestor Rodriguez, *The Effects of U.S. Deportation Policies on Immigrant Families and Communities: Cross-Border Perspectives*, 88 N.C. L. REV. 1799 (2010).

49. Deportation may, of course, also reunite families—albeit under extremely difficult circumstances. A father or son may return, in shame, knowing that not only does he lack a job, but he also bears some responsibility for the added debt, with interest, that his family incurred to send him to the United States. Moreover, the family no longer will receive the remittances that he may have been sending. Daughters and mothers may return to children they have not seen in many years, while leaving behind their other children in the United States. Some may have been raped or otherwise abused and traumatized when they traveled through Central America and Mexico to the United States. Indeed, in recent years, labor migrant streams have become increasingly feminized, a trend referred to by some researchers as "transnational motherhood." Among Salvadorans, for example, it appears that deportees who leave spouses or children behind make up a significant proportion of the total deportee population. This generates substantial return migration pressures among many thousands of deportees. Apart from humane considerations, the implication of this

for future enforcement efforts is that economic controls (i.e., employer sanctions) will not likely impede the re-migration of deportees seeking to return to their spouses or children. P. Hondagneu-Sotelo & E. Avila, *"I'm Here, But I'm There": The Meanings of Transnational Motherhood*, 11(5) GENDER & SOC'Y 548 (1997).

50. Marshall Fitz, Gebe Martinez, & Madura Wijewardena, *The Costs of Mass Deportation Impractical, Expensive, and Ineffective* (Mar. 2010), *available at* http://www.americanprogress.org/issues/2010/03/deportation_cost.html.

51. Raúl Hinojosa-Ojeda, *Raising the Floor for American Workers*, Center for American Progress, Jan. 7, 2010, *available at* http://www.americanprogress.org/issues/2010/01/raising_the_floor.html; Peter B. Dixon & Maureen T. Rimmer, *Restriction or Legalization? Measuring the Economic Benefits of Immigration Reform* (Cato Institute, 2009), *available at* http://www.cato.org/pub_display.php?pub_id=10438.

52. *Id.*

53. Fitz et al., *supra* note 50, at 5.

54. *Id.*

55. *See* DANIEL KANSTROOM, DEPORTATION NATION (Harvard University Press 2007).

56. *See generally* KANSTROOM, DEPORTATION NATION, *id.*

57. *See* subsection *infra*, "Effects of Deportation on the Countries to Which Deportees are Sent."

58. *See* Adam Feibelman, *The Very Uneasy Case Against Remittances: An Ex Ante Perspective*, 88 N.C.L. REV. 1771 (2010) (arguing that the existing literature on remittances almost universally underestimates the overall costs and negative effects of remittances and remittance-driven migration by failing to include various costs and harms borne by migrating workers and their families).

59. BROTHERTON & BARRIOS, *supra* note 18, at 265.

60. *Id.*

61. *See* WALTER LEITNER, INTERNATIONAL HUMAN RIGHTS CLINIC, RETURNEE INTEGRATION SUPPORT CENTER, DEPORTED DIASPORA, REMOVING REFUGEES: U.S. DEPORTATION POLICY AND THE CAMBODIAN-AMERICAN COMMUNITY 18 (Spring 2010).

62. BROTHERTON & BARRIOS, *supra* note 18, at 262.

63. Note that one may be deported as an "aggravated felon," even with a suspended sentence. *See* 8 U.S.C. § 1101(a)(48)(B) (2000).

64. Petition for Review of Final Decision of the Board of Immigration Appeals at 8, Carry v. Ashcroft, No. 02-11752-DD (11th Cir. Aug. 6, 2002). I am grateful to Jenny Landau and Jennifer Moore for bringing this brief to my attention.

65. U.S. Bureau of Citizenship & Immigration Services, *Haiti: Information on Conditions in Haitian Prisons and Treatment of Criminal Deportees (2nd Response)*, Feb. 12, 2002, HTI02001.ASM, *available at* http://www.unhcr.org/refworld/docid/3dec98224.html.

66. *Francois v.* Ashcroft, 343 F. Supp. 2d 327, 329 (D.N.J. 2004).

67. The Convention against Torture and Other Cruel, Inhuman or Degrading Treatment or Punishment (CAT), G.A. Res. 39/46, U.N. Doc. A/RES/39/46 (Dec. 10, 1984). Article 3 of the Torture Convention mandates that signatory states shall not return a person to a country in which there is a substantial likelihood that he or she would be tortured. The Convention protects noncitizens from U.S. deportation via its incorporation into the Foreign Affairs Reform and Restructuring Act of 1998, Pub. L. No. 105-277, div. G, Title XXII, § 2242(b), 112 Stat. 2681-2822 (1998). CAT requests for asylum and withholding of removal need not involve claims of persecution on the basis of race, religion, nationality, membership in a particular social group, or political opinion, because proof of torture, not simply persecution, is required. To obtain relief, an applicant must show that it is more likely than not that he would be tortured if returned to his home country. 8 CFR § 208.16–208.18 (2007). Interpretive trends in CAT claims in the United States are toward increasingly restrictive interpretations. *See* Lori A. Nessel, *Forced to Choose: Torture, Family Reunification and United States Immigration Policy*, 78 TEMPLE L. REV. 897, 900 (2005) (suggesting that the narrow construction placed on CAT may be attributed to the view that the claimants are undesirable); Lori A. Nessel, *"Willful Blindness" to Gender-Based Violence Abroad: United States Interpretation of Article 3 of the United Nations Convention against Torture*, 89 MINN. L. REV. 71, 113 (2004).

68. *See* Mary Holper, *Specific Intent and the Purposeful Narrowing of Victim Protection Under the Convention Against Torture*, 88 Or. L. Rev. 777, 796–801 (2009).

69. Julia Preston, *Losing Asylum, Then His Life*, N.Y. Times, June 28, 2010, *available at* http://www.nytimes.com/2010/06/29/us/29asylum.html.

70. *Id.*

71. *Id.*

72. *Id.*

73. *See* Francisco Díaz Rodríguez & Sidney Blanco. *Deficiencias policiales, fiscales o judiciales en la investigación y juzgamiento causantes de la impunidad*, United Nations Development Program El Salvador, (San Salvador: UNDP May 2007).

74. S-E-G-, 24 I. & N. Dec. 579, Interim Decision #3617 (B.I.A. 2008) (Neither Salvadoran youth who have been subjected to recruitment efforts by the MS-13 gang and who have rejected or resisted membership in the gang based on their own personal, moral, and religious opposition to the gang's values and activities nor the family members of such Salvadoran youth constitute a "particular social group."); E-A-G-, 24 I. & N. Dec. 591, Interim Decision #3618 (B.I.A. 2008) (young Honduran male failed to establish that he was a member of a particular social group of "persons resistant to gang membership"; membership in a criminal gang cannot constitute membership in a particular social group, therefore the respondent could not establish that he was a member of a particular social group of "young persons who are perceived to be affiliated with gangs" based on the incorrect perception by others that he is such a gang member).

75. Deborah Anker (quoted in Preston, *Losing Asylum, supra* note 69).

76. *See generally* Washington Office on Latin America (WOLA), Central American Gang-Related Asylum (2008), *available at* http://www.wola.org/es/node/641.

77. Preston, *Losing Asylum, supra* note 69.

78. *See* Int'l Human Rights Clinic, Human Rights Program, Harvard Law School, No Place to Hide: Gang, State, and Clandestine Violence in El Salvador 95 (Feb. 2007), *available at* http://www.law.harvard.edu/programs/hrp/documents/FinalElSalvadorReport%283-6-07%29.pdf.

79. *Id.* (citing Saca Preocupado por Deportaciones, La Prensa Gráfica, Mar. 16, 2005).

80. *Id.*

81. Law enforcement authorities, apparently often working with Interpol, have subjected arriving deportees to a process known informally as registration. They are photographed and interviewed regarding their criminal history, previous gang associations, and where they plan to live and work. *Id.*

82. *Id.*

83. *Id.* (citing interview with José Miguel Cruz).

84. K. Dingman & R. Rumbaut, *The Immigration-Crime Nexus and Post-Deportation Experiences: Encountering Stereotypes in Southern California and El Salvador*, 31 La Verne L. Rev. 363 (2008).

85. *Id.* at 393.

86. *Id.* at 393–94.

87. Dingman & Rumbaut, *supra* note 84, at 394.

88. *Id.* at 395.

89. *Id.*

90. Julianne Hing, *Home in Name Only*, Oct. 20, 2009 *available at* http://www.colorlines.com/archives/2009/10/home_in_name_only.html.

91. *Id.* (quoting Dr. Myo Oo).

92. *Id.*

93. *Id.*

94. Most ironically, deportees face the assumption that the U.S. system of criminal justice and deportation is so fair and unbiased that the deportees must have engaged in truly heinous crimes to warrant such a harsh sanction. Nina Siulc, Unwelcome Citizens, Criminalized Migrants, and the Quest for Freedom: Deportees in the Dominican Republic, at 62 (May 2009) (unpublished Ph.D. dissertation,) (on file with author).

95. *See* Leitner, *supra* note 61, at 19.

96. Brotherton & Barrios, *supra* note 18, at 278, 331.

97. Charles S. Osborn, *Is Deportation the Cure?* 212 N. Am. Rev. 180 (Jan. 1920).
98. U.N Office on Drugs & Crime, Crime and Development in Central America: Caught in the Crossfire 39 (May 2007) [hereinafter U.N. Crossfire] *available at* http://www.unodc.org/pdf/Central%20America%20Study.pdf.
99. WOLA, *supra* note 76, at 4.
100. U.N. Crossfire, *supra* note 98.
101. *See* Freddy Funes, *Removal of Central American Gang Members: How Immigration Laws Fail to Reflect Global Reality*, 63 U. Miami L. Rev. 301, 310 (2009).
102. Today, the most powerful gangs, *Mara Salvatrucha* (MS 13) and *Mara* 18, have diversified their practices to include kidnapping, extortion, and human and drug trafficking. They are a major force in Central America, Mexico, and most major U.S. cities. *See* Funes, *id.*, at 313. *See also* Jeffrey Corsetti, *Marked for Death: The Maras of Central America and Those Who Flee Their Wrath*, 20 Geo. L. Immigr. L.J. 407 (Spring 2006).
103. *See* Int'l Human Rights Clinic, Human Rights Program, Harvard Law School, No Place to Hide, *supra* note 78.
104. *Id.* (citing U.S. Agency for Int'l Development, Central America and Mexico Gang Assessment 49–50 (2006), *available at* http://www.crin.org/docs/usaid:gang_assessment.pdf; *see also* Joaquín M. Chávez, *An Anatomy of Violence in El Salvador*, in 37(6) North American Congress on Latin America (NACLA) Report on the Americas (May/June 2004); Comisión de la Verdad para El Salvador, de la Locura a la Esperanze: La Guerra de 12 Años en El Salvador (1993), *available at* http://www.usip.org/publications/truth-commission-el-salvador (English version).
105. U.N. Crossfire, *supra* note 98, at 39 (citing ECLAC (CEPAL), *Panorama Social de América Latina 2005* (United Nations 2005)).
106. *Id.* In other countries, remittances amount to about 10 percent of Gross Domestic Product. There has been tremendous dependency on these capital flows as engines of economic growth. The highest percentages in Central America were seen in Nicaragua (18 percent) and El Salvador (16 percent), major sending countries of immigrants to the United States and, more recently, major receiving countries of deportees.
107. U.N. Crossfire, *supra* note 98, at 39–41.
108. *See* Casey Kovacic, Creating a Monster: MS-13 and How United States Immigration Policy Produced "The World's Most Dangerous Criminal Gang," 12 Gonz. J. Int'l L. 2 (2008).
109. Colin McMahon, *Back from L.A. with a Graduate Education in Mayhem; Salvadoran Gang Members Learn From U.S. Mean Streets*, Chicago Tribune, June 2, 1995, at N1.
110. Rich Connell & Robert J. Lopez, *Gang Sweeps Result in 103 Arrests; In a Nationwide Action, Authorities Round Up Members of MS-13, Formed in L.A. and Now Involved in Smuggling, Trafficking, and Murder*, L.A. Times, Mar. 15, 2005, at B1.
111. Cara Buckley, *A Fearsome Gang and Its Wannabes*, N.Y. Times, Aug. 19, 2007, at WK3.
112. O. López, *De 2004 a la fecha, 228 mil han sido expulsados de EE.UU.; la mitad pertenece a pandillas*, Prensa Libre, Mar. 4, 2005.
113. *Gee Officer Krupke* (Leonard Bernstein Music Publishing Company LLC 1956).
114. B. Headley, M. Gordon, & A. MacIntosh, Deported Volume 1: Entry and Exit Findings Jamaicans Returned Home from the U.S. Between 1997 and 2003 (2005). *See generally* Crime, Violence, and Development: Trends, Cost, and Policy Options in the Caribbean, Joint Report by the U.N. Office on Drugs and Crime and the Latin America and the Caribbean Region of the World Bank (Mar. 2007), especially ch. 6, *Case Study: Criminal Deportations and Jamaica*, *available at* http://siteresources.worldbank.org/INTHAITI/Resources/CandVfrontandacknowledgments.pdf.
115. *See* U.N. Crossfire, *supra* note 98 (citing M. Dougherty, D. Wilson, & A. Wu, Annual Report: Immigration Enforcement Actions 2005 (U.S Dep't of Homeland Security 2006)).
116. *See* United Nations Office on Drugs and Crime and the Latin America and the Caribbean Region of the World Bank, *supra* note 114 at 128–36; C. Griffin, *Criminal Deportation: The Unintended Impact of US Anti-crime and Anti-terrorism Policy along Its Third Border*. 30(2) Caribbean Stud. 39–76 (2002).

117. CARICOM, REPORT OF THE TASK FORCE ON CRIME AND SECURITY, GEORGETOWN, 32–38 (2002), *available at* http://www.caricom.org/jsp/community/regional_issues/crime_ and_security.jsp?menu=community.

118. In 2011, the United States Agency for International Development (USAID) and IOM launched a two-year Guatemalan Repatriates Project (GRP) "to provide urgently needed assistance to Guatemalan migrants returned by air from the US and by land from Mexico." The new project will expand the current basic services being provided to those arriving by air at the Fuerza Aerea Airport and will include assistance to those returning from Mexico through the San Marcos land border crossing. The assistance includes the "provision of hygiene kits, psychosocial support, legal advice, transportation to communities of origin, and effective social and economic reintegration through vocational training and job placement by the GRP Referral and Opportunities Centre (CRO) in the capital, Guatemala City." Given the history of USAID in Guatemala, a certain skepticism about this initiative is in order. But, as it is one of the rare instances of organized U.S. government support for deportees, it is worth close observation. *See* IOM Helps Guatemalan Migrants Returned from US and Mexico, Mar. 6, 2011, http://www.iom.int/jahia/Jahia/media/press-brief-ingnotes/pbnAM/cache/offonce/lang/en?entryId=29748.

119. IOM, STORIES OF RETURN (2007), http://www.iom.int/jahia/webdav/shared/shared/mainsite/microsites/IDM/workshops/managing_return_migration_042108/stories_of_return.pdf.

120. RISC MISSION STATEMENT, http://www.risccambodia.org/about/.

121. Julianne Hing, *supra* note 90.

122. Nina Siulc, Unwelcome Citizens, Criminalized Migrants, and the Quest for Freedom: Deportees in the Dominican Republic, at 5 (unpublished Ph.D. dissertation) (May 2009) (on file with author).

123. *Id.*

124. Interview with Kamol Seyha (pseudonym) in Phnom Penh, Cambodia, Mar. 23, 2010, in Feibelman, *The Very Uneasy Case, supra* note 58, at 20.

125. PRESIDENT'S COMM'N ON IMMIGRATION & NATURALIZATION, WHOM WE SHALL WELCOME 202 (1953).

6

Law in the New Diaspora: Deportees and the Space/Time Continuum

The United States is entirely a creature of the Constitution. Its power and authority have no other source.
—Reid v. Covert (1957) *(plurality opinion)*[1]

Legal interpretation takes place in a field of pain and death . . . . A judge articulates her understanding of a text, and as a result, somebody loses his freedom, his property, his children, even his life.
—Robert Cover (1986)[2]

In this chapter we will consider the legal aspects of all that has come before. We can usefully begin with two of the most fundamental legal concepts. The first is territory (the physical space where government action occurred or where the claimant stands). Noncitizens within the United States have well-recognized rights based not only on "their personhood" but also on "their territorial presence."[3] As we have seen, the border and territorial ideas are deeply intertwined with U.S. immigration laws, connecting to the basic distinction between exclusion and deportation. The place where a noncitizen stands can have a wide range of consequences. For example, once a person with a deportation order leaves U.S. soil—voluntarily or otherwise—the order is considered to have been "executed" (or rendered final and effective). The statute says that "any alien ordered deported or removed . . . *who has left the United States*, shall be considered to have been deported or removed in pursuance of law. . . ."[4] Administrative appeals to the BIA are automatically deemed withdrawn if the deportee departs the United States.[5] The most fundamental questions, explored below, concern how territory relates to rights claims and to access to the U.S. legal system.

The second concept is that of time, a vector with many relationships to deportation law.[6] First, the passage of time may be a condition precedent to a legal status, such as naturalization, or for transforming a "conditional" legal status into a permanent one.[7] A second, similar use of time is as a prerequisite to possible discretionary relief from deportation. For example, certain deportees who have lived in the United States since 1972 may apply for legal permanent residence through a mechanism known colloquially as "registry."[8] Other forms of discretionary relief, such as "cancellation of removal" have specific time periods for eligibility.[9]

Time may also be directly protective, as with criminal law statutes of limitations that preclude prosecution after a certain amount of time has passed since the offense was committed.[10] Deportation law does not contain a statute of limitation as such. However, there are specific time periods *after* which some sorts of crime will not result in deportation. For example, a person is subject to deportation for conviction of a crime of moral turpitude if it was committed within five years of the person's admission to the United States.[11] (There are, however, no such time limits for aggravated felonies and for many other crime-based grounds of deportation.)

A deportee may be barred from reentering the United States for particular periods of time, depending upon the reasons for deportation. Indeed, various periods of time spent in "unlawful presence" may also result in long additional bars against legal reentry.[12] Finally, the passage of time affects when a case is "final." A petition for review of a decision of the BIA, for example, must be filed in the federal court of appeals within thirty days.[13] If it is not filed in time, the order will generally be deemed final.

Time, like territory, has long been recognized as both a source of powerful rights claims and a systemic problem. The immigration statutes and courts have seen the passage of time as a link to (if not a proxy for) powerful affiliations, acculturation, and even reliance on nonenforcement.[14] Writing in 1926, Judge Learned Hand poignantly outlined these connections:

> [D]eportation under the circumstances would be deplorable. Whether the relator came here in arms or at the age of ten, he is as much our product as though his mother had borne him on American soil. He knows no other language, no other people, no other habits, than ours; he will be as much a stranger in Poland as any one born of ancestors who immigrated in the seventeenth century. However heinous his crimes, deportation is to him exile, a dreadful punishment, abandoned by the common consent of all civilized peoples.[15]

Soon thereafter, the first "registry" law allowed certain noncitizens (it only applied to those "not ineligible to citizenship"—a euphemism that barred Asian immigrants) to regularize their status if they could show that they had resided in the country continuously since 1921, were not otherwise subject to deportation, and were of "good moral character."[16]

On the other hand, one of Congress's fundamental purposes in enacting the modern judicial review system for immigration law was "to abbreviate the process of judicial review . . . in order to frustrate certain practices . . . whereby persons subject to deportation were forestalling departure by dilatory tactics in the courts."[17] The pre-1996 review system, as we have seen, contained automatic stays of removal while appeals and motions were pending. Thus, every delay was sometimes said to work "to the advantage of the deportable alien who wishes merely to remain in the United States."[18] Congress's intent "was to expedite both the initiation and the completion of the judicial review process."[19] The current system, though it allows direct appeals to be pursued by a deportee abroad, still has a thirty-day filing deadline for appeals as well as time limits for motions.[20]

Deportation law thus combines space, time, and, of course, legal status in complex ways that reflect deep conceptions of state power and individual rights. For example, as we have seen, the Board of Immigration Appeals took a rather mechanical, binary approach to the question of space. As the BIA put it, physical removal under an order of deportation is a "transformative event that fundamentally alters the alien's posture under the law."[21] This proposition is at least partly correct: indeed one might see this "transformative" feature as the essence of deportation law. But should the particular fact of physical removal cause such a fundamental transformation? For the BIA, leaving U.S. soil meant "a nullification of legal status, which leaves [the deportee] in no better position after departure than any other alien who is outside the territory of the United States"?[22] And, "no better position" could mean essentially rightless. To assess the propriety of such a bright-line model, we should consider how territory has historically related to rights claims. Woody Allen once famously said that "eighty percent of success is showing up."[23] This may well capture the essence of a complex jurisprudential history. But that possible residual 20 percent could matter a great deal.

One might think of this as a sort of "social contract" question. In a 2004 legal brief, U.S. government attorneys argued that, because "overseas aliens" are not a part of the "contract that created the United States," they are not "beneficiaries of its protections."[24] Put simply, these lawyers used the social contract device to assert that "overseas aliens" had no constitutional rights at all. Lacking constitutional status, they were, constitutionally speaking, not even "persons" as described in the Fifth Amendment. But such an absolutist approach is hard to reconcile with constitutional ideas of limited government and basic human rights. James Madison once responded to this "no-rights" position by noting that even if aliens were not "parties" to the Constitution, "it does not follow that the Constitution has vested in Congress an absolute power over them. . . ."[25] Madison was referring to noncitizens on U.S. soil, but the rationale would also seem to reject a rigid, territory-based view of deportees' rights.[26] Otherwise, the government could simply violate noncitizens' basic rights domestically, transport them abroad, and then use the territorial limitation to evade judicial oversight.[27] Territory, in short, can never be considered as an absolute or a completely independent criterion, however one views the "social contract." One might accept that implementation of exclusion laws against noncitizens who have never been to the United States, have no connections there, and who are physically abroad are not generally reviewable by U.S. courts.[28] But surely that is very different from the situation of a person who has been forcibly removed from U.S. soil by government action, especially as a matter of *post-entry social control*. As Oliver Wendell Holmes Jr. once noted, "even a dog distinguishes between being stumbled over and being kicked."[29]

To explore the legal debates about the rights of deportees, then, we will first consider the legitimacy of using space or, in more technical parlance, *territoriality* as a determinant of deportees' enforceable rights. If a deportee abroad is in "no better position . . . than any other alien," does this mean that a sort of legal black hole surrounds the individual, in the way that some once described Guantánamo Bay detainees?[30] We can discern two basic contending models. One is rather formalistic and offers bright territorial lines for rights: basically *"in is in and out is out."* The other position requires more nuance and qualification, but it has the convincing virtue of being potentially responsive to compelling rights claims. Its general outline is as follows:

1. *All people* who come into contact with government agents when seeking to enter (or to reenter) a nation-state have *at least certain basic procedural rights*;
2. *Certain defined classes of people*—such as refugees and those who might face torture, serious harm or death—have powerful *substantive rights* as well;
3. Both procedural and substantive rights are greater, and under the U.S. system are constitutionally protected, for long-term residents (especially those who had legal status)—*even if they are outside of U.S. territory*—than they are for most initial entrants or short-term visitors.

This model actually describes much of U.S. immigration law fairly well. But it has faced considerable pressure in recent years.[31] Of course, these are often matters of complex, technical legal interpretation, the full depths of which will not be plumbed in this work. However, they implicate fundamental constitutional and normative principles that call out for more sustained and serious consideration than they have generally received.

Space

Much of U.S. immigration and citizenship law—indeed much of U.S. and international law generally—is based on a territorial, state-based idea, the modern roots of which extend back to a series of seventeenth-century treaties known colloquially as the "Peace of Westphalia."[32] The most well-known example of territoriality goes back even further than this—to the ancient, now constitutionally protected idea of *jus soli* citizenship, i.e., birthright citizenship guaranteed by the place of one's birth.[33] Although scholars question the clarity with which the Westphalian treaties, as such, instantiated the modern state system,[34] one essential principle may be attributed to them—that legal systems are largely congruent with national territorial boundaries. This, as noted earlier, now seems so "intuitive" that it is rarely questioned.[35] We have long accepted the fundamental fact of "a spatial conception of sovereignty,"[36] along with such related principles as a right to self-determination, legal equality between states, and nonintervention by states in the internal affairs of others.[37] On the other hand, of course, contemporary supranational systems such as the European Union, transcendent human rights legal norms, and enforcement regimes such as Interpol[38] render much of the old territorial intuition increasingly problematic.[39] Questions of the modern scope of territoriality are thus at the heart of some of our most compelling current legal dilemmas, from drones to Guantánamo Bay to the "wars" on drugs and terror. Still, as Alex Aleinikoff has noted, much of U.S. constitutional law has remained "largely locked in nineteenth-century conceptions of statehood" derived from the basic Westphalian models.[40] This is especially true of deportation law.

The basic question is whether certain rights guarantees of U.S. law extend to individuals who have been compelled to leave U.S. territory. Does—and should—removal from U.S. territory mean the end of legally enforceable rights? It is very difficult—perhaps impossible—to fully disaggregate this spatial question from that of legal status. Recall that the prior status of deported individuals varies greatly. Deportees may have been undocumented recent border crossers, legally admitted tourists, students, workers and other "nonimmigrants," as well as lawful permanent residents. (There is no question that wrongly deported *citizens* retain powerful rights if they can prove their status.)[41] Still, the deportees' spatial dilemma evokes special problems of extraterritorial application of U.S. law.

The increasing application of U.S. law and power abroad in the context of law enforcement and the "war on terror" raises a powerful question: does U.S. law similarly expand to protect individual rights?[42] A good starting point for our answer is the fact that territoriality has always been a complex and contingent concept, never a formalistic absolute. Consider a simple "private law" question: what law applies if a U.S. corporation injures a U.S. citizen in Mexico, but the victim then sues in the U.S.? The common law rule was that U.S. courts would apply Mexican law to the case. The theory, basically, was that the obligation "follows the person, and may be enforced wherever the person may be found."[43]

U.S. government actions abroad requires us to consider more variables. First is the question of whether extraterritorial jurisdiction may be legitimately extended at all. Second is a long, complicated history of judicial interpretation of potentially extraterritorial statutes. And finally, there is the question of what constitutional rights, if any, people have when affected by U.S. government actions abroad.[44]

As to the first question—whether jurisdiction may be extended abroad—we should begin with international law, as interpreted in the U.S. legal system.[45] Territory is the most well-accepted basis for legal jurisdiction in the Westphalian system: every nation-state has "legislative jurisdiction" or "jurisdiction to prescribe" over events taking place and persons found within its own territory.[46] Territory has been called the "normal" or "primary" basis for jurisdiction.[47] As one well-known treatise puts it: "The starting-point in this part of the law is the proposition that, at least as a presumption, jurisdiction is territorial."[48]

A second, well-accepted basis for extraterritorial jurisdiction is nationality.[49] Nationality has been long recognized by U.S. law as a basis for jurisdiction in many situations.[50] For example, U.S. tax laws apply to U.S. nationals living abroad (as well as to lawful permanent resident aliens). Laws against treason and laws requiring registration for the military draft also apply to U.S. nationals abroad,[51] as do some criminal laws.[52]

Under the so-called "protective principle," states may also seek to extend jurisdiction over extraterritorial conduct that "is directed against the security of the state or against a limited class of other state interests."[53] Under this principle, courts have occasionally upheld immigration-related convictions such as knowingly making a false statement under oath while applying for a visa to an American consular official located in a foreign country.[54] Similarly, U.S. legal jurisdiction may apply to "conduct outside its territory that has or is intended to have substantial effects within its territory."[55] This so-called "objective territorial principle" (a variant is sometimes called the "effects doctrine")[56] can be quite powerful. It has, for example, been applied to sustain the conviction of a defendant for possession of marijuana with intent to distribute even though he was caught on the high seas.[57] Some nation-states also assert jurisdiction over actions that affect their nationals living abroad. This is known as "passive personality" jurisdiction.[58] Finally, international law has long accepted that some criminal offenses, such as slavery, piracy, crimes against humanity, and genocide, may engender "universal jurisdiction," rendering perpetrators subject to prosecution by whichever state captures them.[59]

Before we move to specific questions of U.S. constitutional rights, we should briefly consider the complicated history of interpretive presumptions that have governed this field. Early nineteenth-century Supreme Court cases relating to piracy had stated a general presumption against extraterritorial application.[60] A strong presumption against extraterritorial application of U.S. law was later articulated in a 1909 case known as the *American Banana* case.[61] Justice Holmes, relying more on the field known as "conflict of laws" than public international law, called the idea "rather startling" that an act of Congress (in this case antitrust laws) could apply to actions that occurred "outside the jurisdiction of the United States" or beyond "the territorial limits over which the lawmaker has general and legitimate power."[62] The territorial model, he said, required that "all legislation is *prima facie* territorial in nature," and it was "the general and almost universal rule ... that the character of an act as lawful or unlawful must be determined wholly by the law of the country where the act is done."[63]

Although the strength of this presumption has declined over time, it has not disappeared. In 1922, the Court held that a federal statute criminalizing false claims against the United States or certain corporations applied to actions taken by U.S. nationals in Brazil.[64] A 1949 case, however, considered whether a law that required that every contract to which the United States was a party must provide for time-and-a-half pay for work beyond eight hours a day applied to a U.S. national hired to work on a U.S. construction project in Iran. The Court, applying the presumption, found no evidence that Congress had intended the labor law to reach "beyond places over which the United States has sovereignty or has some measure of legislative control."[65] Over time, Holmes's rather rigid model has often given way to multifactored tests that look to "effects," "interests," "contacts," and various other flexible concepts.[66] The presumption was important, however, in a case involving noncitizens held aboard U.S. ships. President George H. W. Bush had ordered the Coast Guard to intercept vessels outside U.S. territorial waters and to return individuals to Haiti without determining whether they were legally protected as refugees.[67] Advocates argued that this violated both a multilateral treaty and a federal statute that prohibited the return of noncitizens to a country if the Haitians' "life or freedom would be threatened because of race, religion, nationality, political opinion, or membership in a particular group."[68] The Supreme Court held that the U.S. statute did not apply to actions by the Coast Guard outside U.S. territorial waters, largely because of the presumption against extraterritoriality.[69]

Rights claims made by noncitizens outside of U.S. territory are thus especially challenging. But the presumption against extraterritorial application of U.S. laws is not insurmountable. Indeed, in *Rasul v. Bush*, the first Guantánamo case to reach the Supreme Court, the Court applied the federal habeas statute to detainees without even mentioning the presumption.[70] This was particularly significant in that the Court had previously applied the presumption to a U.S. scientific mission in Antarctica and a U.S. Coast Guard vessel on the high seas.[71]

What about deportees? As we have seen, some U.S. laws clearly apply abroad to noncitizens and deportees. For example, direct appeals of deportation cases may be prosecuted from abroad. And all sorts of immigration applications, visas, waivers, etc. may be applied for from foreign soil. The hard questions are how to interpret legal ambiguities in, for example, habeas corpus statutes and how protective of deportees' rights the U.S. constitutional legal system is.

As a normative base, we might consider the connections between deportation law and the legal system's historical approach to chattel slavery.[72] Though this may seem an unduly provocative inquiry, the roots of the modern deportation system are deeply intertwined with the history of slavery.[73] And certain legal dilemmas that arose regarding fugitive and migrating former slaves in the context of antebellum territorial expansion are analogous to those now faced by deportees. For example, a recurring nineteenth-century legal question was whether a master who took a slave to a state or territory where slavery was prohibited had effectively emancipated the slave. What law controlled? Some slave-state courts, as a matter of "comity," had held in favor of emancipation, with variations depending upon the purpose or the length of the travel into free states and territories.[74] In free states, conversely, comity would often be overridden by the general abhorrence of slavery first exemplified by Lord Mansfield's famous declaration in the *Somersett* case, that slavery was "so odious, that nothing can be suffered to support it, but positive law."[75] All ambiguity and all interpretive presumptions would be applied against it. Lord Mansfield had framed the question as "whether any dominion, authority or coercion can be exercised *in this country* [England], on a slave according to the American laws?"[76] The 1772 *Somersett* decision did not outlaw slavery, but it made clear that English law would not protect slaveholders claims as to their "property" *on English soil*, regardless of the length of their stay in England or their legal domicile.[77]

Territoriality thus was mediated by normative values and discretionary principles of comity. The rule in "the general law of nations," as well as among the states, had been that no nation was bound to recognize the state of slavery as to "foreign slaves found within its territorial dominions, when it is in opposition to its own policy and institutions." If it were to do so, it was merely as a matter of comity and "not as a matter of international right." Slavery was limited as a legal rule to the territory of the entity that accepted it.[78]

In the U.S., slaves who were *actually emancipated* under one state's laws (which could happen in either a slave or a free state) and who were then caught in a slave state would seem to present an easier question.[79] Imagine a slaveholder residing in a slave state, who had emancipated his slave through his will. If the emancipated slave chose to "emigrate" to another slave state, even where emancipation by will was not permitted, the person's legal status might well have remained free.[80] The former slave, in effect, could *personally* carry the right to freedom into the new state or territory. In the international sphere, such an outcome could be justified by what was termed *courtesy*: duly executed laws are to have the same effect everywhere, so long as they do not "prejudice . . . the rights of the other governments, or their citizens."[81] In practice, what this meant was that "personal rights or disabilities, obtained or communicated by the laws of any particular place . . . accompany the person wherever he goes."[82]

The tensions among territorial sovereignty, personal rights, and comity/courtesy collided momentously in the case of Dred Scott, a slave owned by John Emerson. Scott had moved with Emerson from Missouri, a slave state, to the free state of Illinois and to the Wisconsin territory, where slavery was prohibited by the Missouri Compromise. Years later, he sued for his freedom, first in state and then in federal court. The Supreme Court of Missouri rejected Scott's personal rights claims and declined his appeals to comity. It held that it would no longer recognize emancipation as it once had, particularly when it had occurred in federal territories.[83] The Missouri majority further opined that the states of the union, although associated for some purposes of government, "have always been regarded as foreign to each other."[84] Territoriality now trumped portable personal rights and comity. Of course, this was not due to the abstract evolution of a territorial principle. It was the fruit of an invigorated, reactionary support for the institution of slavery. "No State," said Missouri's Supreme Court, "is bound to carry into effect enactments conceived in a spirit hostile to that which pervades her own laws." In a dark portent of the terrible violence to come, the court said: "Times now are not as they were when the former decisions on this subject were made."[85]

There are, of course, many differences between Dred Scott's claims and those of deportees. Apart from the brutal fact of slavery, Dred Scott's case involved a claim of right that was asserted *within* a territorial entity (Missouri) based upon the prior acceptance of that claim (either actively or passively) by *another* entity, albeit governed by an arguably transcendent norm. Deportees' claims are against the *same* entity (the U.S. government) that has already declined to recognize their rights. The most basic point for our purposes, though, is that territoriality, like comity, is a malleable, contingent concept, especially in the context of rights claims made by those without citizenship or of questionable citizenship status. Should the *place* where such a claimant happens to stand completely govern the resolution of powerful rights claims? The answer, I suggest, has long been "no."[86]

When the *Dred Scott* case got to the U.S. Supreme Court, the technical legal issues were rather different, but equally relevant to our inquiry. Chief Justice Taney's *Dred Scott* opinion, well described as "the most disastrous" ever issued, was not primarily about comity or courtesy.[87] Rather, it relied on a racist theory of citizenship and personhood that has fortunately been about as thoroughly repudiated as any legal idea can be. But territoriality was a part of Justice Taney's opinion, too, albeit with some strange twists and turns. Taney ironically relied on what might now be considered a rather protective and progressive idea: that the Constitution applied *outside* the existing states of the Union.[88] When legislating for the territories acquired after the founding of the nation, he reasoned, Congress was bound by the Constitution's protections of personal property rights. These property rights, Taney reasoned, included the right to possess human slaves.

The specific content of Taney's application of the Constitution—to protect a citizen [slaveholder] from losing his "property" [another human being] without due process of law because of travel into a free territory—has rightly been definitively repudiated.[89] Taney's constitutional *method*, however, has retained a certain potential force. It is no small irony that those who today seek to extend constitutional rights to detainees at Guantánamo Bay, Bagram Air Base or, perhaps, to deportees in Guatemala may find themselves echoing arguments made not by the abolitionists but by such defenders of slavery as John C. Calhoun, who once pointedly asked: "[I]f all the negative provisions [of the Constitution] apply to the territories, why not the positive?"[90]

The irony would be greater had the formalist underpinnings of the nineteenth-century debates over territoriality been maintained. But, as noted above, they have been largely supplanted by more fluid, functionalist methods. In any case, Justice Taney's view that the Constitution applied in the new territories, fully and "*ex proprio vigore*" (of its own force), did not long survive the Civil War. The legal questions were no longer about slavery but were now tied to such matters as imperial expansion and the legal status of native American Indians.

Following the annexation of all continental territories, Congress sought to extend the Constitution and federal laws to all existing territories.[91] Such constitutional extension soon proved complex, however, as demonstrated by a series of cases known as the *Insular Cases* that dealt with the Philippines, "Porto Rico," and other territorial acquisitions.[92] The question, in contemporary parlance, was often phrased as whether the Constitution "followed the flag?"[93] The debates mixed concerns for the rights of territory residents with anti-imperialist politics, cultural chauvinism, and racism. Some thought that if the courts held that territory residents were entitled to full constitutional protections, it might impel the Congress to relinquish control over them.[94] Others argued that colonized peoples were not ready for U.S.-style constitutional structures and rights.[95]

Ultimately, the Court rejected an absolutist method that would have applied *all* constitutional rights.[96] The focus, for constitutional purposes, was on the relation of the particular territory to the United States.[97] Territories such as Alaska, which had been "incorporated" into the United States, would receive full constitutional protections, including Bill of Rights protections for criminal trials.[98] But in territories that had not been so incorporated—particularly the Philippines and Puerto Rico, only certain "fundamental" constitutional protections would apply. This was a rather functional, multifactored formulation, with some virtues of flexibility. But it lacked clarity and predictability and it required considerable judicial interpretation.[99] Moreover, part of the underlying constitutional proposition— stated directly—remained rather startling: the government—by deciding whether to incorporate a territory—might have discretion to determine the reach of the Constitution.[100] As we shall see, a variant of this problem also applies to deportees abroad.

Problems with the new functional approach were immediately apparent. It was described by one dissenting Justice as "occult."[101] Justice Harlan also wrote powerfully against it:

> The wise men who framed the Constitution, and the patriotic people who adopted it, were unwilling to depend for their safety upon such inherent principles. They proceeded upon the theory—the wisdom of which experience has vindicated—that the only safe guaranty against government oppression was to withhold or restrict the power to oppress.[102]

Judicial interpretation of which rights were fundamental in unincorporated territories also inevitably evoked all manner of underlying prejudices and values. Abbott Lowell, from whose work much of the doctrine was derived, believed in "civic equality," i.e., certain basic civil rights "for all free men." However, he also wrote that the "theory that all men are equal politically is quite a different matter." Indeed, he specifically linked the *Insular Cases* to the earlier debates over "plenary power" to exclude Chinese immigrants, whom he tellingly described as "the first people who were found to be without the pale." Though Lowell had been shocked at the violation of "our fundamental doctrine" when Chinese immigration was first barred, he later concluded that the argument that the Chinese could never be assimilated, and "hence would be an injurious element to the community," was sound. The courts, he asserted, had already decided that the existing naturalization laws, which spoke only of "white persons" and "Africans," did not include Chinese.[103] Lowell further endorsed the post-Reconstruction disenfranchisement of freedmen by Southern states and concluded that political equality did not apply to "to tribal Indians, to Chinese, or to negroes under all conditions." In short, he affirmed, "it seems to apply rigorously only to our own race, and to those people whom we can assimilate rapidly."[104]

With similar reasoning, the Supreme Court held that jury trials were not required in the Philippines. The majority opined that the idea that the Constitution applied in full to all territories would mean that if the United States "shall acquire territory peopled by savages . . . it must establish there the trial by jury." To the Justices, the mere stating of such a proposition demonstrated "the impossibility of carrying it into practice."[105] The possessions could thus be "subject to the jurisdiction of the United States, [but] not *of* the United States,"[106] a troubling formulation that one might well use to describe the current state of deportees' legal rights.

Holding that a U.S. citizen of the United States living in "Porto Rico" did not have a right to trial by jury under the Federal Constitution, Justice Taft wrote that "It is *locality* that is determinative of the application of the Constitution, in such matters as judicial procedure, and not the status of the people who live in it."[107] The key for Taft was *where* the person was—not legal citizenship or immigration status. This was a "curious" doctrine, to say the least, a mix of territoriality, chauvinism, and ostensible cultural sensitivity.[108] It also ignored two rather significant facts. Puerto Ricans, as U.S. citizens, could themselves freely travel to the mainland and could serve on juries there. Second, Puerto Rico had provided for jury trials in felony cases since 1901.[109]

The main importance of the *Insular Cases* for present purposes may be captured in a powerful phrase used by Justice White. Puerto Rico was said to be "foreign to the United States in a domestic sense."[110] Consider the relationship between this strange phrasing and the current approaches to deportees' rights, which often involve a similar metaphorical quality.[111] Ultimately, in such formulations, the rights of people are not clearly protected or even fully justiciable as questions of law—but tend to depend upon such ideas as "humanity," "discretion," and "wise policy."[112] Simply put, the relationship between territory and rights is deeper than a formalist method can handle. As we move to the contemporary dilemmas of deportees, then, we must revisit the additional complicating factor of legal status.

The Particular Problem of Noncitizens Abroad

Beyond the importance of territory to deportees' possible rights claims, our focus must also be on a related question: how much should immigration status matter for extraterritorial constitutional purposes? Here, too, the debates have been fierce, complex, and wide-ranging. In the 1950 case, *Johnson v. Eisentrager*, for example, Justice Robert Jackson dismissed various constitutional claims made by "enemy aliens" held abroad.[113] Distinguishing citizens from noncitizens, he wrote that citizenship, as "a ground of protection was old when Paul invoked it in his appeal to Caesar."[114] Justice Hugo Black, in dissent, strongly disagreed with this formulation, arguing that the U.S. Constitution "has led people everywhere to hope and believe that wherever our laws control, all people, whether our citizens or not, would have an equal chance before the bar of criminal justice."[115] Many variables were at play here. Some are obvious: citizens versus noncitizens, within U.S. territory versus abroad. Others, however, are more subtle: enemy aliens versus "friendly" ones, and rights maintained "before the bar of criminal justice" versus other sorts of constitutional protections.

Even the relatively straightforward question of the rights of U.S. citizens criminally prosecuted abroad has proven difficult for the Supreme Court to unravel. It was considered by the Court in the 1957 case of *Reid v. Covert*.[116] Clarice Covert had killed her husband, an Air Force sergeant, at an airbase in England. She was tried by a court-martial for murder under the Uniform Code of Military Justice (UCMJ).[117] Counsel for Mrs. Covert contended that she was insane at the time she killed her husband, but the military tribunal found her guilty of murder and sentenced her to life imprisonment. The judgment was eventually reversed by the Court of Military Appeals because of errors concerning the insanity defense. While Mrs. Covert was being held for a retrial, her counsel petitioned for a writ of habeas corpus to set her free on the ground that the Constitution prohibited her trial to be conducted by military authorities.[118] Justice Black wrote a plurality opinion as to "basic constitutional issues of the utmost concern."[119] The opinion's ringing first sentences were strangely redolent of Justice Taney and John C. Calhoun, rejecting the idea that when the United States acts against citizens abroad, it can do so free of the Bill of Rights. "The United States," Black wrote, "is entirely a creature of the Constitution. Its power and authority have no other source. It can only act in accordance with *all the limitations* imposed by the Constitution."[120] Citing the *Insular Cases*, Black then noted that courts had long held or asserted that various constitutional limitations apply to the government when it acts outside the continental United States. He rejected the idea that *only* those constitutional rights that are "fundamental" protect Americans abroad, finding no reason for picking and choosing "among the remarkable collection of 'Thou shalt nots,'" which were explicitly fastened on all departments and agencies of the Federal Government by the Constitution and its Amendments."[121] Justice Frankfurter, however, asserted that the *Insular Cases* had provided a more viable method for harmonizing various constitutional provisions that might appear to conflict.

Justice Harlan (differing somewhat with his namesake grandfather) also rejected Black's bright-line absolutist model. He agreed that it was wrong to say that constitutional safeguards are *never* operative outside of the United States. But not "every provision of the Constitution must always be deemed automatically applicable to American citizens in every part of the world." He suggested that the "wise and necessary gloss on our Constitution" holds that there is no rigid and abstract rule that Congress, when exercising power over Americans overseas, is subject to *all* constitutional guarantees, no matter what the conditions and considerations. Sometimes, adherence to a specific provision would be "altogether impracticable and anomalous." The ultimate question, he wrote, is which guarantees of the Constitution should apply in view of "the particular circumstances, the practical necessities, and the possible alternatives which Congress had before it." This is a method that is analogous to the contemporary interpretation of due process, which largely governs the rights of deportees *within* the United States. The question of which specific safeguards of the Constitution are appropriately to be applied in a particular context overseas "can be reduced to the issue of what process is "due" a defendant in the particular circumstances of a particular case."[122] As we shall see, Justice Harlan's formulation would be utilized by the Court in the twenty-first-century Guantánamo cases. Before we explore whether it might also work for post-deportation cases, though, we must also examine certain related constitutional peculiarities of U.S. immigration law.

One of the most basic and venerable concepts of nation-state sovereignty is that each state has the right to determine who may enter and who may remain on its soil. Long before the U.S. Supreme Court began to grapple with the relationship between territoriality and constitutional rights in the *Insular Cases, Johnson v. Eisentrager,* and *Reid v. Covert,* this basic legal principle was well accepted: "Every society possesses the undoubted right to determine who shall compose its members, and it is exercised by all nations, both in peace and war."[123] As one English jurist had put it in 1684, the King had an "absolute power to forbid foreigners . . . from coming within his dominions, both in times of war and in times of peace, according to his royal will and pleasure."[124] Thus, Justice Stephen Field's starting point in the seminal case of U.S. immigration law, known, shamefully, as *The Chinese Exclusion Case*[125] was unsurprising:

> The power of exclusion of foreigners [is] an incident of sovereignty belonging to the government of the United States . . . . [T]he right to its exercise at any time when, in the judgment of the government, the interests of the country require it, cannot be granted away or restrained on behalf of any one. . . .[126]

The basic proposition that such power is both "inherent in sovereignty," and "essential to self-preservation" has been repeated frequently by U.S. courts.[127] As Justice Murphy once wrote, since an alien "obviously" brings with him no constitutional rights, Congress may exclude him "for whatever reason it sees fit." The Bill of Rights, he continued, is a "futile authority for the alien seeking admission for the first time to these shores."[128] Indeed, even when the wife of a U.S. citizen soldier challenged secret exclusion proceedings, the Court held that "Whatever the procedure authorized by Congress is, it is due process as far as an alien denied entry is concerned."[129]

This basic model is still generally accepted, though not without important qualifications derived from international human rights law and with important recognized exceptions for returning lawful permanent residents.[130] Still, as Justice Breyer recited in 2001, the distinction between an alien who has entered the United States and one who has never entered "runs throughout immigration law."[131] It is, he asserted, "well established that certain constitutional protections available to persons inside the United States are unavailable to aliens outside of our geographic borders."[132]

But certain complications cannot be avoided. First, we must reconcile this sovereignty principle with the fact that all persons who are *within* U.S. territory have certain fundamental constitutional rights. Noncitizens within the United States have long been recognized as "persons" for constitutional purposes. In 1886, for example, the Fourteenth Amendment was held to protect Chinese laundry owners against discriminatory enforcement of a San Francisco ordinance.[133] In 1982, the Supreme Court held that the undocumented children of undocumented noncitizens in Texas had a right to public school education. The Court specifically rejected the argument that undocumented "aliens" were not persons with equal protection rights under the Fourteenth Amendment.[134] As Justice Brennan wrote for the majority: "Whatever his status under the immigration laws, an alien is surely a "person" in any ordinary sense of that term." Indeed, even those whose presence in this country is unlawful are guaranteed due process of law.[135] Of course, in the realm of deportation law, as we have seen, such fluid rights principles face significant limitations. Still, as early as 1903, Justice Harlan wrote that as to an "alien who has entered the country and has become subject to its jurisdiction and a part of its population," administrative process must at least comply with certain basic procedural due process norms, characterized, as we have seen, as fundamental fairness.[136] In 1953, the Court stated that "[a]liens who have once passed through our gates, even illegally, may be expelled only after proceedings conforming to traditional standards of fairness encompassed in due process of law."[137] As the Court reiterated in 2001: "once an alien enters the country, the legal circumstance changes."[138]

Anomalous cases or exceptions often force the refinement of an idea.[139] Consider people who are physically on U.S. soil but deemed by legal fiction not to be within the United States. The common technical legal term for this situation is "parole." In the 1953 *Mezei* case, the Supreme Court concluded that physical presence alone does not confer heightened constitutional rights on an alien who is seeking *readmission* to this country.[140] Essentially, such persons were seen to have no constitutional rights regarding their immigration claims.[141] More recent cases, however, have called this formalist "entry fiction" into question. In a 1993 case involving the long-term detention of Cuban parolees, for example, one court "vehemently" disagreed that such detention did not "implicate the Fifth Amendment." The "entry fiction," on this view, did not apply to aliens living in the United States, even if technically they had not been legally admitted.[142] These people had physically entered the United States as refugees and had lived in this country in parolee status for over fifteen years.[143] Thus, their basic territorial claims were enhanced by the realities of their personal stake in U.S. life.

Such tensions among territoriality, personal stakes, and status have not yet been definitively resolved. Perhaps they never can be. But the Supreme Court has recently upheld rights claims made by detained deportees who were awaiting physical deportation.[144] Such noncitizens with final deportation orders who have not yet been deported raised interesting questions. Were they analogous to initial entrants, essentially rightless, and, pursuant to legal fiction, not really "here?" This would seem untenable; the Court has long held that so long as they are within U.S. territory, even deportees with final orders of deportation retain *some* constitutional protections.[145] But what of those in deportation-related detention? Are they, in essence, "reverse parolees"? In 2001, in *Zadvydas v. Davis*, the Court rejected that view. It interpreted a statute to authorize the detention of (formerly legal resident) deportees only so long as it was "reasonably necessary" to effectuate their removal.[146] The key to this interpretation was the Court's recognition that the detainees had *some* constitutional rights to liberty.[147] Should this change the moment they are physically removed?

Equating deported noncitizens with initial entrants who stand at the border, though not illogical, would contradict the historical recognition by the Court of the rights of returning lawful permanent residents. As we have seen, initial entrants generally lack all due process protections. Those who have entered U.S. territory have such rights, and those in parole status may stand somewhere in between. Legal status and various other particularities thus challenge a binary, "on/off" territorial model in which one is either "in" (with rights) or "out" (with no rights).[148] The crucial constitutional question has become: at what point does a lawful permanent resident who leaves U.S. territory lose this precious set of rights? Cases have considered a welter of factors, including the time spent outside the United States, the purpose of the trip, the place of travel, the intent of the noncitizen, conduct abroad, and permissions sought from the government.[149] The current rules remain imprecise. The length of one's trip abroad is significant, but it is not an exact constitutional science.[150] Of course, those who believe that the constitution should generally apply to government action find the very possibility of a binary on/off switch dissatisfying, no matter what factors are considered as triggers. As Henry Hart put it in his famous 1953 Dialogue, such a distinction, between when the Constitution applies and when it does not apply at all, "produces a conflict of basic principle and is inadmissible."[151] Still, this view, as such, has not garnered a Supreme Court majority.

So far, then, we have seen that rights claims by deportees may depend to some degree upon *where* they are physically and upon their former *status*. Might the *nature* of the rights claim also matter? In 1990, the Supreme Court was presented with a rather straightforward but portentous question: whether the Fourth Amendment applies to the search and seizure by United States agents of property that is owned by a "nonresident alien and located in a foreign country."[152]

A majority of the Court in *United States v. Verdugo-Urquidez*,[153] concluded that it did not. But the reasoning, in a concurrence by then newly appointed Justice Anthony Kennedy, has turned out to be at least as important as the majority opinion. The essential facts were that Rene Martin Verdugo-Urquidez, a citizen and resident of Mexico, was believed by the United States Drug Enforcement Agency (DEA) to be one of the leaders of a large and violent organization in Mexico that smuggled narcotics into the United States. The U.S. Government obtained a warrant for his arrest. Mexican police officers then arrested him in Mexico and transported him to the United States for trial. Following Verdugo-Urquidez's arrest, a DEA agent arranged for searches of his Mexican residences, believing that the searches would reveal evidence related to alleged narcotics trafficking activities and his involvement in the kidnapping and torture-murder of a DEA Special Agent.[154] Mexican authorities authorized the searches and agents seized certain documents.

The Court's majority opinion distinguished the Fourth Amendment—which prohibits unreasonable searches and seizures—from the trial rights guaranteed defendants under the Fifth and Sixth Amendments. It mattered for Fourth Amendment purposes that "if there were a constitutional violation, it occurred solely in Mexico."[155] The majority also suggested that constitutional distinctions could be based on the interpretation of the phrase, "the people." On this view, "the people" protected by the Fourth Amendment and certain other provisions[156] "refers to a class of persons who are part of a national community or who have otherwise developed sufficient connection with this country to be considered part of that community."[157] The implications of this approach could be quite negative for many noncitizens, both within and outside the United States. But note that the Fifth Amendment's protections apply not to "*the people*" but to any "*person.*"[158]

Justice Kennedy, foreshadowing much of the reasoning later to become conclusive in the Guantánamo context, approached the case in a somewhat more functional way. He first asserted that the distinction between citizens and aliens meant that neither the Constitution nor "general principles of law" create any juridical relation between our country and some "undefined, limitless class of noncitizens who are beyond our territory." But, echoing James Madison, Kennedy then wrote that this does not necessarily mean that those who, by definition, "did not and could not assent to the Constitution" lack all constitutional rights. As Justice Story had explained in his *Commentaries* more than a century earlier, the fact that a government might originate in the voluntary compact or assent of "the people" of several states, or of "a people" never before united, was not the end or limit of constitutional protections for others.[159] As Justice Kennedy wrote, "the Government may act only as the Constitution authorizes, whether the actions in question are foreign or domestic."[160]

But this principle, while superior to the binary, formalistic alternative, is only a first step. The ultimate question is: what constitutional standards apply when government action "within its sphere of foreign operations" affects an alien? This question required a *functionalist* analysis of whether the extension of Fourth Amendment protections abroad would "be impracticable and anomalous."[161] Justice Kennedy's reasoning thus suggested a middle way between bright-line formalism and the virtually total extension of all constitutional norms abroad.[162]

This sort of method becomes especially complex when courts are asked to order the government to allow a noncitizen with compelling rights claims into the United States or, perhaps, to bring a deportee back. The case of *Kyemba v. Obama* involved a group of Guantánamo detainees who were part of an ethnic and religious minority from China known as Uighurs.[163] Arrested by U.S. forces in Afghanistan, the Uighurs had been cleared of terrorist associations. But they could not be sent to China, their country of nationality, because the U.S. State Department concluded that they could well face torture there.[164] By the time their habeas corpus petitions were adjudicated by District Court Judge Richard Urbina, they had been held at Guantánamo Bay for some seven years, for much of that time in solitary confinement. They ultimately asked to be released into the United States, a request that pit the power of a habeas court to order release from detention directly into conflict with the "plenary power" doctrine of U.S. immigration law pursuant to which it is for the government, not the courts, to decide who may enter U.S. territory. Something, in short, would have to give.

Judge Urbina ruled strongly in favor of the Uighurs. As he put it, in somewhat baroque but strenuous legal prose, the matter was a rather simple one of remedy for an obvious infringement of the Uighurs' right to liberty. "There comes a time," he wrote, "when delayed action prompted by judicial deference to the executive branch's function yields inaction not consistent with the constitutional imperative."[165] Judge Urbina was impressed neither by the plenary power doctrine nor by the government's arguments that the question was nonjusticiable. His view was that "separation-of-powers concerns do not trump the very principle upon which this nation was founded—the unalienable right to liberty."[166] Thus, he ordered the government to release the Uighurs into the United States. His basic theoretical challenge, however, was to explain why such cases as *Mezei* (the 1953 case that had upheld the government's power to detain a returning lawful permanent resident on Ellis Island) did not deprive him of the authority to do what he thought was right. His answer was creative. He conceded that the power to "expel or exclude aliens" is "largely immune from judicial control."[167] But he also asserted that such powers are not absolute. The government must "respect the procedural safeguards of due process....."[168] In his view, this meant that no person could be deprived of liberty without an opportunity, at some time, to be heard about matters upon which that liberty depends."[169] But prior relevant cases had all involved people who—unlike the Uighurs—were *already on U.S. soil.* Although Guantánamo Bay had previously been found to be subject to habeas corpus jurisdiction in the *Rasul* case, it was not U.S. territory for immigration law purposes. Judge Urbina's solution, simply put, was to frame the issue as one of liberty and to reaffirm the power and importance of the "Great Writ" to "safeguard an individual's liberty from unbridled executive fiat." As he majestically put it: "Liberty finds its liberator in the great writ, and the great writ, in turn, finds protection under the Constitution.[170]

The government could not tolerate such a ruling, and so the case made its way to the Court of Appeals, where it was viewed quite differently. The majority began by citing the "ancient principle" that "a nation-state has the inherent right to exclude or admit foreigners and to prescribe applicable terms and conditions for their exclusion or admission."[171] More specifically, the court noted that ever since the decision in the *Chinese Exclusion Case,* the Supreme Court has sustained the "exclusive power of the political branches to decide which aliens may, and which aliens may not, enter the United States, and on what terms."[172] Once the case was framed in this way, the outcome was not in doubt. The appeals court was dismissive of Judge Urbina's reasoning. In its view, he had spoken very generally about "constitutional limits," "constitutional imperative," and "the fundamental right of liberty." But the Fifth Amendment's due process clause could not support the lower court's order of release. The reason takes us back to territoriality: according to the court of appeals, "the due process clause *does not apply to aliens without property or presence in the sovereign territory of the United States.*"[173] This apparently simple assertion, as we have seen, masks much historical complexity. But the appeals court did not tarry long on the point before moving on to a further series of rather restrictive propositions about rights and remedies: "Not every violation of a right yields a remedy, even when the right is constitutional";[174] and "[s]uch words as 'right' are a constant solicitation to fallacy."[175] The key for these two judges was simply that an "alien who seeks admission to this country may not do so under any claim of right."[176] Thus, the matter—a fascinating conflict between two very strong positions—went to the U.S. Supreme Court.

The Court accepted the case,[177] but it was never argued or decided on the merits. The government was able to find countries willing to accept the Uighur detainees. Part of its energy in this regard (which was considerable) was undoubtedly humanitarian. But the Obama administration clearly recognized the potential importance of the issues to a wide range of immigration and deportation situations, and they apparently struggled to keep it away from the Court for that reason, too. Although five detainees rejected the offers of resettlement and were still being held at Guantánamo Bay, the Court ultimately decided simply to remand the case.[178] Unsurprisingly, the D.C. Circuit again ruled against the Uighurs, holding—rather blithely—that "even if petitioners had good reason to reject the offers [such as a fear of being tortured] they would have no right to be released into the United States."[179] The second time around, the Supreme Court denied *certiorari*.[180]

For the Uighurs, the outcome of all this litigation was a mixture of victory and defeat. They did finally get out of Guantánamo Bay, ending up in a variety of willing countries including Bermuda, Palau, and Switzerland—a victory for which their lawyers deserve great praise. But for those who were anticipating a resolution of this deep conflict between these two powerful strains of U.S. law, the cases leave us with only a hint of what the Supreme Court might do. Clearly, at least four justices were not sufficiently persuaded by the D.C. Circuit's plenary power reasoning to deny *certiorari* in the first instance. Beyond that, however, the issues will have to await future cases—perhaps involving deportees—for resolution.

At least two critical differences are apparent between deportees and the Uighurs, however. First, as we have seen, certain former legal residents of the United States have been recognized to have due process rights. Thus, the formalist invocation of territoriality and the plenary power doctrine against deported lawful permanent residents (and perhaps against other former residents) is more problematic. On the other hand, deportees are not in U.S. custody. And finally, for deportees, as we shall see, there is an additional problem of "finality."

Due Process

In due process terms, a wrongly deported deportee's claim seems simple and strong: the person who had been legally admitted has been forced outside the United States because of (arguably illegal) government action. In the *Eisentrager* case, the Court of Appeals offered a line of reasoning that could well be persuasive in the post-deportation context (though it was ultimately rejected by the Supreme Court for certain "enemy aliens"). The basic outline of the argument is as follows:

> First. The Fifth Amendment applies to "any person."
> Second. Action of Government officials in violation of the Constitution is void.
> Third. A basic and inherent function of the judicial branch of a government is to set aside void action by government officials and to restrict executive action to the confines of the constitution. No Government action which is void under the Constitution is exempt from judicial power.

Fourth. The writ of habeas corpus is the established, time-honored process in our law for testing the authority of one who deprives another of his liberty. The writ is the "indispensable implementation of constitutional guarantees in respect to personal liberty."[181]

As the court continued, the "nub of the whole matter" was that constitutional prohibitions apply directly to acts of government or government officials and *are not conditioned upon persons or territory*.[182] Thus, once we reject the idea that the Constitution has a territorial "off-switch," post-deportation constitutional rights are at least theoretically possible. But what might such rights look like?

Deportation, as we have seen, has long been held to be a civil (as opposed to a criminal) system. However, it must comply with constitutional requirements of fundamental fairness and due process.[183] The Due Process Clause applies to all "persons" within the United States, whether their presence here is "lawful, unlawful, temporary, or permanent."[184] Further, returning lawful permanent residents who have left U.S. territory, and who seek to return, may also have due process rights. "[O]nce an alien gains admission to our country and begins to develop the ties that go with permanent residence, his constitutional status changes accordingly."[185] Still, as in other areas of law, the applicability of due process is just the starting point for analysis of exactly what process may be due.[186] Unsurprisingly, post-deportation law (to the extent that cases are even taken up by courts) has inspired particularly parsimonious formulations of due process. For example, the First Circuit has found that allowing a deportation order to stand on the basis of a vacated criminal conviction did not violate due process.[187] The court's vision of due process was that it merely "requires that the alien receive notice of the charges against him, and a fair opportunity to be heard before an executive or administrative tribunal."[188] On this view, the deportee had no right to "continuous opportunities to attack executed removal orders" after his departure from the country. The court felt that "there is a strong public interest in bringing finality to the deportation process,"[189] an issue to which we will return.

But the tide may be turning against such stringent due process models. In 2010, the Supreme Court in *Padilla v. Kentucky*[190] upheld a noncitizen's claim that his criminal defense counsel was ineffective due to allegedly incorrect advice concerning the risk of deportation.[191] This was a pathbreaking decision, virtually unprecedented in the long history of U.S. deportation law. In a formulation that implicitly adopts a strong version of due process protections for deportees, the Court recognized that deportation as a consequence of a criminal conviction has such a close connection to the criminal process that it is now uniquely difficult to classify it as either a "direct or a collateral consequence."[192] The two systems, in short, have become inextricably linked. Further, the Court recognized that "the landscape of federal immigration law has changed dramatically." In the past, there was only a "narrow class of deportable offenses and judges wielded broad discretionary authority to prevent deportation." But now, the regime contains a much expanded class of deportable offenses, and it has limited the authority of judges "to alleviate the harsh consequences of deportation."[193] As a result of these changes, the "drastic measure" of deportation or removal . . . is now *virtually inevitable* for a vast number of noncitizens convicted of crimes.[194] Deportation has become "*an integral part*—indeed, sometimes the most important part—of the penalty that may be imposed on noncitizen defendants who plead guilty to specified crimes."[195] From this logic, one can easily see why substantial due process protections, if not the more specific protections normally tied to the criminal justice system, are warranted.[196]

Padilla was a significant decision, with virtues of both logic and justice. It will likely prevent many avoidable and wrongful deportations. It may also help some deportees who have been wrongly or unjustly deported in the past. Though largely styled as a Sixth Amendment right-to-counsel decision, the case raises many constitutional questions. For one thing, as we have seen, courts have long formalistically distinguished the punishment meted out in criminal courts from deportation. The former, of course, is a criminal sanction, with extensive, specific constitutional protections. The latter has been said to be civil or, at most, quasi-criminal. *Padilla* implicitly challenges this model. It cannot be squared with the historical, formalist relegation of deportation to the realm of civil collateral consequences in which, for example, there is no clear constitutional right to counsel. Indeed, *Padilla* might portend a constitutional reconciliation between the Court's historical formalism and a more appropriate realism. This new constitutional norm for *post-entry social control* deportation, which might be called the *Fifth-and-a-Half Amendment*, embodies both the flexible due process guarantees of the Fifth Amendment and—at least for certain types of deportation—some of the more specific protections of the Sixth Amendment, such as a right to counsel. This is certainly not a simple jurisprudential solution. However, so long as deportation is still formalistically said to be civil and nonpunitive while, in reality, being directly tied to the criminal justice system and highly punitive in effect, it is a construct worth developing.

Habeas Corpus

> The writ is the writ. . . . [T]he rights that may be asserted and the rights
> that may be vindicated will vary with the circumstances. . . .
> —Justice David Souter (2006)[197]

The "Great Writ" of habeas corpus protects a right to judicial process that has been aptly called "the most important human right in the Constitution."[198] In recent

years, the writ's importance for those challenging deportation orders has been profound.[199] This was largely because of limitations on judicial review of deportation
cases in the 1996 laws. As the Supreme Court has confirmed, habeas corpus over-
sees not only the executive detention that accompanies deportation, but it may
also facilitate judicial review of the mechanisms of deportation.[200] In *Boumediene v.
Bush*,[201] the Court further held that the constitution's Suspension Clause—the
basic guarantor of habeas corpus—protected the rights of noncitizens detained at
Guantánamo Bay.[202] Justice Kennedy's majority opinion in *Boumediene* rejected
formalist models of sovereignty and territory and applied a pragmatic, functional
test redolent of his concurrence in *Verdugo-Urquidez*: "questions of extraterritoriality turn on objective factors and practical concerns, not formalism."[203] Indeed,
the Court reaffirmed that even when the United States acts outside its borders
against noncitizens, "its powers are not 'absolute and unlimited' but are subject 'to
such restrictions as are expressed in the Constitution.'"[204] To allow the political
branches the power "to switch the Constitution on or off at will" would permit
what the Court called a "striking anomaly in our tripartite system of government"
in which the most venerable principle of judicial constitutional power would be
threatened: that it is the province of the judiciary to say "what the law is."[205]

Might deportees abroad use habeas corpus to vindicate their rights? Perhaps.
But they would face many obstacles, although some similarities to the Guantánamo cases are apparent.[206] In *Boumediene*, for example, the detainees were permitted to challenge their status as "enemy combatants." For deportees, the status
to be challenged would be that of "deportable aliens." The *Boumediene* Court had
noted serious inadequacies in the status-determination processes at Guantánamo. Analogies might be made to such deficiencies in some deportation adjudications, though formal deportation proceedings are not inherently as
problematic.[207] However, the *Boumediene* decision relied heavily on the particularities of Guantánamo Bay, noting that unlike Landsberg Prison, where the
Eisentrager detainees had been held, Guantánamo Bay "in every practical sense"
is not abroad; but within the "constant jurisdiction of the United States."[208] Deportees obviously can be anywhere, most likely under the jurisdiction of a foreign state (not to mention at liberty). But how much should this factor matter?
Can deportees be said to "carry" certain rights abroad? A long-term legal permanent resident who was arguably wrongly deported might well be able to make a
compelling argument for habeas review. Such a person has arguably been
deprived of many rights by allegedly wrongful government action, perhaps without counsel, in an administrative proceeding. It is hard to see why the fact that the
person has been forced from U.S. territory *by the very same wrongful government
action* should deprive U.S. courts of jurisdiction.[209] Nor would such a claim necessarily infringe on the power or authority of a foreign sovereign. The "practical
obstacles" also seem much less significant in post-deportation cases than in

enemy combatant situations. All relevant evidence will likely be in the United States, as will most witnesses, if necessary, since the issue will be whether the deportation was incorrect. Indeed, the fact that the deportee is not technically detained at the time of the habeas adjudication would reduce problems of detention and transport.[210] Telephonic or video hearings might further enhance efficiency, though they are not without problems.[211] In a serious case of forensic mistake, the strong arguments in favor of such judicial action are obvious.[212] Claims based on subsequent changes in law, however, are harder, involving problems of finality and other technical impediments.[213]

Crucially, though, there is the question of "custody." Habeas at its core is a remedy for unlawful executive detention.[214] The typical remedy is release.[215] Deportees are often not detained abroad (though some are), and thus they might seem ineligible for habeas relief.[216] But the law is not necessarily so mechanical as this. Indeed, detention has long been defined rather broadly in habeas cases. In 1963, the Supreme Court found the habeas custody requirement satisfied not only by actual physical confinement or detention, but also by other "restraints on liberty . . . not shared by the public generally."[217] A decade later, the Court clarified that even "constructive" custody was sufficient, defined as "[c]ustody of a person (such as a parolee or probationer) whose freedom is controlled by legal authority but who is not under direct physical control."[218] Some deportees are detained by the governments to which they have been delivered. The writ cannot directly run to such a detention, where U.S. courts would have no authority to order release. Still, the person is likely being held only because of an arguably wrongful deportation. Thus, a judgment by a U.S. federal court might form the basis for subsequent legal action in, say, Haiti or Cambodia, to release a detained deportee.[219] One might analogize such a situation to "constructive custody."[220]

But, as this brief survey shows, these cases are very difficult. Some federal courts have held that a deportee who has been removed from the United States cannot satisfy the custody requirement.[221] The Eleventh Circuit has specifically rejected the contention that deportation itself, which limits a noncitizen's prospects of lawfully reentering the country, amounts to a sufficiently "severe restraint on [one's] individual liberty."[222] Another court has concluded that deportees are "subject to no greater restraint than any other non-citizen living outside American borders."[223] However, other courts have taken a somewhat broader view. For example, post-removal habeas jurisdiction was recognized where the INS had removed an immigrant in violation of the order of an immigration judge and after interference with his right to counsel.[224] As with so many other aspects of post-deportation law, the meaning of custody in this setting clearly remains a work in progress.[225] Essentially, we should see habeas for deportees as "part of an evolving constitutional tradition." It demands a functional approach that can "adapt its operation to surrounding institutional changes."[226]

Time, Space, and Finality

Dandum semper est tempus: ueritatem dies aperit.
— Lucius Annaeus Seneca (Seneca the Younger)[227]

Finality is death. Perfection is finality.
Nothing is perfect. There are lumps in it.

— James Stephens[228]

As we have seen, time has long been recognized as a source of powerful rights claims for deportees. Its passage may insulate people from deportation, may render them eligible for various types of legal statuses, and may serve as a proxy for powerful affiliations, acculturation, and even reliance on nonenforcement.[229] Conversely, time may also be fictionally "stopped" for legal purposes. For example, so-called "stop-time" rules may apply to certain forms of discretionary relief from removal. Commission of a crime during a required period of "continuous residence" will, in effect, stop time and preclude eligibility.[230]

Deportees, however, must be especially concerned about a particular temporal phenomenon: the idea of "finality." Most specifically, the question is: when is a deportation case completely over and closed and its legal consequences set? Legal finality is more commonly understood as a temporal/jurisdictional concept than as a spatial one. A legal case is typically considered "final" when judgment has been rendered and all possible appeals have been decided or waived. In deportation law, for example, there has been a continuing debate over whether a person may be deported due to a criminal conviction that is still on direct appeal.[231] The Supreme Court in 1955 imposed a *protective* "finality" requirement that precluded such deportations.[232] But statutory changes in 1996 called this ruling into question.[233] Thus, the BIA and courts continue to struggle, as they have for many years, with the question of *when*—during the criminal appeals process—a person may be deported because of a criminal conviction.[234]

Procedural deadlines are taken very seriously in deportation cases. Indeed, courts have allowed deportees to face torture because of untimely court filings.[235] Still, the deportation system has also long had certain safeguards of administrative and judicial review, as well as post-order motions, designed to catch legal and factual mistakes and to remedy other forms of injustice or unfairness. Historically, the use of such safeguards to delay deportation has sometimes caused great consternation.[236] In 1955, for example, the Supreme Court construed the statutory word "final" to mean finality in the administrative process of deportation, rather than as a preclusion of judicial review.[237] As a result, some alleged that deportation cases were unduly delayed while courts reviewed them.[238] As President Eisenhower stated in a message to Congress, "the growing frequency of . . . cases brought for purposes of delay, particularly those involving aliens found to be criminals and traffickers in narcotics and subversion, makes imperative the need for legislation limiting and carefully defining the judicial process."[239] The law that eventually resulted had many restrictive features.[240] Most notably, as we have seen, the statute added a territorial criterion to the temporal idea of finality. It provided that "[a]n order of deportation or exclusion shall not be reviewed . . . if [the alien] has departed from the United States after the issuance of the order."[241] This provision was primarily inspired by the strange case of William Heikkila, a Communist Party member who had come to the United States at the age of 3. He was ordered deported in 1948 but had legally fought his deportation for ten years.[242] On his way home from work one day, Heikkila, then 52, found two men waiting for him. One flashed a badge. "Call my wife," Heikkila yelled to a fellow worker. "Tell her Immigration has picked me up." INS District Director Bruce Barber had been trying for more than a decade to deport Heikkila to Finland. He knew that Heikkila's lawyers had obtained a restraining order against INS, but it was effective the *following* day. Barber saw his chance. Allowing "his heaped-up frustrations" to overpower his judgment, Barber sent Immigration Service agents "to grab Heikkila and haul him away."[243] A U.S. Border Patrol plane took Heikkila to Vancouver, where he was locked in jail to await a plane to Finland. Three days after his arrest, Heikkila landed at "chilly Helsinki with $11.50 in cash, no luggage, no topcoat." But he had become internationally famous. The San Francisco Chronicle colorfully referred to the whole process as *"The Bum's Rush by Immigration."*[244] When Federal District Judge Edward Murphy learned what had happened, he said that Barber's treatment of Heikkila smacked of "the Gestapo, the thumbscrew and the rack." He threatened to hold the INS in contempt of court after which the Justice Department ordered Heikkila to be brought back to the United States. Soon, "smiling happily," he was back home in San Francisco, "reunited with his U.S.-born wife Phyllis."[245] INS Commissioner Joseph M. Swing was, to say the least, unrepentant. He said that deportation authorities must use force sometimes to get rid of "nogoodniks." Most deportees were allowed time to pack up and say their farewells, said Swing, but "there is about 3% of these nogoodniks" who keep on stalling in the courts. Swing vowed to deport Heikkila "if it takes from now until I get kicked out."[246] It took longer. Heikkila achieved true finality when he died in 1960 (still in the United States).

The new legal finality regime, inspired by the *Heikkila* case and a few others such as that of Carlos Marcello, had both a temporal and a spatial dimension. If a person in deportation proceedings left the United States, the case was over.[247] In the following years, few legal challenges were brought to this regime, and those that were brought almost invariably failed.[248] Courts found the statute "clear and unambiguous" and seemed to see no problem with a territorial trigger for the elimination of jurisdiction. However, in a case that presented a serious problem of procedural due process, the Ninth Circuit Court of Appeals came up with a creative—and controversial—legal interpretation. *Mendez v. INS* involved a deported noncitizen whose attorney had not been notified of his deportation.[249] The departure bar nevertheless seemed to render the matter "final." But the court held that for these purposes, "departure" meant only deportations that were "legally executed." The court ordered the INS to readmit Mendez to the United States so that he could pursue his appeal. Though some commentators have criticized the Ninth Circuit's reasoning, there is a deep and compelling logic to it. The court found that Mendez's "right to . . . procedural due process became meaningless when he was deported without notice to his counsel."[250] This required a remedy.

Following *Mendez*, some courts have applied similar reasoning to other types of procedural violations, such as a failure to notify consular authorities,[251] as well as to variations on the theme of vacated convictions.[252] Others, however, have been troubled by the fact that in order to determine *whether* the departure bar ought to apply, the *Mendez* model seemed to require courts to examine the merits of the underlying claim, thus arguably crafting an inevitable breach of the departure bar. The Fifth Circuit expressed "serious reservations" about *Mendez,* describing it rather flamboyantly as "a sinkhole that has swallowed the rule of [the statutory departure bar]."[253] Eventually, the First and Second Circuits also rejected the *Mendez* model, creating a circuit split that has not yet been resolved, mostly because, as we have seen, the whole system was changed in 1996 to allow at least direct judicial appeals, post-departure.[254]

The underlying debate over legal methods, however, is still relevant. As the Ninth Circuit saw it, the interpretation of departure required a functional method, analogous to that which had once been endorsed by the Supreme Court when the question was the meaning of the term "entry."[255] In a 1947 case, for example, a noncitizen had departed on a merchant marine ship, which was then torpedoed. He was later rescued and returned to the United States. Later, he was convicted of robbery and ordered deported because the conviction was within five years of his last "entry" into the United States. The INS argued that he had "entered" the country when he was returned to the United States after being torpedoed. The Supreme Court, however, held that he did not technically "enter" the United States because it was "[t]he exigencies of war, not his voluntary act" that had put him on foreign soil. The Court reasoned that this would be like holding that if he had been kidnapped and taken abroad, he would make a statutory "entry" on his voluntary return. Respect for the law, wrote the Court, "does not thrive on captious interpretations."[256] Similarly, the *Mendez* court determined that for deportations to be immunized from judicial review solely because of physical departure—without regard to the manner in which this "departure" was accomplished—was just such a "captious interpretation."[257]

As we have seen, the most pressing current "finality" problem for deportees is no longer a territorial bar on direct appeals, but on motions.[258] A rigid reliance on this single factor, however, ignores the complex interaction among space, time, and status that has long marked U.S. immigration law.[259] The post-deportation legal system, such as it, raises powerful questions of what the U.S. rule of law requires. Absolute, formalist bars based on territory should be rejected now as they have been in the past. But, as the problem of "finality" illustrates, the issues are never simple. They require a sensitive, nuanced, technically sharp, and functionalist methodology that recognizes the powerful role that interpretation should play in an arena such as this where lives are at stake and powerful legal and moral concerns abound. As Felix Frankfurter once put it, once the "tyranny of literalness is rejected," we should consider all relevant considerations for giving rational content to legal words.[260] In the next chapter, we will consider various sources for such content.

Notes

1. 354 U.S. 1, 5–6 (1957).
2. Robert M. Cover, *Violence and the Word*, 95 YALE L.J. 1601 (1986). The sentences omitted from this quotation are also worth recalling in this context: "Interpretations in law also constitute justifications for violence which has already occurred or which is about to occur. When interpreters have finished their work, they frequently leave behind victims whose lives have been torn apart by these organized, social practices of violence."
3. *See* LINDA BOSNIAK, THE CITIZEN AND THE ALIEN: DILEMMAS OF CONTEMPORARY MEMBERSHIP 3 (2006).
4. 8 U.S.C. § 1101(g) (emphasis added).
5. *See* 8 C.F.R. § 1003.4 (2010) ("Departure from the United States of a person who is the subject of deportation or removal proceedings . . . subsequent to the taking of an appeal, but prior to a decision thereon, shall constitute a withdrawal of the appeal, and the initial decision in the case shall be final to the same extent as though no appeal had been taken."). There is some debate as to whether an involuntary departure would accomplish this result. *See* Mansour v. Gonzales, 470 F.3d 1194 (6th Cir. 2006); Aguilera-Ruiz v. Ashcroft, 348 F.3d 835 (9th Cir. 2003); Mejia-Ruiz v. INS, 51 F.3d 358 (2d Cir. 1995) (requiring a voluntary, intentional departure); *cf.* Long v. Gonzales, 420 F.3d 516 (5th Cir. 2005) (reserving question); Madrigal v. Holder, 572 F.3d 239, 245 (6th Cir. 2009) (distinguishing improper removal); Coyt v. Holder, 593 F.3d 902 (9th Cir. 2010) (same).
6. For a thoughtful and comprehensive consideration of time in this context, see Juliet Stumpf, *Doing Time: Crimmigration Law and the Perils of Haste*, 58 UCLA L. REV. 1705 (2011).
7. 8 U.S.C. § 1427 (five years); 8 U.S.C. § 1430 (three years for spouse of U.S. citizen). *Jus sanguinis* citizenship rules also may involve time. Individuals born abroad may obtain U.S. citizenship at birth if one or both of their U.S. citizen parents resided for fixed periods of time in the United States or its territories. *See also* 8 U.S.C. § 1186(b) (conditional period for certain marriages).
8. 8 U.S.C. § 1259.
9. 8 U.S.C. § 1229(b).
10. There are technical distinctions among a statute of limitation, a statute of repose, and common law *laches* that should be noted but are not relevant for our purposes. *See* Joseph

Mack, *Nullum Tempus: Governmental Immunity to Statutes of Limitation, Laches, and Statutes of Repose*, 73 Def. Couns. J. 180, 181 (2006). *See* Stumpf, *supra* note 6, at 1746.

11. 8 U.S.C. § 1227(a)(2)(A(i).

12. *See, e.g.*, 8 U.S.C. § 1182(a)(9)(b).

13. 8 U.S.C. § 1252(b)(1).

14. *See generally* Hiroshi Motomura, Americans In Waiting: The Lost Story Of Immigration And Citizenship In The United States (2006); Hiroshi Motomura, *We Asked for Workers, but Families Came: Time, Law, and the Family in Immigration and Citizenship*, 14 Va. J. Soc. Pol'y & L. 103, 113 (2006) (at 113 ("[T]he recognition of ties that develop over time—the essence of what I have called immigration as affiliation—is a persuasive basis for both *jus soli* and discretionary relief from removal, even if these two aspects of immigration and citizenship law benefit noncitizens who have violated the conditions of admission or were never admitted at all.").

15. United States *ex rel.* Klonis v. Davis, 13 F.2d 630 (2d Cir. 1926).

16. Some 115,000 people benefited from this law between 1933 and 1940. Secretary of Labor, *Annual Report*, 1933–1940.

17. Foti v. INS, 375 U.S. 217 (1963).

18. INS v. Doherty, 502 U.S. 314, 321–25 (1992); *see also* Stone v. INS, 514 U.S. 386, 399–400 (1995).

19. *Id.* Similarly, as the Court has more recently opined, an alien who requests voluntary departure represents that he or she "has the means to depart the United States and intends to do so" promptly. 8 U.S.C. § 1229c(b)(1)(D); 8 CFR §§ 1240.26(c)(1)–(2) (2007); cf. § 1240.26(c)(3) (the judge may impose additional conditions to "ensure the alien's timely departure from the United States") (emphasis added); Dada v. Mukasey, 554 U.S. 1, 19–20 (2008).

20. *See* INA § 240(c)(6)(B), 8 U.S.C. § 1229(c)(6)(B) (2006) (thirty-day deadline for filing motion to reconsider); INA § 240(c)(7)(C)(i), 8 U.S.C. § 1229a(c)(7)(C)(i)(2006) (ninety-day deadline for motion to reopen).

21. Andres Armendarez-Mendez, Int. Dec. 3626; 24 I. & N. Dec. 646 (B.I.A. 2008).

22. *Id.*

23. Woody Allen, *quoted in* William Safire, On Language; *The Ellision Fields*, N.Y. Times Mag., August 13, 1989, *available at* http://www.nytimes.com/1989/08/13/magazine/on-language-the-elision-fields.html?pagewanted=3&src=pm.

24. Government Response to Petition for Writ of Habeas Corpus and Motion to Dismiss or for Judgment as a Matter of Law and Memorandum in Support at 2, Abdah v. Bush, No. 04-CV-1254 (D.D.C. Oct. 4, 2004) (quoted in Linda Greenhouse, *The Mystery of Guantanamo Bay* (Jefferson Lecture, University of California), 27 Berkeley J. Int'l L. 1, 21 (2009).

25. James Madison, Report on the Virginia Resolutions, 4 Debates, Resolutions and Other Proceedings, in Convention on the Adoption of the Federal Constitution 556 (2d ed. 1836).

26. As Madison said: "If aliens had no rights under the Constitution, they might not only be banished, but even capitally punished, without a jury or the other incidents to a fair trial." *Id. See also* Neuman, Strangers to the Constitution: Immigrants, Borders, and Fundamental Law 58 (Princeton University Press 1996).

27. For a compelling case that comes uncomfortably close to this, see *Arar v. Ashcroft*, 585 F.3d 559 (2d. Cir. 2009), *cert denied*, 130 S. Ct. 3409 (June 14, 2010). Mr. Arar alleged that he was detained while changing planes at Kennedy Airport in New York (based on a warning from Canadian authorities that he was a member of Al Qaeda), mistreated for twelve days while in United States custody, and then removed to Syria via Jordan pursuant to an intergovernmental understanding that he would be detained and interrogated under torture by Syrian officials. He was interrogated for twelve days upon his arrival in Syria and was beaten on his palms, hips, and lower back with a two-inch-thick electric cable and with bare hands. He sued federal officials, alleging a violation of the Torture Victim Protection Act (TVPA) and of his due process rights arising from the conditions of his detention, denial of access to counsel and the courts, and his detention and torture in Syria. The dismissal of his TVPA claim was affirmed because the court found he had failed to allege that the federal officials

possessed power under Syrian law or that his removal to Syria and subsequent torture derived from an exercise of that power. His due process claim was dismissed because he had "failed to specify any culpable action taken by any single federal official and failed to allege the meeting of the minds that a plausible conspiracy claim required." The appellate court also declined to recognize a so-called "Bivens" action in the context of extraordinary rendition as this would have the natural tendency to affect diplomacy, foreign policy, and the security of the nations, thereby counseling hesitation. Rather, said the court, it was up to Congress to create such a remedy.

28. *See, e.g.*, al-Maqaleh v. Gates, 604 F. Supp. 2d 205 (D.D.C. 2009), *rev'd*, 605 F.3d 84 (D.C. Cir. 2010). The case involved detainees at Bagram Air Base. The District court had applied the analysis in *Boumediene* and determined that the Suspension Clause should apply at Bagram, at least where the detainee was not initially detained within Afghanistan. The government argued, notwithstanding *Boumediene*, that section 7(a) of the MCA precluded statutory jurisdiction. First, they argued, Bagram is located in a distant and active war zone. Second, Bagram had been in existence for only a short time, was never part of or carved out of U.S. territory to remain under de facto U.S. sovereignty, and was not intended to serve as a permanent facility. Third, Bagram served the military mission of strengthening Afghan sovereignty, and the government must therefore take into account the views of our allies (most prominently the Afghan government, but also the many other nations whose troops are stationed at Bagram). Unlike at Guantanamo, at Bagram the United States needed the cooperation of both the Afghan government and its coalition allies to achieve its mission. A three-judge panel of the D.C. Circuit unanimously accepted these arguments and held that the practical obstacles were too great to justify extending the protections of the Suspension Clause to noncitizens at Bagram. *See* Stephen I. Vladeck, Symposium: *Presidential Power in the Obama Administration: Early Reflections: The Unreviewable Executive: Kiyemba, Maqaleh, and the Obama Administration*, 26 CONST. COMMENTARY 603, 614–15 (2010).

29. OLIVER WENDELL HOLMES, JR., THE COMMON LAW 3 (Dover Publications, Inc. 1991) (1881).

30. *See* Johan Steyn, *Guantanamo Bay: A Legal Black Hole*, 1 INT'L AND COMP. L.Q. 53 (2004).

31. One major challenge began with George W. Bush's "military order" of November 13, 2001, which authorized indefinite detention and trial by military commission of certain noncitizens. As Giorgio Agamben notes, what was new about President Bush's order was that it radically erased "any status of the individual thus producing a legally unnamable and unclassifiable being." GIORGIO AGAMBEN, STATE OF EXCEPTION 3 (2005).

32. The phrase "Peace of Westphalia" describes a series of peace treaties that ended the Thirty Years' War (1618–1648) in the Holy Roman Empire, and the Eighty Years' War (1568–1648) between Spain and the Dutch Republic. *See* Leo Gross, *The Peace of Westphalia, 1648-1948*, 42 AM. J. INT'L L. 20 (1948).

33. *See* U.S. CONST. amend. XIV ("All persons born or naturalized in the United States, and subject to the jurisdiction thereof, are citizens of the United States and of the State wherein they reside."). The U.S. version of *jus soli* has been recently challenged when applied to the children of undocumented noncitizens. This book will not revisit those debates other than to note the possibility that the protections given to children by virtue of place of birth may, ironically, strengthen the vision of territory as a strong principle upon which basic rights claims may turn. *See also* PETER SCHUCK & ROGERS SMITH, CITIZENSHIP WITHOUT CONSENT: ILLEGAL ALIENS IN THE AMERICAN POLICY (Yale University Press 1985); Gerald L. Neuman, *Back to* Dred Scott?, 24 SAN DIEGO L. REV. 485, 491–92 (1987).

34. *See* Andreas Osiander, *Sovereignty, International Relations, and the Westphalian Myth*, 55 INT'L ORG. 251 (2001).

35. *Id.* at 256.

36. *See, e.g.*, U.N. Charter arts. 1 and 2.

37. Gross, *supra* note 32, at 21.

38. *See* http://www.interpol.int/.

39. *See generally* Kal Raustiala, *The Geography of Justice*, 73 FORDHAM L. REV. 2501 (2005).

40. T. ALEXANDER ALEINIKOFF, SEMBLANCES OF SOVEREIGNTY: THE CONSTITUTION, THE STATE, AND AMERICAN CITIZENSHIP 3 (2002).

41. This illustrates the circularity of their special dilemma: what rights do they have to be heard *in order to prove their status*? As noted above, this was why proof of alienage was once called "a jurisdictional fact." *See* Ng Fung Ho v. White, 259 U.S. 276, 284 (1922); United States *ex rel* Bilokumsky v. Tod, 263 U.S. 149, 153 (1923) ("[A]lienage is a jurisdictional fact, and . . . an order of deportation must be predicated on that finding 'of fact'"); Woodby v. INS, 385 U.S. 276 (1966). It may also prove, logically, that a territorial on/off switch can never be absolute.

42. The Sherman Act, for example, applies to foreign conduct that was meant to produce and in fact did have some substantial effect in the United States. *See* Matsushita Elec. Industrial Co. v. Zenith Radio Corp., 475 U.S. 574, 582 n. 6 (1986); United States v. Aluminum Co. of Am., 148 F.2d 416, 444 (2d Cir. 1945) (L. Hand, J.); RESTATEMENT (THIRD) OF FOREIGN RELATIONS LAW OF THE UNITED STATES [hereinafter RESTATEMENT] § 415, and Reporters' Note 3 (1987). Under § 402 of the Foreign Trade Antitrust Improvements Act of 1982 (FTAIA), 96 Stat. 1246, 15 U.S.C. § 6a, the Sherman Act does not apply to conduct involving foreign trade or commerce, other than import trade or import commerce, unless "such conduct has a direct, substantial, and reasonably foreseeable effect" on domestic or import commerce. § 6a(1)(A). For an interesting Fifth Amendment argument, see Lea Brilmayer and Charles Norchi, *Federal Extraterritoriality and Fifth Amendment Due Process*, 105 HARV. L. REV. 1217 (1992).

43. Slater v. Mexican Nat'l R.R. Co., 194 U.S. 121, 126 (1904); *see also* Larry Kramer, *Vestiges of Beale: Extraterritorial Application of American Law*, 1991 SUP. CT. REV. 179; Aleinikoff, *supra* note 40, at 15.

44. Sarah Cleveland, *Embedded International Law and the Constitution Abroad*, 110 COLUM. L. REV. 225 (2010); *see generally* KAL RAUSTIALA, DOES THE CONSTITUTION FOLLOW THE FLAG? THE EVOLUTION OF TERRITORIALITY IN AMERICAN LAW (Oxford University Press 2009).

45. We should note that these jurisdictional rules may differ depending upon whether one is considering the power to prescribe laws, the power to enforce them, or the power to adjudicate. *See* RESTATEMENT, *supra* note 42, § 401 (distinguishing jurisdiction to prescribe, adjudicate and enforce).

46. RESTATEMENT, *supra* note 42, § 402 cmt. b ("Territoriality is considered the normal . . . basis for the exercise of jurisdiction.").

47. *See, e.g.,* INT'L BAR ASS'N, REPORT OF THE TASKFORCE ON EXTRATERRITORIAL JURISDICTION 11 (2009), *at* http:/www.ibanet.org/ [hereinafter IBA REPORT] ("The starting point for jurisdiction is that all states have competence over events occurring and persons . . . present in their territory. This . . . 'principle of territoriality', is the most common and least controversial basis for jurisdiction.").

48. IAN BROWNLIE, PRINCIPLES OF PUBLIC INTERNATIONAL LAW 297 (6th ed. 2003).

49. *See* RESTATEMENT, *supra* note 42, § 402(2).

50. *See* JOSEPH STORY, COMMENTARIES ON THE CONFLICT OF LAWS § 21, at 22 (1834) (citing treatises by Boullenois (1766) and Vattel (1758)).

51. *See generally* John H. Knox, *A Presumption Against Extrajurisdictionality*, 104 AM. J. INT'L L. 351 (2010); RESTATEMENT, *supra* note 42, §411–413.

52. *See* Knox, *id.,* (citing 18 U.S.C. § 2423(c) (2006), which criminalizes "illicit sexual conduct" "in foreign places" by a U.S. citizen or permanent resident).

53. RESTATEMENT, *supra* note 42, § 402(3); IBA Report, *supra* note 47, at 149–50. *See, e.g.,* United States v. Yousef, 327 F.3d 56 (2d Cir.), *cert. denied,* 540 U.S. 933, *cert. denied,* 540 U.S. 993 (2003) (federal jurisdiction upheld for charges relating to a conspiracy committed outside the United States to bomb American commercial airliners in Southeast Asia and the 1993 bombing of the World Trade Center in New York City).

54. *See* United States v. Pizzarusso, 388 F.2d 8 (2d Cir. 1968) *cert. denied,* 392 U.S. 936 (1968); *see also* Rocha v. United States, 288 F.2d 545 (9th Cir. 1961) (federal jurisdiction exists over offenses committed outside the United States of conspiring with phony brides to secure admission to the United States).

55. RESTATEMENT, *supra* note 42, § 402(1)(c). The IBA notes that "virtually all jurisdictions apply some form of an 'effects' test." IBA REPORT, *supra* note 47, at 63.

56. *See* United States v. Pizzarusso, *supra* note 54, at 10–11 (2nd Cir.), *cert. denied*, 392 U.S. 936 (1968). The objective territorial principle may be distinguished from the protective theory in that in the latter, all the elements of the crime occur in the foreign country, and jurisdiction exists because these actions have a potentially adverse effect upon security or governmental functions, with no actual effect taking place in the country as would be required under the objective territorial principle. *See also* Hartford Fire Ins. Co. v. California, 509 U.S. 764 (1993).

57. United States v. Smith, 680 F.2d 255 (1st Cir. 1982). The objective territorial principle may be distinguished from the protective theory in that in the latter all the elements of the crime occur in the foreign country, and jurisdiction exists because these actions have a potentially adverse effect upon security or governmental functions, with no actual effect taking place in the country as would be required under the objective territorial principle.

58. *See generally* IBA REPORT, *supra* note 47, at 146–49.

59. *See* IBA REPORT, *supra*, at 150–61 (surveying current state practices).

60. *See* G. Edward White, *The Marshall Court and International Law: The Piracy Cases*, 83 AM. J. INT'L L. 727, 730 n.14 (1989); Knox, *supra* note 51, at 362–66 (referring to this as a presumption against "extrajurisdictionality" under international law principles).

61. Am. Banana Co. v. United Fruit Co., 213 U.S. 347 (1909).

62. *See* Larry Kramer, *Vestiges of Beale: Extraterritorial Application of American Law*, 1991 SUP. CT. REV. 179 (1991).

63. *American Banana*, 213 U.S. at 356.

64. United States v. Bowman, 260 U.S. 94 (1922).

65. Foley Bros., Inc. v. Filardo, 336 U.S. 281, 285 (1949).

66. *See* Knox, *supra* note 51, at 371–73. In 1991, however, the Court strengthened the presumption in *EEOC v. Arabian American Oil Co. (Aramco)*, 499 U.S. 244, as the Court considered a claim by a U.S. national that a U.S. corporation had discriminated against him in violation of Title VII of the Civil Rights Act of 1964. *See also* Smith v. United States, 507 U.S. 197 (1993), which involved the widow of a U.S. national who brought a claim under the Federal Tort Claims Act after her husband was killed in Antarctica while working at a U.S. scientific station.

67. A rather cynical and cruel press release issued contemporaneously with Bush's Executive Order No. 12807 (1) urged any Haitians who feared persecution to avail themselves of a refugee processing service at the American Embassy in Haiti and (2) indicated that the American Embassy staff in Haiti would be increased for refugee processing if necessary.

68. Protocol Relating to the Status of Refugees, Art. 33, Jan. 31, 1967, 19 UST 6259, 606 UNTS 267 (incorporating the relevant part of the Convention Relating to the Status of Refugees, July 28, 1951, 189 UNTS 150, to which the United States is not a party); INA §243(h).

69. Sale v. Haitian Ctrs. Council, Inc., 509 U.S. 155, 173–74, 188 (1993). The Court also concluded that both the text and negotiating history of Article 33 indicated that it was not intended to have extraterritorial effect; and that, although the human crisis was compelling, there was no judicial remedy.

70. Rasul v. Bush, 542 U.S. 466, 480 (2004).

71. *See* Knox, *supra* note 51, at 353 (citing Sale v. Haitian Ctrs. Council, Inc., 509 U.S. 155 (1993); Smith v. United States, 507 U.S. 197 (1993)). See also *F. Hoffmann-La Roche v. Empagran*, in which the Court stated that it "ordinarily construes ambiguous statutes to avoid *unreasonable* interference with the sovereign authority of other nations," a rule of construction that "reflects principles of customary international law . . . that (we must assume) Congress ordinarily seeks to follow." The Court concluded that the Sherman Antitrust Act did not apply to claims arising from foreign price-fixing activities. F. Hoffmann-La Roche v. Empagran S.A., 542 U.S. 155, 164 (2004).

72. *See* DANIEL KANSTROOM, DEPORTATION NATION (Harvard University Press 2007).

73. *Id.*

74. *See, e.g.,* Scott v. Emerson, 15 Mo. 576, 590 (1852) (Gamble. J. dissenting) (citing Winney v. Whitesides, 1 Mo. 472 (1824); Le Grange v. Chouteau, 2 Mo. 20 (1828); Ralph v. Duncan, 3 Mo. 194 (1833); Julia v. McKinney, 3 Mo. 270 (1833); Natt v. Ruddle, 3 Mo. 400

(1834); Rachael v. Walker, 4 Mo. 350 (1836); Wilson v. Melvin, 4 Mo. 592(1837). Immigration scholars may note similarities between this body of case law and later immigration cases that involve temporary trips abroad.

75. Somersett v. Stewart, (1772) 98 Eng. Rep. 499, 510 (K.B.). (also sometimes cited as R v Knowles, ex parte Somersett (1772) 20 State Tr 1). The spelling of this name is frequently rendered as "Somerset," but the original had two "t's."

76. *Id.* at 509 (emphasis added). *See generally* Sarah Cleveland, *Foreign Authority, American Exceptionalism, and the Dred Scott Case,* 82 CHI.-KENT L. REV. 393 (2007).

77. *Id.; see also* William M. Wiecek, *Somerset: Lord Mansfield and the Legitimacy of Slavery in the Anglo-American World,* 42 U. CHI. L. REV. 86, 107–08 (1974). *Cf.* Rex v. Allan (The Slave, Grace), (1827) 166 Eng. Rep. 179 (Adm. 1827) (A slave named Grace had been brought from Antigua to live in England for a year. After a return to Antigua, the High Court of Admiralty ruled (Lord Stowell) that the return to Antigua had resurrected Grace's enslaved status. Residence in England did not permanently manumit slaves.).

78. Prigg v. Pennsylvania, 41 U.S. 539, 611 (1842) (a "mere municipal regulation"). In the U.S. federal system, however, such discretionary aspects of comity did not long protect *fugitive* slaves who were subject to a federal system of seizure and recapture, based both upon the Constitution and federal statutes. *See* KANSTROOM, DEPORTATION NATION, *supra* note 72, ch. 2. As Justice Story noted in the 1842 case of *Prigg v. Pennsylvania,* before the adoption of the Constitution, no state had any power over the subject, except within its own territorial limits. Whenever a slave-catcher sought to remove a slave from a free state, the claim would be one of "comity and favour," and not as a matter of obligation or duty. *Prigg,* 411 U.S. at 611. Under the U.S. Constitution, the return of a fugitive slave was rendered "independent of comity, confined to no territorial limits, and bounded by no state institutions or policy." *Prigg,* 411 U.S. at 622–23. For a discussion of how the "full faith and credit clause" is implicated in this general problem, see Robert H. Jackson, *Full Faith and Credit: The Lawyer's Clause of the Constitution,* 45 COLUM. L. REV. 1 (1945). *Available at* http://www.roberthjackson.org/the-man/speeches-articles/speeches/speeches-by-robert-h-jackson/full-faith-and-credit.

79. As a dissenting Missouri judge recalled in 1852:

> As citizens of a slaveholding State, we have no right to complain of our neighbors of Illinois, because they introduce into their State constitution a prohibition of slavery; nor has any citizen of Missouri, who removes with his slave to Illinois, a right to complain that the fundamental law of the State to which he removes, and in which he makes his residence, dissolves the relation between him and his slave.

Scott v. Emerson, 15 Mo. at 590 (Gamble, J. dissenting). Thus, "Whenever the forms . . . are complied with, the emancipation is complete and the slave is free." If the rights of such an emancipated person thus emancipated were subsequently questioned in another State, the matter would be "determined by the law of the State in which he and his former master resided; and when it appears that such law has been complied with, the right to freedom will be fully sustained in the courts of all the slaveholding States . . . ." *Id.*

80. "[T]here is no person so ignorant as to suppose that they would lose their right to freedom by such change of residence." *Id.*

81. Ulrich Huber, *De Conflictu Legum Diversarum in Diversis Imperiis, translated in* Ernest G. Lorenzen, SELECTED ARTICLES ON THE CONFLICT OF LAWS (Yale University Press 1947), *cited in* Emory v. Grenough, 3 U.S. (3 Dall.) 369, 370 n.2 (1797); JOSEPH STORY, COMMENTARIES ON THE CONFLICT OF LAWS § 29, at 28 (1865); *see also* Sarah Cleveland, *Foreign Authority, American Exceptionalism, and the Dred Scott Case,* 82 CHI.-KENT L. REV. 393, 405 (2007).

82. *Id.*

83. The opinion reconsidered the normative limits of comity: "These laws have no force in the States of the Union; they are local and relate to the municipal affairs of the territory . . . ." The key principle now was that "[e]very State has the right of determining how far, in a spirit of comity, it will respect the laws of other States. . . . The respect allowed them will depend altogether on their conformity to the policy of our institutions." JOHN GEORGE NICOLAY & JOHN HAY, ABRAHAM LINCOLN: A HISTORY 61 (The Century Co. 1890).

84. Scott v. Emerson, 15 Mo. at 583.

85. *Scott*, 15 Mo. at 583. The court continued: "Since then not only individuals, but States, have been possessed with a dark and fell spirit in relation to slavery, whose gratification is sought in the pursuit of measures, whose inevitable consequence must be the overthrow and destruction of our government. Under such circumstances it does not behoove the State of Missouri to show the least countenance to any measure which might gratify this spirit." The court also offered a stunning defense of slavery itself:

> As to the consequences of slavery, they are much more hurtful to the master than the slave. There is no comparison between the slave of the United States and the cruel, uncivilized negro in Africa. When the condition of our slaves is contrasted with the state of their miserable race in Africa; when their civilization, intelligence and instruction in religious truths are considered, and the means now employed to restore them to the country from which they have been torn, bearing with them the blessings of civilized life, we are almost persuaded that the introduction of slavery amongst us was, in the providences of God, who makes the evil passions of men subservient to his own glory, a means of placing that unhappy race within the pale of civilized nations.

Scott v. Emerson, 15 Mo. 576, 587 (1852).

86. Even Missouri gave a reason, however odious.

87. Scott v. Sandford, 60 U.S. 393 (1857); *see* ROBERT MCCLOSKEY, THE AMERICAN SUPREME COURT 393 (Chicago University Press 1960); Raustiala, DOES THE CONSTITUTION FOLLOW THE FLAG?, *supra* note 44 at 47.

88. *See* Raustiala, *id.* at 47–48.

89. *See* DONALD E. FEHRENBACHER, THE DRED SCOTT CASE 156 (Oxford University Press 1978); Jack Balkin & Sanford Levinson, *13 Ways of Looking at Dred Scott*, 82 CHI.-KENT LAW REV. 49 (2007); Raustiala, DOES THE CONSTITUTION FOLLOW THE FLAG?, *supra* note 44, at 48. Still, Taney's anti-imperialist and pro-constitution vision was clearly stated. There was, "no power given by the Constitution to the Federal Government to establish or maintain colonies bordering on the United States or at a distance, to be ruled and governed at its own pleasure; nor to enlarge its territorial limits in any way, except by the admission of new States. . . . [N]o power is given to acquire a Territory to be held and governed permanently in that character." Scott v. Sandford, 60 U.S. 393, 446 (1856).

90. *See* FEHRENBACHER, THE DRED SCOTT CASE, *Id.* at 156.

91. *See, e.g.,* An Act to Revise and Consolidate the Statutes of the United States, in Force on the First Day of December, Anno Domini One Thousand Eight Hundred and Seventy-Three § 1891, 18 Stat 1, 333 (1878) ("The Constitution and all laws of the United States which are not locally inapplicable shall have the same force and effect within all the organized Territories, and in every Territory hereafter organized as elsewhere within the United States."). This, of course, did not clarify whether the constitution applied of its own force to the territories; but it indicated the legislative mindset as to whether it should.

92. The *Insular Cases* were a series of cases beginning with *De Lima v. Bidwell*, 182 U.S. 1 (1901), and generally said to culminate in *Balzac v. Porto Rico*, 258 U.S. 298 (1922), which established a framework for selective application of the Constitution to "unincorporated" overseas territories. *See* Christina Duffy Burnett, *A Note on the Insular Cases*, in FOREIGN IN A DOMESTIC SENSE: PUERTO RICO, AMERICAN EXPANSION, AND THE CONSTITUTION 389–92 (Christina Duffy Burnett & Burke Marshall eds., 2001) (positing a more inclusive understanding of which cases fall under the umbrella term "Insular Cases").

93. The expression may originally derive from a pro-trade and pro-imperialist motto, "trade follows the flag." Albert J. Beveridge, *The March of the Flag*, in THE MEANING OF THE TIMES AND OTHER SPEECHES 47–57 (1908). *See also* Finley Peter Dunne: "[N]o matter whether th' constitution follows th' flag, or not, th' supreme coort follows th' ilection returns." *Mr. Dooley's Opinions* 26 (1906).

94. Aleinikoff, *supra* note 40, at 81 (citing Hon. Jose A. Cabranes, *Puerto Rico: Colonialism as Constitutional Doctrine*, 100 HARV. L. REV. 450, 455 (1986) (book review)).

95. *Id.*

96. The new model was first developed by Justice White's concurrence in *Downes v. Bidwell*, 182 U.S. 244, 287 (1901) (White, J., concurring). *See* Dorr v. United States, 195 U.S. 138 (1904). *See* Aleinikoff, *supra* note 40, at 81.

97. *See generally* T. Alexander Aleinikoff, *supra* note 40, at 28; *Dorr*, 195 U.S. at 142.

98. Rasmussen v. United States, 197 U.S. 516, 523 (1905); *cf.* Hawaii v. Manchiki, 190 U.S. 197, 220 (1903) (no jury trial right recognized for Hawaii prior to effective date of a statute that formally organized the territory).

99. Balzac v. Porto Rico, 258 U.S. 298, 306 (1992); *Dorr*, 195 U.S. at 143.

100. *See* Abbot Lowell, *The Status of Our New Possessions—A Third View* 9 HARV. L. REV. 155 (1899).

101. *Downes*, 182 U.S. at 373 (Fuller, J., dissenting).

102. *Id*. at 381 (Harlan, J. dissenting).

103. Abbott Lawrence Lowell, *The Colonial Expansion of the United States*, ATLANTIC MONTHLY, LXXXIII, Feb. 1899, at 145–52 (This is not quite accurate, as these were not really judicial questions but reflected statutory and constitutional provisions.); *see also* Brook Thomas, *The Legal and Literary Complexities of U.S. Citizenship Around 1900*, 22 CARDOZO STUD. L. & LIT. 307, 321 (2010).

104. *Id.*

105. *Dorr*, 195 U.S. at 148; Aleinikoff, *supra* note 40, at 22.

106. Aleinikoff, *supra* note 40, at 23 (citing *Downes*, 182 U.S. at 278).

107. Balzac v. Porto Rico, 258 U.S. 298, 309 (1922) (emphasis added). Puerto Ricans were granted statutory U.S. citizenship in 1917, which was expanded in 1940 and 1952 to include *jus soli*. It is unclear whether the Court meant to invoke a purely formalist territoriality principle or more practical concerns. The opinion seems to embody both. Taft asserted that the jury system needs citizens "trained to the exercise of the responsibilities of jurors." Congress, he continued, had concluded that "a people like the Filipinos or the Porto Ricans, trained to a complete judicial system which knows no juries, living in compact and ancient communities, with definitely formed customs and political conceptions, should be permitted themselves to determine how far they wish to adopt this institution of Anglo-Saxon origin, and when." *Balzac*, 258 U.S. at 310.

108. Aleinikoff, *supra* note 40, at 82.

109. Aleinikoff, *supra* note 40, at 83.

110. Downes v. Bidwell, 182 U.S. 244 (1901) (White, J., concurring).

111. See also John Marshall's paternalistic reference to native American Indians as "domestic dependent nations" in the 1831 case, *Cherokee Nation v. Georgia*, 30 U.S. (5 Pet.) 1 (1831); in Marshall's view, they were so far from equal that he said they were, "in a state of pupilage" with a relation to the United States that resembled that, "of a ward to his guardian." *Id*. at 17; *see also* Raustiala, DOES THE CONSTITUTION FOLLOW THE FLAG?, *supra* note 44, at 84.

112. As Marshall had framed it in 1823:

> The title by conquest is acquired and maintained by force. The conqueror prescribes its limits. Humanity, however, acting on public opinion, has established, as a general rule, that the conquered shall not be wantonly oppressed, and that their condition shall remain as eligible as is compatible with the objects of the conquest. . . .

Johnson v. M'Intosh, 21 U.S. (8 Wheat.) 543, 589 (1823); *see* DEPORTATION NATION, *supra* note 72, at 63–74.

113. *See also* Hirota v. MacArthur, 338 U.S. 197 (1948).

114. *See* Johnson v. Eisentrager, 339 U.S. 763, 769 (1950) (cited in Raustiala, DOES THE CONSTITUTION FOLLOW THE FLAG?, *supra* note 44, at 9 (noting that the analogy to Paul is not entirely apt, as he was in a Roman territory)).

115. Johnson v. Eisentrager, 339 U.S. at 798.

116. 354 U.S. 1 (1957). A companion case involved Mrs. Dorothy Smith who had also killed her husband, an Army officer, at a post in Japan where she was living with him. She was tried for murder by a court-martial, and "despite considerable evidence that she was insane" was found guilty and sentenced to life imprisonment. *Id*. at 4.

117. The charges were brought by Air Force personnel, and the court-martial was composed of Air Force officers.

118. The case was argued twice before the Supreme Court. The first time, a majority of the Court, with three Justices dissenting and one reserving opinion, held that the military trials of Mrs. Smith and Mrs. Covert for their alleged offenses was constitutional. Subsequently, however, the Court granted a petition for rehearing in both cases.

119. *Reid*, 354 U.S. at 3.

120. *Id.* at 6 (emphasis added). In a swipe at his old adversary, Robert Jackson, Justice Black then wrote: "This is not a novel concept. To the contrary, it is as old as government. It was recognized long before Paul successfully invoked his right as a Roman citizen to be tried in strict accordance with Roman law."

121. The plurality noted that *In re Ross*, 140 U.S. 453 (1891), was "one of those cases that cannot be understood except in its peculiar setting." Furthermore, "it seems highly unlikely that a similar result would be reached today." *Reid*, 354 U.S. at 10. The *Insular Cases* were distinguished as having "involved the power of Congress to provide rules and regulations to govern temporarily territories with wholly dissimilar traditions and institutions whereas here the basis for governmental power is American citizenship." Of course, if the broad language of the opinion's opening sentences were taken at face value one might ask why this last criterion would be relevant.

122. *Reid v. Covert*, 354 U.S. 1, 74–75 (1957).

123. WHEATON'S INTERNATIONAL LAW DIGEST, Sec. 206 (1856).

124. Jeffreys, C.J., The East India Co. v. Sandys, 10 Howell's St. Tr 371, 530–31 (1684) (quoted with approval in 10 WILLIAM HOLDSWORTH, A HISTORY OF ENGLISH LAW 395–96 (1938)).

125. Chae Chan Ping v. United States, 130 U.S. 581 (1889).

126. *Id.* at 606.

127. *See, e.g.*, Nishimura Ekiu v. United States, 142 U.S. 651, 659 (1892).

128. Bridges v. Wixon, 326 U.S. 135, 161 (1945) (Murphy, J., concurring) (citations omitted).

129. Knauff v. Shaughnessy, 338 U.S. 537, 544 (1950).

130. *See* Sale v. Haitian Ctrs. Council, Inc., 509 U.S. 155, 179–87 (1993) (discussing Article 33 of the United Nations Convention Relating to the Status of Refugees, July 28, 1951, 19 U.S.T. 6259, T.I.A.S. No. 6577); *Cf.* Regina v. Immigration Officer at Prague Airport [2004] UKHL 55 P 12, at 11 (appeal taken from E.W.C.A. Civ.) (opinion of Lord Bingham of Cornhill) ("[E]ven those fleeing from foreign persecution have had no right to be admitted."); Minister for Immigration v. Ibrahim [2000] H.C.A. 55, P 137 (Austl.) ("[N]o individual, including those seeking asylum, may assert a right to enter the territory of a State of which that individual is not a national.").

131. Zadvydas v. Davis, 533 U.S. 678, 693 (2001) (citing Kaplan v. Tod, 267 U.S. 228 (1925)) (despite nine years' presence in the United States, an "excluded" alien "was still in theory of law at the boundary line and had gained no foothold in the United States"); Leng May Ma v. Barber, 357 U.S. 185, 188–90 (1958) (alien "paroled" into the United States pending admissibility had not effected an "entry").

132. *Zadvydas*, 533 U.S. at 693 (citing United States v. Verdugo-Urquidez, 494 U.S. 259, 269 (1990)) (Fifth Amendment's protections do not extend to aliens outside the territorial boundaries); Johnson v. Eisentrager, 339 U.S. 763, 784 (1950) (same).

133. Yick Wo v. Hopkins, 118 U.S. 356 (1886).

134. Plyler v. Doe, 457 U.S. 202 (1982).

135. *Id.* at 210.

136. Yamataya v. Fisher, 189 U.S. 60 (1903).

137. Shaughnessy, v. United States *ex rel.* Mezei, 345 U.S. 206, 212 (1953). This was a Cold War case rejecting a claim by a noncitizen (a returning lawful resident) named Ignatz Mezei to be released after twenty-one months of confinement on Ellis Island. (The key was the word "expelled," as Mezei was deemed to be seeking readmission.)

138. Zadvydas v. Davis, 533 U.S. 678, 693 (2001).

139. *See generally* GIORGIO AGAMBEN, STATE OF EXCEPTION, *supra* note 31; *see also* GIORGIO AGAMBEN, HOMO SACER SOVEREIGN POWER AND BARE LIFE 11–29 (1998).

140. *Mezei*, 345 U.S. at 213; *see also* Jean v. Nelson, 472 U.S. 846 (1985); Gisbert v. United States, 988 F.2d 1437 (5th Cir. 1993).

141. *See* Duy Dac Ho v. Greene, 204 F.3d 1045, 1058–59 (10th Cir. 2000).

142. Rosales-Garcia v. Holland, 322 F.2d 1437 (6th Cir. 1993).

143. *Duy Dac Ho*, 204 F.3d at 1061 (Broby, J., dissenting).

144. *See* Zadvydas v. Davis, 533 U.S. 678 (2001).

145. In the 1896 case of *Wong Wing v. United States*, for example, the Court considered a statute that imposed a year of hard labor upon noncitizens who were subject to a final deportation order. The Court held that such punitive measures could not be imposed because "all persons within the territory of the United States are entitled to the protection" of the Constitution. *See* Wong Wing v. United States, 163 U.S. 228, 238 (1896) (citing Yick Wo v. Hopkins, 118 U.S. 356, 369 (1886))). *See generally* Daniel Kanstroom, *Deportation, Social Control, and Punishment: Some Thoughts About Why Hard Laws Make Bad Cases,* 113 Harv. L. Rev. 1890–1935 (2000); United States v. Witkovich, 353 U.S. 194, at 199, 201 (1957) (construing statute which applied to aliens ordered deported in order to avoid substantive constitutional problems).

146. The Court further held that the presumptive period during which detention is "reasonably necessary" is six months, and that a deportee must be conditionally released after that time if he can demonstrate that there is "no significant likelihood of removal in the reasonably foreseeable future." 533 U.S. at 701.

147. Still, some Justices continue to compare deportees on U.S. soil to first-time entrants. In his dissent in *Zadvydas*, Justice Scalia wrote that "[a] criminal alien under final order of removal who allegedly will not be accepted by any other country in the reasonably foreseeable future" is like an "inadmissible alien at the border [who] has no right to be in the United States." As he continued: "Insofar as a claimed legal right to release into this country is concerned, an alien under final order of removal stands on an equal footing with an inadmissible alien at the threshold of entry: He has no such right." *Zadvydas*, 533 U.S. 678, 704 (Scalia, J. dissenting). Soon thereafter, though, in the case of two unadmitted Cuban immigrants who had been ordered removed but were detained beyond the statutory removal period, Justice Scalia wrote that the *Zadvydas* reasoning must also apply to such "inadmissible aliens." The Court could not justify giving the same detention provision a different meaning "when such aliens are involved." But this was not a constitutional decision. Justice Scalia thus maintained his deeper position that the two classes of persons (the unadmitted and the deported held on U.S. soil) ought to be viewed as constitutionally analogous, if not identical. Clark v. Martinez, 543 U.S. 371, 380 (2005).

148. For example, Kwong Hai Chew was a Chinese seaman who was legally admitted to the United States, married a U.S. citizen, and ultimately was given permanent resident status. He served in World War II as a merchant marine and applied for citizenship. He set sail as chief steward on a vessel of American registry. When he returned to the United States, however, he was held as "excludable." The Supreme Court saw his case as different from that of Ellen Knauff, the wife of a U.S. soldier seeking to enter the United States about whom the Court had uttered its (in)famous maxim: "Whatever the procedure authorized by Congress is, it is due process as far as an alien denied entry is concerned." Knauff v. Shaughnessy, 338 U.S. 537, 544 (1950). The essential difference was that the Court determined to "assimilate" Kwong's status as a lawful permanent resident for purposes of this constitutional right to due process. Thus, he could not be deprived of life, liberty, or property without due process and—before he could be deported—he was entitled, at the very least, to notice and a hearing with "a fair opportunity to be heard." Kwong Hai Chew v. Colding, 344 U.S. 590 (1953).

149. *See, e.g.,* Rosenberg v. Fleuti, 374 U.S. 449 (1963) (holding that returning lawful permanent resident (LPR) was not making an entry when temporary absence was not "meaningfully interruptive" of permanent residence and trip was "innocent, casual, and brief."); *see also* 8 USC § 1101(a)(13) (prescribing general rule that returning LPR is not "seeking admission" unless certain exceptions apply).

150. *See* Landon v. Plasencia, 459 U.S. 21 (1982) (distinguishing a person who had been gone for some twenty months (*Mezei*) from one who was absent for "only a few days").

151. Hart, *The Power of Congress to Limit the Jurisdiction of the Federal Courts: An Exercise in Dialectic,* 66 Harv. L. Rev. 1362, 1392 (1953).

152. United States v. Verdugo-Urquidez, 494 U.S. 259 (1990).

153. *Id.* at 268.

154. *See* United States v. Verdugo-Urquidez, No. CR-87-422-ER (C.D. Cal. Nov. 22, 1988).

155. *Verdugo-Urquidez*, 494 U.S. at 264. "Whether evidence obtained from respondent's Mexican residences should be excluded at trial in the United States is a remedial question separate from the existence *vel non* of the constitutional violation."

156. These other protective constitutional provisions include the First, Second, Ninth and Tenth Amendments.

157. *Verdugo-Urquidez*, 494 U.S. at 265 (citing an immigration exclusion case, United States *ex rel.* Turner v. Williams, 194 U.S. 279, 292 (1904)).

158. The *Verdugo-Urquidez* majority also cited the *Insular Cases* for the proposition that "not every constitutional provision applies to governmental activity even where the United States has sovereign power." 494 U.S. at 268. Finally, in a passage that might support the claims of some deportees, but that did not help Verdugo-Urquidez, the Court recalled that "aliens receive constitutional protections when they have come within the territory of the United States and developed substantial connections with the country." *Id.* at 271. Verdugo-Urquidez, however, was "an alien who has had no previous significant voluntary connection with the United States, so these cases avail him not." *Id.*

159. *Id.* at 275–76 (citing 1 COMMENTARIES ON THE CONSTITUTION § 365, p. 335 (1833)) (footnote omitted).

160. *Id.* (citing *Reid*, 354 U.S. at 6).

161. *Id.* (citing *Reid*, 354 U.S. at 74) (Harlan, J., concurring)).

162. This had been advocated by Justices Brennan and Marshall in dissent. Justice Stevens relied upon the fact that Verdugo-Urquidez was on U.S. soil for his trial and likely would spend many years in a U.S. prison.

163. 130 S. Ct. 1235 (2010). I authored an *amicus* brief on behalf of law professors.

164. The United States is a party to the Convention Against Torture, which generally prohibits deportations once such a conclusion has been reached.

165. *In re* Guantanamo Bay Litig., 581 F. Supp. 2d 33, 34 (D.D.C. 2008).

166. *Id.*

167. *Id.* at 40 (citing Fiallo v. Bell, 430 U.S. 787, 792 (1977) (citing *Mezei*, 345 U.S. at 210)).

168. *Guantanamo Bay Litig.*, 581 F. Supp. 2d at 40 (citing Galvan v. Press, 347 U.S. 522, 531 (1954)).

169. *Guantanamo Bay Litig.*, 581 F. Supp. 2d at 40 (citing Japanese Immigrant Case, 189 U.S. 86, 101 (1903)).

170. *Guantanamo Bay Litig.*, 581 F. Supp. 2d at 42 (citing INS v. St. Cyr, 533 U.S. 289, 301 (2001)); Wingo v. Wedding, 418 U.S. 461 (1974) (recognizing that "the 'great constitutional privilege' of *habeas corpus* has historically provided a prompt and efficacious remedy for whatever society deems to be intolerable restraints" (internal citation omitted)).

171. Kiyemba v. Obama, 555 F.3d 1022, 1025 (D.C. Cir. 2009) (citing Ekiu v. United States, 142 U.S. 651, 659 (1892); Harisiades v. Shaughnessy, 342 U.S. 580, 596 (1952) (Frankfurter, J., concurring); CLEMENT LINCOLN BOUVÉ, A TREATISE ON THE LAWS GOVERNING THE EXCLUSION AND EXPULSION OF ALIENS 4 & n.3 (1912) and authorities cited therein; II Emmerich de Vattel, *Le Droit Des Gens* §§ 94, 100 (1758).)

172. Kiyemba v. Obama, 555 F.3d at 1025 (citations omitted) (emphasis added).

173. *Kiyemba*, 555 F.3d at 1026.

174. *Id.* at 1027 (citing Wilkie v. Robbins, 551 U.S. 537 (2007)).

175. *Id.* at 1027 (citing Jackman v. Rosenbaum Co., 260 U.S. 22, 31 (1922)).

176. *Kiyemba*, 555 F.3d at 1027.

177. 130 S. Ct. 458 (2009).

178. 130 S. Ct. 1235 (2010).

179. Kiyemba v. Obama, 605 F.3d 1046 (D.C. Cir. 2010); *see also* Kiyemba v. Obama, 561 F.3d 509, 514–16, 385 U.S. App. D.C. 198 (D.C. Cir. 2009) (Kiyemba II) (discussing Munaf v. Geren, 553 U.S. 674 (2008)).

180. 130 S. Ct. 1880 (2010).

181. Eisentrager v. Forrestal, 174 F.2d 961, 963–68 (D.C. Cir. 1949).

182. "Absent constitutional power, neither the objective nor the subject matter of an act is material." *Id.*

183. The fundamental protections of the Fifth Amendment "are universal in their application, to all persons within the territorial jurisdiction" of the United States. Yick Wo v. Hopkins, 118 U.S. 356, 369 (1886).

184. Zadvydas v. Davis, 533 U.S. 678, 693 (2001).

185. Landon v. Plasencia, 459 U.S. 21, 32 (1982); *see also Zadvydas*, 593 U.S. at 694 ("[T]he nature of [due process] protection may vary depending upon status and circumstance.").

186. Despite such constitutional protections, the deportation system remains harsh and anomalous. Thus, as we have seen, deportees do not have the right to appointed counsel, the right to bail, the general right to have illegally seized evidence suppressed, the right against *ex post facto* laws, the right against selective prosecution, or the right to a jury trial. *See infra*, Chapter 1.

187. Pena-Muriel v. Gonzalez, 489 F.3d 438 (1st Cir.), *petitions for reh'g and reh'g en banc denied*, 510 F.3d 350 (1st Cir. 2007), *cert. denied sub. nom.* Pena-Muriel v. Mukasey, 129 S. Ct. 37 (2008). The court distinguished Pena-Muriel's situation from cases that involved convictions that were vacated *before* removal proceedings had terminated and while a deportee remained in the country.

188. *Pena-Muriel*, 489 F.3d at 443 (citing Choeum v. INS, 129 F.3d 29, 38 (1997)).

189. *Id.* (citing Baez v. INS, 41 F.3d 19, 24 (1st Cir. 1994) (noting "Congress's intention to eliminate excessive appeals and lend finality to the deportation process")).

190. Padilla v. Kentucky, 130 S. Ct. 1473, 1478 (2010). *See generally* Daniel Kanstroom, *The Right To Deportation Counsel in Padilla v. Kentucky: The Challenging Construction of the Fifth-And-A-Half Amendment*, 58 UCLA L. Rev. 1461 (2011).

191. The Sixth Amendment provides:

> Rights of the accused. In all criminal prosecutions, the accused shall enjoy the right to a speedy and public trial, by an impartial jury of the State and district wherein the crime shall have been committed, which district shall have been previously ascertained by law, and to be informed of the nature and cause of the accusation; to be confronted with the witnesses against him; to have compulsory process for obtaining witnesses in his favor, and to have the Assistance of Counsel for his defence.

192. *Id. See also Padilla*, 130 S. Ct. at 1482 (emphasis added).

193. *Id.* at 1478.

194. *Id.* 1478 (emphasis added) (citations omitted).

195. *Id.* at 1480.

196. *See generally* Daniel Kanstroom, *Deportation, Social Control, and Punishment: Some Thoughts About Why Hard Laws Make Bad Cases*, 113 HARV. L. REV. 1890 (June 2000).

197. Justice Souter, Transcript of Oral Argument at 59, Hamdan v. Rumsfeld, 548 U.S. 557 (2006), http://www.oyez.org/cases/2000-2009/2005/2005_05_184 (quoted in Steven I. Vladeck, *Deconstructing Hirota: Habeas Corpus, Citizenship, and Article III*, 95 GEO. L.J. 1497, 1502 (2007)).

198. Zechariah Chafee, Jr., *The Most Important Human Right in the Constitution*, 32 B.U. L. REV. 143, 143 (1952).

199. Gerald L. Neuman, *Habeas Corpus, Executive Detention, and the Removal of Aliens*, 98 COLUM. L. REV. 961(1998); *see also* Lenni B. Benson, *Back to the Future: Congress Attacks the Right to Judicial Review of Immigration Proceedings*, 29 CONN. L. REV. 1411 (1997).

200. As the Supreme Court stated in *INS v. St. Cyr*: "[L]eaving aliens without a forum for adjudicating claims such as those raised in this case would raise serious constitutional questions." In *St. Cyr*, the Court construed certain jurisdiction-stripping provisions of the 1996 statutes not to preclude habeas jurisdiction. The *St. Cyr* opinion thus exemplifies the sort of subconstitutional reasoning that has long dominated U.S. deportation law due to the plenary power doctrine. But its implicit constitutional underpinnings might support post-deportation claims. INS v. St. Cyr, 533. U.S. 289 (2001); INS v. Calcano-Martinez, 533 U.S. 348 (2001).

201. 533 U.S. 723 (2008).

202. The United States is not fully sovereign over Guantánamo Bay, occupying that territory under an indefinite lease, which provides that "the United States shall exercise complete jurisdiction and control over and within said areas" during the period of the occupation. The lease agreement was extended by a subsequent 1934 treaty, "[u]ntil the two contracting parties agree to the modification or abrogation of the stipulations." Treaty Between the United States of America and Cuba Defining Their Relations, May 29, 1934, U.S.–Cuba, art. 3, T.S. No. 866.

203. Boumediene v. Bush, 553 U.S. 723 (2008).

204. *Id.* at 765 (citing Murphy v. Ramsey, 114 U.S. 15 (1885)).

205. *Id.* (citing Marbury v. Madison, 5 U.S. 137 (1 Cranch) 137, 177 (1803)).

206. The Court will consider at least four factors: (1) the citizenship and status of the detainee; (2) the adequacy of the process through which that status determination was made; (3) the nature of the sites where apprehension and then detention took place; and (4) the practical obstacles inherent in resolving the prisoner's entitlement to the writ. *Boumediene*, 553 U.S. at 766. *See also* Munaf v. Geren, 533 U.S. 674 (2008) (*Munaf* involved the access of U.S. citizens detained in Iraq to habeas review in U.S. courts. The Court again applied a functional analysis to determine whether there were extraterritorial limits on such U.S. judicial power. The habeas statute extended to American citizens held overseas by American forces operating subject to an American chain of command, even when those forces were part of a multinational coalition. However, under the circumstances of the case, habeas corpus provided petitioners with no relief. Simply put, the extension of habeas jurisdiction does not guarantee any particular result. It does, however, guarantee that courts remain involved.)

207. Although each Guantánamo detainee was assigned a "Personal Representative" to assist him, that person was not the detainee's lawyer "or even his 'advocate.'" Deportees, as we have seen, frequently lack counsel and have no right to appointed counsel. Also, in the Guantánamo setting, the Government's evidence was accorded "a presumption of validity." In many deportation cases, this is also the case; indeed, in many cases, once alienage is proven or conceded, the burden of proof falls upon the noncitizen to disprove "deportability." In Guantánamo, as in deportation proceedings, the detainee was allowed to present "reasonably available' evidence." But, the ability to rebut the government's evidence was seen to be limited by the circumstances of confinement and by lack of counsel. Finally, although the detainee could seek review of his status determination in the Court of Appeals, that review process could not "cure all defects in the earlier proceedings." *Boumediene*, 553 U.S. at 767.

208. *Boumediene*, 553 U.S. at 768 (citing Rasul v. Bush, 542 U.S. 466, 480 (2004)) (Kennedy, J., concurring in judgment).

209. Similar considerations seem to undergird the *Munaf* Court's conclusion that American citizens who were held overseas in the immediate "physical custody" of American soldiers who answered only to an American chain of command had a right to habeas corpus review of their cases. Territory, in short, is a subsidiary factor, compared to status and the authority of the detaining power.

210. Some have seen problems with this approach, though conceding that it is better than bright-line formalism. *See, e.g.*, Christina Duffy Burnett, *A Convenient Constitution? Extraterritoriality After Boumediene*, 109 Colum. L. Rev. 973, 976–77 ("While the test masquerades as a moderate and reasonable 'middle way' between two extremes—strict territoriality on the one hand and what is known as 'universalism' on the other—it actually slips a version of strict territoriality into the analysis through the back door . . . by enabling courts to make decisions respecting the applicability . . . of constitutional provisions abroad based entirely on policy concerns—an approach that would have trouble finding favor domestically, where we take for granted that the Constitution 'applies.'").

211. Habeas corpus review in deportation cases was limited by the Supreme Court in the *St. Cyr* case to "pure questions of law." Thus, some courts have held that discretionary matters, such as eligibility for certain forms of relief from deportation or review of denials of motions to reopen, are not appropriate in the habeas context. I have argued strenuously against this binary approach to law and discretion elsewhere and will not repeat those arguments here, other than to note that this area of law remains unsettled. *See, e.g.*, Negrete v. Holder,

567 F.3d 419 (9th Cir. 2009) (although neither the Court of Appeals nor the district court has jurisdiction to hear discretionary denials of motions to reopen immigration proceedings, this does not present a Suspension Clause problem on petition for habeas relief because review of discretionary determinations was not traditionally available in habeas proceedings). Complications arise because of provisions in the 2005 REAL ID Act, which took away the district court's habeas corpus or similar right of review of administrative removal decisions to remove aliens, and gave it solely to the court of appeals. *See generally* Daniel Kanstroom, *The Better Part of Valor: The REAL ID Act, Discretion, and the "Rule" of Immigration Law*, 51 N.Y. L. Rev. 161 (Fall 2006). Although the REAL ID Act gives the court of appeals jurisdiction over habeas petitions in removal cases, it did not specify what exactly should be done with future habeas petitions filed in district court. Some courts have transferred such cases to the courts of appeals. *See, e.g.,* Ishak v. Gonzales, 422 F.3d 22 (1st Cir. 2005). Others have simply dismissed them. *See, e.g.,* Munoz v. Gonzales, No. 05 Civ. 6056(SHS), 2005 WL 1644165 (S.D.N.Y. July 1, 2005).

212. To be sure, habeas is said to be "governed by equitable principles." Fay v. Noia, 372 U.S. 391, 438 (1963). The habeas statute provides only that a writ of habeas corpus "may be granted" and directs federal courts to "dispose of [habeas petitions] as law and justice require." *See* Danforth v. Minnesota, 552 U.S. 264, 278 (2008). Although statutory limitations do not govern the requisite constitutional minimum, there would still likely arise the question "whether this be a case in which [the habeas power] ought to be exercised." *Ex parte* Watkins, 28 U.S. 193 (1830) (Marshall, C. J.); Munaf v. Geren, 553 U.S. 674 (U.S. 2008).

213. *See* Enwonwu v. Gonzales, 438 F.3d 22 (1st Cir. 2006) (holding that the REAL ID Act did not impermissibly narrow relief available in habeas in violation of the Suspension Clause (U.S. Const. art. I, § 9, cl. 2), where the alien's petition raised only pure questions of law and the REAL ID Act granted the court of appeals full review of constitutional claims or questions of law); *see also* Muka v. Baker, 559 F.3d 480 (6th Cir. 2009) (REAL ID Act's limitation to petition for review does not constitute suspension of writ of habeas corpus and thus does not violate Suspension Clause; petition to court provides adequate and effective remedy to test legality of detention, since it offers the same scope of review as that formerly afforded in habeas corpus: constitutional and legal, but not factual or discretionary, claims); Mohamed v. Gonzales, 477 F.3d 522 (8th Cir. 2007) (similar); Iasu v. Smith, 511 F.3d 881 (9th Cir. 2007) (similar). Furthermore, habeas jurisdiction—pre- or post-departure—will not likely be available for claims that could have been addressed on petitions for review to the circuit courts, though cases involving missed filing deadlines might be reviewable under certain circumstances. *See* Chmakov v. Blackman, 266 F.3d 210 (3d Cir. 2001); Foroglou v. Reno, 241 F.3d 111, 113 (1st Cir. 2001) (recognizing habeas jurisdiction over claims not generally barred from petitioning for review where right to review in the circuit courts was arguably interfered with in violation of due process). Courts have long held, however, that habeas is preserved for those who have no other way to present constitutional or other legal challenges on direct review to a final order of deportation. Wallace v. Reno, 194 F.3d 279, 285 (1st Cir. 1999); Goncalves v. Reno, 144 F.3d 110, 121 (1st Cir. 1998), *cert. denied,* 526 U.S. 1004 (1999). Habeas might also be available if a due process violation frustrated a deportee's right of direct appeal or one's ability to file an appeal with the BIA, a historical prerequisite (called "exhaustion") to many habeas claims. *See* Hernandez v. Reno, 238 F.3d 50, 54 (1st Cir. 2001); Grullon v. Mukasey, 509 F.3d 107 (2d Cir. 2007) (amended Jan. 7, 2008), *cert. denied,* 129 S. Ct. 43 (2008) (statutory exhaustion provision of the INA applies to habeas petitions filed in the district court, which are converted to petitions for review and transferred to the Court Appeals).

214. Hamdi v. Rumsfeld, 542 U.S. 507, 536 (2004).

215. *See, e.g.,* Preiser v. Rodriguez, 411 U.S. 475, 484 (1973).

216. Habeas jurisdiction attaches if the petitioner is in custody (including being under a final order of removal) at the time of filing even if subsequently released from confinement. *See* Spencer v. Kemna, 523 U.S. 1, 7 (1998); United States *ex rel.* Circella v. Sahli, 216 F.2d 33, 37 (7th Cir. 1954) (court's jurisdiction over habeas corpus proceeding, once acquired, is retained). *See* Alison Leal Parker, *In Through the Out Door? Retaining Judicial Review for*

Deported Lawful Permanent Resident Aliens, 101 COLUM. L. REV. 605, 620 (2001) (statutorily imposed collateral consequences can allow a petitioner to satisfy the custody doctrine in the habeas context by showing ongoing injury for the purposes of standing and mootness); Sule v. INS, No. 98, 1090, 1999 U.S. App. LEXIS 20637, *4–5, 189 F.3d 478 (table) (10th Cir. Aug. 27, 1999) ("we strongly suspect that deportation may, as a matter of law, always entail collateral consequences."); Ramirez v. INS, 86 F. Supp. 2d 301, 303 (S.D.N.Y. 1999).

217. As Justice Black wrote, for a unanimous Court, "[h]istory, usage, and precedent can leave no doubt that, besides physical imprisonment, there are other restraints on a man's liberty ... which have been thought sufficient in the English-speaking world to support the issuance of habeas corpus." Jones v. Cunningham, 371 U.S. 236, 240 (1963). For an excellent technical analysis of this body of law, as it stood prior to the 2005 REAL ID Act, *see* Peter Bibring, *Jurisdictional Issues in Post-Removal Habeas Challenges to Orders of Removal*, 17 GEO. IMMIGR. L.J. 135 (2002).

218. Hensley v. Municipal Court, 411 U.S. 345 (1973).

219. Such a judgment might inspire the local courts to release the deportee, who would then, perhaps, have a right to return to the United States. *But see* Mohammed v. Harvey, 456 F. Supp. 2d 115, 121–30 (D.D.C. 2006) ("Because petitioner is in the custody of a multinational entity and not the United States, he cannot invoke this Court's jurisdiction.").

220. Where a person is "in the actual, physical custody of some person or entity who cannot be deemed the United States, but is being held under the authority of the United States or on its behalf." *Id.*

221. *See* Kumarasamy v. Attorney Gen. of U.S., 453 F.3d 169, 173 (3d Cir. 2006); Patel v. U.S. Attorney Gen., 334 F.3d 1259, 1263 (11th Cir. 2003); Miranda v. Reno, 238 F.3d 1156, 1158 (9th Cir. 2001); *see also* Terrado v. Moyer, 820 F.2d 920, 921–22 (7th Cir. 1987) (per curiam) (a previously deported noncitizen was not "in custody" for purposes of *habeas corpus* statute); El-Hadad v. United States, 377 F. Supp. 2d 42, 49 (D.D.C. 2005) (a noncitizen living freely abroad had no right to habeas because he was neither physically restrained nor detained at a point of entry into the United States). *Cf.* Zalawadia v. Ashcroft, 371 F.3d 292, 297 (5th Cir. 2004) (courts may exercise "*habeas* jurisdiction over a deported alien where that alien had been in custody at the time the suit was filed.") As one court rather blithely put it: "The continued harms that [the deportee] alleges—his fear for his life in Togo and the ten-year bar on future entry that the government has 'presumably imposed' on him ... do not constitute 'restraints not shared by the public generally that significantly confine and restrain his freedom.'" Sadhvani v. Chertoff, 460 F. Supp. 2d 114 (D.D.C. 2006), *aff'd*, 279 Fed. Appx. 9 (D.C. Cir. May 13, 2008).

222. *See Patel*, 334 F.3d at 1263.

223. *Miranda*, 238 F.3d at 1159.

224. *Id.* (citing Singh v. Waters, 87 F.3d 346, 349 (9th Cir. 1996)).

225. A look at this problem through the lens of history may be helpful. *See generally* LUCY E. SALYER, LAWS HARSH AS TIGERS: CHINESE IMMIGRANTS AND THE SHAPING OF MODERN IMMIGRATION LAW (1995). As early as 1885, the U.S. Attorney in San Francisco had argued that excluded "aliens" were not deprived of liberty within the meaning of the *habeas corpus* act and that exclusion decisions were therefore unreviewable by federal judges. The courts rejected such arguments. *In re* Jung Ah Lung, 25 F. 141, 142–43 (D. Cal. 1885), *aff'd sub nom.* United States v. Jung Ah Lung, 124 U.S. 621 (1888) (Blatchford, J.); Neuman, *Habeas Corpus, supra* note 199, at 1005–07. The court held the denial of the right to land, had in effect converted the ship into a prison-house, to be followed by his deportation across the sea to a foreign country. If this "be not a restraint of his liberty within the meaning of the habeas corpus act, it is not easy to conceive any case that would fall within its provisions." *Jung Ah Lung*, 25 F. at 142. The Supreme Court later confirmed that the custody attendant to exclusion or deportation, was custody for *habeas* purposes ("It is urged that the only restraint of the party was that he was not permitted to enter the United States. But we are of the opinion that the case was a proper one for the issuing of the writ. The party was in custody ... [pursuant to] an act of Congress. He was, therefore, in custody under or by color of the authority of the United States."). United States v. Jung Ah Lung, 124 U.S. at 626. In 1892, the Court again made clear that an immigrant, prevented from landing by a

government agent, and thereby restrained, was "doubtless entitled to a writ of habeas corpus to ascertain whether the restraint is lawful." Nishimura Ekiu v. United States, 142 U.S. 651, 660 (1892). And as Justice Holmes wrote in 1908, in a proto-realist mode: "We must look at the actual facts. *De facto* he is locked up until carried out of the country against his will." Chin Yow v. United States, 208 U.S. 8, 13 (1908) (Holmes, J.). Even during the height of the Cold War, the Court allowed those excluded from the United States to use the habeas mechanism. In *Mezei*, Justice Clark confirmed that Mezei's "movements are restrained by authority of the United States, and he may by *habeas corpus* test the validity of his exclusion." *See* Neuman, *Habeas Corpus, supra* note 199, at 1017.

226. Neuman, *Habeas Corpus, supra* note 199, at 970. A system in which executive officers can simply round up people and deport them, without judicial review, could certainly be seen as an impermissible "suspension" of the Writ. Courts would be justified, perhaps required, to use the detention that was part of the deportation—or the detention that a deportee would face if he or she tried to return to U.S. soil as the basis for the writ. The current *formal* removal system *does* allow direct judicial review, though. However, judicial review of certain types of issues is precluded. Thus, wherever *habeas* review would provide the indispensible constitutional minimum *pre-deportation*, it would seem also to be required *post-deportation*. Similarly, even in cases for which regular judicial review is available, habeas may still be required for those who have missed the filing deadline for good reasons or who may have other compelling claims that could be raised in a motion to reopen or reconsider.

227. "Time must always be given: the day reveals the truth." *De Ira* (On Anger): Book 2, cap. 22, line 2.

228. JAMES STEPHENS, THE CROCK OF GOLD bk. 1, ch. 4 (1912).

229. *See* KANSTROOM, DEPORTATION NATION, *supra* note 72, ch. 6.

230. The period of continuous residence "shall be deemed to end: (A) . . . when the alien is served a notice to appear under section 1229(a) of this title, or (B) when the alien has committed an offense referred to in section 1182(a)(2) of this title that renders the alien . . . removable from the United States under section 1227(a)(2) or 1227(a)(4) of this title, whichever is earliest." 8 U.S.C. § 1229b(d)(1).

231. *See, e.g.,* Cardenas-Abreu, 24 I. & N. Dec. 795 (B.I.A. May 4, 2009) (holding that a late-reinstated appeal under New York law would not prevent removal), *rev'd sub nom.* Cardenas-Abreu v. Holder, 378 Fed. Appx. 59 (2d Cir. 2010) (an appeal reinstated pursuant to CPL 460.30 was equivalent to any other direct appeal for the purposes of finality). *Cf.* Planes v. Holder, No. 07-70730, 2011 U.S. App. LEXIS 13648 (9th Cir. July 5, 2011) (alien was convicted despite the fact that there had been a remand for a possible resentencing, because the first definition of "conviction" in 8 U.S.C.S. § 1101(a)(48)(A) required only that the trial court enter a formal judgment of guilt, without any requirement that all direct appeals be exhausted or waived).

232. *See* Pino v. Landon, 349 U.S. 901 (1955) (per curiam), *rev'g* Pino v. Nicools, 215 F.2d 237 (1st Cir. 1954) ("On the record here we are unable to say that the conviction has attained such finality as to support an order of deportation").

233. IIRIRA provides that a criminal disposition may be considered a conviction for immigration purposes in the following two circumstances: (1) a "formal judgment of guilt" has been entered by a court, or (2) "adjudication of guilt has been withheld," but "a judge or jury has found the alien guilty or the alien has entered a plea of guilty or nolo contendere or has admitted sufficient facts to warrant a finding of guilt, and the judge has ordered some form of punishment, penalty, or restraint on the alien's liberty to be imposed." *See* INA § 101(a) (48) (A), added by IIRIRA § 322(a).

234. *See generally* David Martin, *Mandel, Cheng Fan Kwok, and Other Unappealing Cases: The Next Frontier of Immigration Reform,* 27 VA. J. INT'L L. 803, 815–19 (1987).

235. *See* Foroglou v. Reno, 241 F.3d 111, 113 (1st Cir. 2001) ("Foroglou's main argument is that the Board's time limit on petitions to reopen is itself invalid because it would result in denying relief to deportees who might then suffer torture, contrary to the Convention Against Torture and to the policies embodied in federal legislation and regulations that implement the convention or otherwise protect the rights of aliens. The short answer to this argument is that Foroglou points to nothing in the convention or legislation that

precludes the United States from setting reasonable time limits on the assertion of claims under the convention in connection with an ongoing proceeding or an already effective order of deportation.").

236. In previous work I have explored the evolution of this problem in the early history of deportation law through its powerful effects on such contentious twentieth-century deportation cases as those of Harry Bridges and Carlos Marcello. The reader is directed to that work for more details than are provided here. *See* Kanstroom, DEPORTATION NATION, *supra* note 72.

237. Shaughnessy v. Pedreiro, 349 U.S. 48, 51 (1955). *See generally* Alison Leal Parker, *In Through the Out Door? Retaining Judicial Review for Deported Lawful Permanent Resident Aliens*, 101 COLUM. L. REV. 605 (2001).

238. For an interesting review of this issue, see Peter J. Spiro, *Leave for Appeal: Departure as a Requirement for Review of Deportation Orders*, 25 SAN DIEGO L. REV. 281 (1988).

239. *See* H.R. DOC. NO. 85, 85TH CONG. (1st Sess. 1957) (message from President Eisenhower, January 31, 1957); *see also* H.R. DOC. NO. 329, 84TH CONG. (2d Sess. 1956) (message from President Eisenhower, February 8, 1956).

240. In particular, it eliminated declaratory and injunctive relief in deportation cases and channeled judicial review of all "final orders" of deportation to the courts of appeals. It limited the period during which an appeal of a deportation order could be filed and it required the exhaustion of administrative remedies.

241. *See* 8 U.S.C. § 1105a. for an overview of the history of the statute; Comment, *Deportation and Exclusion: A Continuing Dialogue Between Congress and the Courts*, 71 YALE L.J. 760, 760–81 (1962). U.S. immigration law previously provided that "any alien ordered deported . . . who has left the United States shall be considered to have been deported in pursuance of law, irrespective of the source from which the expenses of his transportation were defrayed or of the place to which he departed." Act of March 4, 1929, § 1 (b), 45 Stat. 1551, 8 U.S.C. (1940 ed.) § 180 (b). n.4. *See* H. R. REP. NO. 2418, 70TH CONG. (2d Sess.), at 6, which explained the provision as follows:

> Owing to the inadequacy of the appropriations now made for enforcement of deportation provisions under existing law, the Department of Labor has, in many cases, after a warrant of deportation has been issued, refrained from executing the warrant and deporting the alien, at the expense of the appropriation, to the country to which he might be deported, upon the condition that the alien voluntarily, at his own expense, leave the United States. Some doubt exists whether an alien so departing has been "deported." Subsection (b) of section 3 of the bill [the provision quoted above] therefore removes any possible doubt on this question by providing that in such cases the alien shall be considered to have been deported in pursuance of law. *See* Mrvica v. Esperdy, 376 U.S. 560, 563–64 (1964).

242. *See* Spiro, *supra* note 238, 25 SAN DIEGO L. REV. at 283–87

243. *See Immigration: Round Trip to Helsinki*, TIME, May 5, 1958, *available at* http://www.time.com/time/magazine/article/0,9171,863303,00.html. *See also Judicial Review of Deportation and Exclusion Orders: Hearing Before Subcomm. No. I of the Comm. on the Judiciary*, 85th Cong., 2d Sess. 4 (1958) at 20–22.

244. SAN FRANCISCO CHRON., Apr. 22, 1958, *reprinted in* 104 CONG. REC. 7097 (1958).

245. *See Immigration: Round Trip to Helsinki*, *supra* note 243.

246. *Id.*

247. Supporters of that system viewed it in quite rigid terms. In one discussion involving the well-known case of William Heikkila, whose alleged wrongful deportation had become something of a *cause célèbre*, Assistant Attorney General Malcolm Anderson responded to congressional inquiry as follows:

> MR. HILLINGS. This legislation would provide specifically that the deportation order would not be reviewed if the alien had actually departed from the United States-to make it clear, it would not be reviewed if he were outside the United States; is that correct?
>
> MR. ANDERSON. That is what is in the bill.

MR. HILLINGS. If he is out of the country, he could not be returned, or could not return.
MR. ANDERSON. Yes.

See Judicial Review of Deportation and Exclusion Orders, *supra* note 243, at 27 (cited in Spiro, *supra* note 238).

248. *See, e.g.,* Chen v. INS, 418 F.2d 209 (9th Cir. 1969) (petitioner had voluntarily left the United States); *see also* Joehar v. INS, 957 F.2d 887, 888 (D.C. Cir. 1992) (granting INS motion to dismiss due to departure); Sinclair v. INS, No. 98 CIV. 0537, 1998 U.S. Dist. LEXIS 19152, at *5 (S.D.N.Y. Dec. 3, 1998) ("no court may review an order of deportation . . . if the deportee has left the United States"); Kai v. INS, No. 97 CIV. 0869, 1997 WL 786946, at 1 (S.D.N.Y. Dec. 22, 1997) (no jurisdiction to entertain habeas corpus petition because of petitioner's departure from the United States); Borbon v. United States, No. 95 CIV. 1552, 1995 U.S. Dist. LEXIS 9153, at *3 (S.D.N.Y. June 29, 1995) (deportation of petitioner to the Dominican Republic moots habeas petition).

249. 563 F.2d 956 (9th Cir. 1977).

250. *Id.* at 958–59. Still, the opinion did not squarely confront the question of how far such a norm might extend. Nor did the court base its holding squarely on constitutional grounds. Notification to counsel was required by regulations. *See* 8 C.F.R. § 292.5(a) (1987). *Mendez*, 563 F.2d at 958 n.l. The court also found that the failure to notify counsel was a violation of an alien's statutory right to counsel in deportation proceedings. *See id.* at 959 (citing 8 U.S.C. § 1252(b)). Note that Mendez's more substantive claim was that the criminal conviction that had sustained the deportation order had been vacated. Thus, his case, a forerunner of such recent decisions as *Carachuri*, raised the question of whether the vacating of an underlying criminal conviction should permit a deportee to reopen the deportation proceedings. 532 F.2d at 957.

251. INS v. Calderon-Medina, 591 F.2d 529 (9th Cir. 1979).

252. *See* Estrada-Rosales v. INS, 645 F.2d 819 (9th Cir. 1981); *see also* Zepeda-Melendez v. INS, 741 F.2d 285, 289 (9th Cir. 1984) (basing jurisdiction upon failure of INS to notify alien's counsel of deportation); Thorsteinsson v. INS, 724 F.2d 1365, 1367 (9th Cir. 1984) (examining record of deportation hearing upon claim of ineffective assistance of counsel); Newton v. INS, 622 F.2d 1193, 1195 (3d Cir. 1980) (endorsing *Mendez* model); Juarez v. INS, 732 F.2d 58 (6th Cir. 1984) (intimating that if there were due process violations, the BIA could consider an appeal filed from Mexico); Camacho-Bordes v. INS, 33 F.3d 26, 28 (8th Cir. 1994) (holding that there is jurisdiction to "review an order of deportation . . . if the record reveals a colorable due process claim"); Marrero v. INS, 990 F.2d 772, 777 (3rd Cir. 1993) (same). Also, in *Wiedersperg v. INS*, 896 F.2d 1179 (9th Cir. 1990), the court determined that it had jurisdiction to review the denial of the motion to reopen (based on the post-departure bar) where the motion was based on the vacatur of a conviction that occurred subsequent to deportation.

253. Umanzor v. Lambert, 782 F.2d 1299, 1303 n.5 (5th Cir. 1986); *see also* Ortez v. Chandler, 845 F.2d 573, 575 (5th Cir. 1988).

254. *See* Quezada v. INS, 898 F.2d 474, 476 (5th Cir. 1990) (citing Asai v. Castillo, 193 U.S. App. D.C. 68, 593 F.2d 1222 (D.C. Cir. 1978)). The Tenth Circuit ruled that § 1105a(c) was "unequivocal" and that a petitioner's deportation "eliminates our jurisdiction to review his deportation order." Saadi v. INS, 912 F.2d 428, 428 (10th Cir. 1990) (per curiam). The Second Circuit concluded that "[w]e agree with the courts that have criticized *Mendez*. The pertinent language of § 1105a(c) constitutes a clear jurisdictional bar, and admits of no exceptions." Roldan v. Racette, 984 F.2d 85, 90 (2d Cir. 1993). In *Baez v. INS*, 41 F.3d 19 (1st Cir. 1994), the First Circuit found the prohibition on judicial review post-departure from the United States to be "absolute," reflecting "Congress's determination to eliminate repetitive and unjustified appeals." *Id.* at 22.

255. Delgadillo v. Carmichael, 332 U.S. 388 (1947); *see also* Rosenberg v. Fleuti, 374 U.S. 449 (1963) (permanent resident whose absence is "brief, casual, and innocent" would not be deemed to be making an entry). *See* Rachel E. Rosenbloom, *Remedies for the Wrongly Deported: Territoriality, Finality, and the Significance of Departure,* 33 U. HAW. L. REV. 139, 166–67 (2011).

256. *Delgadillo*, 332 U.S. at 391 (footnote omitted).

257. In fact, in a prescient concern with what later became known as "unlawful renditions," the court also wondered about the case "where the alien had been 'kidnapped' and removed." Conversely, the Second Circuit held that the "critical flaw in the *Mendez* rule" was that "an alien need only allege a defective deportation hearing to obtain review of that hearing. To allow the clear intent of Congress . . . to be so easily circumvented is to render the statute virtually without effect . . . ." The Second Circuit also was not troubled by the apparent Suspension Clause problem discussed above, holding that Congress had "ample constitutional authority to enact the jurisdictional limitation at issue in this case." Roldan v. Racette, 984 F.2d 85, 90–91 (2d Cir. N.Y. 1993).

258. *See In re* Vasquez-Muniz, 23 I. & N. Dec. 207, 208 (B.I.A. 2002); *In re* J-J-, 21 I. & N. Dec. 976, 984 (B.I.A. 1997) (justice may require reopening or reconsideration in certain circumstances despite procedural preclusions); *See also* Espinal v. Attorney Gen. of the U.S., No. 10–1473, 2011 U.S. App. LEXIS 15900 (3d Cir. Aug. 3, 2011); Pruidze v. Holder, 632 F.3d 234 (6th Cir. 2011); Marin-Rodriguez v. Holder, 612 F.3d 591, 594–95 (7th Cir. 2010) (agency lacks authority to limit its own jurisdiction); Coyt v. Holder, 593 F.3d 902, 906–07 (9th Cir. 2010) (*ultra vires*); William v. Gonzales, 499 F.3d 329, 332 (4th Cir. 2007) (*ultra vires*); Lin v. Gonzales, 473 F.3d 979 (9th Cir. 2007) (departure bar does not apply to person who has departed the United States subsequent to being ordered removed because such a person is no longer the subject of removal proceedings). *But see* Zhang v. Holder, 617 F.3d 650, 660 (2d Cir. 2010) (upholding departure bar with regard to untimely motions to reopen); Rosillo-Puga v. Holder, 580 F.3d 1147, 1156 (10th Cir. 2009) (upholding departure bar); Ovalles v. Holder, 577 F.3d 288, 296 (5th Cir. 2009) (holding departure bar to be valid with regard to untimely motions to reopen or reconsider); Pena-Muriel v. Gonzales, 489 F.3d 438 (1st Cir. 2007) (upholding departure bar without considering argument that regulation is *ultra vires*).

259. For example, in a recent case, the Supreme Court had to reconcile two conflicting immigration law time/space provisions: the requirement that a motion to reopen be filed within ninety days of the order of deportation versus the requirement that a person granted the right to voluntarily depart (in lieu of formal deportation) must to do so within sixty days. Dada v. Mukasey, 554 U.S. 1 (2008). The government had argued that by requesting voluntary departure, the noncitizen was knowingly surrendering the opportunity to seek reopening. The Court rejected this argument and instead held that the appropriate way to reconcile the voluntary departure and motion to reopen provisions "is to allow an alien to withdraw the request for voluntary departure before expiration of the departure period" and file the motion to reopen. *Id.* at 20. The Court, in reconciling these two provisions, noted that "[a] more expeditious solution to the untenable conflict between the voluntary departure scheme and the motion to reopen might be to permit an alien who has departed the United States to pursue a motion to reopen post-departure." *Id.* at 22. However, because the post-departure regulation was not challenged in that case, the Court did not address it, though an increasing number of lower courts have invalidated the bar for various reasons.

260. United States v. Witkovich, 353 U.S. 194, 199 (1957) (Frankfurter, J.).

7

Reconceptualizing the Law for Deportees: Discretion, Human Rights, and the "Spirit of Fair Play"

> Liberty and security can be reconciled; and in our system they are reconciled within the framework of the law.
> —Justice Anthony Kennedy (2008)[1]

Respect for the "rule of law" has often been said to be one of the main goals of the deportation system. Shortly before the 1996 enactment of the harshest package of U.S. deportation laws since the Alien & Sedition Acts, Barbara Jordan—then Chair of the U.S. Commission on Immigration Reform—said, more broadly: "We are a nation of immigrants, dedicated to the rule of law."[2] More recently, ICE Director John Morton stated that "You've got to have aggressive enforcement against criminal offenders. You have to have a secure border. You have to have some *integrity* in the system."[3] As we have seen, though, the rule of law and systemic integrity are elusive concepts under any circumstances, and especially so in the realm of deportation. Critics of the *Mendez* decision and similar cases described in Chapter 6 (that permitted review of appeals and motions filed by deportees outside the United States) assert that, strictly speaking, these actions have no basis in law. Some see such decisions as classic examples of the courts subverting the legislative will. And yet many critics would also concede that the results are, under certain circumstances, basically just and fair.[4] This, I think, brings us to the nub of the matter: what does the law require during deportation proceedings and after deportation has taken place, particularly for those in the new American diaspora? The answer clearly cannot be "whatever the majority wills" or "whatever the executive enforces." That would countenance government behavior and consequences that we cannot and should not accept. And yet the answer also is not quite "exactly the same rights as U.S. citizens have when facing analogous government enforcement actions;" or "infinite, endless, open-ended review." The best legal solution lies somewhere in between, mediated by moderately flexible ideas of discretion, judicial oversight, and a humane understanding of basic human rights principles, especially those that mandate proportionality and reject arbitrariness whenever state power is brought to bear against people, regardless of their legal status or their location. As one immigration legal treatise has simply but accurately put it, "judicial review is an endless quest for formulas of justice to deal with changing needs."[5] This chapter will consider possible building blocks for a reconceptualized rule of law for deportation. Beginning with the concept of discretion, it will conclude with a look at how international law has moved far ahead of U.S. law in its treatment of such legal questions.

The most basic question, as we have seen, is whether the rule of law extends beyond U.S. territory. Consider in this regard the following excerpt from a 1978 decision by Judge Herbert Stern, who was originally appointed to the bench by Richard Nixon and served as the presiding judge in the case of *United States v. Tiede*, an aircraft hijacking prosecution that was tried in the United States Court for Berlin. In his 1978 opinion, Stern held that the prosecution of a German by U.S. prosecutors outside the United States required at least the constitutional protection of trial by jury. He wrote,

> [W]ho will be here to protect Tiede if I give him to you for four years? Viewing the Constitution as nonexistent, considering yourselves not restrained in any way, who will stand between you and him? What judge? . . . I will not do it. . . . I sentence this defendant to time served. You . . . are a free man right now.[6]

This is an important passage to revisit in the context of post-deportation law because it illustrates at least three basic principles that support judicial review of such cases. First, it clearly rejected government claims that constitutional, civil, and human rights necessarily end at the U.S. border for "aliens." Second, implicitly, it models a functionalist consideration of what sorts of rights must always remain. And finally, it recognizes the judicial responsibility to enforce those rights. Of course, the exact content of such rights is always contestable. But Judge Stern's rejection of a formalist on/off switch at the border is an essential starting point.

Perhaps we should also begin with a rejoinder to those who say things like "They broke the law. Period." The rule of law is not, has never been, and *cannot be* that simple and binary. More nuanced and subtle models have long been available as background norms for a reconceptualized regime of deportation and post-deportation law. One example is the approach to immigration enforcement taken by Frances Perkins who, as Secretary of Labor, found herself in charge of the entire mid-twentieth-century immigration bureaucracy. In 1939, while facing harsh rhetorical attacks and threatened impeachment from the likes of Martin Dies and J. Parnell Thomas, Perkins highlighted a notion that might seem quaint and, perhaps to some, a bit fuzzy.[7] But, in light of the tensions we have considered in previous chapters, I believe it still retains great power. She simply called it, with Roosevelt-era flourish, the "*spirit of fair play.*" Perkins noted that immigration laws have "peculiar significance to the future of our country." It was thus incumbent upon those who administer them to demonstrate to the foreign born "that our American institutions operate without fear or favor and in the spirit of fair play to the stranger within our gates as well as to the native born."[8] What did this mean? For Perkins, who had inherited a widely discredited and often corrupt agency, it meant, in the first instance, clean and honest government action. But there was considerably more to it than that. It also implied a recognition that—even within an adversarial system—the government is bound by strong ethical norms. Government lawyers should not seek every possible litigation advantage simply to win a case. Deportation agents and prosecutors, like those in the criminal justice system, must remain acutely aware of the terrible power they have at their disposal. Tactics that might seem efficient and clever in the short term—such as the use of mass criminal charges in the Postville raids—may be later viewed as cruel, overreaching, and unworthy of our better traditions. Finally, although Perkins was speaking about law "within our gates," a *spirit of fair play* should recognize the complexity and harshness of deportation and not strive to insulate government decisions from judicial review by erecting formalistic, impenetrable territorial barriers.

What might this mean in practice? Gerardo Antonio Mosquera was deported after twenty-nine years of legal U.S. residence because he pled guilty to selling $10 worth of marijuana. His 17-year-old son, a U.S. citizen who helped to care for his younger siblings, became deeply depressed following his father's removal. Three months later, the young man committed suicide. Mr. Mosquera was not permitted to return to the United States to attend his son's funeral.[9] Would a compassionate temporary exception to the bar against returns not have been fair, just, and within the best conception of the rule of law?

Consider, too, a case that arose in New York City.[10] Caroline Jamieson, a U.S. citizen married to Hervé Fonkou Takoulo, a citizen of Cameroon with an outstanding deportation order due to a failed bid for asylum, wrote a poignant letter to President Obama asking for help. She and her husband were scheduled for an interview to regularize his status based on their marriage. However, in order to proceed in that way, they needed ICE Chief Counsel George Maugans to join in a Motion to Reopen. Mr. Maugans refused to do so in part because the visa petition had not yet been approved. Finding herself in a not uncommon "Catch-22" situation. Ms. Jamieson naively suggested to the President that Mr. Maugans should have evaluated her request by considering various factors, not just the technicality. "Without your help," she wrote, "Hervé is probably going to be taken into ICE custody in New York and quickly deported from our country. Hervé only wants a fair consideration of his request. . . ."

What happened next illustrates the intriguing weight of the *"spirit of fair play"* in such situations. In legal terms, what Ms. Jamieson was asking for was transparency and a reasoned exercise of discretion. Soon, however, she got a very different sort of response: two immigration agents stopped her husband in front of the couple's East Village apartment building. One agent reportedly asked, "Did you write a letter to President Obama?" When he acknowledged that his wife had, he was immediately handcuffed and sent to an immigration jail in New Jersey for deportation.

But then the case took a completely different turn. Following a flurry of investigative journalism, publicity, and behind the scenes lobbying, Mr. Takoulo was suddenly released. Officials now said they were investigating how the letter had been improperly used by the agency's "fugitive operations" unit to find and arrest him. The immigration officials acknowledged that their actions seemed to violate a standard practice of not using letters seeking help from elected officials as investigative leads.[11] The agency released Mr. Takoulo on an electronic ankle monitor while his case was reviewed. "ICE has a zero tolerance policy for violations of civil rights," the spokesman said in a statement. Though the case was far from over, it appears that ICE had belatedly decided to adopt a "spirit of fair play," at least insofar as it would not use a plaintive letter from a wife as a basis for choosing whom to arrest.

Of course, discretionary "fair play" can be quite controversial. For example, a memorandum from John Morton to ICE agents in 2011 specifically sought to protect from deportation plaintiffs in "non-frivolous lawsuits regarding civil rights or civil liberties violations" and "individuals engaged in a protected activity" related to civil rights "who may be in a non-frivolous dispute with an employer, landlord, or contractor."[12] Legal advocates said that it would help many noncitizens who face wage- and other work-related issues on the job.[13] The executive director of the American Immigration Lawyers Association described the grim alternative: "When there is a civil rights complaint, one of the best ways to get rid of it was to deport the complainer." Though she did not allege that ICE had ever intentionally done this, she noted that it is "a great way to get rid of cases." But Mark Krikorian of the Center for Immigration Studies, which supports strong immigration enforcement, said the policy would encourage more such claims as a way to prevent deportations. Krikorian said that he had no doubt immigration attorneys would take the hint and use this as a way of keeping their clients from being "sent home."[14]

In some settings, then, the government has opted for "fair play." But what if ICE had decided otherwise? Is fair play somehow *required* by the rule of law? Should judges intervene using fluid equitable principles or compassionate techniques of legal interpretation? This is the difficult terrain where our suggested models of law and discretion converge. Go too far one way and the system seems brittle and cruel. Go too far the other way and one gets judicial decisions that are easy to mock and that test the outer bounds of legitimacy. Potentially infinite review and vague, multifactored analyses add up to an unwieldy, inefficient and un-rule-like system. It is simply not law, one might say, at that point. It has no structure, no predictability, no clarity, and, possibly, no democratic legitimacy. Indeed, some say, both humane prosecutorial discretion and judicial interpretation of the *Mendez* type of case subvert the will of the political branches and, in turn, contradict the will of the people as expressed through their elected representatives. In its strongest versions, this sentiment has sparked sharp critiques of federal enforcement and, as we have seen, highly problematic state and local enforcement measures. For example, Louis Barletta, the mayor of Hazelton, Pennsylvania, once justified his town's attempt to harshly regulate the lives of noncitizens by asserting: "We are targeting illegals. When the quality of life of the city is being destroyed right before your eyes, I cannot sit back and watch it happen to my city."[15] Lou Dobbs responded to Barletta by challenging immigrants' rights organizations' understanding of the rule of law: "I wonder if the ACLU and these activist organizations [would] recommend and participate in lawsuits against federal officials who are refusing to uphold their constitutional oaths of office, and failing . . . to follow the Constitution and enforce existing federal immigration law?"[16]

Can we mediate between these two positions or at least refine our understanding of them? I believe so. First, one might note that when a new presidential administration takes office, the "will of the people" has been expressed in a new way to which the executive branch is surely entitled to respond within the limits of its discretionary powers. Thus, absent a complete abdication of enforcement efforts—which, as we have seen, is hardly the case—the question is not whether the law is being enforced; it is *how* should it be enforced?

Post-deportation law, like pre-deportation law, must take seriously the concept of *judicially overseen* administrative discretion. As I have previously discussed in detail, much of immigration law may well be understood as a "fabric of discretion."[17] This is all the more true of deportation law, notwithstanding the 1996 elimination of some discretionary forms of relief. Certain types of discretion—especially its prosecutorial variety—assumed considerable importance in the Obama administration. But the key question is not whether the rule of law demands the elimination of discretion—that is simply impossible. Rather, the more serious question is: what is the proper relationship among enforcement duties, such as inevitable discretion, basic rights claims, and judicial oversight?[18] Discretion might be described as the flexible shock absorber of the administrative state.[19] It is a venerable and essential component of the rule of law that recognizes the inevitable complexities of enforcement of laws by government agencies.[20] Though it has many technical forms, for present purposes we should focus on three. First, as we have seen, there is the discretion of deportation agents and government lawyers to decide whether to arrest and deport a particular person. This is commonly called *prosecutorial discretion*. Second, there is *interpretive discretion*, which derives both from the complexity of immigration law and from the inevitable task of basing technical interpretations on background norms.[21] As one court has noted, "we are in the never-never land of the Immigration and Nationality Act, where plain words do not always mean what they say."[22] Finally, there is the discretion to recognize unusual circumstances or particular hardships or injustices and to remedy them through adjudication. This *delegated discretion* is seen in the various "waiver" and "relief" provisions that still exist in U.S. immigration law. As Maurice Roberts, former chairman of the Board of Immigration Appeals, once explained: "In terms of human misery, the potential impact of our immigration laws can hardly be overstated."[23] The harshness of deportation law has thus long been mitigated by the possibility of discretion. The basic system, to be sure, was designed "to avoid conferring legal rights on aliens."[24] As one court starkly put it, "No one is entitled to mercy, and there are no standards by which judges may patrol its exercise."[25] But this is surely over-stated. Although delegated discretion was severely restricted by the 1996 laws, it remains an important feature of deportation law.

Discretion, in short, is a two-edged sword. It can cut toward harsh enforcement, or it can cut toward mercy.[26] It is an essential component of the rule of law, but it may seem un-law-like.[27] Most important, though, no form of discretion can ever be completely independent of the basic norms of our legal system, even though it may be insulated from intrusive judicial oversight. As Felix Frankfurter once wrote, discretion is "only to be respected when it is conscious of the traditions which surround it and of the limits which an informed conscience sets to its exercise."[28]

Further, the Supreme Court has long held that discretion, if granted, must *actually be exercised* by the agency to which such authority is given.[29] Statutory eligibility for discretionary relief provides a right to a ruling—a real exercise of discretion.[30] Thus, when the Board of Immigration Appeals took the position that it had no discretion whatsoever to adjudicate a post-deportation claim, it was not only adopting an unduly formalist view of territory, it was also swimming against a powerful historical and jurisprudential tide.[31]

Of course, judges differ greatly as to their willingness to oversee the mechanics of deportation. Consider this rather harsh exchange that took place in

the First Circuit Court of Appeals in a case seeking to enjoin some aspects of the
New Bedford deportation raids.

> JUDGE BOUDIN: This [raid] is unlikely to be repeated. I'm not quite sure
> what you would say to that. . . .
> MR. KAPLAN: . . . there's been an injunction for 25 years. Last week, the
> government filed . . . to lift the injunction. The court refused to do it
> because they still weren't in compliance with the detention standards. If
> they can't get their act together in 25 years with an injunction hanging
> over their head, what the heck—what's going to make them behave? . . .
> [T]here's a government plan. It's called *Endgame*. . . . The government says
> it plans to deport 10 to 12 million people by the year 2012. This is their
> own plan! Is it going to happen again? These raids are happening every
> day! Yes, it is going to happen again. I mean . . . . And it's going to happen
> until this Court says "No!" And we're looking for somebody to stand
> up. . . .
> JUDGE SELYA: Mr. Kaplan, you're looking for someone to stand up. We're
> looking for someone to sit down.[32]

One can surely appreciate the desire of some judges not to become embroiled
in the discretionary minutiae of immigration enforcement discretion. But this
urge cannot legitimately become a rigid or absolute principle. One is reminded
of Robert Cover's assessment of the actions of Judge Stern in Berlin. The judge
refused to accept the proposition that he, as a judge, could defer completely to
executive discretion when liberty was at stake. As Cover put it, Stern's decision
was not simply an "effective, moving plea for judicial independence, a plea
against the subservience which Stern's government tried to impose." It also
revealed the necessity of a "latent role structure" in which judges are *always* part
of the picture.[33]

This, I think, captures quite well what is truly at stake when judges face asser-
tions by the government that certain forms of discretion or certain types of
people, or certain territorial regions are lawless zones. But once we open this door,
we must then struggle with the optimal parameters of such judicial oversight. Let
us therefore consider how such tensions are handled by legal systems that foreground the human rights of deportees in more specific ways than does U.S. law.

International Legal Models

Although international law clearly accepts the basic power of the nation-state to
deport, human rights law has also long recognized the legitimacy and importance
of various rights claims by noncitizens. As Seyla Benhabib has noted, there is not

only a tension, but often also a direct contradiction between human rights principles and nation-states' sovereign claims to control borders and to monitor those who have been admitted or who have entered.[34] Still, few would differ with the basic proposition that "the status of alienage ought not to denude one of fundamental rights."[35] Thus, family unity, procedural regularity,[36] rights against persecution and torture, and a right to proportionality are well-accepted international legal norms, and there is increasing recognition of labor and employment rights for unauthorized migrant workers.[37]

Many deportees would surely foreground the basic ideal of "family unity."[38] The Universal Declaration of Human Rights (UDHR) provides that "The family is the natural and fundamental group unit of society and is entitled to protection by society and the State."[39] It has long been well accepted that an implicit corollary of this principle is a right of family members to live together.[40] Article 17 of the International Covenant on Civil and Political Rights (ICCPR), to which the United States is a party, protects against "arbitrary or unlawful interference with . . . privacy, family, home or correspondence. . . ."[41] When does such interference become "arbitrary"? The dominant view is that deportation itself—particularly *extended border control* deportation—is not necessarily arbitrary even though it may surely separate families. However, deportees must be permitted to plead their cases before competent courts.[42] The principle against arbitrariness guarantees at least that even interference provided for by law should be in accordance with the provisions, aims, and objectives of human rights law and should be, "in any event, *reasonable in the particular circumstances.*"[43]

Human rights law also protects the rights of children to remain with their families. The Convention on the Rights of the Child (CRC), to which the United States is not a party,[44] mandates that states must consider the "best interests of the child." This standard, ironically derived from U.S. family law, is widely applied internationally but routinely disregarded in U.S. deportation proceedings.[45] Still, most Americans, would, I suspect, agree with the basic thrust of the CRC, which cites the family as the "natural environment for the growth and well-being of all its members and particularly children."[46] It also aims to protect "as far as possible, the right [of a child] to know and be cared for by his or her parents," and recognizes the "right of the child to preserve his or her identity, including . . . family relations . . . without unlawful interference."[47] Most specifically, the CRC bars the separation of children from their parents, except under specifically delineated circumstances:

> State Parties shall ensure that a child shall not be separated from his or her parents against their will, except when competent authorities subject to judicial review determine, in accordance with applicable law and procedures, that such separation is necessary for the best interests of the child.[48]

Under the CRC, if parents and children are separated due to "any action initiated by a State Party, such as . . . detention, imprisonment, exile, deportation, or death," the state *must* furnish the parents or children with any available information regarding their family members' whereabouts.[49]

As noted, international human rights law does not unequivocally protect families from separation as a result of deportation. However, the United Nations Human Rights Committee has recognized that deportation from a country in which close family members reside may constitute an *illegal interference with family life*.[50] Thus, what is required is a careful balancing by competent authorities between the interests of the state and that of the individual and his or her family. Most recently, the Human Rights Committee has gone even further than this. In a case with powerful potential implications for U.S. deportees, the Committee majority (there were dissents) held that Australia had violated the right "to enter one's own country"[51] by deporting a man named Nystrom who had lived there since he was 27 days old with a visa status roughly analogous to a U.S. lawful permanent resident alien. This decision, well-described as a "watershed," was based on the Committee majority's recognition that "there are factors other than nationality which may establish close and enduring connections between a person and a country, connections which may be stronger than those of nationality."[52] In such circumstances, deportation is *inherently* arbitrary and thus illegal. The Committee's broad interpretation of one's "own country," though long advocated by some scholars, is obviously controversial and likely to be resisted by[53] governments. Still, it marks an important evolving recognition of the importance of one's identity itself as a limit to deportation.[54]

In the European human rights system, other such limits have been more fully developed. The European Court of Human Rights (ECtHR) has recognized that "contracting states" (to the European Convention on Human Rights) have the right to maintain public order and to control "as a matter of well-established international law . . . the entry, residence and expulsion of aliens."[55] To that end, states have the power to deport noncitizens without legal status or those convicted of criminal offenses. However, Article 8 of the European Convention on Human Rights limits the conditions under which the state may interfere with family and private life.[56] Thus, although governments are granted a considerable "margin of appreciation" (i.e., discretionary leeway)[57] expulsion decisions (as deportations are sometimes known in Europe) must be justified "by a pressing social need" and, in particular, must be "proportionate to the legitimate aim pursued."[58] Indeed, a contracting state may be required to grant family reunion within its territory between a noncitizen and a family member living abroad.[59] The most important distinction from the U.S. model, however, is that illegal entry and lack of status are only elements (though perhaps heavy ones) in a proportionality test. In the United States, the Eighth Amendment proscribes "cruel and unusual punishment." But this, as we have seen, does not apply to deportation under current doctrine because the sanction is deemed inherently nonpunitive.[60] Similarly, the recognition that "disproportionate" civil punitive damages awards may violate the Fifth Amendment's substantive due process guarantees has not been applied by U.S. courts to deportees.[61] Thus, the recognition of proportionality as a protective legal concept in the international realm has been well described as "an important new legal tool to redesign national immigration law from a human rights perspective [that] opens the law for considerations of equity."[62]

How does this work? Basically, European human rights law requires a court to ascertain whether a deportation (expulsion) order "struck a fair balance between the relevant interests, namely the applicant's right to respect for her private and family life, on the one hand, and the prevention of disorder or crime, on the other."[63] The relevant criteria include the nature and seriousness of the crime, the length of the stay in the host country, the time since commission of the crime, other conduct, the nationalities of the various persons concerned, the applicant's family situation, whether the spouse knew about the offense when the relationship began, the age of the children, and the difficulties which the spouse is likely to encounter in the country of origin.[64]

The outcome of such balancing is surely not always favorable to the deportee;[65] indeed many such deportations take place in Europe every day.[66] But the fact that such balancing *must take place* preserves an important measure of respect for human rights norms and a powerful safeguard against arbitrary government actions.[67] The most important point is that the legal system recognizes that the "decision to expel, or indeed not to admit a family member . . . [may constitute] an interference with the right to respect for family life."[68]

In a 2011 ruling with major implications for immigration and citizenship laws throughout Europe, the European Court of Justice (ECJ)[69] held that the parents of children who were born in Belgium must be allowed to live and work in Belgium despite their own lack of legal status.[70] The ruling, which "may be celebrated as a milestone in children's rights in the EU,"[71] involved two Colombian nationals, Mr. and Mrs. Ruiz Zambrano, who were refused asylum in Belgium.[72] The couple had two children who acquired Belgian nationality. Though he did not have a work permit, Mr. Zambrano had worked for a Belgian company, paying taxes and social security. However, when he became unemployed and applied for unemployment benefits, he was denied.[73] The couple then applied for Belgian residency as the parents of Belgian citizens, but their application was rejected.[74] The Court held that EU law precludes national measures that have the effect of depriving citizens (the children in this case) of the "genuine enjoyment of the substance of the rights conferred by virtue of their status as citizens of the union." The refusal to grant the parents the right of residency and a work permit

amounted to such a deprivation. The court also determined that the refusal of
residence would lead to a situation where the children would have to leave EU
territory. Put simply, a *de facto* deportation was impermissible. Moreover, the
refusal of a work permit would lead to a risk of the parents not being able to provide for their citizen children and might force them to leave EU territory. In
those circumstances, the children would be unable to exercise their rights as citizens. From the U.S. perspective, this is truly a remarkable decision. Even in
Europe, where, as we have seen, various human rights norms are more protective
of family unity than in the United States, the case has inspired much discussion
about the relationship between EU law and immigration and citizenship laws of
nation-states themselves.[75]

Could such international developments benefit those deported to the new
American diaspora? Not directly, perhaps. The United States is not, of course,
bound by the European human rights system and, along with Somalia, has not
ratified the Convention on the Rights of the Child. Legal claims against disproportionately harsh sanctions and family separation fare, as we have seen, notably
more poorly under the flexible due process calculus used by U.S. courts. Thus, in
U.S. deportation proceedings, rights to proportionality are largely unrecog-
nized.[76] U.S. courts will almost never consider claims of undue hardship, disproportionality, or family separation if applicable statutes do not empower them to
do so. It is thus fascinating to see how a claim against U.S. deportation law fares
before an international body with authority to analyze it under the rubric of
international law.

Wayne Smith was born in Trinidad and Tobago and came legally to the
United States in 1967 when he was 10 years old, together with his parents who
held diplomatic visas.[77] He became a legal permanent resident of the United
States in 1974. Sixteen years later he was charged with possession of cocaine and
attempted distribution. He pled guilty and served three years in state prison.
After his release, he continued to volunteer for prison ministry, volunteered as a
drug counselor and in other community outreach programs, and finished his
college degree. In 1996 Mr. Smith married Ann Hoyte, a U.S. citizen with whom
he has a U.S. citizen daughter, Karina Ann.[78] Mr. and Mrs. Smith started a small
construction cleaning business together and reportedly hired over fifteen
persons, most of whom were recovering drug addicts. The Smiths reportedly
purchased a family home and paid all their taxes.

The INS began deportation proceedings against Mr. Smith in March 1996,
early in the current deportation delirium. The immigration judge ruled that
he was ineligible for discretionary relief from deportation because he had been
convicted of an "aggravated felony" in 1990. Thus, in 1997, he was ordered
deported. Two years later, Mr. Smith illegally reentered the United States and
returned to his family in Maryland. Stopped for a traffic violation in March 2001,

he was turned over to the INS and was held in jail without bond. Meanwhile, the U.S. Supreme Court held that certain discretionary waivers of deportation (so-called 212(c) waivers) should have been available to noncitizens such as Mr. Smith, who had pled guilty to a criminal offense prior to the enactment of IIRIRA and AEDPA, if they would have been eligible for relief at the time of their guilty plea. Still, in December 2001 Mr. Smith was deported.

According to his lawyers, Mr. Smith's deportation has had deleterious effects on his family. His wife, a breast cancer survivor in need of radiation treatment and continued monitoring, lost her health insurance. She has struggled to support Karina Anne and to pay their basic living expenses. The family has suffered from the loss of Mr. Smith's moral and emotional support. Thinking they had no further remedies under U.S. law, Mr. Smith and his family brought a case before the Inter-American Commission on Human Rights.

Their case was joined with that of Hugo Armendariz, who was born in Mexico and came to the United States in 1972 at the age of 2. He became a legal permanent resident six years later. Except for his first two years, he had resided in the United States his entire life. He is married to a U.S. citizen, has a teenage U.S. citizen daughter, a young U.S. citizen stepdaughter, and many members of his immediate family are U.S. citizens. He had no close relatives living in Mexico, no meaningful ties to that country, and he did not read or write Spanish. In 1995, Mr. Armendariz was convicted of possession of cocaine for sale, possession of drug paraphernalia, and hindering prosecution. Like Mr. Smith, he applied for a 212(c) waiver, but by the time the immigration judge ruled on his application, the 1996 laws had eliminated such relief for persons like him. Therefore, he, too, was ordered deported. Like Mr. Smith, he argued that deportation has had a devastating impact on him and on his family.

As we have seen, U.S. deportation law offers no hope for these deportees. This is particularly true *after* they have been deported. And yet the legal analysis under human rights law was quite different. The rights of family unity, protection of children, and due process were analyzed quite differently based upon various provisions in the American Declaration on the Rights and Duties of Man (the "American Declaration").[79]

The IACHR concluded that the United States was "responsible for violations of Wayne Smith and Hugo Armendariz's rights protected under the American Declaration."[80] The conclusion, a mix of procedural and substantive rights, focused on the fact that the U.S. legal system had eliminated discretionary balancing. The Inter-American Commission further concluded that it was well recognized under international law that a nation state must provide noncitizen residents an opportunity to present a defense against deportation based on humanitarian and other considerations. Each state's administrative or judicial bodies "must be permitted to give meaningful consideration to a non-citizen resident's defense, balance it against the State's sovereign right to enforce reasonable, objective immigration policy, and provided effective relief from deportation if merited."[81]

Note that the *Smith/Armendariz* lawyers did *not* argue that these rights were absolute. They did not suggest that noncitizens with families can never be deported or that deportation is inevitably a human rights violation.[82] Rather, they argued that "[s]tates must show that the impact of the challenged policy or procedure on private or family life is proportionate to the legitimate aim pursued."[83] The stronger an individual's family ties and the longer the duration of residency in the host country, the greater the burden on the State to demonstrate that the deportation is proportionate to the legitimate aim pursued.[84] Courts, on this view, must consider "the extent to which private and family life was or will be ruptured, the existence and nature of the petitioner's links with his or her origin country, the retention of the nationality of his or her country of origin,"[85] as well as "the gravity of the petitioner's offense, persistence of his or her offending behavior, his or her age at time of offense, and his or her medical and psychological status."[86] In short, they demanded a proportional balancing of the nature of criminal conduct, its consequences, and the effects of the deportation sanction.[87]

The lawyers for the U.S. government, of course, saw the matter rather differently. They argued, first, that both "alleged victims" had more than ten years to apply for U.S. citizenship "but chose not to." Further, they argued that the United States has the sovereign right under international law to expel criminal aliens from its territory. The 1996 laws, they continued, were "reasonable and [comported] with the United States' international obligations." Finally, they asserted that the petitioners' interpretation of the American Declaration failed "to take due account of a State's right to take lawful actions that provide for the general welfare and protect the security of other people residing in its territory. . . ."[88] Also, in a series of arguments that might interest U.S. supporters of "family values," the government lawyers argued that family-protective legal norms only protect against "direct state action aimed at harming family life," not against the "secondary consequences of lawful, reasonable state actions."[89]

The U.S. government, in short, emphasized that Mr. Smith and Mr. Armendariz "made choices that had consequences." It said that they could have avoided removal by either "choosing not to commit a serious crime or by availing themselves of the rights and responsibilities of citizenship."[90] The issues were thus fully and fairly presented, and the competing claims could hardly be more dramatically opposed—sovereign power versus rights to family unity; the individuals' alleged responsibility for their "bad choices versus a claim of right to proportionality."

The IACHR ruled strongly in favor of the petitioners and against the U.S. government. It recognized that under international law, states have the right to control the entry, residence, and expulsion of noncitizens.[91] Further, under certain circumstances, individual rights may be limited in the interest of "the security of all, and by the just demands of the general welfare and the advancement of democracy."[92] However, in exercising the right to expel such "aliens," states *must respect certain protections which "enshrine fundamental values of democratic societies*."[93] Immigration policy must imbue "an individual decision with the guarantees of due process; it must respect the right to life, physical and mental integrity, family, and the right of children to obtain special means of protection."[94]

The most basic difference of approach between the IACHR and the U.S. government comes down to whether the power of the state can be seen as absolute in certain realms. No proposition could be more fundamentally contradicted by the very idea of international human rights law. As the IACHR put it, "neither the scope of action of the State nor the rights of a non-citizen are absolute." Instead, "there must be a balancing test, which weighs a State's legitimate interest to protect and promote the general welfare against a non-citizen resident's fundamental rights such as to family life."[95]

The IACHR noted some of the elements considered by the European Court and the U.N. Human Rights Committee in balancing a deportee's rights to remain against a state's interest to protect its citizenry and other individuals under its jurisdiction. Those have included the age at which the noncitizen immigrated; the noncitizen's length of residence; the noncitizen's family ties; the extent of hardship the noncitizen's deportation poses for the family; the extent of the noncitizen's links to the country of origin; the noncitizen's ability to speak the principal language(s) of the country of origin; the nature and severity of the noncitizen's criminal offense(s); the noncitizen's age at the time the criminal offense(s) was/were committed; the time span of the noncitizen's criminal activity; evidence of the noncitizen's rehabilitation from criminal activity; and the noncitizen's efforts to gain citizenship in the host state.[96]

In particular, the IACHR emphasized that that "the best interest of a minor child must be taken into consideration in a parent's removal proceeding."[97] The IACHR asserted that the absence of any procedural opportunity for the best interests of the child to be considered in proceedings involving the removal of a parent or parents "raises serious concern."[98] In light of these conclusions, the IACHR, though it lacked the power to order the U.S. government to do anything, recommended that the United States:

1. Permit Wayne Smith and Hugo Armendariz to return to the United States at the expense of the State;
2. Reopen both men's immigration proceedings and permit them to present their humanitarian defenses to removal from the United States;
3. Allow a competent, independent immigration judge to apply a balancing test that duly considers their humanitarian defenses and can provide meaningful relief; and, most strikingly

4. Implement laws to ensure that noncitizen residents' right to family life are duly protected and given due process on a case-by-case basis in U.S. immigration removal proceedings.

Unfortunately, as one would have predicted, these recommendations have been almost completely ignored by the U.S. government.[99] And yet, as we have seen in other contexts, human rights norms may well influence U.S. judges, even though they are not seen as binding precedent. In *Roper v. Simmons*, for example, the Supreme Court invalidated the juvenile death penalty under the Eighth and Fourteenth Amendments to the Constitution.[100] The Court evaluated "evolving standards of decency" to determine whether a punishment is so disproportionate that it is cruel and unusual and cited, among other sources, human rights law "as evidence of an international consensus prohibiting the juvenile death penalty."[101] Though international consensus did not control the outcome, it provided "respected and significant confirmation for our own conclusions."[102] Earlier, in *Lawrence v. Texas*, Justice Kennedy had cited decisions by the European Court of Human Rights to support the conclusion that liberty protects the "right of homosexual adults to engage in intimate, consensual conduct." He further noted that this right to engage in intimate, consensual conduct has been accepted as an integral part of human freedom in many other countries."[103] Thus, although the idea of "plenary power" remains powerful and most U.S. courts are still reluctant to engage these sorts of arguments on the merits,[104] the international model may well yet influence U.S. deportation law, perhaps as a positive part of the aftermath of our system's recent harshness and rigidity.[105]

Conclusion: Taking Deportation Human Rights and the Rule of Law Seriously

The last major bipartisan study of the U.S. immigration and deportation systems was undertaken by the U.S. Commission on Immigration Reform, which was chaired by the late Barbara Jordan, who died before the report was issued in September 1997. The Commissioners and staff dedicated the report to Ms. Jordan, and, on its first page, they printed the quotation from her with which this chapter began: *"We are a nation of immigrants, dedicated to the rule of law."*[106] This book has examined how deportation has actually functioned in recent years, a study which compels one to ask hard questions about the nature of the rule of law to which we have supposedly been dedicated. These questions are especially hard for those banished to the new American diaspora and for their families.

One might avoid much of the complexity of the problems caused by deportation by adopting one of two strong positions. For those who support open borders, most, if not all, of the deportation dilemma vanishes.[107] Jacqueline Stevens, for example, creatively suggests that we transcend the Weberian understanding of the state as an institution that has a monopoly of the legitimate use of violence and question the rules that hold the state together as a membership organization. Such a focus, she posits, would allow us to imagine the cessation of war and "a truly global politics" that would facilitate "the creative recreation of the planet and its inhabitants (regardless of where or to whom they were born).[108] This alternative vision of a world of "states without nations" marks a particular path by which *all* birthright is eliminated.[109] This, however, is not a position advocated by many scholars, let alone politicians, though its aspirations are surely compelling. Even Joseph Carens, who has long been the most well-known scholarly proponent of open borders, accepts some departures from a pure open borders policy.[110]

There is much to be said for the essentials of the open borders position, whether qualified or not. It seeks to redress the relationship between the accident of place of birth and powerful discrepancies among individuals' life chances. It recognizes and seeks to alleviate historical injustices instantiated by borders, and it responds forcefully to the fact that capital moves freely across borders while labor movement and union organizing are largely constrained by national boundaries. Much of the open borders logic is consonant with the basic principles of justice in Rawlsian liberalism. Those in the "original position" postulated by Rawls would not know their place of birth or whether they were members of one particular society or another.[111] Thus, they would be unlikely to approve of the most hardened versions of borders and, perhaps, would disapprove of them entirely. The "open borders" argument might see such freedom of movement as a Rawlsian "basic liberty" and as a mechanism to ensure the principle of "fair equal opportunity." Open borders might also be required by the "difference principle" (requiring that basic goods (other than liberties) may be distributed unequally only if those who are worst off under this arrangement are nevertheless better off than they would be under any feasible alternative).[112]

Those who see a moral duty to aid persons born into poor states also clearly see the strong attractions of the open borders position. Various religious perspectives thus support a "humanistic discourse that facilitates understanding immigrants as human beings on a physical as well as a spiritual journey."[113]

Conversely, for those who fear that "our society is being overwhelmed" by illegal border crossers and their "anchor babies" or "savaged" by "criminal terrorist aliens," the problem of reconciling deportation with the rule of law is also not especially complex. Many would likely be content with a regime for deportees something like that described by Giorgio Agamben as *homo sacer*, a human being who is consigned to "zones of exemption" from law.[114] The basic answer given to rights claims by such people is simple: "the family of nations . . . keeps the law within itself. That is, the remit of the law, of justice, ends at the borders of the nation-state."[115]

For others of a more reasonable cast, the border and alienage and citizenship statuses—though perhaps not absolute lines—still serve as indispensable bulwarks against a range of threats beyond the control of a single nation-state. Some argue as well that the establishment, preservation, and development of national culture are legitimate goals that require borders, border controls, and membership categories. Deportation may thus be justified as a necessary element of such controls: harsh perhaps, but necessary.

For those of us who believe *both* in the aspirations of liberal constitutionalism and in the more particular ideals of a "nation of immigrants," deportation compels hard thinking about the relationship between power and rights.[116] Even if we accept that "laws designating the criteria for membership in a political community and the key prerogatives that constitute membership—are among the most fundamental of political creations,"[117] we still must ask *how* such laws can legitimately work in space, time, and within our best conceptions of the rule of law. This, after all, is a major part of how such laws "constitute . . . a collective civic identity."[118] Even if one believes that exclusion laws may be justified by the right of communities to self-determination, such rights to exclude and to deport must nevertheless be qualified and constrained. There is surely a compelling obligation to provide aid to others who are in dire need, even if we have no established bonds with them, so long as this can be done without excessive cost to ourselves. And once people are admitted as legal residents or, I would argue, even as participants in the economy, they ought to be entitled to acquire citizenship on reasonable terms.[119]

The legitimate limits of deportation have not been as fully theorized as the problems of borders, citizenship, and castes.[120] My hope is that this book will contribute to this emerging conversation, which, as we have seen, is beginning to gain momentum in various legal arenas. The main question is not only how deep the distinction between members and nonmembers runs (a question of equality and status-rights), but also exactly how it may legitimately be implemented. The answers, of course, can never be absolute.[121]

Deportation law, essentially, is a rickety, swaying bridge between what Mark Tushnet has called those legal rules that "define who is within the polity and who is outside it" and "the heart of liberal constitutionalism," whose concern is the "acceptable distribution of rights, duties, and benefits *within* a liberal polity.[122] Once we reject the indefensible allure of brittle, formalist dichotomies such as "plenary power" or a territorial "on/off" switch for rights, the question of the limits of deportation can be directly and functionally confronted. This obligation is both a normative challenge and a pressing tangible task. This, in short, is what the rule of law must ultimately be about.

What, then, might it mean for the United States to take post-deportation human rights seriously? First, what is clearly needed is a more capacious and generous understanding of the basic idea of the rule of law. This includes recognition of powerful rights to proportionality, anti-arbitrariness, fair process, and protection of family and similar relationships. At the most basic level, there is surely something "deeply wrong in forcing people to leave a place where they have lived for a long time."[123] The task also requires executive policies that take "integrity" seriously along with meaningful judicial review of discretionary decisions. A functionalist approach to questions of finality and territoriality best grapples with the effects of deportation across communities and across borders. It supports a more universal model of membership that is, at least partially, "anchored in transcendent and de-territorialized notions of personal rights."[124] Global migration and the emergent global regime of human rights mean that "the logic of personhood supersedes the logic of national citizenship."[125] There is cause for optimism here, despite the current dismal state of affairs for many deportees. Comprehensive law reform strategies may develop incrementally and through dialogue.[126]

In addition to the obvious gains of justice and fairness, taking post-deportation rights seriously could actually enhance border control. Leaving aside their inaccuracies and collateral effects, *post-entry social control* deportations are, as we have seen, a highly questionable crime control strategy. Absent a comprehensive immigration policy, with workable border controls that respond to the realities of labor migration, *extended border control* deportation has done little to diminish the undocumented population or to dissuade new migrants. The creation of a new, unplanned diaspora population abroad raises serious long-term security concerns in addition to its compelling human rights problems.

In sum, in the aftermath of deportation, we need sustained, serious attention not only to technical legal questions but to the biggest questions as well: should we maintain this system in its current form, or should we fundamentally reform it? The adoption of well-accepted international law models of family unity, proportionality, ameliorative discretion, and judicial review would surely be a good start for reforms. Especially in the cases of long-term legal residents deported due to crimes, we should ponder the ruling by an Australian court in the *Nystrom* case, discussed above. As the federal judges put it:

> [Mr. Nystrom] is only an "alien" by the barest of threads. However, if the decision under challenge here stands he will be deported . . . and permanently banished. . . . That result causes us a . . . sense of disquiet. . . . He has indeed behaved badly, but no worse than many of his age who have also lived as members of the Australian community all their lives but who happen to be citizens. The difference is the barest of technicalities.[127]

Notes

1. Boumediene v. Bush, 553 U.S. 723 (2008).

2. U.S. House of Representatives, Comm. on the Judiciary, Subcomm. on Immigration and Claims (testimony of Barbara Jordan, Chair, U.S. Commission on Immigration Reform, Feb. 24, 1995).

3. Peter Slevin, Deportation of Illegal Immigrants Increases under Obama Administration, WASH. POST, July 26, 2010 (quoting June 30, 2010, memorandum from ICE director John Morton) (emphasis added), available at http://www.washingtonpost.com/wp-dyn/content/article/2010/07/25/AR2010072501790.html?nav=emailpage.

4. See, e.g., Peter J. Spiro, Leave for Appeal: Departure as a Requirement for Review of Deportation Orders, 25 SAN DIEGO L. REV. 281, 282–83 (1988) (noting that in those circuits "where Mendez has not prevailed, an alien with valid grounds for reconsideration may never get his last day in court").

5. GORDON & ROSENFELD, 8 IMMIGRATION LAW AND PROCEDURE § 104.01.

6. 86 F.R.D. 227 (U.S. Court for Berlin 1979); see H. STERN, JUDGMENT IN BERLIN (1984).

7. See DANIEL KANSTROOM, DEPORTATION NATION 165–66 (Harvard University Press 2007).

8. See LILLIAN HOMLEN MOHR, Frances, THAT WOMAN IN FDR'S CABINET 255 (1979) (citing Miss Perkins Tells Committee Bridges Gets No Favoritism, N.Y. TIMES, Feb. 9, 1939).

9. Patrick J. McDonnell, Deportation Shatters Family, L.A. TIMES, Mar. 14, 1998, at B1 (cited in Peter Bibring, Jurisdictional Issues in Post-Removal Habeas Challenges to Orders of Removal, 17 GEO. IMMIGR. L.J. 135 (2002)).

10. See http://www.nytimes.com/2010/06/19/nyregion/19immig.html?src=mv&ref=general.

11. The handling of the case also apparently conflicted with the Obama administration's policy of arresting deportable immigrants only if they have criminal records.

12. This includes union organizing and complaining about employment discrimination or housing conditions.

13. See, e.g., statement of Michael Wishnie in John Christoffersen, Associated Press, Feds Won't Deport Immigrants in Civil Rights Cases, June 22, 2011, available at http://www.foxnews.com/us/2011/06/22/feds-wont-deport-immigrants-in-civil-rights-cases/.

14. Id. Much, it seems, turns on the phrase "non-frivolous."

15. Lou Dobbs Tonight, Aug. 16, 2006, http://transcripts.cnn.com/TRANSCRIPTS/0608/16/ldt.01.html.

16. Id.

17. Daniel Kanstroom, Surrounding the Hole in the Doughnut, 71 TUL. L. REV. 703 (1997).

18. The answers to this dilemma implicate substance as much as process. In many ways, the two categories become inextricably intertwined. The strength of a claim for post-deportation motions turns in large measure on how unjust a deportation would seem without such review.

19. See Daniel Kanstroom, The Better Part of Valor: The REAL ID Act, Discretion, and the "Rule" of Immigration Law, 51 N.Y. L. REV. 161 (Fall 2006).

20. See generally Kanstroom, DEPORTATION NATION, supra note 7, at 231–40.

21. Courts will typically defer to "reasonable" agency interpretations of statutes the meaning of which is not seen as clear. See Chevron, U.S.A., Inc. v. Natural Res. Def. Council, Inc., 467 U.S. 837 (1984) (directing judges to take a two-step approach to review agencies' statutory interpretation. If the intent of Congress is "clear, that is the end of the matter." But if the court decides that Congress has not directly decided the question, then "the question for the court is whether the agency's answer is based on a permissible construction of the statute."). To say the least, this ostensibly clear model has not been consistently applied. See, e.g., INS v. Cardoza-Fonseca, 480 U.S. 421 (1987) (whether the asylum standard was the same as that for withholding of deportation was "a pure question of statutory construction" in which deference to the agency was not required.) See also U.S. v. Mead Corp., 533 U.S. 218 (2001) (administrative implementation of a particular statutory provision qualifies for

deference when it appears that Congress has delegated authority to the agency generally to make rules carrying the force of law, and the agency interpretation claiming deference is promulgated in the exercise of that authority).

22. Yuen Sang Low v. Attorney Gen., 479 F.2d 820, 821 (9th Cir. 1973). See also *INS v. Jong Ha Wang*, in which the issue was the meaning of the term, "extreme hardship," which was, "not self-explanatory, and reasonable men could easily differ as to their construction." The definition was thus committed "in the first instance to the Attorney General and his delegates." Lower courts were instructed not to overturn the agency's interpretation "simply because it may prefer another interpretation of the statute." 450 U.S. 139 (1981); *see also id.* at 144. Cf. *INS v. Phinpathya*, which considered the "continuous presence" requirement for suspension of deportation. Rather than simply deferring to the *interpretive discretion* of the BIA, the Court found that the "plain meaning" of the statute controlled, and the Court simply decided what that meaning was. *Phinpathya*, 464 U.S. 183, 189–96 (1984).

23. Maurice A. Roberts, *The Exercise of Administrative Discretion under the Immigration Laws*, 13 SAN DIEGO L. REV. 144, 146–51 (1975).

24. Kenneth C. Davis, 2 (8.10) ADMINISTRATIVE LAW TREATISE, at 200 (2d ed. 1979).

25. Achacoso-Sanchez v. INS, 779 F.2d 1260, 1265 (7th Cir. 1985) (Easterbrook, J.).

26. One of the lesser-discussed aspects of the DOJ complaint against Arizona's S.B. 1070 was its strong reaffirmation of the significance of federal prosecutorial discretion. The problem, according to DOJ, is that the state law mandates criminal penalties for what is effectively unlawful presence, "even in circumstances where the federal government has decided not to impose such penalties because of federal enforcement priorities or humanitarian, foreign policy, or other federal interests." As stated in the complaint: "Whereas Arizona police (like federal officers and police in other states) formerly had the discretion to decide whether to verify immigration status during the course of a lawful stop, the combination of the verification requirement and the threat of private lawsuits now removes such discretion and mandates verification. This provision also mandates the enforcement of the remaining provisions of S.B. 1070." Complaint ¶ 41, United States v. Arizona, Case No. 10-16645 (D. Ariz. filed July 6, 2010), *available at* www.justice.gov/opa/documents/az-complaint. pdf. This, said DOJ will "necessarily result in countless inspections and detentions of individuals who are lawfully present in the United States [including] citizens." *Id.* ¶¶ 42, 43. This is a quite remarkable statement. It indicates a sophisticated awareness by federal authorities of the dangers of excessively rigid and fast-track enforcement that we have discussed in great detail previously. But it is a politically tricky line to walk, and the Obama administration has faced considerable criticism for its approach. Indeed, in a remarkable resolution of no-confidence, the union that represents ICE agents has repeatedly and publicly challenged John Morton, the head of ICE, by asserting that ICE has "abandoned the agency's core mission of enforcing U.S. immigration laws and providing for public safety," instead directing its attention "to campaigning for programs and policies related to amnesty and the creation of a special detention system for foreign nationals that exceeds the care and services provided to most U.S. citizens similarly incarcerated." Jerry Seper, *Agents' Union Disavows Leaders of ICE*, WASH. TIMES, Aug. 9, 2010, *available at* http://www.washingtontimes.com/news/2010/aug/9/agents-union-disavows-leaders-of-ice/?page=1. Morton has responded vigorously, but with interesting nuance that highlights the Obama administration's use of enforcement discretion. "No Administration in the history of this country," he said, has removed more people. What is different, however, "is a sense of priorities." *See* "*Head of ICE Responds to No Confidence Vote*," uploaded to YouTube Aug. 8, 2010, http://www.youtube.com/watch?v=IiXQK3m0ESg.

27. *See* JACK GOLDSMITH, THE TERROR PRESIDENCY 119–20 (2007) ("The administration chose to push its legal discretion to its limit, and rejected any binding legal constraints on detainee treatment under the laws of war.").

28. Carlson v. Landon, 342 U.S. 524, 562 (1951) (Frankfurter, J., dissenting) (quoting Mark De Wolfe Howe, THE NATION, Jan. 12, 1952, at 30). *See generally* Kanstroom, *The Better Part of Valor, supra* note 19.

29. INS v. St. Cyr, 533 U.S. 289, 307 (2001); Accardi v. Shaughnessy, 347 U.S. 260, 267–68 (1954).

30. *Id.*

31. The Board's own regulations generally require the BIA and immigration judges to exercise "independent judgment and discretion," subject to the orders of the attorney general. *See* 8 C.F.R. 1003.1(d)(2) and 10(b).

32. Aguilar v. ICE, Oral Arguments, Audio recording, Oral Argument Before the First Circuit (Aug. 1, 2007) 21:05–23:00 (transcript reprinted in Gregoire Sauter, Case Study: *Aguilar v. ICE Litigating Workplace Immigration Raids in the Twenty-First Century*, 40(7) BENDER'S IMMIGR. BULL. 9, (Apr. 1, 2009).

33. Robert Cover, *Violence and the Word*, 95 YALE L.J. 1601, 1621 (1986).

34. *See* SEYLA BENHABIB, THE RIGHTS OF OTHERS 2 (2004).

35. *Id.* at 4.

36. *See generally* Kanstroom, *Post Deportation Human Rights Law: Aspiration, Oxymoron or Necessity?* 3 STANFORD J. C.R. & C.L. 195 (Spring 2007). *See also* G.A. Res. 40/144, U.N. Doc. A/RES/40/144 (Dec. 13, 1985) ("An alien lawfully in the territory of a State may be expelled therefrom only in pursuance of a decision reached in accordance with law and shall, except where compelling reasons of national security otherwise require, be allowed to submit the reasons why he or she should not be expelled and to have the case reviewed by, and be represented for the purpose before, the competent authority or a person or persons specially designated by the competent authority. Individual or collective expulsion of such aliens on grounds of race, colour, religion, culture, descent or national or ethnic origin is prohibited.").

37. *See* Beth Lyon, *The Unsigned United Nations Migrant Worker Rights Convention: An Overlooked Opportunity To Change The "Brown Collar" Migration Paradigm* 42 N.Y.U. J. INT'L L. & POL'Y 389 (2010); Beth Lyon, *Colloquium: The Inter-American Court Of Human Rights Defines Unauthorized Migrant Workers' Rights For The Hemisphere: A Comment On Advisory Opinion 18*, 28 N.Y.U. REV. L. & SOC. CHANGE 547 (2004). When such norms are violated, the State may well be obligated to provide a remedy. *See* Sonja Starr & Lea Brilmayer, *Family Separation as a Violation of International Law*, 21 BERKELEY J. INT'L L. 213, 242, 278 (2003). To be sure, noncitizens have powerful rights claims against being deported to countries where they may face persecution and torture, and many of these norms have been incorporated into U.S. law. But even the most compelling asylum claims are frequently denied if the noncitizen has even a minor criminal record. *See* 8 U.S.C. § 1158(b)(2)(A)(3) and § 1158(b)(2)(B)(i) (2000); *see also* 8 U.S.C. § 1231(b)(3)(B) (2000) (barring withholding of removal).

38. *See generally* Sonja Starr & Lea Brilmayer, *supra* note 37 (noting the inconsistency of international law regarding protection of family unity but identifying a "patchwork of treaty provisions and the glimmerings of a developing customary norm against the involuntary separation of families"). *See also* Juridical Condition and Rights of the Undocumented Migrants, Advisory Opinion OC-18, Inter-Am. Ct. H.R. (Ser. A) No. 18 (Sept. 17, 2003).

39. Universal Declaration of Human Rights, Article 16, G.A. Res. 217A, at 71, U.N. GAOR, 3d Sess., 1st. plen. mtg., U.N. Doc A/810 (Dec. 12, 1948). *See also* International Covenant on Civil and Political Rights, G.A. Res. 2200A (XXI), art. 23(1), at 52, U.N. Doc. A/6316 (Mar. 23, 1976); Organization of American States, American Convention on Human Rights, art. 17(1), Nov. 22, 1969, O.A.S.T.S No. 36, 1144 U.N.T.S. 123.

40. *See* Human Rights Comm., *Protection of the Family, the Right to Marriage and Equality of the Spouses*, General Comment, U.N. Doc. CCPR/C/21/Rev. 1/Add.2 (Sept. 19, 1990). UDHR Article 12 also states: "No one shall be subjected to arbitrary interference with his privacy, family, home. . . . Everyone has the right to the protection of the law against such interference."

41. International Covenant on Civil and Political Rights, *supra* note 39. *See also* Organization of American States, American Convention on Human Rights, art. 11, Nov. 22, 1969, 1144 U.N.T.S. 123; Convention on the Rights of the Child, G.A. Res. 44/25, art. 16, Annex, U.N. Doc. A/44/49/Annex (1989); Article 10 of the Organization of African Unity, African Charter on the Rights and Welfare of the Child, art. 10, Nov. 29, 1999, O.A.U. Doc. CAB/LEG/24.9/49; Organization of African Unity, African (Banjul) Charter on Human and Peoples' Rights, June 27, 1981, OAU Doc. CAB/LEG/67/3 rev. 5, 21 I.L.M. 58.

The African Commission on Human and Peoples' Rights has held that family separation under certain circumstances may constitute inhuman and degrading treatment. *See* Modise v. Botswana, Afr. Comm'n Human & Peoples' Rights, Comm. No. 97/93 (2000).

42. The African Commission on Human and Peoples' Rights has indicated that it: "[D]oes not wish to call into question nor is it calling into question the right of any State to take legal action against illegal immigrants and deport them to their countries of origin, if the competent courts so decide. It is however of the view that it is unacceptable to deport individuals without giving them the possibility to plead their case before the competent national courts as this is contrary to the spirit and letter of the Charter [the African Charter of Human and Peoples' Rights] and international law." Union Inter Africaine des Droits de l'Homme, Federation Internationale des Ligues des Droits de l'Homme and Others v. Angola, African Comm'n Human & Peoples' Rights, Comm. No. 159/96, ¶ 20 (Nov. 11, 1997).

43. General Comment 16, U.N. Human Rights Committee, U.N. Doc. HRI/GEN/1/Rev.1 (1994) (emphasis added). Obviously, a concept such as reasonableness requires careful consideration of the facts of each case as well as judicial review.

44. Although the United States is not a party to this Convention, some of its protections may be binding as customary international law.

45. *See generally* Philip Alston, *The Best Interests Principle: Towards a Reconciliation of Culture and Human Rights*, 8 INT'L J. L. & FAM. 1, 4 (1994); Hendriks v. Netherlands, App. No. 8427/78, 5 Eur. Comm'n H.R. Dec. & Rep. (1982).

46. Convention on the Rights of the Child (CRC), Preamble.

47. CRC art. 7(1) & art. 8(1).

48. CRC art. 9(1). Examples of such a proper determination include cases involving abuse or neglect of the child by the parents, or where the parents are living separately and a decision must be made as to the child's place of residence.

49. Convention on the Rights of the Child, G.A. Res. 44/25, Annex, art. 9, ¶ 4, U.N. Doc. A/44/49 (1989). Further, states must allow sufficient freedom of movement to enable the families to see one another regularly *Id.* at art. 10, ¶ 2. They also must act in a "positive, humane, and expeditious manner" upon applications by children or parents "to enter or leave a State Party for the purpose of family reunification." *Id.* art. 10, ¶ 1. Article 10 does not explicitly require states to permit entry for the purpose of family reunification, however. Article 10(2) grants children whose parents reside in different countries the right of "personal relations and direct contacts with both parents." States Parties must also "respect the right of the child and his or her parents to leave any country, including their own, and to enter their own country."

50. *See* Aumeeruddy-Cziffra v. Mauritius, Communication No. R.9/35, U.N. Human Rights Comm., U.N. Doc. No. A/36/40 at 134 (1981).

51. *See* ICCPR 12(4) ("[n]o one shall be arbitrarily deprived of the right to enter *his own country.*"). The International Law Commission has noted that, "the principle of non-expulsion of nationals" is a general principle that is "widely recognized as applicable to the expulsion of aliens." Maurice Kamto, Int'l Law Comm'n, *Third Report on the Expulsion of Aliens*, [11], UN Doc A/CN.4/581 (2007).

52. Nystrom v. Australia, UN Doc CCPR/C/102/D/1557/2007 (August 18, 2011). Mr. Nystrom, who had a very substantial criminal record, had lived all his life in Australia with his mother and sister. Apparently, he thought he was an Australian citizen. He had no close ties to Sweden, his country of birth; he did not speak Swedish, and he had no direct contact with his family there. *See* Jason Pobjoy, Human Rights Law Centre, *There's No Place Like Home: The Case of Mr. Nystrom* (2011), *available at* http://www.hrlc.org.au/court-tribunal/un-human-rights-committee/nystrom-v-australia-un-doc-ccprc102d15572007-18-august-2011/.

53. *See, e.g.,* HURST HANNUM, THE RIGHT TO LEAVE AND RETURN IN INTERNATIONAL LAW AND PRACTICE 58–59 (1987) (arguing that the proper interpretation of this phrase "includes nationals, citizens and permanent residents" and is "most consistent with the ordinary meaning of the words in the text, and with at least portions of the *travaux preparatoires*"); *see also* MANFRED NOWAK, UN COVENANT ON CIVIL AND POLITICAL RIGHTS: CCPR COMMENTARY 287 (2nd ed. 2005).

54. *See generally* Michelle Foster, *An "Alien" By The Barest Of Threads—The Legality of the Deportation of Long-Term Residents from Australia*, 33 MELBOURNE U. L. REV. 483, 520 (2009).

55. Moustaquim v. Belgium, App. No. 12313/86, 13 Eur. H.R. Rep. 802, 813–815 (1991), par. 43.

56. "There shall be no interference by a public authority with the exercise of this right except such as is in accordance with the law and is necessary in a democratic society in the interests of national security, public safety or the economic well-being of the country, for the prevention of disorder or crime, for the protection of health or morals, or for the protection of the rights and freedoms of others." European Convention for the Protection of Human Rights and Fundamental Freedoms, Nov. 4, 1950, 213 U.N.T.S. 222.

57. *See* Clare Ovey, *The Margin of Appreciation and Article 8 of the Convention* 19 HUM. RTS. L.J. 10–12 (1998). As the ECtHR has stated: "Article 8 cannot be considered to impose on a State a general obligation to respect the choice by married couples of the country of their matrimonial residence and to authorise family reunion in its territory." ECtHR, judgment of Feb. 19, 1996, No 23218/94, Gül v. Switzerland, para. 38.

58. *Moustaquim, supra* note 55 at ¶ 43; see also *Dalia v. France*, 1998–I Eur. Ct. H.R. 52–53. In fact, five European countries (Austria, Belgium, Hungary, Portugal, and Sweden) prohibit the deportation of noncitizens who arrived during childhood, even if they are later convicted of crimes. *See* Uner v Netherlands, 45 EHRR 421, 429. (2007) (describing these laws).

59. ECtHR, judgment of Dec. 21, 2001, No 31465/96, Sen v. the Netherlands; *see also* ECtHR, judgment of May 28, 1985, No 9214/80, 9473/81 & 9474/81, Abdulaziz v. United Kingdom, paras. 85–86. Such family rights have sometimes been construed rather broadly in this system. Article 8 may even relate to "ties between near relatives, for instance those between grandparents and grandchildren, since such relatives may play a considerable part in family life." ECtHR, judgment of June 13, 1979, No 6833/74, Marckx v. Belgium, para. 45. This view of family life was applied to the deportation of a deaf/mute adult in ECtHR, judgment of July 13, 1995, No 19465/92, Nasri v. France, para. 34. Cf. ECtHR, decision of July 3, 2001, No 47390/99, Javeed v. the Netherlands (declining to apply it to an aunt who had looked after her nieces and nephews before their full age where the court found no "further elements of dependency involving more than the normal emotional ties.").

60. *See* Daniel Kanstroom, *Deportation, Social Control, and Punishment: Some Thoughts About Why Hard Laws Make Bad Cases*, 113 HARV. L. REV. 1890 (2000); *see also* Lockyer v. Andrade, 538 U.S. 63, 72 (2003) ("grossly disproportionate criminal sentences violate the Eighth Amendment").

61. *See* State Farm Mut. Auto. Ins. Co. v. Campbell, 538 U.S. 408 (2003); Hudson v. United States, 522 U.S. 93 (1997); BMW v. Gore, 517 U.S. 559 (1996); United States v. Ursery, 518 U.S. 267 (1996); Dep't of Revenue v. Kurth Ranch, 511 U.S. 767 (1994); Austin v. United States, 509 U.S. 602 (1993).

62. Daniel Thym, *Respect for Private and Family Life Under Article 8 ECHR in Immigration Cases: A Human Right to Regularize Illegal Stay?*, 57 INT'L & COMP. L.Q. 8.

63. *Id.* at 87, 96 (2008) (explaining court's balancing of family unity and public order).

64. In Europe, of course, a "foreigner" may have been born in the host country. In such cases, or where the "foreigner" had moved there in early childhood, the court will only consider the three first criteria, resulting in still greater protection for the person facing expulsion. *Id.* (citing ECtHR, judgment of Aug. 2, 2001, No 54273/00, Boultif v. Switzerland, para. 48. ECtHR, judgment of Oct. 18, 2006 (GC), No 46410/99, Üner v. the Netherlands, para. 57–58; ECtHR, judgment of July 10, 2003, No 53441/99, Benhebba v. France, para. 33).

65. *See, e.g.*, Stewart v. Canada, Communication No. 538/1993, U.N. Human Rights Committee, U.N. Doc. No. CCPR/C/58/D/538/1993 (1996) (affirming the deportation of a person convicted of various offenses, most petty, despite separation from his entire family).

66. The criteria are derived from ECtHR, judgment of Aug. 2, 2001, No 54273/00, Boultif v. Switzerland, para. 48.

67. Such balancing also takes place in the European system pursuant to Article 3 of the European Convention, which may preclude Member States from deporting a person who could be exposed to torture or inhuman treatment in the receiving country. *See, e.g.*, Bensaid

v. United Kingdom, 33 Eur. Ct. H.R. 205, 217–18 (2001) (considering applicant's schizophrenia, but finding that the risk that his condition would deteriorate if he was deported to Algeria was speculative); D. v. United Kingdom, 24 Eur. Ct. H.R. 423, 447–48 (1997) (finding that it would violate Article 3 to deport applicant with AIDS to St. Kitts). *See generally* Ann Sherlock, *Deportation of Aliens and Article 8 ECHR*, 23 Eur. L. Rev. 62 (1998).

68. *Id.* See also ECtHR, judgment of Jan. 31, 2006, No 50435/99, Rodrigues Da Silva & Hoogkamer v. the Netherlands (separation of mother and child would infringe the obligations of the Netherlands under Article 8); ECtHR, judgment of Oct. 9, 2003 (GC), No 48321/99, Slivenko v. Latvia (the family had developed "uninterruptedly since birth, the network of personal, social and economic relations that make up the private life of every human being." In these circumstances, "the applicants' removal from Latvia constituted an interference with their 'private life' and their 'home' within the meaning of Article 8 § 1 of the Convention."). The court places the burden of establishing that the family could relocate on the expelling authorities before assessing the proportionality of the interference. *See* Mehemi v. France, App. No. 25017/94, 30 Eur. H.R. Rep. 739, 750–51, 753 (1997); Beldjoudi v. France, App. No. 12083/86, 14 Eur. H.R. Rep. 801, 830–31, 833–34 (1992); Moustaquim v. Belgium, App. No. 12313/86, 13 Eur. H.R. Rep. 802, 813–15 (1991); Nicola Rogers, *Immigration and the European Convention on Human Rights: Are New Principles Emerging?*, 2003 Eur. Hum. Rts. L. Rev. 1, 53–64 (2003).

69. The European Court of Justice (officially the Court of Justice), is the highest court in the European Union in matters of European Union law. As a part of the Court of Justice of the European Union institution, it is tasked with interpreting EU law and ensuring its equal application across all EU member states.

70. Gerardo Ruiz Zambrano v. Office national de l'emploi (ONEm), Case C-34/09, ECJ (2010).

71. Elspeth Guild, *The Court of Justice of the European Union and Citizens of the Union: A Revolution Underway? The Zambrano judgment March 8, 2011*, *available at* cmr.jur.ru.nl/cmr/docs/Zambrano.pdf.

72. The court concluded that Article 20 of the TFEU precludes a member state from refusing a third-country national upon whom his minor children, who are European Union citizens, are dependent, a right of residence in the member state of residence and nationality of those children, and from refusing to grant a work permit to that third-country national, in so far as such decisions deprive those children of the genuine enjoyment of the substance of the rights attaching to the status of European Union citizens.

73. He was denied because he did not comply with Belgian residence requirements and was not entitled to work there.

74. The Brussels Employment Tribunal, to which the application was brought, asked the European Court of Justice whether he could rely on European Union law, even though in this case the children were not exercising their right of free movement within the EU. The court ruled that while a member state has sole jurisdiction to lay down the conditions for the acquisition of citizenship, it was undisputed that the children were of Belgian nationality. They therefore enjoyed the status of citizens of the European Union.

75. On the other hand, it is important to note that the basis for the Court's decision was the fact that the children had, in fact, obtained citizenship in Belgium due to their birth there. An example of how this background legal regime may change is seen in Ireland. Prior to the 2005 Citizenship Referendum, any person born on the island of Ireland was entitled to Irish citizenship. Since the referendum, where a child is born in Ireland to nonnational parents, one of those parents must have been lawfully resident in Ireland for three out of the previous four years, other than as an asylum seeker or a student, in order for the child to acquire Irish citizenship. *See* Statement by Minister for Justice, Equality and Defence, Mr. Alan Shatter, TD, on the implications of the recent ruling of the Court of Justice of the European Union in the case of Ruiz Zambrano, *available at* http://www.justice.ie/en/JELR/Pages/PR11000019.

76. *See, e.g.*, Beharry v. Reno, 183 F. Supp. 2d 584, 604 (E.D.N.Y. 2002) (customary international law requires that, under 8 U.S.C. § 1182(h), the Attorney General grant a "compassionate

hearing" prior to deporting certain lawful permanent residents who have resided in the United States for more than seven years, who have been convicted of a crime that was categorized as an aggravated felony only after its commission, and whose families would suffer "extreme hardship" if the deportation were carried out), *rev'd for failure to exhaust administrative alternatives sub nom.* Beharry v. Ashcroft, 329 F.3d 51 (2d Cir. 2003); Beharry v. Ashcroft, 329 F.3d 51 (2d Cir. 2003), *criticized by* Guaylupo-Moya v. Gonzales, 423 F.3d 121, 124–25 (2d Cir. 2005) ("we now find that the *Beharry* decision, while commendable for its efforts and concern for human interests, cannot support the remedy it attempted to provide. In its most doctrinally sound form, *Beharry* urges that where a statute is ambiguous, we should construe the statute to conform to the principles of international law. Congress, however, plainly provided that IIRIRA's restriction on 212(h) relief and expanded definition of an aggravated felony should apply retroactively. Because Congress's intent is clear, it displaces any inconsistent norms of customary international law or prior treaty obligations.").

77. IACHR, Report No. 81/10 CASE 12.562; Smith, Armendariz, et al. v. United States (July 12, 2010).

78. Apparently, he also has two older daughters from a prior relationship who live in the United States. *See id.* (citing petitioners' submission dated Dec. 7, 2006, page 24).

79. *See* American Declaration on the Rights and Duties of Man ("American Declaration") Articles I (right to life, liberty and personal security), V (right to private and family life), VI (right to family), VII (right to protection for mothers and children), IX (right to inviolability of the home), XVIII (right to fair trial), and XXVI (right to due process of law).

80. American Declaration Articles V, VI, VII, XVIII, and XXVI.

81. *See* IACHR, Report on the Situation of Human Rights of Asylum Seekers within the Canadian Refugee Determination System [hereinafter "Canada Report"], *available at* http://www1.umn.edu/humanrts/iachr/country-reports/canada2000.html.

82. IACHR, Canada Report, *id.*; *see also* Eur. Ct. H.R., Berrehab v. Netherlands, Judgment of June 21, 1988, No. 10730/84, para. 23; Eur. Ct. H.R., Moustaquim v. Belgium, Judgment of Feb. 19, 1991, No. 12313/86; Eur. Ct. H.R., Beldjoudi v. France, Judgment of Mar. 26, 1992, No. 12083/86; Eur. Ct. H.R. Nasri v. France, Judgment of July 13, 1995, No. 19465/92; Eur. Ct. H.R., Boughanemi v. France, Judgment of Apr. 24, 1996, No. 22070/93, Rep. 1996–II, fasc. 8, para. 32; Eur. Ct. H.R., C. v. Belgium, June 24, 1996, No. 35/1995/541/627; Eur. Ct. H.R., Bouchelkia v. France, Judgment of Jan. 1, 1997, No. 230078/93, Rep. 1997–I, fasc. 28; Eur. Ct. H.R., Boudjaidi v. France, Judgment of Sept. 26, 1997, 123/1996/742/941, Rep. 1997–VI, fasc. 51; Eur. Ct. H.R., Boujlifa v. France, Judgment of Oct. 21, 1997, 122/1996/741/940, Rep. 1997–VI, fasc. 54; Mehemi v. France (No. 2), Judgment of Apr. 10, 2003, No. 53470/99 (sect. 3) (bil.), ECHR 2003–IV; U.N. C.C.P.R. Human Rights Committee, Stewart v. Canada, Judgment of Dec. 1996, No. 538/1993, para. 12.10; U.N.C.C.P.R. Human Rights Committee, Winata and Li v. Australia, Aug. 16, 2001, No. 930/2000.

83. *See* Berrehab v. Netherlands, Judgment of June 21, 1988, No. 10730/84, para. 29.

84. *See Beldjoudi, Berrehab, supra* note 82 and *Moustaquim, supra* note 68.

85. *See Beldjoudi, Berrehab, Mehemi, Boughanemi, Boujlifa, supra* note 82.

86. IACHR Report, Smith, Armendariz, et al. v. United States, *supra* note 77 (citing *Moustaquim, Bouchelkia,* and *Nasri*).

87. They cited the fact that the U.N. Human Rights Committee has long employed a similar balancing test that considers whether "due consideration was given in the deportation proceedings to the deportee's family connections." Petitioners' submission dated Dec. 7, 2006, at 49–50 (citing U.N.C.C.P.R). The Human Rights Committee has held that a State must provide "ample opportunity [for the petitioner] to present evidence of his family connections." Human Rights Committee, Stewart v. Canada, Judgment of Dec. 1996, No. 538/1993, para. 12.10.

88. *See* State's response dated Aug. 28, 2008, at 5 (citing Convention on the Status of Aliens ("Havana Convention"), art. 1, 6, adopted Feb. 20, 1928, 132 L.N.T.S. 301, T.S. 815, 46 Stat. 2753), 2 Bevans, 4 Malloy 4722 ("for reasons of public order or safety, states may expel foreigners domiciled, resident, or merely in transit through their territory.").

89. Further, it argued that the rights to family and private life under the American Declaration are inherently limited by the legitimate exercise of state authority, whereas under Article 8 of the European Convention, these individual rights must be given full effect unless the state can prove that it has acted within one of the enumerated exceptions. It also argued that even though Article 8 of the European Convention creates more restrictions on state action to remove criminal noncitizens, there are a number of analogous European Court precedents that demonstrate that it is permissible for a State to deport criminal noncitizens with family ties in the deporting country. *See* State's response dated Aug. 28, 2008, at 16 (citing Bouchelkia v. France, Judgment of Jan. 1, 1997, No. 230078/93, Rep. 1997–I, fasc. 28; Eur. Ct. H.R., Boudjaidi v. France, Judgment of Sept. 26, 1997, 123/1996/742/941, Rep. 1997–VI, fasc. 51).

90. State's response dated Aug. 28, 2008, at 19 (citing U.N. C.C.P.R. Human Rights Committee, Stewart v. Canada, Judgment of Dec. 1996, No. 538/1993, para. 12.8) ("Countries like Canada, which enable immigrants to become nationals after a reasonable period of residence, have a right to expect such immigrants will in due course acquire all the rights and assume all the obligations that nationality entails. Individuals who do not take advantage of this opportunity and thus escape the obligations nationality imposes can be deemed to have opted to remain aliens in Canada. They have every right to do so, but must also bear the consequences.").

91. *See* IACHR, Canada Report, *supra* note 81; Inter-Am. Ct. H.R., Juridical Condition and Rights of the Undocumented Migrants, Advisory Opinion OC-18/03, para. 119 (Sept. 17, 2003).

92. American Declaration on the Rights and Duties of Man, art. XXVIII (1948).

93. Case of Andrea Mortlock, Report No. 63/08 (admissibility and merits report), Case No. 12.534, para. 78, July 25, 2008 (United States) (emphasis added).

94. *Id.* (citing IACHR, Canada Report, *supra* note 81).

95. As the Commission had previously stated: "[W]here decision-making involves the potential separation of a family, the resulting interference with family life may only be justified where necessary to meet a pressing need to protect public order, and where the means are proportional to that end.... [T]his balancing must be made on a case by case basis, and ... the reasons justifying interference with family life must be very serious indeed." IACHR, Canada Report, *supra* note 81 at para. 166.

96. *See generally* Eur. Ct. H.R., Berrehab v. Netherlands, Judgment of June 21, 1988, No. 10730/84, para. 23; Eur. Ct. H.R., Moustaquim v. Belgium, Judgment of Feb. 19, 1991, No. 12313/86; Eur. Ct. H.R., Beldjoudi v. France, Judgment of Mar. 26, 1992, No. 12083/86; Eur. Ct. H.R. Nasri v. France, Judgment of July 13, 1995, No. 19465/92; Eur. Ct. H.R., Boughanemi v. France, Judgment of Apr. 24, 1996, No. 22070/93, Rep. 1996–II, fasc. 8, para. 32; Eur. Ct. H.R. C. v. Belgium, June 24, 1996, No. 35/1995/541/627; Eur. Ct. H.R., Bouchelkia v. France, Judgment of Jan. 1, 1997, No. 230078/93, Rep. 1997–I, fasc. 28; Eur. Ct. H.R., Boudjaidii v. France, Judgment of Sept. 26, 1997, Rep. 1997–VI, fasc. 51; Eur. Ct. H.R., Boujlifa v. France, Judgment of Oct. 21, 1997, 122/1996/741/940, Rep. 1997–VI, fasc. 54; Mehemi v. France (no. 2), Judgment of Apr. 10, 2003, No. 53470/99 (sect. 3) (bil.), ECHR 2003–IV; U.N. C.C.P.R. Human Rights Committee, Stewart v. Canada, Judgment of Dec. 1996, No. 538/1993, para. 12.10; U.N.C.C.P.R. Human Rights Committee, Winata v. Australia, Aug. 16, 2001, No. 930/2000.

97. Article VII of the American Declaration states that "all children have the right to special protection, care and aid." As a component of this special protection afforded children, in the context of legal proceedings that may impact a child's right to family life, "special protection" requires that the proceedings duly consider the best interests of the child. Inter-Am. Ct. H.R., Juridical Condition and Human Rights of the Child, Advisory Opinion OC-17/02, Series A No. 17, paras. 62–77, 92–103 (Aug. 28, 2002).

98. IACHR Report, Smith, Armendariz, et al. v. U.S. *supra* note 77 at para. 56–57. The European Court has repeatedly held that the "best interest and well-being of the children" of a noncitizen must be taken into consideration in a removal proceeding. *See, e.g.,* Eur. Ct. H.R. Maslov v. Austria, Judgment of June 23, 2008, No. 1638/03, para. 82 (citing Eur. Ct. H.R., Üner v. Netherlands, Judgment of Oct. 18, 2006, No. 46410/99, para. 58).

99. For discussions of whether the IACHR—and human rights norms more generally—ought to be taken more seriously by U.S. courts in this context, see Melissa A. Waters, *Creeping Monism: The Judicial Trend Toward Interpretive Incorporation of Human Rights Treaties*, 107 COLUM. L. REV. 628 (2007); Shayana Kadidal, *"Federalizing" Immigration Law: International Law as a Limitation on Congress's Power to Legislate in the Field of Immigration*, 77 FORDHAM L. REV. 501 (2008); Kenneth Roth, *The Charade of US Ratification of International Human Rights Treaties*, 1 CHI. J. INT'L L. 347 (2000); Michael Scaperlanda, *Polishing the Tarnished Golden Door*, 1993 WIS. L. REV. 964 (1993); Louis Henkin, *The Constitution and United States Sovereignty: A Century of Chinese Exclusion and its Progeny*, 100 HARV. L. REV. 853 (1987); James A. R. Nafziger, *The General Admission of Aliens Under International Law*, 77 AM. J. INT'L L. 804, 805 (1983).

100. Roper v. Simmons, 543 U.S. 551 (2005).

101. *See* Corinna Lain, *The Unexceptionalism of "Evolving Standards,"* 57 UCLA L. REV. 365 (2009); Corinna Lain, *Deciding Death*, 57 DUKE L.J. 1 (2007).

102. *Roper*, 543 U.S. at 578.

103. Lawrence v. Texas, 539 U.S. 558, 576–77 (2003).

104. *See, e.g.*, Naoum v. Attorney Gen. of U.S., 300 F. Supp.2d 521, 526 (N.D. Ohio 2004); Fernandez v. INS., No. 03-CV-2623, 2004 WL 951491 (E.D.N.Y. 2004); El Zoul v. Bur. Citizenship & Immigration Serv., No. 04-4349, 2006 WL 526091 (2d. Cir. 2006) (unpublished decision); Guaylupo-Maya v. Gonzales, 423 F. 3d 121 (2d Cir. 2005); Taveras-Lopez v. Reno, 127 F. Supp. 2d 598 (M.D. Pa. 2000).

105. In *Maria v. McElroy* and *Beharry v. Reno*, for example, Judge Weinstein used human rights treaties as aids in interpreting the INA, concluding that individualized hearings were required. Maria v. McElroy, 68 F. Supp. 2d 206 (E.D.N.Y. 1999); Beharry v. Reno, 183 F. Supp. 2d 584 (E.D.N.Y. 2002). *But see* Guaylupo-Moya v. Gonzales, 423 F.3d 121 (2d Cir. 2005) (immigration laws that postdate ratification of the ICCPR displace conflicting treaty provisions).

106. Hon. Barbara Jordan, August 1995 (quoted in BECOMING AN AMERICAN: IMMIGRATION AND IMMIGRATION POLICY, U.S. COMM'N ON IMMIGRATION REFORM, Sept. 30, 1997), full report *available at* http://www.utexas.edu/lbj/uscir/becoming/full-report.pdf.

107. Jacqueline Stevens, for example, views nation-states as simply "the sovereign units that make up the 'us' and 'them' comprising the affinities and enmities of enduring inter-state inequality and systemically violent conflict." Jacqueline Stevens *Recreating the State*, 27 THIRD WORLD Q. 755–66 (2006); *see also* JACQUELINE STEVENS, STATES WITHOUT NATIONS: CITIZENSHIP FOR MORTALS (Columbia University Press 2009); JACQUELINE STEVENS, REPRODUCING THE STATE (Princeton University Press 1999).

108. Stevens, *Recreating the State*, 27 THIRD WORLD Q. at 758. The ultimate question, Stevens notes, is whether the "state-nation," with membership rules based on "the artifice of kinship and its fantasies of primordial connections and origins," can ever be dismantled.

109. It entails not only the re-creation of citizenship based on residence instead of birth, but also many other major changes that she well recognizes as "dramatic."

110. *See* Joseph H. Carens, *Aliens and Citizens: The Case for Open Borders*, 49 REV. POL. 251 (1987).

111. *See* Carens, *id. see also* PETER SINGER, ONE WORLD THE ETHICS OF GLOBALIZATION (Yale University Press 2002)

112. *See* Frederick G. Whelan, *Citizenship and Freedom of Movement An Open Admission Policy?* in OPEN BORDERS? CLOSED SOCIETIES? THE ETHICAL AND POLITICAL ISSUES 7–11 (Mark Gibney ed. 1988).

113. *See, e.g.*, Richard Ryscavage, *Strangers as Neighbors: Religious Language and the Response to Immigrants in the United States* 3 (Fairfield University Center for Faith & Public Life 2009); PIERRETTE HONDAGNEU-SOTELO, GOD'S HEART HAS NO BORDERS: HOW RELIGIOUS ACTIVISTS ARE WORKING FOR IMMIGRANT RIGHTS (University of California Press 2008).

114. GIORGIO AGAMBEN, HOMO SACER: SOVEREIGN POWER AND BARE LIFE 71–74 (1998).

115. Prem Kumar Rajaram & Carl Grundy-Warr, *The Irregular Migrant as Homo Sacer: Migration and Detention in Australia, Malaysia, and Thailand*, 42 INT'L MIGRATION 33, 34 (2004).

116. As Joseph Carens once stated: "To argue for or against open borders on the basis of fundamental principles is perhaps to go too deep too soon." *Nationalism and the Exclusion of Immigrants Lessons from Australian Immigration Policy*, in OPEN BORDERS 42, *supra* note 112.

117. ROGERS M. SMITH, CIVIC IDEALS: CONFLICTING VISIONS OF CITIZENSHIP IN U.S. HISTORY 30 (1997)

118. *Id.* at 31.

119. This may be grounded both in dignity claims and those of equality. History has shown the dangers of fixed castes all too clearly.

120. As Joseph Carens has noted: "To say that membership is open to all who wish to join is not to say that there is no distinction between members and nonmembers." Joseph H. Carens, *Aliens and Citizens: The Case for Open Borders*, 49(2) REV. OF POLITICS 251, 273 (Spring 1987).

121. For example, newly recognized states or governments such as Bosnia and Herzogovina or the Republic of South Sudan may not simply expel existing inhabitants even if they are regarded as "alien" by the majority of the population. *See* MICHAEL WALZER, SPHERES OF JUSTICE (Basic Books 1983).

122. Mark Tushnet, *Essay Review: United States Citizenship Policy and Liberal Universalism*, 12 GEO. IMMIGR. L.J. 311(1998).

123. JOSEPH CARENS, IMMIGRANTS AND THE RIGHT TO STAY 55 (2010).

124. YASEMIN SOYSAL, LIMITS OF CITIZENSHIP: MIGRANTS AND POSTNATIONAL MEMBERSHIP IN EUROPE 3, 164 (University of Chicago Press 1994); *see also* DAVID JACOBSON, RIGHTS ACROSS BORDERS: IMMIGRATION AND THE DECLINE OF CITIZENSHIP (1996) (arguing that "universal personhood" means that rights are increasingly based on residency more than on citizen status, which erodes distinction between citizen and alien, as well as the link between territorially bounded national sovereignty and citizenship).

125. *See* SEYLA BENHABIB, THE RIGHTS OF OTHERS (2004).

126. Certain classes of cases warrant particular immediate attention:
    • wrongful deportations of citizens;
    • torture or persecution of deportees;
    • clear errors in deportation proceedings;
    • changes in the law after deportation, especially the vacating of convictions;
    • claims based on unadjudicated eligibility for statutory waivers; and
    • claims of particularly extreme and unforeseen hardship, such as family separation, illness, and loss of custody.

127. *See* Nystrom v. Minister for Immigration & Multicultural & Indigenous Affairs (2005) 143 FCR 420, 422 (Moore and Gyles, JJ). The decision was overturned by the High Court in *Nystrom* (2006) 228 CLR 566, 57–72 (Gleeson CJ), 592 (Gummow and Hayne JJ), 616–17 (Heydon and Crennan JJ).

INDEX

Administrative appeals, power, and practices, 32, 51, 63, 65, 98, 111, 156, 164, 178, 184, 186, 188, 214–15, 221
Administrative Procedure Act, 95
Administrative removal, 65, 100
Agamben, Giorgio, xiiin5, 193n31, 199n139, 225, 236n114
Aggravated felony, 3, 4, 19n4, 25n98, 39, 41, 48n96, 49n110, 65, 77n113, 106, 108–10, 113, 129nn191, 195, 130nn204, 205, 138, 160n63, 165, 220, 234n76
Alabama, 53, 73nn33, 35
Alamanni de Carrillo, Beatrice, 150
Aleinikoff, T. Alexander, 26n114, 48n104, 168, 194n43, 197n94, 198nn96, 97, 105, 106, 108, 109
Alien and Sedition Acts, xi, 61–62, 70, 210
Aliens, 40, 61–62, 94, 99, 156, 166, 178, 180–82, 189, 211, 215, 218
    arriving, 104
    criminal, 39, 41, 85, 90, 92, 106, 109, 111, 222–23, 225
    detained, 90, 94
    deportable, 30, 33, 34–35, 67–68, 70, 186
    enemy, 175, 183
    fugitive, 71
    illegal or undocumented, 5, 7, 42, 84, 90, 178
    lawful permanent resident, 169
    overseas, 166
    removed, 114
American Banana case, 169
American Civil Liberties Union (ACLU), 68, 71, 93, 214
Anderson, George, W., 64
Anderson, nancy, 151
Anti-Drug Abuse Act (1988), 129n191
Antiterrorism and Effective Death Penalty Act, (1996) (AEDPA), 12, 221
Arellano, Elvira, 56, 69

Arendt, Hannah, 58
Arizona, 15, 32, 35–36, 53, 58, 91
Armendarez-Mendez, Andres, 113–14
Armendariz, Hugo, 221–23
Ashcroft, John, 64

Balderrama, David, 136–37
Banishment, x, 6, 8, 11, 145, 156
Barletta, Louis, 214
Barrios, Luis, 137
Benhabib, Seyla, x, 216
Bernstein, nina, 91, 122n68, 123n77, 124n91, 125n119, 126n124, 127nn158, 159, 161
Black, Hugo, 175–76, 205n217
Board of Immigration Appeals (BIA), 11, 51, 97, 101, 103, 109, 111–15, 138, 148–49, 164–66, 188, 215
Boumedienne v. Bush, 186, 228n1
Brennan, William J., 178
Breuer, Lanny, 39
Breyer, Stephen G., 177
Brotherton, David, C., 137, 139
Brubaker, Rogers, 8, 20nn39, 41, 21nn45, 47, 49, 51
Bush, George H.W., 170
Bush, George W., 10, 12, 35, 54, 56, 68, 85–86, 91

Calhoun, John C., 173, 176
Camarota, Steven, 56, 119n9
Camayd-Freixas, Erik, 57
Cambodia, xi, xiii, 19n7, 140, 146, 151, 156, 157n2, 163n124, 187
Cancellation of removal, 49n109, 109, 117–18, 165
Carachuri-Rosendo, Jose, 7, 110–11
Carens, Joseph, 22n57, 225, 236n110, 237nn116, 120, 123
Carry, Kervence Video, 147–48
Chacon, Jennifer, xiii, 22n56, 61, 75n68, 158n27

Chae Chan Ping v. United States, 177, 182, 199n125

Chafee, Jr., Zechariah, 64, 76n86, 77n108, 202n198

Chavez, Dale, 137

Chertoff, Michael, 36, 54, 83

Chinese Exclusion Case, See Chae Chan Ping v. United States

Citizenship: birthright, 22n57, 29, 168, 225

Clinton, William J., 10, 35

Cole, David, 63, 76n94

Comprehensive Immigration Reform (CIR), 12, 54

Constitution, xi, 8, 11, 38, 51–52, 61–63, 114, 164, 166–69, 171–86, 211, 224, 226
  equal protection, 178
  Fifth Amendment due process, 114, 183–84
  Fourth Amendment, 59
  Sixth Amendment, 184–85

Convention on the Rights of the Child (CRC), 217, 218, 220, 231nn41, 46, 47, 48, 49

Cornelius, Wayne, 34, 45n47, 120n19

Corrections Corporation of America, 91

Coutin, Susan Bibler, xiii, 18, 20n37, 27n122

Cover, Robert, 164, 191n2, 216, 230n33

Cox, Christopher, 96, 125n112

Crane, Chris, 53

Customs and border patrol, 34–36, 83–84, 101, 189

Customs and Border Protection (U.S. CBP), 31, 50, 81

D'Amato, Alfonse, 39, 48n93

Demjanjuk, John, 38–39

Department of Homeland Security (DHS), x, 6, 36, 51, 61, 65, 67, 70–71, 83–84, 96, 99, 102, 105, 110, 141

Deportation: *extended border control*, 5, 31, 33–34, 36–37, 61, 81–85, 89, 217, 227
  post-entry social control, 31, 37–40, 61, 85–89, 108, 136, 145–46, 167, 185, 227
  deformalized, 52, 65–67, 84, 115
  disabled, 102–4, 107
  de facto deportation of U.S. citizens, 135, 141
  wrongful deportation of U.S. citizens, 14, 99–102

Detention, x, 3, 8, 11–12, 15–16, 36, 39, 52, 55, 64, 68, 70, 71, 89–94, 98–106, 139–40, 142–43, 145, 178–79, 181, 186–87, 216, 218

Diaspora, xi, 6, 8, 9, 145–46, 150, 152, 164, 210, 220, 224, 227

Discretion, generally, 6, 8, 11, 29, 33, 51, 62, 99, 105, 112–14, 118, 164, 171, 174–75, 185, 211, 213–16, 218, 227
  relief from deportation, 4, 12, 37, 39, 66, 108–9, 113, 115, 117, 143, 156, 165, 185, 188, 214–15, 220–21

prosecutorial, 6, 37, 143, 214–16
  interpretive, 215
  delegated, 215
  motions, 111

Dobbs, Lou, 214

Dominican Republic, xi, 14, 88, 104, 137–38, 151, 154, 156

Dow, Mark, 90, 92

Dred Scott case, 172–73

Dummermuth, Matt, 57

Ecuador, xiii, 16, 146, 153

Eisenhower, Dwight D., 188

El Salvador, 16–18, 41, 148–50, 153–54

European Court of Human Rights (ECtHR), 218, 223–24

European Court of Justice (ECJ), 219

Exclusion, xi, 4, 10, 12, 28, 29, 30–31, 62, 89, 113, 164, 167, 177, 182, 189, 226

Executive Office for Immigration Review (EOIR), 103–4

Expedited removal, *See* Removal, expedited

Ex post facto laws, 52

Extended border control, *See* Deportation, *extended border control*

Ewing, Walter, 88, 121n44

Fernandez-Vargas v. Gonzales, 115–16, 118

Field, Stephen J., 3, 177

Finality, 8, 112, 183–84, 187–91, 227

Florence Immigration and Refugee Rights Project, 99

Fong Yue Ting v. United States, 18n1

Fonkou Takoulo, Hervé, 212–13

Force multipliers, 67, 90, 106–7

Frankfurter, Felix, 176, 191

Giuliani, Rudy, 41

Golden Venture, 90

Grant, Edwin, 41

Guantánamo Bay, 167–68, 170, 173, 177, 180–83, 186

Guatemala, xi, xiii, 17–18, 39, 55, 57, 93, 101, 106–7, 142, 146, 153–54, 173

Guerrier, Wildrick, 8

Guthrie, Woody, xii, 55, 71n1, 74n47

Guzman, Pedro, 14–15, 99

Habeas corpus, 93, 170–71, 176, 181–87

Haiti, xi, 8, 16, 108, 146–48, 154, 187
  Haitian refugees, 90
  Haitian interdiction, 170

Hand, Learned, 165

Hannity, Sean, 58

Harlan, John Marshall, 174

Harlan, John Marshall II, 176–78

Hart, Henry, 179

Headley, Bernard, 151, 155

Heikkila, William, 189
Hing, Julianne, 150, 158n28, 161n90,
    163n121
Holmes, Jr., Oliver Wendell, 63, 167, 169–70
Hoover, J. Edgar, 145
Hughes, Charles Evans, 61–62
Human Rights Watch, 86, 139

Illegal Immigration Reform and Immigrant
    Responsibility Act, (1996) (IIRIRA), 12,
    70, 221
Immigration Act, (1917), 33
Immigration and Customs Enforcement (ICE),
    3, 12, 14, 31, 36, 38–40, 50–55, 59–60, 67,
    69–71, 84–86, 90–94, 99–103, 106–13,
    135, 143, 210, 212–14
Immigration and nationality Act, (1952), 62
Immigration and Naturalization Service (INS),
    82, 89, 91, 94–96, 108–9, 137, 140, 187,
    189–90, 220–21
Immigration Reform and Control Act, (1986)
    (IRCA), 95
INS v. St. Cyr, 108
Insular Cases, 173–77
Inter-American Commission on Human Rights,
    221–24
Internal Security Act, (1950) (McCarran Act),
    62, 115
International Covenant on Civil and Political
    Rights, (ICCPR), 123n75, 217, 231n51,
    236n105
International Organization for Migration, 155

Jackson, Robert, 95, 175, 196n78, 199n120
Jamaica, 150–51, 155
James, Calvin, 150–51
Jamieson, Caroline, 212–23
Jefferson, Thomas, xii, 62
Jiménez, Luis Alberto, 107
Jiménez, Quelino Ojeda, 107
Johnson v. Eisentrager, 175, 177, 183, 186
Johnson, Yvonne, 140
Jordan, Barbara, 210, 224
Judicial review, 12, 39, 52, 77n117, 111,
    125n103, 129n193, 132nn250, 252,
    133n257, 165–66, 186, 188, 190,
    202n199, 204n216, 206n226, 207nn237,
    240, 243, 208n254, 211–12, 217, 227,
    231n43
Justice, Department of (DOJ), 32, 38, 51, 61, 96,
    104–5, 112–13

Kang, Jinyu, 97
Kennedy, Anthony M., 118, 180–81, 186, 210,
    224
King, Steve, 32
Kiyemba v. Obama, 201nn171–79
Krikorian, Mark, 213

Landon v. Plasencia, 72nn17, 20, 200n150,
    202n185
Lawrence v. Texas, 224, 236n103
Lemkin, Raphael, xii, xvnn21–22
Leocal, Josue, 108–9, 111
Leon, Erica, 98
Lofgren, Zoe, 99
Lopez, Jose Antonio, 109–10
Lopez v. Gonzales, 19n4, 25n98, 111, 130n205
Lowell, Abbott, 174
Lun, Loeun, 140
Lyttle, Mark, 101–2

Madison, James, xii, 62, 166, 180
Massachusetts, 9, 40, 55, 92
Maugans, George, 212–13
McCarran Act, (1950), *See* Internal Security Act,
    (1950)
McCarran-Walter Act, (1952), *See*, Immigration
    and Nationality Act, (1952)
McKeon, Edward, 83
Mead, Gary, 99
Mendez v. INS, 190, 210, 214
Mexico, xi, xiii, 7, 14, 17, 34–35, 82–83,
    100–101, 107, 109–10, 115, 136–37, 142,
    154, 168, 180, 221
Mexicans in the U.S., 31–32, 56, 60, 107, 137,
    140, 150
Moral turpitude, 33, 165
Morton, John, 39, 52, 210, 213
Mosquera, Gerald Antonio, 212
Murphy, Frank, 50, 177
Myers, Julie, 84–85

Napolitano, Janet, 36
Naturalization, 4, 38–39, 95–96, 108, 164, 174
Neuman, Gerald, xiii, 20n36, 22n59, 42n4,
    192n26, 193n33, 202n199, 205n225,
    206n226
Nelson, Alan C., 95–96
Ngai, Mae, 34, 44nn44–45
*Nystrom v. Minister for Immigration &
    Multicultural & Indigenous Affairs*,
    218, 227, 231n52, 237n127

Obama, Barack, 6, 10, 12, 31, 36–37, 39, 40, 54,
    58, 60, 66, 85, 86, 94, 182, 212–14
Office of Immigration Litigation (OIL), 97
Operation Endgame, 68–71, 81, 145, 216
Operation Last Call, 137
Osborne, Charles S., 152, 154
Owusu, Emmanuel, 91–92

Padilla v. Kentucky, 184–85, 202nn190–95
Palmer, Mitchell, 63
Palmer Raids, 61, 64
Pearce, Russell, 53
Pelta, Eleanor, 52

Perkins, Frances, xii, 94, 211–12
Pew Hispanic Center, 24nn85, 89, 83, 119n12, 120n23
Piceno, Adam, 68–69
Plenary power doctrine, 174, 181, 183, 224, 226
Plyler v. Doe, 117, 199n134
Portes, Alejandro, 88, 121nn46–47
Posner, Richard A., 149
Post deportation law, 11, 113, 117–18, 177, 183–84, 186–87, 191, 211, 214–15, 227
Post Deportation Human Rights Project, 104
Post-entry social control, *See* Deportation, *post-entry social control*
Post, Louis, xii, 63, 76nn84, 87
Postville raids, 57–58, 65, 93, 212
Pregerson, Harry, 143
Presidential Commission on Immigration & Naturalization, (1953), 156
Proportionality, 5, 8, 11, 13, 20n35, 21n52, 110, 137, 146, 156, 211, 217–20, 222, 227, 233n68, 235n95

Quota laws, 34

RAND Corporation, 81, 87
Rankin, John, 62, 64
Rasul v. Bush, 170, 182
Raustiala, Kal, 11, 23n69, 193n39, 194n44, 197nn87–89, 198nn111, 114
Rawls, John, xiiin4, 19n15, 225
Reagan, Ronald, 90
Registry, 165
Reid v. Covert, 164, 176–77, 199nn121–22, 201nn160–61
Removal, expedited, 52, 65, 90, 98, 104–6, 128nn164–65, 169
    reinstatement of, 65–66, 77n117, 84–85, 115–18, 120nn24, 26, 132n241, 133nn256–57, 134n269
    stipulated orders of, 65, 78n119 *See also* Deportation
Rendell, Marjorie O., 97
Roberts, Barbara, 31, 44n29
Roberts, Maurice, 215, 229n23
Roosevelt, Theodore, 33
Roper v. Simmons, 224, 236nn100, 102
Rule of law, x, xi, 6, 10, 11, 19n21, 52–53, 56, 71, 81, 89, 157, 191, 210–12, 214–15, 224–27
Rumbaut, Rubén, 88–89, 120n29, 121nn37, 44, 46, 51, 158n34, 161nn84, 87

Salvatierra, Alexia, 56
Sampson, Robert J., 87, 121n42
Scott v. Sandford, see Dred Scott Case
Secure Borders Initiative (SBI), 36

Secure Communities, 39, 40–41, 48nn96, 98, 100–101, 106, 128n173
Slaughter, Jimmy and Sheila, 58
Slavery, 171–73
Smith, Armendariz, et al. v. United States, 220–23, 234nn77, 86, 235n98
Smith, Lamar, 46n67, 47n82, 63, 76n92
Smith, Rogers, 193n33, 237n117
Smith, Wayne, 220–23
Somersett case, 171, 196n75
Stern, Herbert, 211, 216
Stevens, Jacqueline, xiii, 14, 22n57, 24n91, 44n30, 93, 99–100, 102, 111, 126nn133, 136, 139, 141–43, 225, 236nn107–8
Stevens, John Paul, 116–17, 133n266, 201, 162

Taft, William Howard, 175
Taney, Roger, 172–73, 176
Tangeman, Anthony S., 68–69, 78n130
Texas, 55, 93, 101, 104, 110, 117
Tocqueville, Alexis de, x, xivn12
Torres, John, 38
Trinidad and Tobago, 155, 220
Triveline, Glenn, 69
Tushnet, Mark, xvn19, 226, 237n122

Uighurs, 181–83
United States v. Mendoza-Lopez, 114–15, 132nn248–50
United States v. Tiede, 211
United States v. Verdugo-Urquidez, 180, 186
Universal Declaration of Human Rights (UDHR), 217, 230n40
Urbina, Richard, 181–82
USA PATRIOT Act, 64, 90
Utah, 53

Voluntary Departure, 43n24, 66, 68, 84, 191n5, 192n19, 209n259

Washington, George, 156
Westphalia, Peace of, 168–69, 193n32
Williams, Diane, 100
Williams, Juan, 58
Wilson, Woodrow, 63, 76n83

Yamataya v. Fisher, 199n136
Yick Wo v. Hopkins, 72n18, 199n133, 200n145, 202n183
Young, Jock, 88, 121n50

Zadvydas v. Davis, 122n63, 129n188, 179, 199nn131, 138, 200nn144, 147, 202n184
Zaldívar, Benito, 148–49, 154
Zambrano, Ruiz, 219–20, 233nn70, 71, 233n75
Zhou, Min, 88, 121nn46–47